Praise for the first edition of
Black Feminist Thought

"The book argues convincingly that black feminists be given, in the words immortalized by Aretha Franklin, a little more R-E-S-P-E-C-T. . . . Those with an appetite for scholarese will find the book delicious."
—*Black Enterprise*

"With the publication of *Black Feminist Thought*, black feminism has moved to a new level. Collins' work sets a standard for the discussion of black women's lives, experiences, and thought that demands rigorous attention to the complexity of these experiences and an exploration of a multiplicity of responses."
—*Women's Review of Books*

"Patricia Hill Collins' new work [is] a marvelous and engaging account of the social construction of black feminist thought. Historically grounded, making excellent use of oral history, interviews, music, poetry, fiction, and scholarly literature, Hill proposes to illuminate black women's standpoint. . . . Those already familiar with black women's history and literature will find this book a rich and satisfying analysis. Those who are not well acquainted with this body of work will find Collins' book an accessible and absorbing first encounter with excerpts from many works, inviting fuller engagement. As an overview, this book would make an excellent text in women's studies, ethnic studies, and African-American studies courses, especially at the upper-division and graduate levels. As a meditation on the deeper implications of feminist epistemology and sociological practice, Patricia Hill Collins has given us a particular gift."
—*Signs*

"Patricia Hill Collins has done the impossible. She has written a book on black feminist thought that combines the theory with the most immediate in feminist practice. Collins' book is a must for any feminist's library."
—Rosemarie Tong

"Finding her own voice and sharing with us the voices of other African-American women, Collins brilliantly explicates our unique standpoint. As a black feminist, Collins traverses both old and new territories. She explores the familiar themes of oppression, family, work, and activism and also examines new areas of cultural images and sexual politics. Collins gently challenges white feminist dominance of feminist theory and nurtures an appreciation for diversity in positions reflecting different race, class, and gender junctures. Her work is an example of how academics can make their work accessible to the wider public."
—Elizabeth Higginbotham, Professor of Sociology, University of Delaware, and co-editor of *Women and Work: Exploring Race, Ethnicity, and Class* (Volume 6)

BLACK FEMINIST THOUGHT

Knowledge,
Consciousness,
and the
Politics of
Empowerment

Second Edition

Patricia Hill Collins

Routledge

New York and London

Published in 2000 by
Routledge
29 West 35th Street
New York, NY 10001

Published in Great Britain by
Routledge
11 New Fetter Lane
London EC4P 4EE

Printed in the United States of America on acid-free paper.
Designed and typeset by The Whole Works®, New York

10 9 8 7 6 5 4

Library of Congress Cataloging-in-Publication Data

Collins, Patricia Hill, 1948–
    Black feminist thought : knowledge, consciousness, and the
politics of empowerment / Patricia Hill Collins. — 2nd ed.
        p.   cm. — (Perspectives on gender)
    Includes bibliographical references and index.
    ISBN 0-415-92483-9 (hb). — ISBN 0-415-92484-7 (pb)
    1. Feminism—United States. 2. Afro-American women. 3. United
States—Race relations.   I. Title   II. Series: Perspectives on
gender (New York, N.Y.)
HQ1426.C633   1999
305.42'01—dc21   99–29144
                                                        CIP

CONTENTS

Preface
to
First
Edition

When I was five years old, I was cho-
sen to play Spring in my preschool pageant. Sitting on my throne, I proudly
presided over a court of children portraying birds, flowers, and the other, "lesser"
seasons. Being surrounded by children like myself—the daughters and sons of
laborers, domestic workers, secretaries, and factory workers—affirmed who I
was. When my turn came to speak, I delivered my few lines masterfully, with
great enthusiasm and energy. I loved my part because I was Spring, the season of
new life and hope. All of the grown-ups told me how vital my part was and con-
gratulated me on how well I had done. Their words and hugs made me feel that
I was important and that what I thought, and felt, and accomplished mattered.

As my world expanded, I learned that not everyone agreed with them.
Beginning in adolescence, I was increasingly the "first," or "one of the few," or
the "only" African-American and/or woman and/or working-class person in my
schools, communities, and work settings. I saw nothing wrong with being who
I was, but apparently many others did. My world grew larger, but I felt I was
growing smaller. I tried to disappear into myself in order to deflect the painful,
daily assaults designed to teach me that being an African-American, working-
class woman made me lesser than those who were not. And as I felt smaller, I
became quieter and eventually was virtually silenced.

This book reflects one stage in my ongoing struggle to regain my voice. Over
the years I have tried to replace the external definitions of my life forwarded by
dominant groups with my own self-defined viewpoint. But while my personal
odyssey forms the catalyst for this volume, I now know that my experiences are
far from unique. Like African-American women, many others who occupy societally denigrated categories have been similarly silenced. So the voice that I now
seek is both individual and collective, personal and political, one reflecting the
intersection of my unique biography with the larger meaning of my historical
times.

I share this part of the context that stimulated this book because that context
influenced my choices concerning the volume itself. First, I was committed to
making this book intellectually rigorous, well researched, and accessible to more

than the select few fortunate enough to receive elite educations. I could not write a book about Black women's ideas that the vast majority of African-American women could not read and understand. Theory of all types is often presented as being so abstract that it can be appreciated only by a select few. Though often highly satisfying to academics, this definition excludes those who do not speak the language of elites and thus reinforces social relations of domination. Educated elites typically claim that only they are qualified to produce theory and believe that only they can interpret not only their own but everyone else's experiences. Moreover, educated elites often use this belief to uphold their own privilege.

I felt that it was important to examine the complexity of ideas that exist in both scholarly and everyday life and present those ideas in a way that made them not less powerful or rigorous but accessible. Approaching theory in this way challenges both the ideas of educated elites and the role of theory in sustaining hierarchies of privilege. The resulting volume is theoretical in that it reflects diverse theoretical traditions such as Afrocentric philosophy, feminist theory, Marxist social thought, the sociology of knowledge, critical theory, and post-modernism; and yet the standard vocabulary of these traditions, citations of their major works and key proponents, and these terms themselves rarely appear in the text. To me the ideas themselves are important, not the labels we attach to them.

Second, I place Black women's experiences and ideas at the center of analysis. For those accustomed to having subordinate groups such as African-American women frame our ideas in ways that are convenient for the more powerful, this centrality can be unsettling. For example, White, middle-class, feminist readers will find few references to so-called White feminist thought. I have deliberately chosen not to begin with feminist tenets developed from the experiences of White, middle-class, Western women and then insert the ideas and experiences of African-American women. While I am quite familiar with a range of histori-cal and contemporary White feminist theorists and certainly value their contri-butions to our understanding of gender, this is not a book about what Black women think of White feminist ideas or how Black women's ideas compare with those of prominent White feminist theorists. I take a similar stance regarding Marxist social theory and Afrocentric thought. In order to capture the intercon-nections of race, gender, and social class in Black women's lives and their effect on Black feminist thought, I explicitly rejected grounding my analysis in any sin-gle theoretical tradition.

Oppressed groups are frequently placed in the situation of being listened to only if we frame our ideas in the language that is familiar to and comfortable for a dominant group. This requirement often changes the meaning of our ideas and works to elevate the ideas of dominant groups. In this volume, by placing African-American women's ideas in the center of analysis, I not only privilege those ideas but encourage White feminists, African-American men, and all oth-ers to investigate the similarities and differences among their own standpoints and those of African-American women.

Third, I deliberately include numerous quotations from a range of African-American women thinkers, some well known and others rarely heard from. Explicitly grounding my analysis in multiple voices highlights the diversity, richness, and power of Black women's ideas as part of a long-standing African-American women's intellectual community. Moreover, this approach counteracts the tendency of mainstream scholarship to canonize a few Black women as spokespersons for the group and then refuse to listen to any but these select few. While it is certainly appealing to receive recognition for one's accomplishments, my experiences as the "first," "one of the few," and the "only" have shown me how effective selecting a few and using them to control the many can be in stifling subordinate groups. Assuming that only a few exceptional Black women have been able to do theory homogenizes African-American women and silences the majority. In contrast, I maintain that theory and intellectual creativity are not the province of a select few but instead emanate from a range of people.

Fourth, I used a distinctive methodology in preparing this manuscript which illustrates how thought and action can work together in generating theory. Much of my formal academic training has been designed to show me that I must alienate myself from my communities, my family, and even my own self in order to produce credible intellectual work. Instead of viewing the everyday as a negative influence on my theorizing, I tried to see how the everyday actions and ideas of the Black women in my life reflected the theoretical issues I claimed were so important to them. Lacking grants, fellowships, release time, or other benefits that allow scholars to remove themselves from everyday life and contemplate its contours and meaning, I wrote this book while fully immersed in ordinary activities that brought me into contact with a variety of African-American women. Through caring for my daughter, mentoring Black women undergraduates, assisting a Brownie troop, and engaging in other "unscholarly" activities, I reassessed my relationships with a range of African-American women and their relationships with one another. Theory allowed me to see all of these associations with fresh eyes, while concrete experiences challenged the worldviews offered by theory. During this period of self-reflection, work on this manuscript inched along, and I produced little "theory." But without this involvement in the everyday, the theory in this volume would have been greatly impoverished.

Fifth, in order to demonstrate the existence and authenticity of Black feminist thought, I present it as being coherent and basically complete. This portrayal is in contrast to my actual view that theory is rarely this smoothly constructed. Most theories are characterized by internal instability, are contested, and are divided by competing emphases and interests. When I considered that Black feminist thought is currently embedded in a larger political and intellectual context that challenges its very right to exist, I decided not to stress the contradictions, frictions, and inconsistencies of Black feminist thought. Instead I present Black feminist thought as overly coherent, but I do so because I suspect that this approach is more appropriate for this historical moment. I hope to see other volumes emerge which will be more willing to present Black feminist thought as a shifting mosaic of competing ideas and interests. I have focused on the pieces of the mosaic—perhaps others will emphasize the disjunctures distinguishing the pieces of the mosaic from one another.

Finally, writing this book has convinced me of the need to reconcile subjectivity and objectivity in producing scholarship. Initially I found the movement between my training as an "objective" social scientist and my daily experiences as an African-American woman jarring. But reconciling what we have been trained to see as opposites, a reconciliation signaled by my inserting myself in the text by using "I," "we," and "our" instead of the more distancing terms "they" and "one," was freeing for me. I discovered that the both/and conceptual stance of Black feminist thought allowed me to be both objective and subjective, to possess both an Afrocentric and a feminist conciousness, and to be both a respectable scholar and an acceptable mother.

When I began this book, I had to overcome my reluctance concerning committing my ideas to paper. "How can I as one person speak for such a large and complex group as African-American women?" I asked myself. The answer is that I cannot and should not because each of us must learn to speak for herself. In the course of writing the book I came to see my work as being part of a larger process, as one voice in a dialogue among people who have been silenced. I know that I will never again possess the curious coexistence of naiveté and unshakable confidence that I had when I portrayed Spring. But I hope to recapture those elements of the voice of Spring that were honest, genuine, and empowering. More important, my hope is that others who were formerly and are currently silenced will find their voices. I, for one, certainly want to hear what they have to say.

Preface
to
Second
Edition

I initially wrote *Black Feminist Thought* in order to help empower African-American women. I knew that when an individual Black woman's consciousness concerning how she understands her everyday life undergoes change, she can become empowered. Such consciousness may stimulate her to embark on a path of personal freedom, even if it exists initially primarily in her own mind. If she is lucky enough to meet others who are undergoing similar journeys, she and they can change the world around them. If ideas, knowledge, and consciousness can have such an impact on individual Black women, what effect might they have on Black women as a group? I suspected that African-American women had created a collective knowledge that served a similar purpose in fostering Black women's empowerment. *Black Feminist Thought* aimed to document the existence of such knowledge and sketch out its contours.

My goal of examining how knowledge can foster African-American women's empowerment remains intact. What has changed, however, is my understanding of the meaning of empowerment and of the process needed for it to happen. I now recognize that empowerment for African-American women will never occur in a context characterized by oppression and social injustice. A group can gain power in such situations by dominating others, but this is not the type of empowerment that I found within Black women's thinking. Reading Black women's intellectual work, I have come to see how it is possible to be both centered in one's own experiences and engaged in coalitions with others. In this sense, Black feminist thought works on behalf of Black women, but does so in conjunction with other similar social justice projects.

My deepening understanding of empowerment stimulated more complex arguments of several ideas introduced in the first edition. For one, throughout this revision, I emphasize Black feminist thought's purpose, namely, fostering *both* Black women's empowerment *and* conditions of social justice. Both of these themes were in the first edition, but neither was as fully developed as they are here. This enhanced emphasis on empowerment and social justice permeates the revised volume and is especially evident in Chapter 2. There I replace my efforts to "define" Black feminist thought with a discussion that identifies its distinguishing features. This shift allowed me to emphasize particular dimensions that characterize Black feminist thought but are not unique to it. It also created space for other groups engaged in similar social justice projects to recognize dimensions of their own thought and practice. I tried to reject the binary thinking that frames so many Western definitions, including my earlier ones of Black feminist thought and of Black feminist epistemology. Rather than drawing a firm line around Black feminist thought that aims to classify entities as *either* being Black feminist *or* not, I aimed for more fluidity without sacrificing logical rigor.

My analysis of oppression is also more complex in this edition, in part because neither empowerment nor social justice can be achieved without some sense of what one is trying to change. Whereas both editions rely on a paradigm of intersecting oppressions to analyze Black women's experiences, this edition provides a more comprehensive treatment. Race, class, and gender studies were being established when I wrote the first edition. Just as this area of inquiry has greatly expanded since that writing, so has my treatment of this framework. For example, in this edition, I broaden my analysis beyond race, class, and gender and include sexuality as a form of oppression. Issues of social class and culture also receive a more complex analysis in this edition. The first edition was especially concerned with issues of Black culture yet said less about social class. Culture and class were both there, but not in the balance that characterizes this edition. My arguments have not substantially changed, but I think they are more effectively developed.

In this edition, I also place greater emphasis on the *connections* between knowledge and power relations. I have always seen organic links between Black feminism as a social justice project and Black feminist thought as its intellectual center. Stated differently, the relationship between African-American women's activism and Black feminist thought as an intellectual and political philosophy integral to that endeavor for me are inextricably linked. These links continue, but as social conditions change, these ties must be rethought.

Rethinking empowerment also led me to incorporate new themes in this edition. For example, this volume says much more about nation as a form of oppression. Incorporating ideas about nation allowed me to introduce a transnational, global dimension. Whereas the discussion here of transnational politics and the global economy remains preliminary, I felt that it was important to include it. U.S. Black women must continue to struggle for our empowerment, but at the same time, we must recognize that U.S. Black feminism participates in a larger context of struggling for social justice that transcends U.S. borders. In particular, U.S. Black feminism should see commonalities that join women of African descent as well as differences that emerge from our diverse national histories. Whereas this edition remains centered on U.S. Black women, it raises questions concerning African-American women's positionality within a global Black feminism.

Providing more complex analyses of these themes required trying to retain the main arguments of the first edition while changing their time-bounded expression. Just as political and intellectual contexts change, so does the language used to describe them. Some changes in terminology reflect benign shifts in usage. Others signal more deep-seated political issues. The cases that are most interesting occur when the same language continues to be used, whereas the meaning attached to it changes. This type of shift certainly affected the term *Afrocentrism,* a term that I used in the first edition. As understood in the 1970s and 1980s, *Afrocentrism* referred to African influences on African-American culture, consciousness, behavior, and social organization. Despite considerable diversity among thinkers who embraced this paradigm, Afrocentric analyses typically claimed that people of African descent have created and re-created a valuable system of ideas, social practices, and cultures that have been essential to Black survival. In the 1990s, however, news media and some segments of U.S. higher education attacked the term as well as all who used it. Effectively discrediting it, as of this writing, the term Afrocentrism refers to the ideas of a small group of Black Studies professionals with whom I have major areas of disagreeement, primarily concerning the treatment of gender and sexuality. For me, the main ideas of Afrocentrism, broadly defined, continue to have merit, but the term itself is too value laden to be useful. Readers familiar with the first edition may notice that I have retained the main ideas of a broadly defined Afrocentrism, but have substituted other terms.

Providing more complex analyses while trying to retain the main arguments of the first edition led me to modify the overall organization of the volume. In order to strengthen my analyses, I moved blocks of text and even some chapters, all the while being careful to omit very little from the first edition. For example, because of the developments in the field of sexuality, I expanded the two chapters dealing with the sexual politics of Black womanhood and moved them earlier in the volume. This new placement allowed me to strengthen ideas about sexuality in the remainder of the volume. Similarly, I moved much of the material in the final chapter of the first edition into earlier chapters. In its place, here I present a new chapter on the politics of empowerment that provides a new capstone for the entire book. Readers familiar with the first edition will find that the three chapters in Part III have been most affected by this reorganization of text. These changes in Part III, however, enabled me to present a more theoretically rich analysis of the connections between knowledge and power than that provided in the first edition. Overall, the arguments from the first edition are here as well, but may appear in new and unexpected places.

I have learned much from revising the first edition of *Black Feminist Thought.* In particular, the subjective experience of writing the first edition in the mid-1980s and revising it now has been markedly different. I can remember how difficult it was for me to write the first edition. Then my concerns centered on coming to voice, especially carving out the intellectual and political space that would enable me to be heard. As the preface to the first edition points out, I saw my individual struggles as emblematic of Black women's collective struggles to claim a similar intellectual and political space. The events surrounding the publication of the first edition certainly involved considerable struggle. One month before *Black Feminist Thought* was to be released, the entire staff that had worked on it was summarily fired, victims of a corporate takeover. We were all in shock. During its first year with its new publisher, the book received little promotion. Despite its media invisibility, *Black Feminist Thought* quickly exhausted its initial print run. I was despondent. I had worked so hard, and it all seemed to have been taken away so quickly. Fortunately, during that awful year before the book was sold yet again to its current publisher, *Black Feminist Thought*'s readers kept it alive. People shared copies, Xeroxed chapters, and engaged in effective word-of-mouth advertising. To this day, I remain deeply grateful to all of the readers of the first edition because without them, this book would have disappeared.

I am in another place now. I remain less preoccupied with coming to voice because I know how quickly voice can be taken away. My concern now lies in finding effective ways to use the voice that I have claimed while I have it. Just as I confront new challenges, new challenges also face U.S. Black women and Black feminist thought as our self-defined knowledge. Because Black feminist thought is created under greatly changed conditions, I worry about its future. However, as long as Black feminist thought, or whatever terms we choose in the future to name this intellectual work, remains dedicated to fostering both Black women's empowerment and broader social justice, I plan on using my voice to support it. I recognize that the struggle for justice is larger than any one group, individual, or social movement. It certainly transcends any one book, including my own. For me, social injustice is a collective problem that requires a collective solution. When it comes to my work, the only thing that is essential is that it contribute toward this end.

Acknowledgments

Writing this book was a collaborative effort, and I would like to thank those most essential to its completion. For the three years that it took me to write the first edition, my husband, Roger L. Collins, and daughter, Valerie L. Collins, lived with my uncertainty and struggles. During that time we all ate far too much fast food and certainly did not reside in a spotless house. But despite this book—or perhaps because of it—we are a stronger family.

I also wish to thank those individuals who could not be with me while I produced this volume but whose contributions are reflected on every page. I drew much of my inspiration from the many Black women who have touched my life. They include my aunts, Mildred Walker, Marjorie Edwards, and Bertha Henry; teachers, friends, and othermothers who helped me along the way, Pauli Murray, Consuelo, Eloise "Muff" Smith, and Deborah Lewis; and countless Black women ancestors, both famous and anonymous, whose struggles created the foundation that nurtured me. I especially acknowledge the spirit of my mother, Eunice Randolph Hill. Often when I became discouraged, I thought of her and told myself that if she could persist despite the obstacles that she faced, then so could I. One great regret of my life is that my mother and my daughter will never meet. I hope these pages will bring them closer together.

Many of my colleagues listened to partially articulated ideas, read earlier drafts of chapters, and generally offered the encouragement and intellectual stimulation that enabled me remain critical my own work yet persevere. Special thanks to Margaret L. Andersen, Elsa Barkley Brown, Lynn Weber Cannon, Bonnie Thornton Dill, Cheryl Townsend Gilkes, Evelyn Nakano Glenn, Sandra Harding, Deborah K. King, and Maxine Baca Zinn for their enthusiastic support. I am especially indebted to the Center for Research on Women at Memphis State Univerity for providing resources, ideas, and overall assistance. Also, I am deeply grateful to Elizabeth Higginbotham and Rosemarie Tong for reading this manuscript in its entirety and offering helpful suggestions.

I have many people to thank for permission to reproduce copyright materals. Earlier versions of Chapters 2 and 10 appeared in *Signs* 14 (4), Summer 1989, pp.

745–73, and *Social Problems* 33 (6), Oct./Dec., 1986, pp. S14–S32. I also thank June Jordan and South End Press for *On Call,* 1985, and Marilyn Richardson and Indiana University Press for *Maria W. Stewart, America's First Black Women Political Writer,* edited by Marilyn Richardson, 1987. This book takes materials from *Drylongso, A Self-Portrait of Black America,* by John Langston Gwaltney, copyright 1980 by John Langston Gwaltney, reprinted by permission of Random House, Inc.; "Strange Fruit," by Lewis Allan, copyright 1939, Edward B. Marks Music Company, copyright renewed, used by permission, all rights reserved; and "Respect," lyrics and music by Otis Redding, copyright 1965 and 1967 by Irving Music, Inc. (BMI), international copyright secured, all rights reserved.

One special person participated in virtually every phase of the first edition of this project. As a research assistant, she prepared literature reviews, read and commented on chapter drafts, and skillfully located even the most obscure materials. Her contributions often surpassed the scholarly—she provided child care so I could work and even fed my family's cats. During our many long conversations, she patiently listened to my ideas, bravely shared parts of her life that profoundly influenced my thinking, and in many unspoken ways told me on a daily basis how important it was that I keep going. Special thanks therefore go out to Patrice L. Dickerson, an emerging Black feminist intellectual, a future colleague, and always a solid sister-friend.

For the institutional support that I needed to work on this second edition, I thank Joseph Caruso, Dean of the College of Arts and Sciences at the University of Cincinnati, John Brackett, Head of the Department of African-American Studies, and Robin Sheets, Director of the Women's Studies Program. The Charles Phelps Taft fund at the University of Cincinnati also made an important contribution to this project. The research budget that accompanied my being named Charles Phelps Taft Professor of Sociology funded part of the expenses incurred in final manuscript preparation.

My students at the University of Cincinnati were also important in helping me complete this project. The undergraduate majors in the Department of African-American Studies proved to be invaluable in helping me clarify arguments concerning power that became important in the second edition. I also thank the graduate students in Women's Studies who enrolled in my graduate seminars "Black Feminism: Issues and Challenges" and "Black Women and the Politics of Sexuality." The students in these courses greatly enriched my understanding of issues of global feminism and of the significance of sexuality. Special thanks goes out to Amber Green, my research assistant for the year. We were both under considerable stress, but we both made it through the year.

The staff at Routledge has been wonderful. Heidi Freund, my editor at Routledge, who politely yet persistently kept asking me to do this revision until I finally agreed to do it, deserves special credit. Also, I thank Shea Settimi, Anthony Mancini, and other members of the staff at Routledge for making the production process so positive for me. I also thank Norma McLemore for meticulous copyediting of the manuscript. As any writer knows, a good copyeditor is important.

Finally, I remain grateful for the numerous invitations that I have received over the years to lecture on college campuses and at professional meetings. These trips enabled me to work through the ideas in the second edition with diverse audiences. Whereas the list of colleagues and new friends that I met during these visits is too long to list, I appreciate all of the ideas that people shared with me. I especially thank the students, parents, poets, high school teachers, activists, and ministers whom I met on my trips. The conversations that I was able to have with you proved to be invaluable. I thank you all, and hope that you each see a bit of yourselves in these pages.

1 THE POLITICS OF BLACK FEMINIST THOUGHT

In 1831 Maria W. Stewart asked, "How long shall the fair daughters of Africa be compelled to bury their minds and talents beneath a load of iron pots and kettles?" Orphaned at age five, bound out to a clergyman's family as a domestic servant, Stewart struggled to gather isolated fragments of an education when and where she could. As the first American woman to lecture in public on political issues and to leave copies of her texts, this early U.S. Black woman intellectual foreshadowed a variety of themes taken up by her Black feminist successors (Richardson 1987).

Maria Stewart challenged African-American women to reject the negative images of Black womanhood so prominent in her times, pointing out that race, gender, and class oppression were the fundamental causes of Black women's poverty. In an 1833 speech she proclaimed, "Like King Solomon, who put neither nail nor hammer to the temple, yet received the praise; so also have the white Americans gained themselves a name . . . while in reality we have been their principal foundation and support." Stewart objected to the injustice of this situation: "We have pursued the shadow, they have obtained the substance; we have performed the labor, they have received the profits; we have planted the vines, they have eaten the fruits of them" (Richardson 1987, 59).

Maria Stewart was not content to point out the source of Black women's oppression. She urged Black women to forge self-definitions of self-reliance and independence. "It is useless for us any longer to sit with our hands folded, reproaching the whites; for that will never elevate us," she exhorted. "Possess the spirit of independence. . . . Possess the spirit of men, bold and enterprising, fearless and undaunted" (p. 53). To Stewart, the power of self-definition was essential, for Black women's survival was at stake. "Sue for your rights and privileges. Know the reason you cannot attain them. Weary them with your importunities. You can but die if you make the attempt; and we shall certainly die if you do not" (p. 38).

Stewart also challenged Black women to use their special roles as mothers to forge powerful mechanisms of political action. "O, ye mothers, what a responsibility rests on you!" Stewart preached. "You have souls committed to your charge. . . . It is you that must create in the minds of your little girls and boys a thirst for knowledge, the love of virtue, . . . and the cultivation of a pure heart." Stewart recognized the magnitude of the task at hand. "Do not say you cannot make any thing of your children; but say . . . we will try" (p. 35).

Maria Stewart was one of the first U.S. Black feminists to champion the utility of Black women's relationships with one another in providing a community for Black women's activism and self-determination. "Shall it any longer be said of the daughters of Africa, they have no ambition, they have no force?" she questioned. "By no means. Let every female heart become united, and let us raise a fund ourselves; and at the end of one year and a half, we might be able to lay the corner stone for the building of a High School, that the higher branches of knowledge might be enjoyed by us" (p. 37). Stewart saw the potential for Black women's activism as educators. She advised, "Turn your attention to knowledge and improvement; for knowledge is power" (p. 41).

Though she said little in her speeches about the sexual politics of her time, her advice to African-American women suggests that she was painfully aware of the sexual abuse visited upon Black women. She continued to "plead the cause of virtue and the pure principles of morality" (p. 31) for Black women. And to those Whites who thought that Black women were inherently inferior, Stewart offered a biting response: "Our souls are fired with the same love of liberty and independence with which your souls are fired. . . . [T]oo much of your blood flows in our veins, too much of your color in our skins, for us not to possess your spirits" (p. 40).

Despite Maria Stewart's intellectual prowess, the ideas of this extraordinary woman come to us only in scattered fragments that not only suggest her brilliance but speak tellingly of the fate of countless Black women intellectuals. Many Maria Stewarts exist, African-American women whose minds and talents have been suppressed by the pots and kettles symbolic of Black women's subordination (Guy-Sheftall 1986).[1] Far too many African-American women intellectuals have labored in isolation and obscurity and, like Zora Neale Hurston, lie buried in unmarked graves.

Some have been more fortunate, for they have become known to us, largely through the efforts of contemporary Black women scholars (Hine et al. 1993; Guy-Sheftall 1995b). Like Alice Walker, these scholars sense that "a people do not throw their geniuses away" and that "if they are thrown away, it is our duty as artists, scholars, and witnesses for the future to collect them again for the sake of our children, . . . if necessary, bone by bone" (Walker 1983, 92).

This painstaking process of collecting the ideas and actions of "thrown away" Black women like Maria Stewart has revealed one important discovery. Black women intellectuals have laid a vital analytical foundation for a distinctive

standpoint on self, community, and society and, in doing so, created a multifaceted, African-American women's intellectual tradition. While clear discontinuities
in this tradition exist—times when Black women's voices were strong, and others when assuming a more muted tone was essential—one striking dimension of
the ideas of Maria W. Stewart and her successors is the thematic consistency of
their work.

If such a rich intellectual tradition exists, why has it remained virtually invisible until now. In 1905 Fannie Barrier Williams lamented, "The colored girl . . .
is not known and hence not believed in; she belongs to a race that is best designated by the term 'problem,' and she lives beneath the shadow of that problem
which envelops and obscures her" (Williams 1987, 150). Why are African-
American women and our ideas not known and not believed in?

The shadow obscuring this complex Black women's intellectual tradition is
neither accidental nor benign. Suppressing the knowledge produced by any
oppressed group makes it easier for dominant groups to rule because the seeming absence of dissent suggests that subordinate groups willingly collaborate in
their own victimization (Scott 1985). Maintaining the invisibility of Black
women and our ideas not only in the United States, but in Africa, the Caribbean,
South America, Europe, and other places where Black women now live, has been
critical in maintaining social inequalities. Black women engaged in reclaiming
and constructing Black women's knowledges often point to the politics of suppression that affect their projects. For example, several authors in Heidi Mirza's
(1997) edited volume on Black British feminism identify their invisibility and
silencing in the contemporary United Kingdom. Similarly, South African busi-
nesswoman Danisa Baloyi describes her astonishment at the invisibility of
African women in U.S. scholarship: "As a student doing research in the United
States, I was amazed by the [small] amount of information on Black South
African women, and shocked that only a minuscule amount was actually written by Black women themselves" (Baloyi 1995, 41).

Despite this suppression, U.S. Black women have managed to do intellectual
work, and to have our ideas matter. Sojourner Truth, Anna Julia Cooper, Ida B.
Wells-Barnett, Mary McLeod Bethune, Toni Morrison, Barbara Smith, and countless others have consistently struggled to make themselves heard. African women
writers such as Ama Ata Aidoo, Buchi Emecheta, and Ellen Kuzwayo have used
their voices to raise important issues that affect Black African women (James
1990). Like the work of Maria W. Stewart and that of Black women transnationally, African-American women's intellectual work has aimed to foster Black
women's activism.

This dialectic of oppression and activism, the tension between the suppression of African-American women's ideas and our intellectual activism in the face
of that suppression, constitutes the politics of U.S. Black feminist thought. More
important, understanding this dialectical relationship is critical in assessing how
U.S. Black feminist thought—its core themes, epistemological significance, and

connections to domestic and transnational Black feminist practice—is fundamentally embedded in a political context that has challenged its very right to exist.

The Suppression of Black Feminist Thought

The vast majority of African-American women were brought to the United States to work as slaves in a situation of oppression. Oppression describes any unjust situation where, systematically and over a long period of time, one group denies another group access to the resources of society. Race, class, gender, sexuality, nation, age, and ethnicity among others constitute major forms of oppression in the United States. However, the convergence of race, class, and gender oppression characteristic of U.S. slavery shaped all subsequent relationships that women of African descent had within Black American families and communities, with employers, and among one another. It also created the political context for Black women's intellectual work.

African-American women's oppression has encompassed three interdependent dimensions. First, the exploitation of Black women's labor essential to U.S. capitalism—the "iron pots and kettles" symbolizing Black women's long-standing ghettoization in service occupations—represents the economic dimension of oppression (Davis 1981; Marable 1983; Jones 1985; Amott and Matthaei 1991). Survival for most African-American women has been such an all-consuming activity that most have had few opportunities to do intellectual work as it has been traditionally defined. The drudgery of enslaved African-American women's work and the grinding poverty of "free" wage labor in the rural South tellingly illustrate the high costs Black women have paid for survival. The millions of impoverished African-American women ghettoized in Philadelphia, Birmingham, Oakland, Detroit, and other U.S. inner cities demonstrate the continuation of these earlier forms of Black women's economic exploitation (Brewer 1993; Omolade 1994).

Second, the political dimension of oppression has denied African-American women the rights and privileges routinely extended to White male citizens (Burnham 1987; Scales-Trent 1989; Berry 1994). Forbidding Black women to vote, excluding African-Americans and women from public office, and withholding equitable treatment in the criminal justice system all substantiate the political subordination of Black women. Educational institutions have also fostered this pattern of disenfranchisement. Past practices such as denying literacy to slaves and relegating Black women to underfunded, segregated Southern schools worked to ensure that a quality education for Black women remained the exception rather than the rule (Mullings 1997). The large numbers of young Black women in inner cities and impoverished rural areas who continue to leave school before attaining full literacy represent the continued efficacy of the political dimension of Black women's oppression.

Finally, controlling images applied to Black women that originated during the slave era attest to the ideological dimension of U.S. Black women's oppression (King 1973; D. White 1985; Carby 1987; Morton 1991). Ideology refers to the body of ideas reflecting the interests of a group of people. Within U.S. culture, racist and sexist ideologies permeate the social structure to such a degree that they become hegemonic, namely, seen as natural, normal, and inevitable. In this context, certain assumed qualities that are attached to Black women are used to justify oppression. From the mammies, jezebels, and breeder women of slavery to the smiling Aunt Jemimas on pancake mix boxes, ubiquitous Black prostitutes, and ever-present welfare mothers of contemporary popular culture, negative stereotypes applied to African-American women have been fundamental to Black women's oppression.

Taken together, the supposedly seamless web of economy, polity, and ideology function as a highly effective system of social control designed to keep African-American women in an assigned, subordinate place. This larger system of oppression works to suppress the ideas of Black women intellectuals and to protect elite White male interests and worldviews. Denying African-American women the credentials to become literate certainly excluded most African-American women from positions as scholars, teachers, authors, poets, and critics. Moreover, while Black women historians, writers, and social scientists have long existed, until recently these women have not held leadership positions in universities, professional associations, publishing concerns, broadcast media, and other social institutions of knowledge validation. Black women's exclusion from positions of power within mainstream institutions has led to the elevation of elite White male ideas and interests and the corresponding suppression of Black women's ideas and interests in traditional scholarship (Higginbotham 1989; Morton 1991; Collins 1998a, 95–123). Moreover, this historical exclusion means that stereotypical images of Black women permeate popular culture and public policy (Wallace 1990; Lubiano 1992; Jewell 1993).

U.S. and European women's studies have challenged the seemingly hegemonic ideas of elite White men. Ironically, Western feminisms have also suppressed Black women's ideas (duCille 1996, 81–119). Even though Black women intellectuals have long expressed a distinctive African-influenced and feminist sensibility about how race and class intersect in structuring gender, historically we have not been full participants in White feminist organizations (Giddings 1984; Zinn et al. 1986; Caraway 1991). As a result, African-American, Latino, Native American, and Asian-American women have criticized Western feminisms for being racist and overly concerned with White, middle-class women's issues (Moraga and Anzaldua 1981; Smith 1982a; Dill 1983; Davis 1989).

Traditionally, many U.S. White feminist scholars have resisted having Black women as full colleagues. Moreover, this historical suppression of Black women's ideas has had a pronounced influence on feminist theory. One pattern of suppression is that of omission. Theories advanced as being universally applicable to women as a group upon closer examination appear greatly limited by the White, middle-class, and Western origins of their proponents. For example, Nancy Chodorow's (1978) work on sex role socialization and Carol Gilligan's (1982) study of the moral development of women both rely heavily on White, middle-class samples. While these two classics made key contributions to feminist theory, they simultaneously promoted the notion of a generic woman who is White and middle class. The absence of Black feminist ideas from these and other studies placed them in a much more tenuous position to challenge the hegemony of mainstream scholarship on behalf of all women.

Another pattern of suppression lies in paying lip service to the need for diversity, but changing little about one's own practice. Currently, some U.S. White women who possess great competence in researching a range of issues acknowledge the need for diversity, yet omit women of color from their work. These women claim that they are unqualified to understand or even speak of "Black women's experiences" because they themselves are not Black. Others include a few safe, "hand-picked" Black women's voices to avoid criticisms that they are racist. Both examples reflect a basic unwillingness by many U.S. White feminists to alter the paradigms that guide their work.

A more recent pattern of suppression involves incorporating, changing, and thereby depoliticizing Black feminist ideas. The growing popularity of postmodernism in U.S. higher education in the 1990s, especially within literary criticism and cultural studies, fosters a climate where symbolic inclusion often substitutes for bona fide substantive changes. Because interest in Black women's work has reached occult status, suggests Ann duCille (1996), it "increasingly marginalizes both the black women critics and scholars who excavated the fields in question and their black feminist 'daughters' who would further develop those fields" (p. 87). Black feminist critic Barbara Christian (1994), a pioneer in creating Black women's studies in the U.S. academy, queries whether Black feminism can survive the pernicious politics of resegregation. In discussing the politics of a new multiculturalism, Black feminist critic Hazel Carby (1992) expresses dismay at the growing situation of symbolic inclusion, in which the texts of Black women writers are welcome in the multicultural classroom while actual Black women are not.

Not all White Western feminists participate in these diverse patterns of suppression. Some do try to build coalitions across racial and other markers of difference, often with noteworthy results. Works by Elizabeth Spelman (1988), Sandra Harding (1986, 1998), Margaret Andersen (1991), Peggy McIntosh (1988), Mab Segrest (1994), Anne Fausto-Sterling (1995), and other individual U.S. White feminist thinkers reflect sincere efforts to develop a multiracial, diverse feminism. However, despite their efforts, these concerns linger on.

Like feminist scholarship, the diverse strands of African-American social and political thought have also challenged mainstream scholarship. However, Black social and political thought has been limited by both the reformist postures toward change assumed by many U.S. Black intellectuals (Cruse 1967; West 1977–78) and the secondary status afforded the ideas and experiences of African-American women. Adhering to a male-defined ethos that far too often equates racial progress with the acquisition of an ill-defined manhood has left much U.S. Black thought with a prominent masculinist bias.

In this case the patterns of suppressing Black women's ideas have been similar yet different. Though Black women have played little or no part in dominant academic discourse and White feminist arenas, we have long been included in the organizational structures of Black civil society. U.S. Black women's acceptance of subordinate roles in Black organizations does not mean that we wield little authority or that we experience patriarchy in the same way as do White women in White organizations (Evans 1979; Gilkes 1985). But with the exception of Black women's organizations, male-run organizations have historically either not stressed Black women's issues (Beale 1970; Marable 1983), or have done so under duress. For example, Black feminist activist Pauli Murray (1970) found that from its founding in 1916 to 1970, the *Journal of Negro History* published only five articles devoted exclusively to Black women. Evelyn Brooks Higginbotham's (1993) historical monograph on Black women in Black Baptist churches records African-American women's struggles to raise issues that concerned women. Even progressive Black organizations have not been immune from gender discrimination. Civil rights activist Ella Baker's experiences in the Southern Christian Leadership Conference illustrate one form that suppressing Black women's ideas and talents can take. Ms. Baker virtually ran the entire organization, yet had to defer to the decision-making authority of the exclusively male leadership group (Cantarow 1980). Civil rights activist Septima Clark describes similar experiences: "I found all over the South that whatever the man said had to be right. They had the whole say. The woman couldn't say a thing" (C. Brown 1986, 79). Radical African-American women also can find themselves deferring to male authority. In her autobiography, Elaine Brown (1992), a participant and subsequent leader of the 1960s radical organization the Black Panther Party for Self-Defense, discusses the sexism expressed by Panther men. Overall, even though Black women intellectuals have asserted their right to speak both as African-Americans and as women, historically these women have not held top leadership positions in Black organizations and have frequently struggled within them to express Black feminist ideas (Giddings 1984).

Much contemporary U.S. Black feminist thought reflects Black women's increasing willingness to oppose gender inequality within Black civil society. Septima Clark describes this transformation:

> I used to feel that women couldn't speak up, because when district meetings were being held at my home . . . I didn't feel as if I could tell them what I had in mind . . . But later on, I found out that women had a lot to say, and what they had to say was really worthwhile. . . . So we started talking, and have been talking quite a bit since that time. (C. Brown 1986, 82)

African-American women intellectuals have been "talking quite a bit" since 1970 and have insisted that the masculinist bias in Black social and political thought, the racist bias in feminist theory, and the heterosexist bias in both be corrected (see, e.g., Bambara 1970; Dill 1979; Jordan 1981; Combahee River Collective 1982; Lorde 1984).

Within Black civil society, the increasing visibility of Black women's ideas did not go unopposed. The virulent reaction to earlier Black women's writings by some Black men, such as Robert Staples's (1979) analysis of Ntozake Shange's (1975) choreopoem, *For Colored Girls Who Have Considered Suicide*, and Michele Wallace's (1978) controversial volume, *Black Macho and the Myth of the Superwoman,* illustrates the difficulty of challenging the masculinist bias in Black social and political thought. Alice Walker encountered similarly hostile reactions to her publication of *The Color Purple.* In describing the response of African-American men to the outpouring of publications by Black women writers in the 1970s and 1980s, Calvin Hernton offers an incisive criticism of the seeming tenacity of a masculinist bias:

> The telling thing about the hostile attitude of black men toward black women writers is that they interpret the new thrust of the women as being "counter-productive" to the historical goal of the Black struggle. Revealingly, while black men have achieved outstanding recognition throughout the history of black writing, black women have not accused the men of collaborating with the enemy and setting back the progress of the race. (1985, 5)

Not all Black male reaction during this period was hostile. For example, Manning Marable (1983) devotes an entire chapter in *How Capitalism Underdeveloped Black America* to how sexism has been a primary deterrent to Black community development. Following Marable's lead, work by Haki Madhubuti (1990), Cornel West (1993), Michael Awkward (1996), Michael Dyson (1996), and others suggests that some U.S. Black male thinkers have taken Black feminist thought seriously. Despite the diverse ideological perspectives expressed by these writers, each seemingly recognizes the importance of Black women's ideas.

Black Feminist Thought as Critical Social Theory

Even if they appear to be otherwise, situations such as the suppression of Black women's ideas within traditional scholarship and the struggles within the critiques of that established knowledge are inherently unstable. Conditions in the wider political economy simultaneously shape Black women's subordination and foster activism. On some level, people who are oppressed usually know it. For African-American women, the knowledge gained at intersecting oppressions of race, class, and gender provides the stimulus for crafting and passing on the subjugated knowledge[2] of Black women's critical social theory (Collins 1998a, 3–10).

As an historically oppressed group, U.S. Black women have produced social thought designed to oppose oppression. Not only does the form assumed by this thought diverge from standard academic theory—it can take the form of poetry, music, essays, and the like—but the *purpose* of Black women's collective thought is distinctly different. Social theories emerging from and/or on behalf of U.S. Black women and other historically oppressed groups aim to find ways to escape from, survive in, and/or oppose prevailing social and economic injustice. In the United States, for example, African-American social and political thought analyzes institutionalized racism, not to help it work more efficiently, but to resist it. Feminism advocates women's emancipation and empowerment, Marxist social thought aims for a more equitable society, while queer theory opposes heterosexism. Beyond U.S. borders, many women from oppressed groups also struggle to understand new forms of injustice. In a transnational, postcolonial context, women within new and often Black-run nation-states in the Caribbean, Africa, and Asia struggle with new meanings attached to ethnicity, citizenship status, and religion. In increasingly multicultural European nation-states, women migrants from former colonies encounter new forms of subjugation (Yuval-Davis 1997). Social theories expressed by women emerging from these diverse groups typically do not arise from the rarefied atmosphere of their imaginations. Instead, social theories reflect women's efforts to come to terms with lived experiences within intersecting oppressions of race, class, gender, sexuality, ethnicity, nation, and religion (see, e.g., Alexander and Mohanty 1997; Mirza 1997).

Black feminist thought, U.S. Black women's critical social theory, reflects similar power relationships. For African-American women, critical social theory encompasses bodies of knowledge and sets of institutional practices that actively grapple with the central questions facing U.S. Black women as a collectivity. The need for such thought arises because African-American women as a *group* remain oppressed within a U.S. context characterized by injustice. This neither means that all African-American women within that group are oppressed in the same way, nor that some U.S. Black women do not suppress others. Black feminist thought's identity as a "critical" social theory lies in its commitment to justice, both for U.S. Black women as a collectivity and for that of other similarly oppressed groups.

Historically, two factors stimulated U.S. Black women's critical social theory. For one, prior to World War II, racial segregation in urban housing became so entrenched that the majority of African-American women lived in self-contained Black neighborhoods where their children attended overwhelmingly Black schools, and where they themselves belonged to all-Black churches and similar community organizations. Despite the fact that ghettoization was designed to foster the political control and economic exploitation of Black Americans (Squires 1994), these all-Black neighborhoods simultaneously provided a separate space where African-American women and men could use African-derived ideas to craft distinctive oppositional knowledges designed to resist racial oppression.

Every social group has a constantly evolving worldview that it uses to order and evaluate its own experiences (Sobel 1979). For African-Americans this worldview originated in the cosmologies of diverse West African ethnic groups (Diop 1974). By retaining and reworking significant elements of these West African cultures, communities of enslaved Africans offered their members explanations for slavery alternative to those advanced by slave owners (Gutman 1976; Webber 1978; Sobel 1979). These African-derived ideas also laid the foundation for the rules of a distinctive Black American civil society. Later on, confining African-Americans to all-Black areas in the rural South and Northern urban ghettos fostered the solidification of a distinctive ethos in Black civil society regarding language (Smitherman 1977), religion (Sobel 1979; Paris 1995), family structure (Sudarkasa 1981b), and community politics (Brown 1994). While essential to the survival of U.S. Blacks as a group and expressed differently by individual African-Americans, these knowledges remained simultaneously hidden from and suppressed by Whites. Black oppositional knowledges existed to resist injustice, but they also remained subjugated.

As mothers, othermothers, teachers, and churchwomen in essentially all-Black rural communities and urban neighborhoods, U.S. Black women participated in constructing and reconstructing these oppositional knowledges. Through the lived experiences gained within their extended families and communities, individual African-American women fashioned their own ideas about the meaning of Black womanhood. When these ideas found collective expression, Black women's self-definitions enabled them to refashion African-influenced conceptions of self and community. These self-definitions of Black womanhood were designed to resist the negative controlling images of Black womanhood advanced by Whites as well as the discriminatory social practices that these controlling images supported. In all, Black women's participation in crafting a constantly changing African-American culture fostered distinctively Black and women-centered worldviews.

Another factor that stimulated U.S. Black women's critical social theory lay in the common experiences they gained from their jobs. Prior to World War II, U.S. Black women worked primarily in two occupations—agriculture and domestic work. Their ghettoization in domestic work sparked an important contradiction. Domestic work fostered U.S. Black women's economic exploitation, yet it simultaneously created the conditions for distinctively Black and female forms of resistance. Domestic work allowed African-American women to see White elites, both actual and aspiring, from perspectives largely obscured from Black men and from these groups themselves. In their White "families," Black women not only performed domestic duties but frequently formed strong ties with the children they nurtured, and with the employers themselves. On one level this insider relationship was satisfying to all concerned. Accounts of Black domestic workers stress the sense of self-affirmation the women experienced at seeing racist ideology demystified. But on another level these Black women knew that they could never belong to their White "families." They were economically exploited workers and thus would remain outsiders. The result was being placed in a curious *outsider-within* social location (Collins 1986b), a peculiar marginality that stimulated a distinctive Black women's perspective on a variety of themes (see, e.g., Childress 1986).

Taken together, Black women's participation in constructing African-American culture in all-Black settings and the distinctive perspectives gained from their outsider-within placement in domestic work provide the material backdrop for a unique Black women's standpoint. When armed with cultural beliefs honed in Black civil society, many Black women who found themselves doing domestic work often developed distinct views of the contradictions between the dominant group's actions and ideologies. Moreover, they often shared their ideas with other African-American women. Nancy White, a Black inner-city resident, explores the connection between experience and beliefs:

> Now, I understand all these things from living. But you can't lay up on these flowery beds of ease and think that you are running your life, too. Some women, white women, can run their husband's lives for a while, but most of them have to . . . see what he tells them there is to see. If he tells them that they ain't seeing what they know they *are* seeing, then they have to just go on like it wasn't there! (in Gwaltney 1980, 148)

Not only does this passage speak to the power of the dominant group to suppress the knowledge produced by subordinate groups, but it illustrates how being in outsider-within locations can foster new angles of vision on oppression. Ms. White's Blackness makes her a perpetual outsider. She could never be a White middle-class woman lying on a "flowery bed of ease." But her work of caring for White women allowed her an insider's view of some of the contradictions between White women thinking that they are running their lives and the patriarchal power and authority in their households.

Practices such as these, whether experienced oneself or learned by listening to African-American women who have had them, have encouraged many U.S. Black women to question the contradictions between dominant ideologies of American womanhood and U.S. Black women's devalued status. If women are allegedly passive and fragile, then why are Black women treated as "mules" and assigned heavy cleaning chores? If good mothers are supposed to stay at home with their children, then why are U.S. Black women on public assistance forced to find jobs and leave their children in day care? If women's highest calling is to become mothers, then why are Black teen mothers pressured to use Norplant and Depo Provera? In the absence of a viable Black feminism that investigates how intersecting oppressions of race, gender, and class foster these contradictions, the angle of vision created by being deemed devalued workers and failed mothers could easily be turned inward, leading to internalized oppression. But the legacy of struggle among U.S. Black women suggests that a collectively shared, Black women's oppositional knowledge has long existed. This collective wisdom in turn has spurred U.S. Black women to generate a more specialized knowledge, namely, Black feminist thought as critical social theory. Just as fighting injustice lay at the heart of U.S. Black women's experiences, so did analyzing and creating imaginative responses to injustice characterize the core of Black feminist thought.

Historically, while they often disagreed on its expression—some U.S. Black women were profoundly reformist while more radical thinkers bordered on the revolutionary—African-American women intellectuals who were nurtured in social conditions of racial segregation strove to develop Black feminist thought as critical social theory. Regardless of social class and other differences among U.S. Black women, all were in some way affected by intersecting oppressions of race, gender, and class. The economic, political, and ideological dimensions of U.S. Black women's oppression suppressed the intellectual production of individual Black feminist thinkers. At the same time, these same social conditions simultaneously stimulated distinctive patterns of U.S. Black women's activism that also influenced and was influenced by individual Black women thinkers. Thus, the dialectic of oppression and activism characterizing U.S. Black women's experiences with intersecting oppressions also influenced the ideas and actions of Black women intellectuals.

The exclusion of Black women's ideas from mainstream academic discourse and the curious placement of African-American women intellectuals in feminist thinking, Black social and political theories, and in other important thought such as U.S. labor studies has meant that U.S. Black women intellectuals have found themselves in outsider-within positions in many academic endeavors (Hull et al. 1982; Christian 1989). The assumptions on which full group membership are based—Whiteness for feminist thought, maleness for Black social and political thought, and the combination for mainstream scholarship—all negate Black women's realities. Prevented from becoming full insiders in any of these areas of inquiry, Black women remained in outsider-within locations, individuals whose marginality provided a distinctive angle of vision on these intellectual and political entities.

Alice Walker's work exemplifies these fundamental influences within Black women's intellectual traditions. Walker describes how her outsider-within location influenced her thinking: "I believe . . . that it was from this period—from my solitary, lonely position, the position of an outcast—that I began really to see people and things, really to notice relationships" (Walker 1983, 244). Walker realizes that "the gift of loneliness is sometimes a radical vision of society or one's people that has not previously been taken into account" (p. 264). And yet marginality is not the only influence on her work. By reclaiming the works of Zora Neale Hurston and in other ways placing Black women's experiences and culture at the center of her work, she draws on alternative Black feminist worldviews.

Developing Black Feminist Thought

Starting from the assumption that African-American women have created independent, oppositional yet subjugated knowledges concerning our own subordination, contemporary U.S. Black women intellectuals are engaged in the struggle to reconceptualize all dimensions of the dialectic of oppression and activism as it applies to African-American women. Central to this enterprise is reclaiming Black feminist intellectual traditions (see, e.g., Harley and Terborg-Penn 1978; Hull et al. 1982; James and Busia 1993; and Guy-Sheftall 1995a, 1995b).

For many U.S. Black women intellectuals, this task of reclaiming Black women's subjugated knowledge takes on special meaning. Knowing that the minds and talents of our grandmothers, mothers, and sisters have been suppressed stimulates many contributions to the growing field of Black women's studies (Hull et al. 1982). Alice Walker describes how this sense of purpose affects her work: "In my own work I write not only what I want to read—understanding fully and indelibly that if I don't do it no one else is so vitally interested, or capable of doing it to my satisfaction—I write all the things *I should have been able to read*" (Walker 1983, 13).

Reclaiming Black women's ideas involves discovering, reinterpreting, and, in many cases, analyzing for the first time the works of individual U.S. Black women thinkers who were so extraordinary that they did manage to have their ideas preserved. In some cases this process involves locating unrecognized and unheralded works, scattered and long out of print. Marilyn Richardson's (1987) painstaking editing of the writings and speeches of Maria Stewart, and Mary Helen Washington's (1975, 1980, 1987) collections of Black women's writings typify this process. Similarly, Alice Walker's (1979a) efforts to have Zora Neale Hurston's unmarked grave recognized parallel her intellectual quest to honor Hurston's important contributions to Black feminist literary traditions.

Reclaiming Black women's ideas also involves discovering, reinterpreting, and analyzing the ideas of subgroups within the larger collectivity of U.S. Black women who have been silenced. For example, burgeoning scholarship by and about Black lesbians reveals a diverse and complex history. Gloria Hull's (1984) careful compilation of the journals of Black feminist intellectual Alice Dunbar-Nelson illustrates the difficulties of being closeted yet still making major contributions to African-American social and political thought. Audre Lorde's (1982) autobiography, *Zami*, provides a book-length treatment of Black lesbian communities in New York. Similarly, Kennedy and Davis's (1994) history of the formation of lesbian communities in 1940s and 1950s Buffalo, New York, strives to understand how racial segregation influenced constructions of lesbian identities.

Reinterpreting existing works through new theoretical frameworks is another dimension of developing Black feminist thought. In Black feminist literary criticism, this process is exemplified by Barbara Christian's (1985) landmark volume on Black women writers, Mary Helen Washington's (1987) reassessment of anger and voice in *Maud Martha,* a much-neglected work by novelist and poet Gwendolyn Brooks, and Hazel Carby's (1987) use of the lens of race, class, and gender to reinterpret the works of nineteenth-century Black women novelists. Within Black feminist historiography the tremendous strides that have been made in U.S. Black women's history are evident in Evelyn Brooks Higginbotham's (1989) analysis of the emerging concepts and paradigms in Black women's history, her study of women in the Black Baptist Church (1993), Stephanie Shaw's (1996) study of Black professional women workers during the Jim Crow era, and the landmark volume *Black Women in the United States: An Historical Encyclopedia* (Hine et al. 1993).

Developing Black feminist thought also involves searching for its expression in alternative institutional locations and among women who are not commonly perceived as intellectuals. As defined in this volume, Black women intellectuals are neither all academics nor found primarily in the Black middle class. Instead, all U.S. Black women who somehow contribute to Black feminist thought as critical social theory are deemed to be "intellectuals." They may be highly educated. Many are not. For example, nineteenth-century Black feminist activist Sojourner Truth is not typically seen as an intellectual.[3] Because she could neither read nor write, much of what we know about her has been recorded by other people. One of her most famous speeches, that delivered at the 1851 women's rights convention in Akron, Ohio, comes to us in a report written by a feminist abolitionist some time after the event itself (Painter 1993). We do not know what Truth actually said, only what the recorder claims that she said. Despite this limitation, in that speech Truth reportedly provides an incisive analysis of the definition of the term *woman* forwarded in the mid-1800s:

> That man over there says women need to be helped into carriages, and lifted over ditches, and to have the best place everywhere. Nobody ever helps me into carriages, or over mud puddles, or gives me any best place! And ain't I a woman? Look at me! Look at my arm! I have ploughed, and planted, and gathered into barns, and no man could head me! And ain't I a woman? I could work as much and eat as much as a man—when I could get it—and bear the lash as well! And ain't I a woman? I have borne thirteen children, and seen them most all sold off to slavery, and when I cried out with my mother's grief, none but Jesus heard me! And ain't I a woman? (Loewenberg and Bogin 1976, 235)

By using the contradictions between her life as an African-American woman and the qualities ascribed to women, Sojourner Truth exposes the concept of woman as being culturally constructed. Her life as a second-class citizen has been filled with hard physical labor, with no assistance from men. Her question, "and ain't I a woman?" points to the contradictions inherent in blanket use of the term *woman*. For those who question Truth's femininity, she invokes her status as a mother of thirteen children, all sold off into slavery, and asks again, "and ain't I a woman?" Rather than accepting the existing assumptions about what a woman is and then trying to prove that she fit the standards, Truth challenged the very standards themselves. Her actions demonstrate the process of deconstruction—namely, exposing a concept as ideological or culturally constructed rather than as natural or a simple reflection of reality (Collins 1998a, 137–45). By deconstructing the concept *woman,* Truth proved herself to be a formidable intellectual. And yet Truth was a former slave who never learned to read or write.

Examining the contributions of women like Sojourner Truth suggests that the concept of *intellectual* must itself be deconstructed. Not all Black women intellectuals are educated. Not all Black women intellectuals work in academia. Furthermore, not all highly educated Black women, especially those who are employed in U.S. colleges and universities, are *automatically* intellectuals. U.S. Black women intellectuals are not a female segment of William E. B. DuBois's notion of the "talented tenth." One is neither born an intellectual nor does one become one by earning a degree. Rather, doing intellectual work of the sort envisioned within Black feminism requires a process of self-conscious struggle on behalf of Black women, regardless of the actual social location where that work occurs.

These are not idle concerns within new power relations that have greatly altered the fabric of U.S. and Black civil society. Race, class, and gender still constitute intersecting oppressions, but the ways in which they are now organized to produce social injustice differ from prior eras. Just as theories, epistemologies, and facts produced by any group of individuals represent the standpoints and interests of their creators, the very definition of who is legitimated to do intellectual work is not only politically contested, but is changing (Mannheim 1936; Gramsci 1971). Reclaiming Black feminist intellectual traditions involves much more than developing Black feminist analyses using standard epistemological criteria. It also involves challenging the very terms of intellectual discourse itself.

Assuming new angles of vision on which U.S. Black women are, in fact, intellectuals, and on their seeming dedication to contributing to Black feminist thought raises new questions about the production of this oppositional knowledge. Historically, much of the Black women's intellectual tradition occurred in institutional locations other than the academy. For example, the music of working-class Black women blues singers of the 1920 and 1930s is often seen as one important site outside academia for this intellectual tradition (Davis 1998). Whereas Ann duCille (1993) quite rightly warns us about viewing Black women's blues through rose-colored glasses, the fact remains that far more Black women listened to Bessie Smith and Ma Rainey than were able to read Nella

Larsen or Jessie Fauset. Despite impressive educational achievements that have allowed many U.S. Black women to procure jobs in higher education and the media, this may continue to be the case. For example, Imani Perry (1995) suggests that the music of Black women hip-hop artists serves as a new site of Black women's intellectual production. Again, despite the fact that hip-hop contains diverse and contradictory components (Rose 1994) and that popularity alone is insufficient to confer the title "intellectual," many more Black women listen to Queen Latifah and Salt 'N' Pepa than read literature by Alice Walker and Toni Morrison.

Because clarifying Black women's experiences and ideas lies at the core of Black feminist thought, interpreting them requires collaborative leadership among those who participate in the diverse forms that Black women's communities now take. This requires acknowledging not only how African-American women outside of academia have long functioned as intellectuals by representing the interests of Black women as a group, but how this continues to be the case. For example, rap singer Sister Souljah's music as well as her autobiography *No Disrespect* (1994) certainly can be seen as contributing to Black feminist thought as critical social theory. Despite her uncritical acceptance of a masculinist Black nationalist ideology, Souljah is deeply concerned with issues of Black women's oppression, and offers an important perspective on contemporary urban culture. Yet while young Black women listened to Souljah's music and thought about her ideas, Souljah's work has been dismissed within feminist classrooms in academia as being "nonfeminist." Without tapping these nontraditional sources, much of the Black women's intellectual tradition would remain "not known and hence not believed in" (Williams 1987, 150).

At the same time, many Black women academics struggle to find ways to do intellectual work that challenges injustice. They know that being an academic and an intellectual are not necessarily the same thing. Since the 1960s, U.S. Black women have entered faculty positions in higher education in small but unprecedented numbers. These women confront a peculiar dilemma. On the one hand, acquiring the prestige enjoyed by their colleagues often required unquestioned acceptance of academic norms. On the other hand, many of these same norms remain wedded to notions of Black and female inferiority. Finding ways to temper critical responses to academia without unduly jeopardizing their careers constitutes a new challenge for Black women who aim to be intellectuals within academia, especially intellectuals engaged in developing Black feminist thought (Collins 1998a, 95–123).

Surviving these challenges requires new ways of doing Black feminist intellectual work. Developing Black feminist thought as critical social theory involves including the ideas of Black women not previously considered intellectuals—many of whom may be working-class women with jobs outside academia—as well as those ideas emanating from more formal, legitimated scholarship. The ideas we share with one another as mothers in extended families, as othermothers in Black communities, as members of Black churches, and as teachers to the Black community's children have formed one pivotal area where African-American women have hammered out a multifaceted Black women's standpoint. Musicians, vocalists, poets, writers, and other artists constitute another group from which Black women intellectuals have emerged. Building on African-influenced oral traditions, musicians in particular have enjoyed close association with the larger community of African-American women constituting their audience. Through their words and actions, grassroots political activists also contribute to Black women's intellectual traditions. Producing intellectual work is generally not attributed to Black women artists and political activists. Especially in elite institutions of higher education, such women are typically viewed as objects of study, a classification that creates a false dichotomy between scholarship and activism, between thinking and doing. In contrast, examining the ideas and actions of these excluded groups in a way that views them as subjects reveals a world in which behavior is a statement of philosophy and in which a vibrant, both/and, scholar/activist tradition remains intact.

Objectives of the Volume

African-American women's social location as a collectivity has fostered distinctive albeit heterogeneous Black feminist intellectual traditions that, for convenience in this volume, I call *Black feminist thought*. Investigations of four basic components of Black feminist thought—its thematic content, its interpretive frameworks, its epistemological approaches, and its significance for empowerment—constitute the core of this volume. All four components have been shaped by U.S. Black women's placement in a political context that is undergoing considerable change. Thus, Black feminist thought's core themes, interpretive frameworks, epistemological stances, and insights concerning empowerment will reflect and aim to shape specific political contexts confronting African-American women as a group.

In this volume, I aim to describe, analyze, explain the significance of, and contribute to the development of Black feminist thought as critical social theory. In addressing this general goal, I have several specific objectives. First, I summarize selected core themes in Black feminist thought by surveying their historical and contemporary expression. Drawing primarily on the works of African-American women scholars and on the thought produced by a wide range of Black women intellectuals, I explore several core themes that preoccupy Black women thinkers. The vast majority of thinkers discussed in the text are, to the best of my knowledge, U.S. Black women. I cite a range of Black women thinkers not because I think U.S. Black women have a monopoly on the ideas presented but because I aim to demonstrate the range and depth of thinkers who exist in U.S. Black civil society. Placing the ideas of ordinary African-American women as well as those of better-known Black women intellectuals at the center of analysis produces a new angle of vision on Black women's concerns. At the same time, Black feminist thought cannot be developed in isolation from the thought and actions of other groups. Thus, I also include the ideas of diverse thinkers who make important contributions to developing Black feminist thought. Black women must be in charge of Black feminist thought, but being in charge does not mean that others are excluded.

Using and furthering an interpretive framework or paradigm that has come to be known as race, class, and gender studies constitute a second objective of *Black Feminist Thought*. Rejecting additive models of oppression, race, class, and gender studies have progressed considerably since the 1980s.[4] During that decade, African-American women scholar-activists, among others, called for a new approach to analyzing Black women's experiences. Claiming that such experiences were shaped not just by race, but by gender, social class, and sexuality, works such as *Women, Race and Class* by Angela Davis (1981), "A Black Feminist Statement" drafted by the Combahee River Collective (1982), and Audre Lorde's (1984) classic volume *Sister Outsider* stand as groundbreaking works that explored interconnections among systems of oppression. Subsequent work aimed to describe different dimensions of this interconnected relationship with terms such as *intersectionality* (Crenshaw 1991) and *matrix of domination*. In this volume, I use and distinguish between both terms in examining how oppression affects Black women. Intersectionality refers to particular forms of intersecting oppressions, for example, intersections of race and gender, or of sexuality and nation. Intersectional paradigms remind us that oppression cannot be reduced to one fundamental type, and that oppressions work together in producing injustice. In contrast, the matrix of domination refers to how these intersecting oppressions are actually organized. Regardless of the particular intersections involved, structural, disciplinary, hegemonic, and interpersonal domains of power reappear across quite different forms of oppression.

My third objective is to develop an epistemological framework that can be used both to assess existing Black feminist thought and to clarify some of the underlying assumptions that impede its development. This issue of epistemology raises some difficult questions. I see the need to define the boundaries that delineate Black feminist thought from other arenas of intellectual inquiry. What criteria, if any, can be applied to ideas to determine whether they are in fact Black and feminist? What essential features does Black feminist thought share with other critical social theories, particularly Western feminist theory, Afrocentric theory, Marxist analyses, and postmodernism? Do African-American women implicitly rely on alternative standards for determining whether ideas are true? Traditional epistemological assumptions concerning how we arrive at "truth" simply are not sufficient to the task of furthering Black feminist thought. In the same way that concepts such as woman and intellectual must be challenged, the process by which we arrive at truth merits comparable scrutiny. While I provide a book-length treatment of these theoretical concerns in *Fighting Words: Black Women and the Search for Justice,* here I focus on the distinguishing features of a Black feminist epistemology.

I aim to use this same epistemological framework throughout the volume. Alice Walker describes this process as one whereby "to write the books one wants to read is both to point the direction of vision and, at the same time, to follow it" (1983, 8). This was a very difficult process for me, one requiring that I not only develop standards and guidelines for assessing U.S. Black feminist thought but that I then apply those same standards and guidelines to my own work while I was creating it. For example, in Chapters 2 and 10 I argue that Black women intellectuals best contribute to a Black women's group standpoint by using their experiences as situated knowers. To adhere to this epistemological tenet required that, when appropriate, I reject the pronouns "they" and "their" when describing U.S. Black women and our ideas and replace these terms with the terms "we," "us," and "our." Using the distancing terms "they" and "their" when describing my own group and our experiences might enhance both my credentials as a scholar and the credibility of my arguments in some academic settings. But by taking this epistemological stance that reflects my disciplinary training as a sociologist, I invoke standards of certifying truth about which I remain ambivalent.

In contrast, by identifying my position as a participant in and observer of Black women's communities, I run the risk of being discredited as being too subjective and hence less scholarly. But by being an advocate for my material, I validate epistemological tenets that I claim are fundamental for Black feminist thought, namely, to equip people to resist oppression and to inspire them to do it (Collins 1998a, 196–200). To me, the suppression of Black women's intellectual traditions has made this process of feeling one's way an unavoidable epistemological stance for Black women intellectuals. As Walker points out, "she must be her own model as well as the artist attending, creating, learning from, realizing the model, which is to say, herself" (1983, 8).

Finally, I aim to further Black feminist thought's contributions to empowering African-American women. Empowerment remains an illusive construct and developing a Black feminist politics of empowerment requires specifying the domains of power that constrain Black women, as well as how such domination can be resisted. Ideally, Black feminist thought contributes ideas and analytical frameworks toward this end. Moreover, it is important to remember that Black women's full empowerment can occur only within a transnational context of social justice. While focused on U.S. Black women, U.S. Black feminism constitutes one of many historically specific social justice projects dedicated to fostering the empowerment of groups within an overarching context of justice. In this sense, Black feminist thought constitutes one part of a much larger social justice project that goes far beyond the experiences of African-American women.

2 DISTINGUISHING FEATURES OF BLACK FEMINIST THOUGHT

I am a product of an intellectual tradition which until twenty-five years ago did not exist within the academy. Like patchwork in a quilt, it is a tradition gathered from meaningful bits and pieces. My tradition has no name, because it embraces more than womanism, Blackness, or African studies, although those terms will do for now.   —Barbara Omolade 1994, ix

It seems I am running out of words these days. I feel as if I am on a linguistic tread-mill that has gradually but unmistakably increased its speed, so that no word I use to positively describe myself or my scholarly projects lasts for more than five seconds. I can no longer justify my presence in academia, for example, with words that exist in the English language. The moment I find some symbol of my presence in the rarefied halls of elite institutions, it gets stolen, co-opted, filled with negative meaning.   —Patricia Williams 1995, 27

U.S. Black women's struggles on this "linguistic treadmill" to name this tradition with "no name" reveal the difficulties of making do with "terms [that] will do for now." Widely used yet increasingly difficult to define, U.S. Black feminist thought encompasses diverse and often contradictory meanings. Despite the fact that U.S. Black women, in particular, have expended considerable energy on naming Black women's knowledge, definitional tensions not only persist but encounter changing political climates riddled with new obstacles. When the very vocabulary used to describe Black feminist thought comes under attack, Black women's self-definitions become even more difficult to achieve. For example, despite continued acceptance among many African-Americans of Afrocentrism as a term referencing traditions of Black consciousness and racial solidarity, academics and media pundits maligned the term in the 1980s and 1990s. Similarly, the pejorative meanings increasingly attached to the term feminist seem designed to discredit a movement dedicated to women's empowerment. Even the term *Black* fell victim to the deconstructive moment, with a growing number of "Black" intellectuals who do "race" scholarship questioning the very terms used to describe both themselves and their political struggles (see, e.g., Gilroy 1993). Collectively, these developments produced a greatly changed political and intellectual context for defining Black feminist thought.

Despite these difficulties, finding some sort of common ground for thinking through the boundaries of Black feminist thought remains important because, as U.S. Black feminist activist Pearl Cleage reminds us, "we have to see clearly that we are a unique group, set undeniably apart because of race and sex with a unique set of challenges" (Cleage 1993, 55). Rather than developing definitions and arguing over naming practices—for example, whether this thought should be called Black feminism, womanism, Afrocentric feminism, Africana woman-ism, and the like—a more useful approach lies in revisiting the reasons why Black feminist thought exists at all. Exploring six distinguishing features that characterize Black feminist thought may provide the common ground that is so sorely needed both among African-American women, and between African-American women and all others whose collective knowledge or thought has a similar purpose. Black feminist thought's distinguishing features need not be unique and may share much with other bodies of knowledge. Rather, it is the *convergence* of these distinguishing features that gives U.S. Black feminist thought its distinctive contours.

Why U.S. Black Feminist Thought?

Black feminism remains important because U.S. Black women constitute an oppressed group. As a collectivity, U.S. Black women participate in a *dialectical* relationship linking African-American women's oppression and activism. Dialectical relationships of this sort mean that two parties are opposed and opposite. As long as Black women's subordination within intersecting oppres-sions of race, class, gender, sexuality, and nation persists, Black feminism as an activist response to that oppression will remain needed.

In a similar fashion, the overarching purpose of U.S. Black feminist thought is also to resist oppression, both its practices and the ideas that justify it. If inter-secting oppressions did not exist, Black feminist thought and similar opposi-tional knowledges would be unnecessary. As a critical social theory, Black femi-nist thought aims to empower African-American women within the context of social injustice sustained by intersecting oppressions. Since Black women cannot be fully empowered unless intersecting oppressions themselves are eliminated, Black feminist thought supports broad principles of social justice that transcend U.S. Black women's particular needs.

Because so much of U.S. Black feminism has been filtered through the prism of the U.S. context, its contours have been greatly affected by the specificity of American multiculturalism (Takaki 1993). In particular, U.S. Black feminist thought and practice respond to a fundamental contradiction of U.S. society. On the one hand, democratic promises of individual freedom, equality under the law, and social justice are made to all American citizens. Yet on the other hand, the reality of differential group treatment based on race, class, gender, sexuality, and citizenship status persists. Groups organized around race, class, and gender in and of themselves are not inherently a problem. However, when African-Americans, poor people, women, and other groups discriminated against see little hope for group-based advancement, this situation constitutes social injustice.

Within this overarching contradiction, U.S. Black women encounter a distinctive set of social practices that accompany our particular history within a unique matrix of domination characterized by intersecting oppressions. Race is far from being the only significant marker of group difference—class, gender, sexuality, religion, and citizenship status all matter greatly in the United States (Andersen and Collins 1998). Yet for African-American women, the effects of institutionalized racism remain visible and palpable. Moreover, the institutionalized racism that African-American women encounter relies heavily on racial segregation and accompanying discriminatory practices designed to deny U.S. Blacks equitable treatment. Despite important strides to desegregate U.S. society since 1970, racial segregation remains deeply entrenched in housing, schooling, and employment (Massey and Denton 1993). For many African-American women, racism is not something that exists in the distance. We encounter racism in everyday situations in workplaces, stores, schools, housing, and daily social interaction (St. Jean and Feagin 1998). Most Black women do not have the opportunity to befriend White women and men as neighbors, nor do their children attend school with White children. Racial segregation remains a fundamental feature of the U.S. social landscape, leaving many African-Americans with the belief that "the more things change, the more they stay the same" (Collins 1998a, 11–43). Overlaying these persisting inequalities is a rhetoric of color blindness designed to render these social inequalities invisible. In a context where many believe that to talk of race fosters racism, equality allegedly lies in treating everyone the same. Yet as Kimberle Crenshaw (1997) points out, "it is fairly obvious that treating different things the same can generate as much inequality as treating the same things differently" (p. 285).

Although racial segregation is now organized differently than in prior eras (Collins 1998a, 11–43), being Black and female in the United States continues to expose African-American women to certain common experiences. U.S. Black women's similar work and family experiences as well as our participation in diverse expressions of African-American culture mean that, overall, U.S. Black women as a group live in a different world from that of people who are not Black and female. For individual women, the particular experiences that accrue to living as a Black woman in the United States can stimulate a distinctive consciousness concerning our own experiences and society overall. Many African-American women grasp this connection between what one does and how one thinks. Hannah Nelson, an elderly Black domestic worker, discusses how work shapes the perspectives of African-American and White women: "Since I have to work, I don't really have to worry about most of the things that most of the white women I have worked for are worrying about. And if these women did their own work, they would think just like I do—about this, anyway" (Gwaltney 1980, 4). Ruth Shays, a Black inner-city resident, points out how variations in men's and women's experiences lead to differences in perspective. "The mind of the man and the mind of the woman is the same" she notes, "but this business of living makes women use their minds in ways that men don't even have to think about" (Gwaltney 1980, 33).

A recognition of this connection between experience and consciousness that shapes the everyday lives of individual African-American women often pervades the works of Black women activists and scholars. In her autobiography, Ida B. Wells-Barnett describes how the lynching of her friends had such an impact on her worldview that she subsequently devoted much of her life to the anti-lynching cause (Duster 1970). Sociologist Joyce Ladner's discomfort with the disparity between the teachings of mainstream scholarship and her experiences as a young Black woman in the South led her to write *Tomorrow's Tomorrow* (1972), a groundbreaking study of Black female adolescence. Similarly, the trans-formed consciousness experienced by Janie, the light-skinned heroine of Zora Neale Hurston's (1937) classic *Their Eyes Were Watching God,* from obedient granddaughter and wife to a self-defined African-American woman, can be directly traced to her experiences with each of her three husbands. In one scene Janie's second husband, angry because she served him a dinner of scorched rice, underdone fish, and soggy bread, hits her. That incident stimulates Janie to stand "where he left her for unmeasured time" and think. And in her thinking "her image of Jody tumbled down and shattered. . . . [S]he had an inside and an out-side now and suddenly she knew how not to mix them" (p. 63).

Overall, these ties between what one does and what one thinks illustrated by *individual* Black women can also characterize Black women's experiences and ideas as a *group*. Historically, racial segregation in housing, education, and employment fostered group commonalities that encouraged the formation of a group-based, collective standpoint.[1] For example, the heavy concentration of U.S. Black women in domestic work coupled with racial segregation in housing and schools meant that U.S. Black women had common organizational networks that enabled them to share experiences and construct a collective body of wisdom. This collective wisdom on how to survive as U.S. Black women constituted a dis-tinctive Black women's standpoint on gender-specific patterns of racial segrega-tion and its accompanying economic penalties.

The presence of Black women's collective wisdom challenges two prevail-ing interpretations of the consciousness of oppressed groups. One approach claims that subordinate groups identify with the powerful and have no valid independent interpretation of their own oppression. The second assumes the oppressed are less human than their rulers, and are therefore less capable of interpreting their own experiences (Rollins 1985; Scott 1985). Both approaches see any independent consciousness expressed by African-American women and other oppressed groups as being either not of our own making or inferior to that of dominant groups. More importantly, both explanations suggest that the alleged lack of political activism on the part of oppressed groups stems from our flawed consciousness of our own subordination.[2]

Historically, Black women's group location in intersecting oppressions produced commonalities among individual African-American women. At the same time, while common experiences may predispose Black women to develop a distinctive group consciousness, they guarantee neither that such a consciousness will develop among all women nor that it will be articulated as such by the group. As historical conditions change, so do the links among the types of experiences Black women will have and any ensuing group consciousness concerning those experiences. Because group standpoints are situated in, reflect, and help shape unjust power relations, standpoints are not static (Collins 1998a, 201–28). Thus, common challenges may foster similar angles of vision leading to a group knowledge or standpoint among African-American women. Or they may not.

Diverse Responses to Common Challenges within Black Feminism

A second distinguishing feature of U.S. Black feminist thought emerges from a tension linking experiences and ideas. On the one hand, all African-American women face similar challenges that result from living in a society that historically and routinely derogates women of African descent. Despite the fact that U.S. Black women face common challenges, this neither means that individual African-American women have all had the same experiences nor that we agree on the significance of our varying experiences. Thus, on the other hand, despite the common challenges confronting U.S. Black women as a group, diverse responses to these core themes characterize U.S. Black women's group knowledge or standpoint.

Despite differences of age, sexual orientation, social class, region, and religion, U.S. Black women encounter societal practices that restrict us to inferior housing, neighborhoods, schools, jobs, and public treatment and hide this differential consideration behind an array of common beliefs about Black women's intelligence, work habits, and sexuality. These common challenges in turn result in recurring patterns of experiences for individual group members. For example, African-American women from quite diverse backgrounds report similar treatment in stores. Not every *individual* Black woman consumer need experience being followed in a store as a potential shoplifter, ignored while others are waited on first, or seated near restaurant kitchens and rest rooms, for African-American women as a collectivity to recognize that differential *group* treatment is operating.

Since standpoints refer to group knowledge, recurring patterns of differential treatment such as these suggest that certain themes will characterize U.S. Black women's group knowledge or standpoint. For example, one core theme concerns multifaceted legacies of struggle, especially in response to forms of violence that accompany intersecting oppressions (Collins 1998d). Katie Cannon observes, "[T]hroughout the history of the United States, the interrelationship of white supremacy and male superiority has characterized the Black woman's reality as a situation of struggle—a struggle to survive in two contradictory worlds simultaneously, one white, privileged, and oppressive, the other black, exploited, and oppressed" (1985, 30). Black women's vulnerability to assaults in the workplace, on the street, at home, and in media representations has been one factor fostering this legacy of struggle.

Despite differences created by historical era, age, social class, sexual orientation, skin color, or ethnicity, the legacy of struggle against the violence that permeates U.S. social structures is a common thread binding African-American women. Anna Julia Cooper, an educated, nineteenth-century Black woman intellectual, describes Black women's vulnerability to sexual violence:

> I would beg . . . to add my plea for the *Colored Girls* of the South:—that large, bright, promising fatally beautiful class . . . so full of promise and possibilities, yet so sure of destruction; often without a father to whom they dare apply the loving term, often without a stronger brother to espouse their cause and defend their honor with his life's blood; in the midst of pitfalls and snares, waylaid by the lower classes of white men, with no shelter, no protection. (Cooper 1892, 240)

Yet during this period Cooper and other middle-class U.S. Black women built a powerful club movement and numerous community organizations (Giddings 1984, 1988; Gilkes 1985).

Stating that a legacy of struggle exists does not mean that all U.S. Black women share its benefits or even recognize it. For example, for African-American girls, age often offers little protection from assaults. Far too many young Black girls inhabit hazardous and hostile environments (Carroll 1997). In 1975 I received an essay titled "My World" from Sandra, a sixth-grade student who was a resident of one of the most dangerous public housing projects in Boston. Sandra wrote, "My world is full of people getting rape. People shooting on another. Kids and grownups fighting over girlsfriends. And people without jobs who can't afford to get a education so they can get a job . . . winos on the streets raping and killing little girls." Her words poignantly express a growing Black feminist sensibility that she may be victimized by racism, misogyny, and poverty. They reveal her awareness that she is vulnerable to rape as a form of sexual violence. Despite her feelings about her neighborhood, Sandra not only walked the streets daily but managed safely to deliver three siblings to school. In doing so she participated in a Black women's legacy of struggle. Sandra prevailed, but at a cost. Unlike Sandra, others simply quit.

This legacy of struggle constitutes one of several core themes of a Black women's standpoint. Efforts to reclaim U.S. Black women's intellectual traditions have revealed Black women's long-standing attention to additional core themes first recorded by Maria W. Stewart (Richardson 1987). Stewart's perspective on intersecting oppressions, her call for replacing derogated images of Black womanhood with self-defined images, her belief in Black women's activism as mothers, teachers, and Black community leaders, and her sensitivity to sexual politics are all core themes advanced by a variety of Black feminist intellectuals.

Despite the common challenges confronting African-American women as a group, individual Black women neither have identical experiences nor interpret experiences in a similar fashion. The existence of core themes does not mean that African-American women respond to these themes in the same way. Differences among individual Black women produce different patterns of experiential knowledge that in turn shape individual reactions to the core themes. For example, when faced with controlling images of Black women as being ugly and unfeminine, some women—such as Sojourner Truth—demand, "Ain't I a woman?" By deconstructing the conceptual apparatus of the dominant group, they challenge notions of Barbie-doll femininity premised on middle-class White women's experiences (duCille 1996, 8–59). In contrast, other women internalize the controlling images and come to believe that they are the stereotypes (Brown-Collins and Sussewell 1986). Still others aim to transgress the boundaries that frame the images themselves. Jaminica, a 14-year-old Black girl, describes her strategies: "Unless you want to get into a big activist battle, you accept the stereotypes given to you and just try and reshape them along the way. So in a way, this gives me a lot of freedom. I can't be looked at any worse in society than I already am—black and female is pretty high on the list of things not to be" (Carroll 1997, 94–95).

Many factors explain these diverse responses. For example, although all African-American women encounter institutionalized racism, social class differences among African-American women influence patterns of racism in housing, education, and employment. Middle-class Blacks are more likely to encounter a pernicious form of racism that has left many angry and disappointed (Cose 1993; Feagin and Sikes 1994). A young manager who graduated with honors from the University of Maryland describes the specific form racism can take for middle-class Blacks. Before she flew to Cleveland to explain a marketing plan for her company, her manager made her go over it three or four times in front of him so that she would not forget *her* marketing plan. Then he explained how to check luggage at an airport and how to reclaim it. "I just sat at lunch listening to this man talking to me like I was a monkey who could remember but couldn't think," she recalled. When she had had enough, "I asked him if he wanted to tie my money up in a handkerchief and put a note on me saying that I was an employee of this company. In case I got lost I would be picked up by Traveler's Aid, and Traveler's Aid would send me back" (Davis and Watson 1985, 86). Most middle-class Black women do not encounter such blatant incidents, but many working-class Blacks do. Historically, working-class Blacks have struggled with forms of institutionalized racism directly organized by White institutions and by forms mediated by some segments of the Black middle class. Thus, while it shares much with middle-class Black women, the legacy of struggle by working-class Blacks (Kelley 1994) and by working-class Black women in particular will express a distinctive character (Fordham 1993).

Sexuality signals another important factor that influences African-American women's varying responses to common challenges. Black lesbians have identified heterosexism as a form of oppression and the issues they face living in homo-phobic communities as shaping their interpretations of everyday events (Shockley 1974; Lorde 1982, 1984; Clarke et al. 1983; Barbara Smith 1983, 1998; Williams 1997). Beverly Smith describes how being a lesbian affected her perceptions of the wedding of one of her closest friends: "God, I wish I had one friend here. Someone who knew me and would understand how I feel. I am mas-querading as a nice, straight, middle-class Black 'girl' " (1983, 172). While the majority of those attending the wedding saw only a festive event, Beverly Smith felt that her friend was being sent into a form of bondage. In a similar fashion, varying ethnic and citizenship statuses within the U.S. nation-state as well also shape differences among Black women in the United States. For example, Black Puerto Ricans constitute a group that combines categories of race, nationality, and ethnicity in distinctive ways. Black Puerto Rican women thus must negotiate a distinctive set of experiences that accrue to being racially Black, holding a spe-cial form of American citizenship, and being ethnically Latino.

Given how these factors influence diverse response to common challenges, it is important to stress that no homogeneous Black *woman's* standpoint exists. There is no essential or archetypal Black woman whose experiences stand as normal, normative, and thereby authentic. An essentialist understanding of a Black woman's standpoint suppresses differences among Black women in search of an elusive group unity. Instead, it may be more accurate to say that a Black *women's* collective standpoint does exist, one characterized by the tensions that accrue to different responses to common challenges. Because it both recognizes and aims to incorporate heterogeneity in crafting Black women's oppositional knowledge, this Black *women's* standpoint eschews essentialism in favor of democracy. Since Black feminist thought both arises within and aims to articu-late a Black *women's* group standpoint regarding experiences associated with intersecting oppressions, stressing this group standpoint's heterogeneous com-position is significant.

Moreover, in thinking through the contours of a Black women's standpoint, it is equally important to recognize that U.S. Black women also encounter the same challenges (and correspondingly different expressions) as women of African descent within a Black diasporic context. This context in turn is situated within a transnational, global context. The term *diaspora* describes the experiences of people who, through slavery, colonialism, imperialism, and migration, have been forced to leave their native lands (Funani 1998, 417). For U.S. Black women and other people of African descent, a diasporic framework suggests a dispersal from Africa to societies in the Caribbean, South America, North America, and Europe. Understandings of African-American womanhood thus reflect a distinctive pattern of dispersal associated with forced immigration to the United States and subsequent enslavement (Pala 1995). Since a diasporic framework is not normative, it should not be used to assess the authenticity of people of African descent in reference to an assumed African norm. Rather, Black diasporic frameworks center analyses of Black women within the context of common challenges experienced transnationally.

The version of Black feminism that U.S. Black women have developed certainly must be understood in the context of U.S. nation-state politics. At the same time, U.S. Black feminism as a social justice project shares much with comparable social justice projects advanced not only by other U.S. racial/ethnic groups (see, e.g., Takaki 1993), but by women of African descent across quite diverse societies. In the context of an "intercontinental Black women's consciousness movement" (McLaughlin 1995, 73), women of African descent are dispersed globally, yet the issues we face may be similar. Transnationally, women encounter recurring social issues such as poverty, violence, reproductive concerns, lack of education, sex work, and susceptibility to disease (*Rights of Women* 1998). Placing African-American women's experiences, thought, and practice in a transnational, Black diasporic context reveals these and other commonalities of women of African descent while specifying what is particular to African-American women.

Black Feminist Practice and Black Feminist Thought

A third distinguishing feature of Black feminist thought concerns the connections between U.S. Black women's experiences as a heterogeneous collectivity and any ensuing group knowledge or standpoint. One key reason that standpoints of oppressed groups are suppressed is that self-defined standpoints can stimulate resistance. Annie Adams, a Southern Black woman, describes how she became involved in civil rights activities:

> When I first went into the mill we had segregated water fountains. . . . Same thing about the toilets. I had to clean the toilets for the inspection room and then, when I got ready to go to the bathroom, I had to go all

> the way to the bottom of the stairs to the cellar. So I asked my boss man, "what's the difference? If I can go in there and clean them toilets, why can't I use them?" Finally, I started to use that toilet. I decided I wasn't going to walk a mile to go to the bathroom. (Byerly 1986, 134)

In this case Ms. Adams found the "boss man's" point of view inadequate, developed one of her own, and acted on it. On the individual level, her actions illustrate the connections among lived experiences with oppression, developing one's own point of view concerning those experiences, and the acts of resistance that can follow. A similar relationship characterizes African-American women's group knowledge. U.S. Black women's collective historical experiences with oppression may stimulate a self-defined Black women's standpoint that in turn can foster Black women's activism.

As members of an oppressed group, U.S. Black women have generated alternative practices and knowledges that have been designed to foster U.S. Black women's group empowerment. In contrast to the dialectical relationship linking oppression and activism, a *dialogical* relationship characterizes Black women's collective experiences and group knowledge. On both the individual and the group level, a dialogical relationship suggests that changes in thinking may be accompanied by changed actions and that altered experiences may in turn stimulate a changed consciousness. For U.S. Black women as a collectivity, the struggle for a self-defined Black feminism occurs through an ongoing dialogue whereby action and thought inform one another.

U.S. Black feminism itself illustrates this dialogical relationship. On the one hand, there is U.S. Black feminist practice that emerges in the context of lived experience. When organized and visible, such practice has taken the form of overtly Black feminist social movements dedicated to the empowerment of U.S. Black women. Two especially prominent moments characterize Black feminism's visibility. Providing many of the guiding ideas for today, the first occurred at the turn of the century via the Black women's club movement. The second or modern Black feminist movement was stimulated by the antiracist and women's social justice movements of the 1960s and 1970s and continues to the present. However, these periods of overt political activism where African-American women lobbied in our own behalf remain unusual. They appear to be unusual when juxtaposed to more typical patterns of quiescence regarding Black women's advocacy.

Given the history of U.S. racial segregation, Black feminist activism demonstrates distinctive patterns. Because African-Americans have long been relegated to racially segregated environments, U.S. Black feminist practice has often occurred within a context of Black community development efforts and other Black nationalist-inspired projects. Black nationalism emerges in conjunction with racial segregation—U.S. Blacks living in a racially integrated society would most likely see less need for Black nationalism. As a political philosophy, Black nationalism is based on the belief that Black people constitute a people or "nation" with a common history and destiny. Black solidarity, the belief that Blacks have common interests and should support one another, has long permeated Black women's political philosophy. Thus, Black women's path to a "feminist" consciousness often occurs within the context of antiracist social justice projects, many of them influenced by Black nationalist ideologies. In describing how this phenomenon affects Black women in global context, Andree Nicola McLaughlin contends, "[A]mong activist Black women, it is generally recognized that nationalist struggle provides a rich arena for developing a woman's consciousness" (McLaughlin 1995, 80). To look for Black feminism by searching for U.S. Black women who self-identify as "Black feminists" misses the complexity of how Black feminist practice actually operates (Collins 1993a).

Similar views have been expressed about the feminism of women in Africa. When a colleague asked Obioma Nnaemeka to describe African feminists' definition of African feminism, her off-the-cuff response was telling: "[T]he majority of African women are not hung up on 'articulating their feminism'; they just do it." In Nnaemeka's view, "It is *what* they do and *how* they do it that provide the 'framework'; the 'framework' is not carried to the theater of action as a definitional tool. . . . Attempts to mold 'African feminism' into an easily digestible ball of pointed yam not only raise definitional questions but create difficulties for drawing organizational parameters and unpacking complex modes of engagement" (Nnaemeka 1998a, 5). Here Nnaemeka provides a compelling argument concerning the interconnectedness of experiences and ideas, one that differs markedly from accepted models of how one defines social justice movements. Her model references the dialogical relationship, and points to a different way of thinking about Black feminist thought as knowledge. Specifically, Black feminist practice requires Black feminist thought, and vice versa.

When it comes to the dialogical relationship within U.S. Black feminism, on the other hand, there is U.S. Black feminist thought as a critical social theory. Critical social theory constitutes theorizing about the social in defense of economic and social justice. As critical social theory, Black feminist thought encompasses bodies of knowledge and sets of institutional practices that actively grapple with the central questions facing U.S. Black women as a group. Such theory recognizes that U.S. Black women constitute one group among many that are differently placed within situations of injustice. What makes critical social theory "critical" is its commitment to justice, for one's own group and for other groups.

Within these parameters, knowledge for knowledge's sake is not enough—Black feminist thought must both be tied to Black women's lived experiences and aim to better those experiences in some fashion. When such thought is sufficiently grounded in Black feminist practice, it reflects this dialogical relationship. Black feminist thought encompasses general knowledge that helps U.S. Black women survive in, cope with, and resist our differential treatment. It also includes more specialized knowledge that investigates the specific themes and challenges of any given period of time. Conversely, when U.S. Black women cannot see the connections among themes that permeate Black feminist thought and those that influence Black women's everyday lives, it is appropriate to question the strength of this dialogical relationship. Moreover, it is also reasonable to question the validity of that particular expression of Black feminist thought. For example, during slavery, a special theme within Black feminist thought was how the institutionalized rape of enslaved Black women operated as a mechanism of social control. During the period when Black women worked primarily in agriculture and service, countering the sexual harassment of live-in domestic workers gained special importance. Clear connections could be drawn between the content and purpose of Black feminist thought and important issues in Black women's lives.

The potential significance of Black feminist thought goes far beyond demonstrating that African-American women can be theorists. Like Black feminist practice, which it reflects and which it seeks to foster, Black feminist thought can create collective identity among African-American women about the dimensions of a Black women's standpoint. Through the process of *rearticulation,* Black feminist thought can offer African-American women a different view of ourselves and our worlds (Omi and Winant 1994, 99). By taking the core themes of a Black women's standpoint and infusing them with new meaning, Black feminist thought can stimulate a new consciousness that utilizes Black women's everyday, taken-for-granted knowledge. Rather than raising consciousness, Black feminist thought affirms, rearticulates, and provides a vehicle for expressing in public a consciousness that quite often already exists. More important, this rearticulated consciousness aims to empower African-American women and stimulate resistance.

Sheila Radford-Hill stresses the importance of rearticulation as an essential ingredient of an empowering Black feminist theory in her essay "Considering Feminism as a Model for Social Change." In evaluating whether Black women should espouse feminist programs, Radford-Hill suggests, "[T]he essential issue that black women must confront when assessing a feminist position is as follows: If I, as a black woman, 'become a feminist,' what basic tools will I gain to resist my individual and group oppression?" (1986, 160). For Radford-Hill, the relevance of feminism as a vehicle for social change must be assessed in terms of its "ability to factor black women and other women of color into alternative conceptions of power and the consequences of its use" (p. 160). Thus Black feminist thought as critical social theory aims to aid African-American women's struggles against intersecting oppressions.

At first glance, these connections between Black feminist practice and Black feminist thought might suggest that only African-American women can participate in the production of Black feminist thought and that only Black women's experiences can form the content of that thought. But this model of Black feminism is undermined as a critical perspective by being dependent on those who are biologically Black and female. Exclusionary definitions of Black feminism which confine "black feminist criticism to black women critics of black women artists depicting black women" (Carby 1987, 9) are inadequate because they are inherently separatist. Instead, the connections here aim for autonomy. Given this need for self-definition and autonomy—an important objective of "an intellectual tradition which until twenty-five years ago did not exist within the academy" (Omolade 1994, ix)—what is the significance of Black women intellectuals within Black feminist thought?

Dialogical Practices and Black Women Intellectuals

A fourth distinguishing feature of Black feminist thought concerns the essential contributions of African-American women intellectuals. The existence of a Black women's standpoint does not mean that African-American women, academic or otherwise, appreciate its content, see its significance, or recognize its potential as a catalyst for social change. One key task for Black women intellectuals of diverse ages, social classes, educational backgrounds, and occupations consists of asking the right questions and investigating all dimensions of a Black women's standpoint with and for African-American women. Historically, Black women intellectuals stood in a special relationship to the larger community of African-American women, a relationship that framed Black feminist thought's contours as critical social theory. Whether this relationship will persist depends, ironically, on Black women intellectuals' ability to analyze their own social locations.

Very different kinds of "thought" and "theories" emerge when abstract thought is joined with pragmatic action. Denied positions as scholars and writers which allow us to emphasize purely theoretical concerns, the work of most Black women intellectuals has been influenced by the merger of action and theory. The activities of nineteenth-century educated Black women intellectuals such as Anna J. Cooper, Frances Ellen Watkins Harper, Ida B. Wells-Barnett, and Mary Church Terrell exemplify this tradition of merging intellectual work and activism. These women both analyzed the intersecting oppressions that circumscribed Black women's lives and worked for social justice. The Black women's club movement they created was both an activist and an intellectual endeavor. Working-class Black women also engaged in a parallel joining of ideas and activism. But because they were denied formal educations, the form of their activism as well as the content of the ideas they developed differed from those of middle-class Black women. The live performances of classic Black women blues singers in the 1920s can be seen as one important arena where working-class women gathered and shared ideas especially germane to them (Davis 1998).

Many contemporary Black women intellectuals continue to draw on this tradition of using everyday actions and experiences in our theoretical work. Black feminist historian Elsa Barkley Brown describes the importance her mother's ideas played in the scholarship she eventually produced on African-American washerwomen. Initially Brown used the lens provided by her training as a historian and saw her sample group as devalued service workers. But over time she came to understand washerwomen as entrepreneurs. By taking the laundry to whoever had the largest kitchen, they created a community and a culture among themselves. In explaining the shift of vision that enabled her to reassess this portion of Black women's history, Brown notes, "It was my mother who taught me how to ask the right questions—and all of us who try to do this thing called scholarship on a regular basis are fully aware that asking the right questions is the most important part of the process" (1986, 14).

This special relationship of Black women intellectuals to the community of African-American women parallels the existence of two interrelated levels of knowledge (Berger and Luckmann 1966). The commonplace, taken-for-granted knowledge shared by African-American women growing from our everyday thoughts and actions constitutes a first and most fundamental level of knowledge. The ideas that Black women share with one another on an informal, daily basis about topics such as how to style our hair, characteristics of "good" Black men, strategies for dealing with White folks, and skills of how to "get over" provide the foundations for this taken-for-granted knowledge.

Experts or specialists who participate in and emerge from a group produce a second, more specialized type of knowledge. Whether working-class or middle-class, educated or not, famous or everyday, the range of Black women intellectuals discussed in Chapter 1 are examples of these specialists. Their theories that facilitate the expression of a Black women's standpoint form the specialized knowledge of Black feminist thought. The two types of knowledge are interdependent. While Black feminist thought articulates the often taken-for-granted knowledge shared by African-American women as a group, the consciousness of Black women may be transformed by such thought. Many Black women blues singers have long sung about taken-for-granted situations that affect U.S. Black women. Through their music, they not only depict Black women's realities, they aim to shape them.

Because they have had greater opportunities to achieve literacy, middle-class Black women have also had greater access to the resources to engage in Black feminist scholarship. Education need not mean alienation from this dialogical relationship. The actions of educated Black women within the Black women's club movement typify this special relationship between one segment of Black women intellectuals and the wider community of African-American women:

> It is important to recognize that black women like Frances Harper, Anna Julia Cooper, and Ida B. Wells were not isolated figures of intellectual genius; they were shaped by and helped to shape a wider movement of Afro-American women. This is not to claim that they were representative of all black women; they and their counterparts formed an educated, intellectual elite, but an elite that tried to develop a cultural and historical per-

spective that was organic to the wider condition of black womanhood. (Carby 1987, 115)

The work of these women is important because it illustrates a tradition of joining scholarship and activism. Because they often lived in the same neighborhoods as working-class Blacks, turn-of-the-century club women lived in a Black civil society where this dialogical relationship was easier to establish. They saw the problems. They participated in social institutions that encouraged solutions. They fostered the development of a "cultural and historical perspective that was organic to the wider condition of black womanhood." Contemporary Black women intellectuals face similar challenges of fostering dialogues, but do so under greatly changed social conditions. Whereas racial segregation was designed to keep U.S. Blacks oppressed, it fostered a form of racial solidarity that flourished in all-Black neighborhoods. In contrast, now that Blacks live in economically heterogeneous neighborhoods, achieving the same racial solidarity raises new challenges.

Black women intellectuals are central to Black feminist thought for several reasons. First, our experiences as African-American women provide us with a unique angle of vision concerning Black womanhood unavailable to other groups, should we choose to embrace it. It is more likely for Black women, as members of an oppressed group, to have critical insights into the condition of our oppression than it is for those who live outside those structures. One of the characters in Frances Ellen Watkins Harper's 1892 novel, *Iola Leroy*, expresses this belief in the special vision of those who have experienced oppression:

> Miss Leroy, out of the race must come its own thinkers and writers. Authors belonging to the white race have written good books, for which I am deeply grateful, but it seems to be almost impossible for a white man to put himself completely in our place. No man can feel the iron which enters another man's soul. (Carby 1987, 62)

Only African-American women occupy this center and can "feel the iron" that enters Black women's souls, because while U.S. Black women's experiences resemble others, such experiences remain unique. The importance of Black women's leadership in producing Black feminist thought does not mean that others cannot participate. It does mean that the primary responsibility for defining one's own reality lies with the people who live that reality, who actually have those experiences.

Second, Black women intellectuals both inside and outside the academy are less likely to walk away from Black women's struggles when the obstacles seem overwhelming or when the rewards for staying diminish. In discussing Black women's involvement in the feminist movement, Sheila Radford-Hill stresses the significance of taking actions in one's own behalf:

> Black women now realize that part of the problem within the movement was our insistence that white women do for/with us what we must do

> for/with ourselves: namely, frame our own social action around our own agenda for change. . . . Critical to this discussion is the right to organize on one's own behalf. . . . Criticism by black feminists must reaffirm this principle. (1986, 162)

For most U.S. Black women, engaging in Black feminist research and scholarship is not a passing fad—these issues affect both contemporary daily life and inter-generational realities.

Third, Black women intellectuals from all walks of life must aggressively push the theme of self-definition because speaking for oneself and crafting one's own agenda is essential to empowerment. As Black feminist sociologist Deborah K. King succinctly states, "Black feminism asserts self-determination as essential" (1988, 72). Black feminist thought cannot challenge intersecting oppressions without empowering African-American women. Because self-definition is key to individual and group empowerment, ceding the power of self-definition to other groups, no matter how well-meaning or supportive of Black women they may be, in essence replicates existing power hierarchies. As Patrice L. Dickerson con-tends, "A person comes into being and knows herself by her achievements, and through her efforts to become and know herself, she achieves" (personal corre-spondence 1988). Like Dickerson, individual African-American women have long displayed varying types of consciousness regarding our shared angle of vision. When these individual expressions of consciousness are articulated, argued through, contested, and aggregated in ways that reflect the heterogeneity of Black womanhood, a collective group consciousness dedicated to resisting oppression becomes possible. Black women's ability to forge these individual, often unarticulated, yet potentially powerful expressions of everyday conscious-ness into an articulated, self-defined, collective standpoint is key to Black women's survival. As Audre Lorde points out, "It is axiomatic that if we do not define ourselves for ourselves, we will be defined by others—for their use and to our detriment" (1984, 45).

Fourth, Black women intellectuals are central in the production of Black fem-inist thought because we alone can foster the group autonomy that fosters effec-tive coalitions with other groups. Recall that Black women intellectuals need not be middle-class, educated, middle-aged, or recognized as such by academia or other establishments. Black women intellectuals constitute a highly diverse group. Rather than assuming that Black women intellectuals constitute a Black female version of William E. B. DuBois's Talented Tenth—a common mispercep-tion advanced by some elitist academics who apparently have difficulty imagin-ing everyday Black women as bona fide intellectuals (see, e.g., Gilroy 1993, 53)—the type of intellectual leadership envisioned here requires collaboration among diverse Black women to think through what would constitute Black women's autonomy. Moreover, although Black feminist thought originates within Black women's communities, it cannot flourish isolated from the experiences and ideas of other groups. Black women intellectuals must find ways to place our own heterogeneous experiences and consciousness at the center of any serious efforts to develop Black feminist thought without having our thought become separatist and exclusionary.

This autonomy is quite distinct from separatist positions whereby Black women withdraw from other groups and engage in exclusionary politics. In her introduction to *Home Girls, A Black Feminist Anthology,* Barbara Smith describes this difference: "Autonomy and separatism are fundamentally different. Whereas autonomy comes from a position of strength, separatism comes from a position of fear. When we're truly autonomous we can deal with other kinds of people, a multiplicity of issues, and with difference, because we have formed a solid base of strength" (1983, xl). As mothers, college presidents, grassroots activists, teachers, musicians, and corporate executives, Black women intellectuals who contribute to articulating an autonomous, self-defined standpoint are in a position to examine the usefulness of coalitions with other groups, both scholarly and activist, in order to develop new models for social change. Autonomy to develop a self-defined, independent analysis means neither that Black feminist thought has relevance only for African-American women nor that we must confine ourselves to analyzing our own experiences. As Sonia Sanchez points out, "I've always known that if you write from a black experience, you're writing from a universal experience as well. . . . I know you don't have to whitewash yourself to be universal" (Tate 1983, 142).

By advocating, refining, and disseminating Black feminist thought, individuals from other groups who are engaged in similar social justice projects—Black men, African women, White men, Latinas, White women, and members of other U.S. racial/ethnic groups, for example—can identify points of connection that further social justice projects. Very often, however, engaging in the type of coalition envisioned here requires that individuals become "traitors" to the privileges that their race, class, gender, sexuality, or citizenship status provide them. For example, in *Memoir of a Race Traitor,* Mab Segrest (1994) writes of how coming to terms with her lesbian identity spurred her recognition of how her Whiteness gave her unearned privileges. Unlike most U.S. White women, Segrest turned her back on this privilege, embraced her new identity as a "race traitor," and came to see her role as confronting social injustice.[3] Similarly, sociologist Joe Feagin's antiracist scholarship exemplifies a similar rejection of the unearned privileges of Whiteness. Feagin chooses to use benefits that may accrue to him as a White male to engage in collaborative scholarship with Black men (Feagin and Sikes 1994) and with Black women (St. Jean and Feagin 1998). While many might see Segrest and Feagin as "race traitors," their intellectual work illustrates how coalition building that advances Black feminist thought might operate.

Just as African-American women who aim to advance Black feminism as a social justice project can support other social justice projects—U.S. Black women who are respectful of the importance of Latina autonomy to Latina social justice projects can study, learn from, research, and teach about Latinas if they do so in non-exploitative ways—so can others approach Black feminist thought in a similar fashion. Thus, U.S. Black feminist thought fully actualized is a collaborative enterprise. It must be open to coalition building with individuals engaged in similar social justice projects.

Coalition building such as this requires simultaneous if not prior dialogues among Black women intellectuals and within the larger African-American women's community. Exploring the common themes of a Black women's standpoint is an important first step. Moreover, finding ways of handling internal dissent is especially important for building Black women's intellectual communities. Evelynn Hammonds describes how maintaining a united front for Whites stifles her thinking: "What I need to do is challenge my thinking, to grow. On white publications sometimes I feel like I'm holding up the banner of black womanhood. And that doesn't allow me to be as critical as I would like to be" (in Clarke et al. 1983, 104). Cheryl Clarke observes that she has two dialogues: one with the public and the private ones in which she feels free to criticize the work of other Black women. Clarke states that the private dialogues "have changed my life, have shaped the way I feel . . . have mattered to me" (p. 103).

Coalition building also requires dialogues with groups engaged in similar social justice projects. Black women intellectuals can use our outsider-within location in building effective coalitions and stimulating dialogue with others who are similarly located. Barbara Smith suggests that Black women develop dialogues from a "commitment to principled coalitions, based not upon expediency, but upon our actual need for each other" (1983, xxxiii). Dialogues among and coalitions with a range of groups, each with its own distinctive set of experiences and specialized thought embedded in those experiences, form the larger, more general terrain of intellectual and political discourse necessary for furthering Black feminism. Through dialogues exploring how domination is maintained and changed, parallels between Black women's experiences and those of other groups become the focus of investigation.

Dialogues associated with ethical, principled coalition building create possibilities for new versions of truth. Alice Walker's answer to the question of what she felt were the major differences between the literature of African-Americans and Whites offers a provocative glimpse of the types of truths that might emerge through epistemologies that embrace dialogues and coalition building. Walker did not spend much time considering this question, since it was not the difference between them that interested her, but, rather, the way Black writers and White writers seemed to be writing one immense story, with different parts of the story coming from a multitude of different perspectives. In a conversation with her mother, Walker refines this epistemological vision: "I believe that the truth about any subject only comes when all sides of the story are put together, and all their different meanings make one new one. Each writer writes the missing parts to the other writer's story. And the whole story is what I'm after" (1983, 49). Her mother's response to Walker's vision of the possibilities of dialogues and coalitions hints at the difficulty of sustaining such dialogues across differences in power: " 'Well, I doubt if you can ever get the *true* missing parts of anything away from the white folks,' my mother says softly, so as not to offend the waitress who is mopping up a nearby table; 'they've sat on the truth so long by now they've mashed the life out of it' " (1983, 49).

Black Feminism as Dynamic and Changing

A fifth distinguishing feature of U.S. Black feminist thought concerns the significance of change. In order for Black feminist thought to operate effectively within Black feminism as a social justice project, both must remain dynamic. Neither Black feminist thought as a critical social theory nor Black feminist practice can be static; as social conditions change, so must the knowledge and practices designed to resist them. For example, stressing the importance of Black women's centrality to Black feminist thought does not mean that all African-American women desire, are positioned, or are qualified to exert this type of intellectual leadership. Under current conditions, some Black women thinkers have lost contact with Black feminist practice. Conversely, the changed social conditions under which U.S. Black women now come to womanhood—class-segregated neighborhoods, some integrated, far more not—place Black women of different social classes in entirely new relationships with one another.

African-American women as a group may have experiences that provide us with a unique angle of vision. But expressing a collective, self-defined Black feminist consciousness is problematic precisely because dominant groups have a vested interest in suppressing such thought. As Hannah Nelson notes, "I have grown to womanhood in a world where the saner you are, the madder you are made to appear" (Gwaltney 1980, 7). Ms. Nelson realizes that those who control school curricula, television programs, government statistics, and the press typically prevail in establishing their viewpoint as superior to others.

An oppressed group's experiences may put its members in a position to see things differently, but their lack of control over the ideological apparatuses of society makes expressing a self-defined standpoint more difficult. Elderly domestic worker Rosa Wakefield assesses how the standpoints of the powerful and those who serve them diverge:

> If you eats these dinners and don't cook 'em, if you wears these clothes and don't buy or iron them, then you might start thinking that the good fairy or some spirit did all that. . . . Black folks don't have no time to be thinking like that. . ... But when you don't have anything else to do, you can think like that. It's bad for your mind, though. (Gwaltney 1980, 88)

Ms. Wakefield has a self-defined perspective growing from her experiences that enables her to reject standpoints advanced by more powerful groups. And yet ideas like hers are typically suppressed by dominant groups. Groups unequal in power are correspondingly unequal in their ability to make their standpoint known to themselves and others.

The changing social conditions that confront African-American women stimulate the need for new Black feminist analyses of the common differences that characterize U.S. Black womanhood. Some Black women thinkers are already engaged in this process. Take, for example, Barbara Omolade's (1994) insightful analysis of Black women's historical and contemporary participation in mammy work. Most can understand mammy work's historical context, one where Black women were confined to domestic service, with Aunt Jemima created as a controlling image designed to hide Black women's exploitation. Understanding the limitations of domestic service, much of Black women's progress in the labor market has been measured by the move out of domestic service. Currently, few U.S. Black women work in domestic service in private homes. Instead, a good deal of this work in private homes is now done by undocumented immigrant women of color who lack U.S. citizenship; their exploitation resembles that long visited upon African-American women (Chang 1994). But, as Omolade points out, these changes do not mean that U.S. Black women have escaped mammy work. Even though few Aunt Jemimas exist today, and those that do have been cosmetically altered, leading to the impression that mammy work has disappeared, Omolade reminds us that mammy work has assumed new forms. Within each segment of the labor market—the low-paid jobs at fast-food establishments, nursing homes, day-care centers, and dry cleaners that characterize the secondary sector, the secretaries and clerical workers of the primary lower tier sector, or the teachers, social workers, nurses, and administrators of the primary upper tier sector—U.S. Black women still do a remarkable share of the emotional nurturing and cleaning up after other people, often for lower pay. In this context, the task for contemporary Black feminist thought lies in explicating these changing relationships and developing analyses of how these commonalities are experienced differently.

The changing conditions of Black women's work overall has important implications for Black women's intellectual work. Historically, the suppression of Black feminist thought has meant that Black women intellectuals have traditionally relied on alternative institutional locations to produce specialized knowledge about a Black women's standpoint. Many Black women scholars, writers, and artists have worked either alone, as was the case with Maria W. Stewart, or within African-American community organizations, the case for Black women in the club movement and in Black churches. The grudging incorporation of work on Black women into curricular offerings of historically White colleges and universities, coupled with the creation of a critical mass of African-American women writers such as Toni Morrison, Alice Walker, and Gloria Naylor within these institutional locations, means that Black women intellectuals can now find employment within academia. Black women's history and Black feminist literary criticism constitute two focal points of this renaissance in Black women's intellectual work (Carby 1987). Moreover, U.S. Black women's access to the media remains unprecedented, as talk show hostess Oprah Winfrey's long-running television show and forays into film production suggest.

The visibility provided U.S. Black women and our ideas via these new institutional locations has been immense. However, one danger facing African-American women intellectuals working in these new locations concerns the potential isolation of individual thinkers from Black women's collective experiences—lack of access to other U.S. Black women and to Black women's communities. Another is the pressure to separate thought from action—particularly political activism—that typically accompanies training in standard academic disciplines or participating in allegedly neutral spheres like the "free" press. Yet another involves the inability of some Black women "superstars" to critique the terms of their own participation in these new relations. Blinded by their self-proclaimed Black feminist diva aspirations, they feel that they owe no one, especially other Black women. Instead, they become trapped within their own impoverished Black feminist universes. Despite these dangers, these new institutional locations provide a multitude of opportunities for enhancing Black feminist thought's visibility. In this new context, the challenge lies in remaining dynamic, all the while keeping in mind that a moving target is more difficult to hit.

U.S. Black Feminism and Other Social Justice Projects

A final distinguishing feature of Black feminist thought concerns its relationship to other projects for social justice. A broad range of African-American women intellectuals have advanced the view that Black women's struggles are part of a wider struggle for human dignity, empowerment, and social justice. In an 1893 speech to women, Anna Julia Cooper cogently expressed this worldview:

> We take our stand on the solidarity of humanity, the oneness of life, and the unnaturalness and injustice of all special favoritisms, whether of sex, race, country, or condition. . . . The colored woman feels that woman's cause is one and universal; and that . . . not till race, color, sex, and condition are seen as accidents, and not the substance of life; not till the universal title of humanity to life, liberty, and the pursuit of happiness is conceded to be inalienable to all; not till then is woman's lesson taught and woman's cause won—not the white woman's nor the black woman's, not the red woman's but the cause of every man and of every woman who has writhed silently under a mighty wrong. (Loewenberg and Bogin 1976, 330–31)

Like Cooper, many African-American women intellectuals embrace this perspective regardless of particular political solutions we propose, our educational backgrounds, our fields of study, or our historical periods. Whether we advocate working through autonomous Black women's organizations, becoming part of women's organizations, running for political office, or supporting Black community institutions, African-American women intellectuals repeatedly identify political actions such as these as a *means* for human empowerment rather than ends in and of themselves. Thus one important guiding principle of Black feminism is a recurring humanist vision (Steady 1981, 1987).[4]

Alice Walker's preference for the term *womanist* addresses this notion of the solidarity of humanity. "Womanist is to feminist as purple is to lavender," she writes. To Walker, one is "womanist" when one is "committed to the survival and wholeness of entire people, male and female." A womanist is "not a separatist, except periodically for health" and is "traditionally universalist, as is 'Mama, why are we brown, pink, and yellow, and our cousins are white, beige, and black?' Ans.: 'Well, you know the colored race is just like a flower garden, with every color flower represented' " (1983, xi). By redefining all people as "people of color," Walker universalizes what are typically seen as individual struggles while simultaneously allowing space for autonomous movements of self-determination.[5]

In assessing the sexism of the Black nationalist movement of the 1960s, lawyer Pauli Murray identifies the dangers inherent in separatism as opposed to autonomy, and also echoes Cooper's concern with the solidarity of humanity:

> The lesson of history that all human rights are indivisible and that the failure to adhere to this principle jeopardizes the rights of all is particularly applicable here. A built-in hazard of an aggressive ethnocentric movement which disregards the interests of other disadvantaged groups is that it will become parochial and ultimately self-defeating in the face of hostile reactions, dwindling allies, and mounting frustrations. . . . Only a broad movement for human rights can prevent the Black Revolution from becoming isolated and can insure ultimate success. (Murray 1970, 102)

Without a commitment to human solidarity and social justice, suggests Murray, any political movement—whether Black nationalist, feminist, or anti-elitist—may be doomed to ultimate failure.

Former congresswoman Shirley Chisholm also points to the need for self-conscious struggle against the stereotypes that support social injustice. In "working toward our own freedom, we can help others work free from the traps of their stereotypes," she notes. "In the end, antiblack, antifemale, and all forms of discrimination are equivalent to the same thing—antihumanism. . . . We must reject not only the stereotypes that others have of us but also those we have of ourselves and others" (1970, 181).

This humanist orientation within U.S. Black feminism also resembles similar stances taken with Black diasporic feminisms. Ama Ata Aidoo, a former minister of education in Ghana and author of novels, poetry, and short stories, describes the inclusive nature of her political philosophy:

> When people ask me rather bluntly every now and then whether I am a feminist, I not only answer yes, but I go on to insist that every woman and every man should be a feminist—especially if they believe that Africans should take charge of African land, African wealth, African lives, and the burden of African development. It is not possible to advocate independence for the African continent without also believing that African women must have the best that the environment can offer. For some of us, this is the crucial element in our feminism. (Aidoo 1998, 39)

Aidoo recognizes that neither African nor U.S. Black women nor any other group will ever be empowered in situations of social injustice. Social justice projects are not either/or endeavors where one can say, "We have our movement and you have yours—our movements have nothing to do with one another." Instead, such projects counsel, "We have our movement, and we support yours." In a context of intersecting oppressions, Black feminism requires searching for justice not only for U.S. Black women, but for everyone.

The words and actions of these diverse Black women intellectuals may address markedly different audiences. Yet in their commitment to Black women's empowerment within a context of social justice, they advance the strikingly similar theme of the oneness of all human life. Perhaps the most succinct version of the humanist vision in U.S. Black feminist thought is offered by Fannie Lou Hamer, the daughter of sharecroppers and a Mississippi civil rights activist. While sitting on her porch, Ms. Hamer observed, "Ain' no such thing as I can hate anybody and hope to see God's face" (Jordan 1981, xi).

3 WORK, FAMILY, AND BLACK WOMEN'S OPPRESSION

Honey, de white man is the de ruler of everything as fur as Ah been able tuh find out. Maybe it's some place way off in de ocean where de black man is in power, but we don't know nothin' but what we see. So de white man throw down de load and tell de nigger man tuh pick it up. He pick it up because he have to, but he don't tote it. He hand it to his womenfolks. De nigger woman is de mule uh de world so fur as Ah can see. —Zora Neale Hurston 1937, 16

With these words Nanny, an elderly African-American woman in Zora Neale Hurston's *Their Eyes Were Watching God,* explains Black women's "place" to her young, impressionable granddaughter. Nanny knows that being treated as "mules uh de world" lies at the heart of Black women's oppression. Thus, one core theme in U.S. Black feminist thought consists of analyzing Black women's work, especially Black women's labor market victimization as "mules." As dehumanized objects, mules are living machines and can be treated as part of the scenery. Fully human women are less easily exploited. As mill worker Corine Cannon observes, "Your work, and this goes for white people and black, is what you are . . . your work is your life" (Byerly 1986, 156).

In general, Black feminist analyses of Black women's work emphasize two themes. On the one hand, much scholarship investigates how Black women's paid work is organized within intersecting oppressions of race, class, and gender. Documenting Black women's labor market status in order to see the general patterns of race and gender inequality is one primary area of analysis (Higginbotham 1983; Jones 1985; Amott and Matthaei 1991). This research is supplemented by studies of Black women's work during specific historical eras, such as slavery (Jones 1985; D. White 1985) and the urbanizing South (Clark-Lewis 1985), and their positions in specific occupational niches, primarily domestic work (Dill 1980, 1988a; Rollins 1985), in unions (Sacks 1988), and in the professions (Moses 1989; Essed 1991; Higginbotham 1994). Within Black feminist-influenced scholarship, African-American women are often presented as constrained but empowered figures, even in extremely difficult labor market settings (Terborg-Penn 1985). Studying the conditions of Black women's employment, especially racial discrimination at work, also provides new knowledge on the significance of Black women's work (St. Jean and Feagin 1998, 40–72). Despite the scholarship's insights concerning Black women's resilience, Black feminist-influenced scholarship points out that for far too many U.S. Black women, Maria Stewart's claim that "let our girls possess whatever amiable qualities of soul they may . . . it is impossible for scarce an individual of them to rise above the condition of servants" (Richardson 1987, 46) remains true (Omolade 1994). U.S. Black women may have migrated out of domestic service in private homes, but as their overrepresentation as nursing home assistants, day-care aides, dry-cleaning workers, and fast-food employees suggests, African-American women engaged in low-paid service work is far from a thing of the past.

A less developed but equally important theme concerns how Black women's unpaid family labor is simultaneously confining and empowering for Black women. In particular, research on U.S. Black women's unpaid labor within extended families remains less fully developed in Black feminist thought than does that on Black women's paid work. By emphasizing African-American women's contributions to their families' well-being, such as keeping families together and teaching children survival skills (Martin and Martin 1978; Davis 1981), such scholarship suggests that Black women see the unpaid work that they do for their families more as a form of resistance to oppression than as a form of exploitation by men. Despite these views, investigating how Black women's unpaid labor is exploited within African-American family networks, for example, by boyfriends, relatives, and even government-supported social policies, remains a neglected topic. In the context of Black family studies that either castigate Black mothers or glorify them, the theme of how hard Black women *work* is often overlooked.

When combined, Black feminist-inspired analyses of paid and unpaid work performed both in the labor market and in families stimulate a better appreciation of the powerful and complex interplay that shapes Black women's position as "de mule uh de world." They also promise to shed light on ongoing debates concerning connections between work and family.

Family and Work: Challenging the Definitions

When Dan Quayle, then U.S. vice president, used the term *family values* near the end of a speech at a political fund-raiser in 1992, he apparently touched a national nerve. Following Quayle's speech, close to 300 articles with "family values" in their titles appeared in the popular press. Despite the range of polit-ical perspectives expressed on family values, one thing remained clear: Family values, however defined, seemed important to national well-being, and Quayle had tapped much deeper feelings about the significance of ideas about family if not actual families themselves in the United States.

Dan Quayle's and similar understandings of family depend heavily on who controls the definitions. And the definitions advanced by elite groups in the United States uniformly work to the detriment of African-American women. Situated in the center of family values debates is an imagined traditional family ideal. Formed through a combination of marital and blood ties, "normal" fami-lies should consist of heterosexual, racially homogeneous couples who produce their own biological children. Such families should have a specific authority structure, namely, a father-head earning an adequate family wage, a stay-at-home wife and mother, and children. Idealizing the traditional family as a private haven from a public world, family is seen as being held together through primary emo-tional bonds of love and caring. Assuming a relatively fixed sexual division of labor, wherein women's roles are defined as primarily in the home with men's in the public world of work, the traditional family ideal also assumes the separa-tion of work and family. Defined as a natural or biological arrangement based on heterosexual attraction, instead this monolithic family type is actually supported by government policy. It is organized not around a biological core, but a state-sanctioned, heterosexual marriage that confers legitimacy not only on the fami-ly structure itself but on children born in this family (Andersen 1991; Thorne 1992). In general, everything the imagined traditional family ideal is thought to be, African-American families are not.[1]

Two elements of the traditional family ideal are especially problematic for African-American women. First, the assumed split between the "public" sphere of paid employment and the "private" sphere of unpaid family responsibilities has never worked for U.S. Black women. Under slavery, U.S. Black women worked without pay in the allegedly public sphere of Southern agriculture and had their family privacy routinely violated. Second, the public/private binary separating the family households from the paid labor market is fundamental in explaining U.S. gender ideology. If one assumes that real men work and real women take care of families, then African-Americans suffer from deficient ideas concerning gender. In particular, Black women become less "feminine," because they work outside the home, work for pay and thus compete with men, and their work takes them away from their children.

Framed through this prism of an imagined traditional family ideal, U.S. Black women's experiences and those of other women of color are typically deemed deficient (Higginbotham 1983; Glenn 1985; Mullings 1997). Rather than trying to explain why Black women's work and family patterns deviate from the seem-ing normality of the traditional family ideal, a more fruitful approach lies in challenging the very constructs of work and family themselves (Collins 1998b).

Understandings of work, like understandings of family, vary greatly depending on who controls the definitions. In the following discussion of the distinction between work and measures of self, May Madison, a participant in John Gwaltney's study of inner-city African-Americans, alludes to the difference between work as an instrumental activity and work as something for self:

> One very important difference between white people and black people is that white people think you *are* your work. . . . Now, a black person has more sense than that because he knows that what I am doing doesn't have anything to do with what I want to do or what I do when I am doing for myself. Now, black people think that my work is just what I have to do to get what I want. (Gwaltney 1980, 174)

Ms. Madison's perspective criticizes definitions of work that grant White men more status and human worth because they are employed in better-paid occupations. She recognizes that work is a contested construct and that evaluating individual worth by the type of work performed is a questionable practice in systems based on race and gender inequality.

Work might be better conceptualized by examining the range of work that African-American women actually perform. Work as alienated labor can be economically exploitative, physically demanding, and intellectually deadening—the type of work long associated with Black women's status as "mule." Alienated labor can be paid—the case of Black women in domestic service, those Black women working as dishwashers, dry-cleaning assistants, cooks, and health-care assistants, as well as some professional Black women engaged in corporate mammy work; or it can be unpaid, as with the seemingly never-ending chores of many Black grandmothers and Black single mothers. But work can also be empowering and creative, even if it is physically challenging and appears to be demeaning. Exploitative wages that Black women were allowed to keep and use for their own benefit or labor done out of love for the members of one's family can represent such work. Again, this type of work can be either paid or unpaid.

What is the connection between U.S. Black women's work both in the labor market and in African-American family networks? Addressing this question for four key historical periods in Black political economy uses this broader understanding of Black women's work to further Black feminist analyses of U.S. Black women's oppression.

The Process of Enslavement

Historically African-American families have been economically exploited and politically disenfranchised within the U.S. political economy (Berry 1994). This neither means that all African-Americans have been poor, nor that most are today. But diversity among U.S. Blacks in the historical and contemporary contours of intersecting oppressions of race and class does not erase the fundamental relationship of injustice. This unjust context has affected U.S. Blacks as a group and thus provides a framework for understanding Black women's work experiences both in kin networks and in the labor market (Mullings 1997, 20–51).

During the shift to industrialization in the early nineteenth century, White immigrants, landowners, and Whites of all social classes and citizenship categories had the legal right to maintain families and, if needed, to work for pay. In contrast, the majority of African-Americans were enslaved. They had great difficulty maintaining families and family privacy in public spheres that granted them no citizenship rights. Enslaved Africans were property (Burnham 1987), and one way that many resisted the dehumanizing effects of slavery was by re-creating African notions of family as extended kin units (Webber 1978; Sobel 1979). Bloodlines carefully monitored in West African societies were replaced by a notion of "blood" whereby enslaved Africans drew upon notions of family to redefine themselves as part of a Black community consisting of their enslaved "brothers" and "sisters" (Gutman 1976). This slave community stood in opposition to a White male–controlled public sphere of the capitalist political economy. In this way, the line separating enslaved African women and men from White women and men stimulated the creation of an important yet subjugated Black civil society (Brown 1994). This racial divide served as a more accurate marker delineating public and private spheres for African-Americans than that separating Black households from the Black community overall.

Prior to U.S. enslavement and African colonization, women in African societies apparently combined work and family without seeing much conflict between the two. In West African societies, women's fundamental family responsibilities revolved around motherhood, and they routinely combined child care with their contributions to precapitalist political economies. In agricultural societies dependent on female farmers, children accompanied their mothers to the fields. Women entrepreneurs took their children with them when conducting business in the marketplace. When old enough, children contributed to family-based production by caring for siblings, running errands, and generally helping out. Working did not detract from West African women's mothering. Instead, being economically productive and contributing to the family-based economy was an integral part of motherhood (Sudarkasa 1981a). This does not mean that male domination was absent from such societies (see, e.g., Imam et al. 1997), only that women's activities with work and family differed from those they encountered under slavery.

For African women enslaved in the United States, these basic ideas concerning work, family, and motherhood were retained, yet changed by two fundamental demands of enslavement. First, whereas African women worked on behalf of their families and children, enslaved African-American women's labor benefited their owners. Second, the nature of work performed was altered. Women did not retain authority over their time, technology, workmates, or type or amount of work they performed. In essence, their forced incorporation into a capitalist political economy as slaves meant that West African women became economically exploited, politically powerless units of labor.

Gender roles were similarly shaped under slavery. Black women generally performed the same work as men. This enabled them to recraft West African traditions whereby women were not limited to devalued family labor (Jones 1985; D. White 1985). However, unlike African precolonial political economies, where women's labor benefited their lineage group and their children, under slavery neither men nor women got to keep what they produced. Under U.S. capitalism, slavery also established the racial division of labor whereby African-Americans were relegated to dirty, manual, nonintellectual jobs. Despite slavery's burdens, African-Americans did not perceive work as the problem but, rather, the exploitation inherent in the work they performed. A saying among enslaved Africans, "It's a poor dog that won't wag its own tail," alludes to popular perceptions among Blacks that Whites were lazy and did not value work as much as African-Americans themselves.

Black women's work affected the organization of child care. Perceptions of motherhood as an unpaid occupation in the home comparable to paid male occupations in the public sector advanced by the traditional family ideal never became widespread among the majority of African-American women (Mullings 1997). By denying enslaved African women marriage, citizenship, and even humanity, slavery provided no social context for issues of privatized motherhood as a stay-at-home occupation. Instead, communal child-care arrangements substituted for individualized maternal care—a few women were responsible for caring for all children too young to work, and women as a group felt accountable for one another's children (D. White 1985).

African-American women's experiences as mothers have been shaped by the dominant group's efforts to harness Black women's sexuality and fertility to a system of capitalist exploitation. Efforts to control U.S. Black women's reproduction were important to the maintenance of the race, class, and gender inequality characterizing the slave order in at least three ways. First, the biological notions of race underpinning the racial subordination of the slave system required so-called racial purity in order to be effective. Since children followed the condition of their mothers, children born of enslaved Black women were slaves. Forbidding Black men to have sexual relations with White women of any social class reduced the possibility that children of African descent would be born to White mothers. Any children born of such liaisons must be seen as being the product of rape. Motherhood and racism were symbolically intertwined, with controlling the sexuality and fertility of both African-American and White women essential in reproducing racialized notions of American womanhood (King 1973).

Second, motherhood as an institution occupies a special place in transmitting values to children about their proper place. On the one hand, a mother can foster her children's oppression if she teaches them to believe in their own inferiority. On the other hand, the relationship between mothers and children can serve as a private sphere in which cultures of resistance and everyday forms of resistance are learned (Scott 1985). When Black slave mothers taught their children to trust their own self-definitions and value themselves, they offered a powerful tool for resisting oppression.

Finally, controlling Black women's reproduction was essential to the creation and perpetuation of capitalist class relations. Slavery benefited certain segments of the U.S. population by economically exploiting others. As Black feminist intellectual Frances Ellen Watkins Harper argued, "How can we pamper our appetites upon luxuries drawn from reluctant fingers. Oh, could slavery exist long if it did not sit on a commercial throne?" (Sterling 1984, 160). Under such a system in which the control of property is fundamental, enslaved African women were valuable commodities (Williams 1991). Slaveowners controlled Black women's labor and commodified Black women's bodies as units of capital. Moreover, as mothers, Black women's fertility produced the children who increased their owner's property and labor force (Davis 1981; Burnham 1987).

Efforts to control Black women's sexuality were tied directly to slave owners' efforts to increase the number of children their female slaves produced. Historian Deborah Gray White (1985) writes, "Slave masters wanted adolescent girls to have children, and to this end they practiced a passive, though insidious kind of breeding" (p. 98). Techniques such as assigning pregnant women lighter workloads, giving pregnant women more attention and rations, and rewarding prolific women with bonuses were all used to increase Black women's reproduction. Punitive measures were also used. Infertile women could expect to be treated "like barren sows and be passed from one unsuspecting buyer to the next" (D. White 1985, 101).

The relative security that often accompanied motherhood served to reinforce its importance. Childbearing was a way for enslaved Black women to anchor themselves in a place for an extended period and maintain enduring relationships with husbands, family, and friends. Given the short life expectancy of slave women—33.6 years—and the high mortality rates of Black children—from 1850 to 1860 fewer than two of three Black children survived to the age of 10—enslaved women's ability to bear many healthy children was often the critical element in the length and stability of slave marriages (Giddings 1984). Similarly, the refusal of women to bear children and cases of Black infanticide can be interpreted as acts of resistance (Hine and Wittenstein 1981).

Deborah Gray White contends that slaveholders' efforts to increase fertility encouraged Black women to elevate motherhood over marriage. At the same time, it paralleled African-derived cultural patterns where women were expected to provide for their children:

> Relationships between mother and child . . . superseded those between husband and wife. Slaveholder practice encouraged the primacy of the mother-child relationship, and in the mores of the slave community

> motherhood ranked above marriage. . . . Women in their roles as mothers
> were the central figures in the nuclear slave family. (1985, 159)

Black women's centrality in Black family networks should not be confused with
matriarchal or female-dominated family units (Collins 1989; Dickerson 1995b).
Matriarchy theses assume that someone must "rule" in order for households to
function effectively. Neither Black men nor Black women ruled Black family networks (Davis 1981; Burnham 1987). Rather, African-American men's and
women's positions within slave political economies made it unlikely that either
patriarchal or matriarchal domination could take root.

The Transition to "Free" Labor

For African-Americans the period between emancipation and subsequent migrations to southern and northern cities was characterized by two distinct models
of community. Each offered a different version of the connections between work
and family. The model of community advanced by dominant White society
reflected capitalist market economies of competitive, industrial, and monopoly
capitalism (Amott and Matthaei 1991). Firmly rooted in an exchange-based
marketplace with its accompanying assumptions of rational economic decision
making and White male control of the marketplace, this model of community
stressed the rights of individuals to make decisions in their own self-interest,
regardless of the impact on the larger society. Composed of a collection of
unequal individuals who compete for greater shares of money as the medium
of exchange, this model of community legitimates relations of domination
either by denying they exist or by treating them as inevitable (Hartsock 1983b).

   Under slavery, African-Americans paradoxically were well integrated within,
yet excluded from, the economic and political benefits of the market economy
and its version of community. Slave notions of Black community, while African-
influenced, were also supported by the common conditions of exclusion from
the market economy. Upon emancipation, Blacks became wage laborers and were
thrust into these exchange relationships in which individual gain was placed
ahead of collective good. Anna Julia Cooper describes this larger setting as the
Accumulative Period, and challenged its basic assumptions about community
and women's role in it:

> At the most trying time of what we have called the Accumulative Period,
> when internecine war, originated through man's love of gain and his
> determination to subordinate national interests and black men's rights
> alike to the considerations of personal profit and loss, was drenching our
> country with its own best blood, who shall recount the name and fame of
> the women on both sides of the senseless strife? (Cooper 1892, 128)

Cooper's ideas are key in that they not only link racism, economic exploitation after emancipation, and the violence needed to maintain both, but they clearly label the public sphere and its community as a male-defined arena. By asking, "Who shall recount the name and fame of the women?" she questions the role of gender in structuring women's subordination generally, and Black women's work and family roles in particular.

During this period, revitalized political and economic oppression of African-Americans in the South influenced U.S. Blacks' actions and ideas about family and community. Racial segregation became legally entrenched during this period (Berry 1994). Within Black civil society, notions of interpersonal relations forged during slavery endured—such as equating family with extended family, of treating community as family, and of seeing dealings with Whites as elements of public discourse and dealings with Blacks as part of family business (Brown 1994). In a climate of state-sanctioned racial violence, Black solidarity became highly important and worked to suppress bona fida differences among U.S. Blacks. As a result, African-American definitions of community emerged that differed from public, market-driven, exchange-based community models. Whether adhered to as a remnant of the African past or responding to the exigencies of political and economic disenfranchisement in the post–Reconstruction South, Black communities as places of collective effort and will stood in contrast to the public, market-driven, exchange-based dominant political economy in which they were situated.

For African-American women the issue was less one of achieving economic parity with their Black male counterparts and more one of securing an adequate overall family income. Denying U.S. Black men a family wage meant that Black women continued working for pay. Motherhood as a privatized, female "occupation" never predominated in Black civil society because no social class foundation could be had to support it (Dill 1988b). Communal child care within extended families continued (Martin and Martin 1978; Jones 1985). Beginning with the landmark *Plessy v. Ferguson* Supreme Court decision, the legalization of racial segregation in housing, education, employment, and public accommodations erected rigid boundaries between African-Americans and White Americans. At the same time, the more fluid boundaries characterizing the relationships among households, Black family networks, and Black community organizations such as Black churches persisted. Within African-American communities social class–specific gender ideology developed during this period (Higginbotham 1989, 1993).

For at least 75 years after emancipation, the vast majority of Black families remained in the South (Jones 1985). Black women workers were confined to two major occupations. The majority of Black women worked in the fields, with the male head of the extended family unit receiving any wages earned by the family unit. Such work was hard, exhausting, and represented little change from the work done by enslaved African-American women. Sara Brooks began full-time work in the fields at age 11 and remembers, "We never was lazy cause we used to really work. We used to work like mens. Oh, fight sometime, fuss sometime, but worked on" (Simonsen 1986, 39).

Domestic work constituted the other primary occupation for Black women's wage labor. Seeing such work as inevitable, families tried to prepare young Black girls. An 87-year-old North Carolina woman remembers her training: "No girl I know wasn't trained for work out by ten. You washed, watched, and whipped somebody the day you stopped crawling. From the time a girl can stand, she's being made to work" (Clark-Lewis 1985, 7). Such work was low paid and exposed Black girls and women to the constant threat of sexual harassment. One African-American woman describes the lack of protection for Black women domestic workers in the South: "I remember . . . I lost my place because I refused to let the madam's husband kiss me. . . . When my husband went to the man who had insulted me, the man cursed him, and slapped him, and—had him arrested!" (Lerner 1972, 155–56). Even though she testified in court, her husband was fined $25 and was told by the presiding judge, "This court will never take the word of a nigger against the word of a white man" (p. 156).

The sexual harassment of African-American women by White men contributed to images of Black women as fair game for all men. The difficulty of the environment prompted one Southern Black women to remonstrate:

> We poor colored women wage-earners in the South are fighting a terrible battle. . . . On the one hand, we are assailed by white men, and on the other hand, we are assailed by black men, who should be our natural protectors; and, whether in the cook kitchen, at the washtub, over the sewing machine, behind the baby carriage, or at the ironing board, we are little more than pack horses, beasts of burden, slaves! (Lerner 1972, 157)

African-American women who were the wives and daughters of able-bodied men often withdrew from both field labor and domestic service in order to concentrate on domestic duties in their own homes. In doing so they were "severely criticized by whites for removing themselves from field labor because they were seen to be aspiring to a model of womanhood that was inappropriate to them" (Dill 1988b, 422). Black women wanted to withdraw from the labor force, not to mimic middle-class White women's domesticity but, rather, to strengthen the political and economic position of their families. Their actions can be seen as a sustained effort to remove themselves from the exploited labor force in order to return the value of their labor to their families and to find relief from the sexual harassment they endured in domestic service. While many women tried to leave the paid labor force, the limited opportunities available to African-American men made it virtually impossible for the majority of Black families to survive on Black male wages alone. Even though she was offered work only as a maid, Elsa Barkley Brown's college-educated mother was fortunate. From Brown's perspective, her mother's "decision to be a wife and mother first in a world which defined Black women in so many other ways, the decision to make her family the most important priority, was an act of resistance" (1986, 11). Far too many Black women could not make this choice—they continued to work for pay, and their work profoundly affected African-American family life, communities, and the women themselves (Jones 1985).

Urbanization and Domestic Work

Black women's move to Southern and Northern cities in the early 1900s continued virtually unabated until after World War II (Marks 1989). Migration stimulated substantial shifts in Black women's labor market activities, especially those of working-class women, as well as changes in African-American family patterns and community organization. While racial segregation in housing separated African-American from White Americans, gender relations within Black civil society separated men from women. Male space included the streets, barber shops, and pool halls; female arenas consisted of households and churches. "Women, who blurred the physical boundaries of gender, did so at the jeopardy of respectability within their communities" (Higginbotham 1989, 59). Moreover, class differences among U.S. Blacks existed, but were masked by the force of racial segregation. The vast majority of U.S. Blacks were poor or working class.

During this period, historical employment patterns persisted whereby African-American men were able to locate higher-paying yet less secure work while Black women found lower-paying, more plentiful work. For example, Black men employed in low-skilled manufacturing occupations typically received wages higher than the wages earned by their wives working in domestic service. But because Black men competed directly with White male workers, they were more vulnerable to layoffs. Although Black men made higher wages when they found work, few guarantees existed that their wages were consistently available to their families. In contrast, Black women received substantially lower wages in domestic work, but could count on receiving them. This classic pattern of exploitation, differentiated by gender, has often been misrepresented in arguments suggesting that Black women or Black men have a labor market "advantage" over the other. What these approaches fail to realize is that both African-American women and men were disadvantaged in urban labor markets, with gender differences structuring distinctive patterns of economic vulnerability in employment.

Black women migrants encountered urban labor markets segmented along lines of race and gender (Amott and Matthaei 1991). For the vast majority of African-American women, urbanization meant migration out of agricultural work and into domestic work. One benefit of urbanization was that it allowed Black domestic workers to shift the conditions of their work from those of live-in servant to day work. A common migration pattern was for Black girls to train for domestic work in the South by doing chores and taking care of siblings.

Around age 10, they went to Northern cities to assist working relatives (Clark-Lewis 1985). At first girls might take care of their relatives' children. They eventually—often after years of search—found employment in day work. Moving to a larger marketplace where domestics could leave employers when demands were inappropriate allowed African-American women to make the transition from live-in to day work. One 83-year-old respondent in Elizabeth Clark-Lewis's study recounts how she viewed this shift as a move toward better working conditions: "The living-in jobs just kept you running; never stopped. Day or night you'd be getting something for somebody. You'd serve them. It was never a minute's peace. . . . But when I went out days on my jobs, I'd get my work done and be gone. I guess that's it. This work had a end" (Clark-Lewis 1985, 1).

While an improvement, the shift to day work maintained some of the more negative features of the employer/employee relationship. Despite their removal from the particular form control took in the South, domestic workers in Northern cities were economically exploited even under the best of circumstances. At its worst, domestic work approximated conditions the women had left behind in the South. Florence Rice describes how the 1930s New York City "Bronx slave market" operated, where women stood in an assigned spot and waited for employers to drive by and offer them day work: "I always remember my domestic days. Some of the women, when they didn't want to pay, they'd accuse you of stealing. . . . It was like intimidation" (Lerner 1972, 275). Although sexual harassment was less pervasive, it too remained a problem. Ms. Rice remembers a male employer who "picked me up and said his wife was ill and then when I got there his wife wasn't there and he wanted to have an affair" (p. 275).

Judith Rollins (1985) contends that what makes domestic work more "profoundly exploitative than other comparable occupations" is the precise element that makes it unique: the personal relationship between employer and employee. Rollins reports that employers do not rank work performance as their highest priority in evaluating domestic workers. Rather, the "personality of the worker and the kinds of relationships employers were able to establish with them were as or more important considerations" (p. 156).

Deference mattered, and those women who were submissive or who successfully played the role of obedient servant were more highly valued by their employers, regardless of the quality of the work performed. When domestic worker Hannah Nelson reports, "Most people who have worked in service have to learn to talk at great length about nothing," she identifies the roles domestics must play in order to satisfy their employers' perceptions of a good Black domestic. She continues, "I never have been very good at that, so I don't speak, normally. . . . Some people I have worked for think I am slow-witted because I talk very little on the job" (Gwaltney 1980, 6).

Employers used a variety of means to structure domestic work's power relationship and solicit the deference they so desired. Techniques of linguistic deference included addressing domestics by their first names, calling them "girls," and requiring that the domestic call the employer "ma'am." Employers routinely questioned domestics about their lifestyle, questions they would hesitate to ask members of their own social circle. Gifts of used clothing and other household items highlighted the economic inequality separating domestic and employer. Employers used domestics as confidantes, another behavior that reinforced the notion that domestics were outsiders (Rollins 1985).

Physical markers reinforced the deference relationship. One technique was to require that domestics wear uniforms. One respondent in Clark-Lewis's study explains why her employers liked uniforms: "Them uniforms just seemed to make them know you was theirs. Some say you wore them to show different jobs you was doing. This in grey, other serving in black. But mostly them things just showed you was always at they beck and call. Really that's all them things means!" (Clark-Lewis 1985, 16). The use of space was also a major device in structuring deference behaviors. Domestics were confined to one area of the house, usually the kitchen, and were expected to make themselves invisible when in other areas of the house. Judith Rollins recounts her reactions to being objectified in this fashion, to being treated as invisible while her employers had a conversation around her:

> It was this aspect of servitude I found to be one of the strongest affronts to my dignity as a human being. To Mrs. Thomas and her son, I became invisible; their conversation was private with me, the black servant, in the room as it would have been with no one in the room. . . . These gestures of ignoring my presence were not, I think, intended as insults; they were expressions of the employer's ability to annihilate the humanness and even, at times, the very existence of me, a servant and a black woman. (Rollins 1985, 209)

Some African-American women were fortunate enough to locate work in manufacturing. In the South, Black women entered tobacco factories, cotton mills, and flour manufacturing. Some of the dirtiest jobs in these industries were offered to African-American women. In the cotton mills Black women were employed as common laborers in the yards, as waste gatherers, and as scrubbers of machinery (Glenn 1985). With Northern migration, some Black women entered factory employment, primarily in steam laundries and the rest in unmechanized jobs as sweepers, cleaners, and ragpickers. Regardless of their location, African-American women faced discrimination (Terborg-Penn 1985). For example, Luanna Cooper, an employee for the Winston Leaf Tobacco Storage company, describes her reactions to the effort to organize segregated unions in her plant: "They're trying to have jimcrow unions. But I'm telling you jimcrow unions aren't good. They wanted me to join. I told them: 'I get jimcrow free. I won't pay for that' " (Lerner 1972, 268).

The shift to day work among domestic workers and the incorporation of some Black women into the manufacturing sector paralleled changes in African-American family and community structures. Even though the hours were long and the pay low in the occupations where Black women remained concentrated, they did have more time to devote to their families and communities than that available to live-in domestic workers. During the first wave of urbanization, African-Americans re-created the types of communities they had known in their Southern rural communities (Gutman 1976). Racial segregation in housing and employment meant that African-Americans continued to live in self-contained communities even after migration to Northern cities. As a result, the public/private split separating Black communities from what were frequently hostile White neighborhoods remained a salient feature framing Black women's work and family relationships, especially among working-class women. The cooperative networks that these women created under slavery and that they sustained in the rural South often endured. Black women domestic workers who rode buses together shared vital information essential to their survival. On occasion, they attempted unionization (Terborg-Penn 1985). Neighbors took care of one another's children, and churches typically formed the core of many Black women's community activities (Clark-Lewis 1985; Dill 1988a)

Black Women's Work and the Post–World War II Political Economy

As long as African-Americans lived in self-contained albeit racially segregated urban neighborhoods, Black community institutions aided U.S. Blacks in responding to changes in wider society. After 1945, a changing global economy in conjunction with the emergence of a new postcolonial, transnational context fostered significant shifts in Black civil society. Globally, numerous groups waged successful anticolonial struggles that resulted in new nation-states in Africa and Asia. Within the United States, the Black activism of the 1950s–1970s stimulated the dismantling of de jure and de facto racial segregation. When combined, these international and domestic political shifts greatly affected the relationship between work and family for African-American women.

The post–World War II period reflects several contradictions. On the one hand, the period has been marked by substantial gains in formal political rights for U.S. Blacks as a collectivity. From the end of the war to the mid-1970s, U.S. Blacks acquired unprecedented access to education, housing, and jobs long denied under legal segregation. From the founding of the National Association for the Advancement of Colored People (NAACP) in 1910 to the passage of the landmark Civil Rights Act in 1964 and the Voting Rights Act in 1965, U.S. Blacks pursued a policy of gaining civil rights and equal treatment in housing, schools, jobs, and public accommodation. This changed political climate led to Black civil society's becoming more stratified by social class.[2] The sizable working class that had long formed the core of Black civil society expanded upward. From this working-class "center," many Blacks experienced social mobility into the fledgling Black middle class.

On the other hand, it became increasingly clear that many problems that U.S. Blacks faced were not due solely to racial discrimination. While many African-Americans benefited from the changed legislative climate, many others did not. Class factors were equally important. Many Blacks endured downward social mobility from the working-class center. The downwardly mobile—those who lost their jobs and failed to find new ones—joined a growing population of poor Blacks that had been on the bottom all along. This growing group on the bottom, often referred to as the "Black underclass," was not the cause of Black economic disadvantage but, instead, constituted one outcome.

During this period, Black civil society underwent considerable change, much of it influenced by gender-specific patterns of Black incorporation in an increasingly global political economy (Brewer 1993; Squires 1994; Wilson 1996). In general, work for Black men in manufacturing disappeared. Black women could find work, but it was often part time, low paid, and lacking in security and benefits (Wilson 1996). Moreover, the introduction of crack cocaine in urban Black neighborhoods in the early 1980s incorporated men and women into the informal economy in gender-specific ways. Drugs became a major employer of young Black men, and young Black women looked to these men for financial assistance.

Many young U.S. Blacks grew up in communities that were markedly different than those prior to the 1980s. Extended family networks weakened (see, e.g., Kaplan 1997), and while U.S. Blacks became more class stratified, the racial segregation in housing that fosters inequities of education and employment also persisted (Massey and Denton 1993). Many young Black men came to see their futures only in terms of being rap stars, basketball players, or drug dealers. Many young Black women saw few options other than motherhood. Overall, young Black men and women could not see the optimism of the diverse antiracist social justice projects of the 1950s and 1960s but instead encountered the pessimism of shrinking opportunities. Ostensibly the beneficiaries of the previous generation's Black activism, they learned to live with new forms of control introduced by an expanding criminal justice system (Davis 1997) and a punitive social welfare bureaucracy (Brewer 1994). For many young U.S. Black men and women, access to African-American intellectual and political traditions, feminist and otherwise, remained elusive. Instead, they found themselves living in impoverished economic and intellectual environments.

Several factors stimulated these and other dramatic changes in Black civil society that in turn have affected African-American women's work and family experiences. At the center of these changes is a restructured global political economy. Job export to nonunionized American and foreign markets, job de-skilling, the shift from manufacturing to service occupations, and job creation in suburban communities all allow firms to find cheaper substitutes for Black American labor (Wilson 1987, 1996). As Black feminist sociologist Rose Brewer points out, "Capitalist firms do not have to depend upon black labor, either male or female. Low-wage, low-cost labor can be found all over the world" (Brewer 1993, 19). Moreover, legal victories did not mean that all segments of U.S. society were willing to enforce antidiscrimination legislation. Beginning in the 1980s, and throughout the 1990s, conservative politicians advanced a series of racial projects designed to limit if not eliminate the social gains of the 1960s (Omi and Winant 1994). White backlash also emerged as a formidable factor, some of it crystallizing in the growth of new White supremacist organizations (Daniels 1997; Ferber 1998). When combined with deeply entrenched patterns of racial segregation in housing that reflect an "American apartheid" (Massey and Denton 1993), worsening and chronic unemployment in many Black urban neighborhoods persisted. Overall, Black political activism of the 1950s and 1960s in the context of a changing global political economy fostered the emergence of a comfortable yet vulnerable new Black middle class. It also led to the growth of a reorganized Black working class segmented by its ability to find steady, well-paid work.

Just Holding On: Working-Class Black Women

A crucial factor in contemporary African-American civil society is not simply Black men's marginalization from work but changes affecting Black women's paid and unpaid work (Brewer 1993). Two major changes affect U.S. Black women's paid labor. The first is Black women's movement from domestic service to industrial and clerical work. The second is Black women's integration into the international division of labor in low-paid service work, which does not provide sufficient income to support a family. When combined, these two factors segment Black working-class women into two subgroups. African-American women holding good jobs in industry and the government sector constitute the core of the Black working class. Black women who can find only low-paid, intermittent service work become part of the working poor, that segment of the Black working class most likely to end up in poverty. Both groups work, and the nature of the jobs they hold determines their work and family experiences.

More Black feminist–influenced studies that examine how intersections of race and gender influence the work experiences of working-class Black women are sorely needed. In this regard, Rose Brewer's (1993) analysis of Black women's participation in Southern textile industries illustrates how examining Black women's participation in one industry reveals how U.S. Black women have been affected by global economic restructuring. Barbara Omolade (1994) points to a framework of new relationships among African-American women, one that she calls a "three-tiered Black female work site: Black female professionals who supervise Black female clerks who then serve Black female clients" (p. 62). Black working-class women "clerks" sandwiched between the professionals and their clients may find themselves subject to deference relationships reminiscent of Judith

Rollins's (1985) study of Black domestic workers. Yet these relationships among U.S. Black women across social class differences break entirely new ground. Consider Alice Walker's experiences when trying to visit Dessie Woods, a Black woman incarcerated in the Georgia penal system for defending herself against a White rapist. Walker describes her arrival at the prison, where she was turned away, not by White male guards, but by a Black woman very much like herself:

> We look at each other hard. And I "recognize" her, too. She is very black and her neck is stiff and her countenance has been softened by the blows. All day long, while her children are supported by earnings here, she sits isolated in this tiny glass entranceway, surrounded by white people who have hired her, as they always have, to do their dirty work for them. It is no accident that she is in this prison, too. (Walker 1988, 23)

Barbara Omolade advances a similar argument: "Unlike the slave plantation, which brought different kinds of workers together in an oppositional community of resistance, today's triple-tiered, Black female work site does not foster community" (1994, 63).

The disappearance of well-paid manufacturing jobs for Black working-class men suggests that young African-American women view the dual-income, working-class family as a hoped-for, albeit difficult-to-achieve, option. The alternative open to past generations of Blacks—intact marriages based on reasonably steady, adequately paid jobs for Black men and reliable yet lesser-paid jobs for Black women—is less available in the advanced capitalist welfare state. Black working-class women, especially those employed in the government sector as clerical workers, are more likely to find steady employment. But the income of Black working-class wives cannot compensate for the loss of Black men's incomes. Despite expressing support for dominant "family values" ideology, Black working-class women may find themselves as single mothers. Aggravated by Black men's inability to find well-paid work, rates of separation and divorce have increased. More significantly, many young Black women do not marry in the first place. For many Black working-class families, the economic vulnerability of Black men is one fundamental factor spurring increasing poverty among Black working-class women (Burnham 1985).

Despite its size and significance, the Black working class has been rendered mostly invisible within contemporary U.S. Black feminist thought. While many factors stimulate this outcome, Rose Brewer points to one important definitional concern: "Although there has been an assault on the Black working class, there is still a working class. It is conflated with the working poor. It is highly exploited and has experienced heavy assaults on its wage. It is a class which is often poor and female" (Brewer 1993, 25).

The New Working Poor: Black Single Mothers

Black women who work yet remain poor form an important segment of the

Black working class. Labor market trends as well as changes in federal policies toward the poor have left this group economically marginalized (Zinn 1989). Ironically, gender differences in the jobs held by working-poor Black women and men are becoming less pronounced. On average, approximately one-third of Black women and men who find employment work in jobs characterized by low wages, job instability, and poor working conditions. These jobs are growing rapidly, spurred by the increasing need for cooks, waitresses, waiters, laundry workers, health aides, and domestic servants to service the needs of affluent middle-class families. While plentiful, these jobs are mostly in neighborhoods far from the inner-city communities where poor Black women live. Moreover, few of these jobs offer the wages, stability, or advancement potential of disappearing manufacturing jobs.

The work performed by employed poor Black women resembles duties long associated with domestic service. During prior eras, domestic service was confined to private households. In contrast, contemporary cooking, cleaning, nursing, and child care have been routinized and decentralized in an array of fast-food restaurants, cleaning services, day-care centers, and service establishments. Black women perform similar work, but in different settings. The location may have changed, but the work has not. Moreover, the treatment of Black women resembles the interpersonal relations of domination reminiscent of domestic work. Mabel Lincoln, an inner-city resident, describes how the world looks to her as a working woman:

> If you are a woman slinging somebody else's hash and busting somebody else's suds or doing whatsoever you might do to keep yourself from being a tramp or a willing slave, you will be called out of your name and asked out of your clothes. In this world most people will take whatever they think you can give. It don't matter whether they want it or not, whether they need it or not, or how wrong it is for them to ask for it. (Gwaltney 1980, 68)

Many Black women turn to the informal labor market and to government transfer payments to avoid being called out of their names and asked out of their clothes. Many Black women over age 16 are not employed, in many cases because they cannot find jobs, because they are in school, have children to care for, are retired, or are in poor health. A considerable proportion support themselves through varying combinations of low-wage jobs and government transfer payments.

The employment vulnerability of working-class African-Americans in the post–World War II political economy, the relative employment equality of poor Black women and men, and the gender-specific patterns of dependence on the informal economy all have substantial implications for U.S. Black women who find themselves among the working poor. One effect has been the growth of families maintained by Black single mothers. As the testimonies of numerous

African-Americans raised by their mothers suggest, such families are not inherently a problem. Rather, the alarming trend is the persistent poverty of African-American women and children living in such households (Dickerson 1995a).

The increase in unmarried Black adolescent parents is only one indication of the effects that changes in the broader political economy are having on work and family patterns not just of poor Black women but of many other segments of the U.S. population. Rates of adolescent pregnancy are actually *decreasing* among young Black women. The real change has been a parallel decrease in marital rates of Black adolescents, a decision linked directly to how Black teens perceive opportunities to support and sustain independent households. A sizable proportion of families maintained by Black single women are created by unmarried adolescent mothers. This decline in marital rates, a post–World War II trend that accelerated after 1960, is part of changes in African-American community structures overall (Wilson 1987). The communal child-care networks of the slave era, the extended family arrangements of the rural South, and the cooperative family networks of prior eras of Black urban migration have eroded. These shifts portend major problems for African-American women and point to a continuation of Black women's oppression, but structured through new institutional arrangements.

The effects of these changes are convincingly demonstrated in Ladner and Gourdine's (1984) replication study of *Tomorrow's Tomorrow,* Joyce Ladner's (1972) study of Black female adolescents. The earlier investigation examined poor Black teenage girls' values toward motherhood and Black womanhood. The girls in the original study encountered the common experiences of urban poverty—they became mothers quite young, lived in substandard housing, attended inferior schools, and generally had to grow up quickly in order to survive. But despite the harshness of their environments, the girls in the earlier sample still "had high hopes and dreams that their futures would be positive and productive" (Ladner and Gourdine 1984, 24).

The findings from the replication study are quite different. Ladner and Gourdine maintain that "the assessments the teenagers and their mothers made of the socioeconomic conditions and their futures are harsher and bleaker than a similar population a generation ago" (p. 24). In talking with young grandmothers, all of whom looked older than they were even though the majority were in their 30s and the youngest was age 29, Ladner and Gourdine found that all became single parents through divorce or had never married. The strong Black grandmothers of prior generations were not in evidence. Instead, Ladner and Gourdine found that these young grandmothers complained about their own unmet emotional and social needs. They appeared to feel "powerless in coping with the demands made by their children. They comment frequently that their children show them no respect, do not listen to their advice, and place little value on their role as parents" (p. 23).

Sociologist Elaine Bell Kaplan's important (1997) study of 32 teen mothers and adult women who were once teen mothers reports similar findings. By the

1980s, reports Kaplan, so many young Black girls were "pushing strollers around inner-city neighborhoods that they became an integral part of both the reality and the myth concerning the sexuality of Black underclass culture" (p. xx). Kaplan describes a threadbare, overstretched Black extended family system where Black mothers could not support the emotional needs of their daughters. In the absence of support, teenagers got pregnant and decided to keep their babies. Just at a point in life when young Black girls most needed affection, many felt unloved by their mothers, ignored by their schools, and rejected by their fathers and boyfriends. The girls' mothers had their own needs. Often in poor health, anxious, distracted, and generally worn down by the struggle to raise their families in harsh urban neighborhoods, mothers routinely saw their daughters' pregnancies as one more responsibility for them to bear.

Middle-Class Black Women

Increased access to managerial and professional positions enabled sizable numbers of African-American women to move into the middle class in the post–World War II political economy. Members of the new middle class work for corporations and in the government sector, just as blue-collar workers do, and may earn generous incomes and enjoy substantial prestige. This new Black middle class occupies a contradictory location in the American political economy. As is the case for their White counterparts, being middle class requires U.S. Black professionals and managers to enter into specific social relations with owners of capital and with workers. In particular, the middle class dominates labor and is itself subordinate to capital. It is this simultaneous dominance and subordination that puts it in the "middle" (Vanneman and Cannon 1987, 57). Like owners, it exercises economic control. Professionals and managers also exercise political controls over the conditions of their own work and that of workers. Finally, members of the new middle class exercise ideological control of knowledge: They are the planners of work and framers of society's ideas.

On all three dimensions of middle-class power—economic, political, and ideological—the Black middle class differs from its White counterpart. Persistent racial discrimination means that Black middle-class women and men are less economically secure than White middle-class individuals (Oliver and Shapiro 1995). Members of the Black middle class, most of whom became middle class through social mobility from working-class origins, may express more ambivalence concerning their function as controllers of working-class employees, especially working-class Blacks. While some aspire to manage working-class Blacks, others aim to liberate them from racial oppression and poverty, while still others aim to distance themselves from Black working-class concerns. Similarly, though many middle-class Blacks defend dominant group ideologies, others challenge race, gender, and class ideologies and practices.

Black feminist theorist Barbara Omolade's (1994) three-tiered Black female work site not only explores the needs of the clerks and clients, it points to the new demands placed on Black women professionals. According to Omolade, these women's work involves a new version of "mammification," one where the legacy of Black women's work in domestic service weaves itself into the very fabric of professional Black women's jobs. Elizabeth Higginbotham (1994) notes that Black women professionals are disproportionately employed in the government sector, making them especially vulnerable to political changes such as government downsizing of the 1980s and 1990s. Moreover, within this sector, their work can resemble that of "modern mammies," namely, the care of the personal needs of the destitute and the weak in public institutions. Black women professionals are expected to fix systems which are in crisis due to underfunding, infrastructure deterioration, and demoralized staffs. As Barbara Omolade (1994) points out, "New mammies, especially those educated after the civil rights movement era, have a hard time pointing to the source of their alienation and depression or clearly identifying with a base and constituency within the Black community. Black professional women are often in high-visibility positions which require them to serve white superiors while quieting the natives" (p. 55).

Elaine Kaplan found the Black professional women she interviewed who worked with Black adolescent mothers expressed ambivalence about their jobs. By the time Kaplan finished her fieldwork at one counseling center, most of the White staff had left, and it was being run by a predominantly Black staff. Kaplan's description of the reactions of the Black staff to their new status echoes Omolade's arguments about mammification:

> The Black staff also wanted to leave but felt they would have difficulty finding other jobs to match their skills and expertise, a problem they attributed to racist White employers. Several Black women were promoted at the Center as a result of the turnover. The newly promoted women also feared the neighborhood, but for them the central issue was one of being disadvantaged while at the same time having to work with the disadvantaged. (Kaplan 1997, 154)

When the traditional gender differences in Black employment patterns are combined with the economic, political, and ideological vulnerability of the Black middle class caused by race, some interesting patterns emerge for African-American women. Black women and men alike are more vulnerable than Whites to being excluded from professional and managerial occupations. Fewer Black men have such positions, but those who do have them are in higher-paying, higher-status jobs. Greater numbers of Black women than men work in professional and managerial positions, but theirs are lower-paying, lower-status jobs.

For Black women, most of whom are not born into the Black middle class but who have recently arrived in it through social class mobility, dealing with the demands of work and family as well as those of Black civil society can be unsettling (Dumas 1980; Higginbotham and Weber 1992). Consider the case of

Leanita McClain, an African-American woman journalist raised in segregated Chicago public housing who eventually became a feature writer for a major Chicago newspaper (McClaurin-Allen 1989). In a widely cited piece titled "The Middle-Class Black's Burden," Ms. McClain laments, "I am not comfortably middle class; I am uncomfortably middle class. I have made it, but where?" (1986, 13). A substantial source of Ms. McClain's frustration stemmed from her marginal status in a range of settings. She notes, "My life abounds in incongruities. . . . Sometimes when I wait at the bus stop with my attaché case, I meet my aunt getting off the bus with other cleaning ladies on their way to do my neighbor's floors" (p. 13). No wonder Ms. McClain felt compelled to say, "I am a member of the black middle class who has had it with being patted on the head by white hands and slapped in the face by black hands for my success" (p. 12).

U.S. Black professional women report increasing difficulty in finding middle-class Black men interested in marrying them. The smaller number of Black men than Black women in professional and managerial positions represents one important issue facing Black heterosexual women who want to marry Black men. Given that separated and divorced Black women professionals are much less likely to remarry than their White counterparts, higher rates of separation and divorce may become a special problem for married Black women professionals. When faced with the prospect of never getting married to a professional Black man, whether by choice or by default, many professional Black women simply go it alone.

Black Feminist Questions

In prior eras, African-American women's relegation to agricultural and domestic work more uniformly structured Black women's oppression as "mules uh de world." At the turn of the twenty-first century, work still matters, but is organized via social class formations that often place working-class and middle-class women in new, uncharted territories. Black women's ability to cooperate across class lines for collective empowerment is not new, but the ways in which those class lines have been redrawn within a global political economy is. All African-American women encounter the common theme of having our work and family experiences shaped by intersecting oppressions of race, gender, and class. But this commonality is experienced differently by working-class women such as Mabel Lincoln and by middle-class women such as Leanita McClain.

Large numbers of U.S. Black women in the working poor are employed as cooks, laundry workers, nursing home aides, and child-care workers. These women serve not only U.S. Whites, but more affluent U.S. Blacks, other people of color, and recent immigrants. Dependent on public services of all sorts—public schools for their children, health-care clinics for their checkups, buses and other public transportation to get them to work, and social welfare bureaucracies to fill in the gap between paychecks and monthly bills—these women can encounter

Black middle-class teachers, nurses, bus drivers, and social workers who are as troublesome to them as White ones. Far too many Black single mothers living in inner-city neighborhoods remain isolated and encounter middle-class Black women primarily as police officers, social workers, teachers, or on television. How will these working-class Black women, many of whom feel stuck in the working poor, view their more privileged sisters?

Middle-class women face a distinctive set of challenges in thinking through this new social context so profoundly restructured by class. In prior eras the precarious political and social position of the small numbers of middle-class Black women encouraged them to work on behalf of "race uplift" and fostered Black solidarity among all African-American women. But contemporary middle-class Black women seem to have a choice. Will they continue to value Black solidarity with their working-class sisters, even if creating that solidarity might place them at odds with their proscribed "mammification" duties? Or will they see their newly acquired positions as theirs alone and thus perpetuate working-class Black women's subordination?

There has never been a uniformity of experience among African-American women, a situation that is more noticeable today. What remains as a challenge to Black feminist thinkers, working-class and middle-class alike, is to analyze how these new structures of oppression differentially affect Black women. If this does not occur, some U.S. Black women may in fact become instrumental in fostering other Black women's oppression.

4 MAMMIES, MATRIARCHS, AND OTHER CONTROLLING IMAGES

Called Matriarch, Emasculator and Hot Momma. Sometimes Sister, Pretty Baby, Auntie, Mammy and Girl. Called Unwed Mother, Welfare Recipient and Inner City Consumer. The Black American Woman has had to admit that while nobody knew the troubles she saw, everybody, his brother and his dog, felt qualified to explain her, even to herself. —Trudier Harris 1982, 4

Intersecting oppressions of race, class, gender, and sexuality could not continue without powerful ideological justifications for their existence. As Cheryl Gilkes contends, "Black women's assertiveness and their use of every expression of racism to launch multiple assaults against the entire fabric of inequality have been a consistent, multifaceted threat to the status quo. As punishment, Black women have been assaulted with a variety of negative images" (1983a, 294). Portraying African-American women as stereotypical mammies, matriarchs, welfare recipients, and hot mommas helps justify U.S. Black women's oppression. Challenging these controlling images has long been a core theme in Black feminist thought.

As part of a generalized ideology of domination, stereotypical images of Black womanhood take on special meaning. Because the authority to define societal values is a major instrument of power, elite groups, in exercising power, manipulate ideas about Black womanhood. They do so by exploiting already existing symbols, or creating new ones. Hazel Carby suggests that the objective of stereotypes is "not to reflect or represent a reality but to function as a disguise, or mystification, of objective social relations" (1987, 22). These controlling images are designed to make racism, sexism, poverty, and other forms of social injustice appear to be natural, normal, and inevitable parts of everyday life.

Even when the initial conditions that foster controlling images disappear, such images prove remarkably tenacious because they not only subjugate U.S. Black women but are key in maintaining intersecting oppressions (Mullings

1997, 109–30). African-American women's status as outsiders becomes the point from which other groups define their normality. Ruth Shays, a Black inner-city resident, describes how the standpoint of a subordinate group is discredited: "It will not kill people to hear the truth, but they don't like it and they would much rather hear it from one of their own than from a stranger. Now, to white people your colored person is always a stranger. Not only that, we are supposed to be dumb strangers, so we can't tell them anything!" (Gwaltney 1980, 29). As the "Others" of society who can never really belong, strangers threaten the moral and social order. But they are simultaneously essential for its survival because those individuals who stand at the margins of society clarify its boundaries. African-American women, by not belonging, emphasize the significance of belonging.

The Objectification of Black Women as the Other

Black feminist critic Barbara Christian asserts that in the United States, "the enslaved African woman became the basis for the definition of our society's *Other*" (1985, 160). Maintaining images of U.S. Black women as the Other provides ideological justification for race, gender, and class oppression. Certain basic ideas crosscut these and other forms of oppression. One such idea is binary thinking that categorizes people, things, and ideas in terms of their difference from one another (Keller 1985, 8). For example, each term in the binaries white/black, male/female, reason/emotion, culture/nature, fact/opinion, mind/body, and subject/object gains meaning only in *relation* to its counterpart (Halpin 1989).

Another basic idea concerns how binary thinking shapes understandings of human difference. In such thinking, difference is defined in oppositional terms. One part is not simply different from its counterpart; it is inherently opposed to its "other." Whites and Blacks, males and females, thought and feeling are not complementary counterparts—they are fundamentally different entities related only through their definition as opposites. Feeling cannot be incorporated into thought or even function in conjunction with it because in binary oppositional thinking, feeling retards thought and values obscure facts.

Objectification is central to this process of oppositional difference. In binary thinking, one element is objectified as the Other, and is viewed as an object to be manipulated and controlled. Social theorist Dona Richards (1980) suggests that Western thought requires objectification, a process she describes as the "separation of the 'knowing self' from the 'known object'" (p. 72). Intense objectification is a "prerequisite for the despiritualization of the universe," Richards writes, "and through it the Western cosmos was made ready for ever increasing materialization" (p. 72). A Marxist assessment of the culture/nature binary argues that history can be seen as that in which human beings constantly objectify the natural world in order to control and exploit it (Brittan and Maynard 1984, 198). Culture is defined as the opposite of an objectified nature. If undomesticated, this wild and primitive nature might destroy more civilized culture.[1] Feminist scholarship points to the identification of women with nature as being central to women's subsequent objectification and conquest by men (McClintock 1995). Black studies scholarship and postcolonial theory both suggest that defining people of color as less human, animalistic, or more "natural" denies African and Asian people's subjectivity and supports the political economy of domination that characterized slavery, colonialism, and neocolonialism (Torgovnick 1990; Chow 1993, 27–54; Said 1993; Bannerji 1995, 55–95).

Domination always involves attempts to objectify the subordinate group. "As subjects, people have the right to define their own reality, establish their own identities, name their history," asserts bell hooks (1989, 42). "As objects, one's reality is defined by others, one's identity created by others, one's history named only in ways that define one's relationship to those who are subject" (p. 42). The treatment afforded U.S. Black women domestic workers exemplifies the many forms that objectification can take. Making Black women work as if they were animals or "mules uh de world" represents one form of objectification. Deference rituals such as calling Black domestic workers "girls" enable employers to treat their employees like children, as less capable human beings. Objectification can be so severe that the Other simply disappears, as was the case when Judith Rollins's employer treated her as if she were invisible.

Finally, because oppositional binaries rarely represent different but equal relationships, they are inherently unstable. Tension may be temporarily relieved by subordinating one half of the binary to the other. Thus Whites rule Blacks, men dominate women, reason is thought superior to emotion in ascertaining truth, facts supersede opinion in evaluating knowledge, and subjects rule objects. The foundations of intersecting oppressions become grounded in interdependent concepts of binary thinking, oppositional difference, objectification, and social hierarchy. With domination based on difference forming an essential underpinning for this entire system of thought, these concepts invariably imply relationships of superiority and inferiority, hierarchical bonds that mesh with political economies of race, gender, and class oppression.

African-American women occupy a position whereby the inferior half of a series of these binaries converge, and this placement has been central to our subordination. The allegedly emotional, passionate nature of Black women has long been used to justify Black women's sexual exploitation. Similarly, restricting Black women's literacy, then claiming that we lack the facts for sound judgment, relegates African-American women to the inferior side of the fact/opinion binary. Denying Black women status as fully human subjects by treating us as the objectified Other within multiple binaries demonstrates the power that binary thinking, oppositional difference, and objectification wield within intersecting oppressions.

Despite its seeming permanence, this way of thinking, by fostering injustice, can also stimulate resistance. For example, U.S. Black women have long recognized the fundamental injustice of a system that routinely and from one generation to the next relegates U.S. Black women to the bottom of the social hierarchy. When faced with this structural injustice targeted toward the group, many Black women have insisted on our right to define our own reality, establish our own identities, and name our history. One significant contribution of work on domestic workers is that it documents Black women's everyday resistance to this attempted objectification.

Analyzing the particular controlling images applied to African-American women reveals the specific contours of Black women's objectification as well as the ways in which oppressions of race, gender, sexuality, and class intersect. Moreover, since the images themselves are dynamic and changing, each provides a starting point for examining new forms of control that emerge in a transnational context, one where selling images has increased in importance in the global marketplace.

Controlling Images and Black Women's Oppression

"Black women emerged from slavery firmly enshrined in the consciousness of white America as 'Mammy' and the 'bad black woman,'" contends Cheryl Gilkes (1983a, 294). The dominant ideology of the slave era fostered the creation of several interrelated, socially constructed controlling images of Black womanhood, each reflecting the dominant group's interest in maintaining Black women's subordination. Moreover, since Black and White women were both important to slavery's continuation, controlling images of Black womanhood also functioned to mask social relations that affected all women.

According to the cult of true womanhood that accompanied the traditional family ideal, "true" women possessed four cardinal virtues: piety, purity, submissiveness, and domesticity. Propertied White women and those of the emerging middle class were encouraged to aspire to these virtues. African-American women encountered a different set of controlling images.

The first controlling image applied to U.S. Black women is that of the mammy—the faithful, obedient domestic servant. Created to justify the economic exploitation of house slaves and sustained to explain Black women's long-standing restriction to domestic service, the mammy image represents the normative yardstick used to evaluate all Black women's behavior. By loving, nurturing, and caring for her White children and "family" better than her own, the mammy symbolizes the dominant group's perceptions of the ideal Black female relationship to elite White male power. Even though she may be well loved and may wield considerable authority in her White "family," the mammy still knows her "place" as obedient servant. She has accepted her subordination.

Black women intellectuals have aggressively criticized the image of African-American women as contented mammies. Literary critic Trudier Harris's (1982) volume *From Mammies to Militants: Domestics in Black American Literature* investigates prominent differences in how Black women have been portrayed by others in literature and how they portray themselves. In her work on the difficulties faced by Black women leaders, Rhetaugh Dumas (1980) describes how Black women executives are hampered by being treated as mammies and penalized if they do not appear warm and nurturing. Striking a similar chord, Barbara Omolade's (1994) description of the "mammification" of Black professional women also takes aim at the imagined Black woman mammy. But despite these works, the mammy image lives on in scholarly and popular culture. Audre Lorde's account of a shopping trip offers a powerful example of its tenacity: "I wheel my two-year-old daughter in a shopping cart through a supermarket in ... 1967, and a little white girl riding past in her mother's cart calls out excitedly, 'Oh look, Mommy, a baby maid!'" (1984, 126).[2]

The mammy image is central to intersecting oppressions of race, gender, sexuality, and class. Regarding racial oppression, controlling images like the mammy aim to influence Black maternal behavior. As the members of African-American families who are most familiar with the skills needed for Black accommodation, Black mothers are encouraged to transmit to their own children the deference behavior that many are forced to exhibit in their mammified jobs. By teaching Black children their assigned place in White power structures, Black women who internalize the mammy image potentially become effective conduits for perpetuating racial oppression. Ideas about mammy buttress racial hierarchies in other ways. Employing Black women in mammified occupations supports the racial superiority of White employers, encouraging middle-class White women in particular to identify more closely with the racial and class privilege afforded their fathers, husbands, and sons. In a climate where, as Patricia Williams (1995) puts it, "those blacks who do indeed rise into the middle class end up being figured only as those who were *given* whatever they enjoy, and the black 'underclass' becomes those whose sole life activity is *taking*" (p. 61), no wonder that working-class Whites expect Black women to exhibit deferential behavior, and deeply resent those who do not. Mammy is the public face that Whites expect Black women to assume for them.

The mammy image also serves a symbolic function in maintaining oppressions of gender and sexuality. Black feminist critic Barbara Christian argues that images of Black womanhood serve as a reservoir for the fears of Western culture, "a dumping ground for those female functions a basically Puritan society could not confront" (1985, 2). Juxtaposed against images of White women, the mammy image as the Other symbolizes the oppositional difference of mind/body and culture/nature thought to distinguish Black women from everyone else. Christian comments on the mammy's gender significance: "All the functions of mammy are magnificently physical. They involve the body as sensuous, as funky, the part of woman that white southern America was profoundly afraid of. Mammy, then, harmless in her position of slave, unable because of her all-giving nature to do harm, is needed as an image, a surrogate to contain all those fears of the physical female" (1985, 2). The mammy image buttresses the ideology of the cult of true womanhood, one in which sexuality and fertility are severed. "Good" White mothers are expected to deny their female sexuality. In contrast, the mammy image is one of an asexual woman, a surrogate mother in blackface whose historical devotion to her White family is now giving way to new expectations. Contemporary mammies should be completely committed to their jobs.

No matter how loved they were by their White "families," Black women domestic workers remained poor because they were economically exploited workers in a capitalist political economy. The restructured post–World War II economy, in which African-American women moved from service in private homes to jobs in the low-paid service sector and to jobs in clerical work and mammified professions, has produced similar yet differently organized economic exploitation. Historically, many White families in both the middle class and working class were able to maintain their class position because they used Black women domestic workers as a source of cheap labor (Rollins 1985; Byerly 1986). The mammy image was designed to mask this economic exploitation of social class (King 1973). Currently, while the mammy image becomes more muted as Black women move into better jobs, the basic economic exploitation where U.S. Black women either make less for the same work or work twice as hard for the same pay persists. U.S. Black women and African-American communities pay a price for this exploitation. Removing Black women's labor from African-American families and exploiting it denies Black extended family units the benefits of both decent wages and Black women's emotional labor in their homes. Moreover, as the attention to issues of stress in Black feminist analyses of U.S. Black women's health suggest, participating in this chronically undercompensated and unrecognized labor takes its toll (White 1994, 11–14).

For reasons of economic survival, U.S. Black women may play the mammy role in paid work settings. But within African-American families and neighborhoods these same women often teach their own children something quite different. Bonnie Thornton Dill's (1980) work on child-rearing patterns among Black domestics shows that while the participants in her study showed deference behavior at work, they discouraged their children from believing that they should be deferential to Whites and encouraged their children to avoid domestic work. Barbara Christian's analysis of the mammy in Black slave narratives reveals that, "unlike the white southern image of mammy, she is cunning, prone to poisoning her master, and not at all content with her lot" (1985, 5).

The fact that the mammy image by itself cannot control Black women's behavior is tied to the creation of the second controlling image of Black womanhood. Though a more recent phenomenon, the image of the Black matriarch fulfills similar functions in explaining Black women's placement in intersecting oppressions. Ironically, Black scholars such as William E. B. DuBois (1969) and E. Franklin Frazier (1948) described the connections among higher rates of female-headed households in African-American communities, the importance that women assume in Black family networks, and the persistence of Black poverty. However, neither scholar interpreted Black women's centrality in Black families as a *cause* of African-American social class status. Both saw so-called matriarchal families as an *outcome* of racial oppression and poverty. During the eras when DuBois and Frazier wrote, the political disenfranchisement and economic exploitation of African-Americans was so entrenched that control over Black women could be maintained without the matriarchal stereotype. But what began as a muted theme in the works of these earlier African-American scholars grew into a full-blown racialized image in the 1960s, a time of significant political and economic mobility for African-Americans. Racialization involves attaching racial meaning to a previously racially unclassified relationship, social practice, or group (Omi and Winant 1994). Prior to the 1960s, Black communities contained higher percentages of families maintained by single mothers than White ones, but an ideology that racialized female-headedness as one important cause of Black poverty had not emerged. Interestingly, the insertion of the Black matri-archy thesis into discussions of Black poverty came in the midst of considerable Black activism. Moreover, the public depiction of U.S. Black women as unfeminine matriarchs came at precisely the same moment that the women's movement advanced its critique of U.S. patriarchy (Gilkes 1983a, 296).

While the mammy typifies the Black mother figure in White homes, the matriarch symbolizes the mother figure in Black homes. Just as the mammy represents the "good" Black mother, the matriarch symbolizes the "bad" Black mother. Introduced and widely circulated via a government report titled *The Negro Family: The Case for National Action,* the Black matriarchy thesis argued that African-American women who failed to fulfill their traditional "womanly" duties at home contributed to social problems in Black civil society (Moynihan 1965). Spending too much time away from home, these working mothers ostensibly could not properly supervise their children and thus were a major contributing factor to their children's failure at school. As overly aggressive, unfeminine women, Black matriarchs allegedly emasculated their lovers and husbands. These men, understandably, either deserted their partners or refused to marry the mothers of their children. From the dominant group's perspective, the matriarch represented a failed mammy, a negative stigma to be applied to African-American women who dared reject the image of the submissive, hardworking servant.

Black women intellectuals who study African-American families and Black motherhood typically report finding few matriarchs and even fewer mammies (Myers 1980; Sudarkasa 1981b; Dill 1988b). Instead they portray African-American mothers as complex individuals who often show tremendous strength under adverse conditions, or who become beaten down by the incessant demands of providing for their families. In *A Raisin in the Sun,* the first play presented on Broadway written by a Black woman, Lorraine Hansberry (1959) examines the struggles of widow Lena Younger to actualize her dream of purchasing a home for her family. In *Brown Girl, Brownstones,* novelist Paule Marshall (1959) presents Mrs. Boyce, a Black mother negotiating a series of relationships with her husband, her daughters, the women in her community, and the work she must perform outside her home. Ann Allen Shockley's *Loving Her* (1974) depicts the struggle of a lesbian mother trying to balance her needs for self-actualization with the pressures of child-rearing in a homophobic community.

Like these fictional analyses, Black women's scholarship on Black single mothers also challenges the matriarchy thesis, but finds far fewer Lena Youngers or Mrs. Boyces (Ladner 1972; Brewer 1988; Jarrett 1994; Dickerson 1995a; Kaplan 1997). In her study of Black teenage mothers, Elaine Bell Kaplan (1997) learned that the reactions of mothers to their teenaged daughters' pregnancies were far from the image of the superstrong Black mother. Mothers in the new working poor felt their pregnant teenage daughters had failed them. Until their daughters' pregnancies, these mothers hoped that their daughters would do better with their lives. The mothers who came from humble beginnings and who had worked hard to achieve a modicum of middle-class respectability felt cheated when their daughters became pregnant. Among both groups of mothers, adjusting to their daughters' pregnancies brought on much hardship.

Like the mammy, the image of the matriarch is central to intersecting oppressions of class, gender, and race. While at first glance the matriarch may appear far removed from issues in U.S. capitalist development, this image is actually important in explaining the persistence of Black social class outcomes. Assuming that Black poverty in the United States is passed on intergenerationally via the values that parents teach their children, dominant ideology suggests that Black children lack the attention and care allegedly lavished on White, middle-class children. This alleged cultural deficiency seriously retards Black children's achievement. Such a view diverts attention from political and economic inequalities that increasingly characterize global capitalism. It also suggests that anyone can rise from poverty if he or she only received good values at home. Inferior housing, underfunded schools, employment discrimination, and consumer racism all but disappear from Black women's lives. In this sanitized view of American society, those African-Americans who remain poor cause their own victimization. In this context, portraying African-American women as matriarchs allows White men and women to blame Black women for their children's failures in school and with the law, as well as Black children's subsequent poverty. Using images of bad Black mothers to explain Black economic disadvantage links gender ideology to explanations for extreme distributions of wealth that characterize American capitalism.

One source of the matriarch's failure is her inability to model appropriate gender behavior. Thus, labeling Black women unfeminine and too strong works to undercut U.S. Black women's assertiveness. Many U.S. Black women who find themselves maintaining families by themselves often feel that they have done something wrong. If only they were not so strong, some reason, they might have found a male partner, or their sons would not have had so much trouble with the law. This belief masks the culpability of the U.S. criminal justice system, described by Angela Davis (1997) as an "out of control punishment industry" that locks up a disproportionate number of U.S. Blacks. African-Americans are almost eight times more likely to be imprisoned than Whites (p. 267), a social policy that leaves far fewer men for Black women to marry than the proportion of White men available to White women. Moreover, not only does the image of the Black matriarch seek to regulate Black women's behavior, it also seems designed to influence White women's gendered identities. In the post–World War II era, increasing numbers of White women entered the labor market, limited their fertility, and generally challenged their proscribed roles as subordinate helpmates in their families and workplaces. In this context, the image of the Black matriarch serves as a powerful symbol for both Black and White women of what can go wrong if White patriarchal power is challenged. Aggressive, assertive women are penalized—they are abandoned by their men, end up impoverished, and are stigmatized as being unfeminine. The matriarch or overly strong Black woman has also been used to influence Black men's understandings of Black masculinity. Many Black men reject Black women as marital partners, claiming that Black women are less desirable than White ones because we are too assertive.

The image of the matriarch also supports racial oppression. Much social science research implicitly uses gender relations in African-American communities as one seeming measure of Black cultural disadvantage. For example, the Moynihan Report (1965) contends that slavery destroyed Black families by creating reversed roles for men and women. Black family structures are seen as being deviant because they challenge the patriarchal assumptions underpinning the traditional family ideal. Moreover, the absence of Black patriarchy is used as evidence for Black cultural inferiority (Collins 1989). Under scientific racism, Blacks have been construed as inferior, and their inferiority has been attributed either to biological causes or cultural differences. Thus, locating the source of cultural difference in flawed gender relations provides a powerful foundation for U.S. racism. Black women's failure to conform to the cult of true womanhood can then be identified as one fundamental source of Black cultural deficiency. Advancing ideas about Black cultural disadvantage via the matriarchal image worked to counter efforts by African-Americans who identified political and social policies as one important source of Black economic disadvantage. The image of Black women as dangerous, deviant, castrating mothers divided the Black community at a critical period in the Black liberation struggle. Such images fostered a similar reaction within women's political activism and created a wider gap between the worlds of Black and White women at an equally critical period in women's history (Gilkes 1983a).

Taken together, images of the mammy and the matriarch place African-American women in an untenable position. For Black women workers in service occupations requiring long hours and/or substantial emotional labor, becoming the ideal mammy means precious time and energy spent away from husbands and children. But being employed when Black men have difficulty finding steady work exposes African-American women to the charge that Black women emasculate Black men by failing to be submissive, dependent, "feminine" women. This image ignores gender-specific patterns of incorporation into the capitalist economy, where Black men have greater difficulty finding work but make higher wages when they do work, and Black women find work with greater ease yet earn much less. Moreover, Black women's financial contributions to Black family well-being have been cited as evidence supporting the matriarchy thesis (Moynihan 1965). Many Black women are the sole support of their families, and labeling these women "matriarchs" erodes their self-confidence and ability to confront oppression. In essence, African-American women who must work encounter pressures to be submissive mammies in one setting, then are stigmatized again as matriarchs for being strong figures in their own homes.

A third, externally defined, controlling image of Black womanhood—that of the welfare mother—appears tied to working-class Black women's increasing access to U.S. welfare state entitlements. At its core, the image of the welfare mother constitutes a class-specific, controlling image developed for poor, working-class Black women who make use of social welfare benefits to which they are entitled by law. As long as poor Black women were denied social welfare benefits, there was no need for this stereotype. But when U.S. Black women gained more political power and demanded equity in access to state services, the need arose for this controlling image.

Essentially an updated version of the breeder woman image created during slavery, this image provides an ideological justification for efforts to harness Black women's fertility to the needs of a changing political economy. During slavery the breeder woman image portrayed Black women as more suitable for having children than White women. By claiming that Black women were able to produce children as easily as animals, this image provided justification for interference in enslaved Africans' reproductive lives. Slave owners wanted enslaved Africans to "breed" because every slave child born represented a valuable unit of property, another unit of labor, and, if female, the prospects for more slaves. The controlling image of the breeder woman served to justify slave owners' intrusion into Black women's decisions about fertility (King 1973; Davis 1981; D. White 1985).

In the post–World War II political economy, African-Americans struggled for and gained rights denied them in former historical periods (Squires 1994). Contrary to popular belief, U.S. Black women were not "given" unearned entitlements, but instead had to struggle for rights routinely offered to other American citizens (Amott 1990; Quadagno 1994). African-Americans successfully acquired basic political and economic protections from a greatly expanded social welfare state, particularly Social Security, unemployment compensation, school feeding programs, fellowships and loans for higher education, affirmative action, voting rights, antidiscrimination legislation, child welfare programs, and the minimum wage. Despite sustained opposition by Republican administrations in the 1980s, these social welfare programs allowed many African-Americans to reject the subsistence-level, exploitative jobs held by their parents and grandparents. However, these Black citizenship rights came at a time of shrinking economic opportunities in U.S. manufacturing and agriculture. Job export, de-skilling, and increased use of illegal immigrants have all been used to replace the cheap, docile labor force that U.S. Blacks used to be (Nash and Fernandez-Kelly 1983; Brewer 1993; Squires 1994). Until the mid-1990s, the large numbers of undereducated, unemployed African-Americans ghettoized in U.S. inner cities, most of whom were women and children, could not be forced to work. This surplus population no longer represented cheap labor but instead, from the perspective of elites, signified a costly threat to political and economic stability. African-American men increasingly became targeted by a growing punishment industry (Davis 1997). In the absence of legitimate jobs, many men worked in the informal sector, serving as low-level employees of a growing, global drug industry that introduced crack cocaine into U.S. Black neighborhoods in the 1980s. For many, becoming entangled with the punishment industry was one cost of doing business.

Controlling Black women's fertility in this political and economic context became important to elite groups. The image of the welfare mother fulfills this function by labeling as unnecessary and even dangerous to the values of the country the fertility of women who are not White and middle class. A closer look at this controlling image reveals that it shares some important features with its mammy and matriarch counterparts. Like the matriarch, the welfare mother is labeled a bad mother. But unlike the matriarch, she is not too aggressive—on the contrary, she is not aggressive enough. While the matriarch's unavailability contributed to her children's poor socialization, the welfare mother's accessibility is deemed the problem. She is portrayed as being content to sit around and collect welfare, shunning work and passing on her bad values to her offspring. The image of the welfare mother represents another failed mammy, one who is unwilling to become "de mule uh de world."

The image of the welfare mother provides ideological justifications for intersecting oppressions of race, gender, and class. African-Americans can be racially stereotyped as being lazy by blaming Black welfare mothers for failing to pass on the work ethic. Moreover, the welfare mother has no male authority figure to assist her. Typically portrayed as an unwed mother, she violates one cardinal tenet of White, male-dominated ideology: She is a woman alone. As a result, her treatment reinforces the dominant gender ideology positing that a woman's true worth and financial security should occur through heterosexual marriage. Finally, on average, in the post–World War II political economy, one of every three African-American families has been officially classified as poor. With such high levels of Black poverty, welfare state policies supporting poor Black mothers and their children have become increasingly expensive. Creating the controlling image of the welfare mother and stigmatizing her as the cause of her own poverty and that of African-American communities shifts the angle of vision away from structural sources of poverty and blames the victims themselves. The image of the welfare mother thus provides ideological justification for the dominant group's interest in limiting the fertility of Black mothers who are seen as producing too many economically unproductive children (Davis 1981).

With the election of the Reagan administration in 1980, the stigmatized welfare mother evolved into the more pernicious image of the welfare queen (Lubiano 1992). To mask the effects of cuts in government spending on social welfare programs that fed children, housed working families, assisted cities in maintaining roads, bridges, and basic infrastructure, and supported other basic public services, media images increasingly identified and blamed Black women for the deterioration of U.S. interests. Thus, poor Black women simultaneously become symbols of what was deemed wrong with America and targets of social policies designed to shrink the government sector. Wahneema Lubiano describes how the image of the welfare queen links Black women with seeming declines in the quality of life:

> "Welfare queen" is a phrase that describes economic dependency—the lack of a job and/or income (which equal degeneracy in the Calvinist United States); the presence of a child or children with no father and/or husband (moral deviance); and, finally, a charge on the collective U.S. treasury—a human debit. The cumulative totality, circulation, and effect of these meanings in a time of scarce resources among the working class and the lower middle class is devastatingly intense. The welfare queen represents moral aberration and an economic drain, but the figure's problematic status becomes all the more threatening once responsibility for the destruction of the American way of life is attributed to it. (Lubiano 1992, 337–38)

In contrast to the welfare mother who draws upon the moral capital attached to American motherhood, the welfare queen constitutes a highly materialistic, domineering, and manless working-class Black woman. Relying on the public dole, Black welfare queens are content to take the hard-earned money of taxpaying Americans and remain married to the state. Thus, the welfare queen image signals efforts to use the situation of working-class Black women as a sign of the deterioration of the state.

During this same period, the welfare queen was joined by another similar yet class-specific image, that of the "Black lady" (Lubiano 1992). Because the Black lady refers to middle-class professional Black women who represent a modern version of the politics of respectability advanced by the club women (Shaw 1996), this image may not appear to be a controlling image, merely a benign one. These are the women who stayed in school, worked hard, and have achieved much. Yet the image of the Black lady builds upon prior images of Black womanhood in many ways. For one thing, this image seems to be yet another version of the modern mammy, namely, the hardworking Black woman professional who works twice as hard as everyone else. The image of the Black lady also resembles aspects of the matriarchy thesis—Black ladies have jobs that are so all-consuming that they have no *time* for men or have forgotten how to treat them. Because they so routinely compete with men and are successful at it, they become less feminine. Highly educated Black ladies are deemed to be *too* assertive—that's why they cannot get men to marry them.

Upon first glance, Black ladies also seem far removed from charges of unearned dependency on the state that are so often leveled at working-class U.S. Black women via the welfare queen image. Yet here, too, parallels abound. Via affirmative action, Black ladies allegedly take jobs that should go to more worthy Whites, especially U.S. White men. Given a political climate in the 1980s and 1990s that reinterpreted antidiscrimination and affirmative action programs as examples of an unfair "reverse racism," no matter how highly educated or demonstrably competent Black ladies may be, their accomplishments remain questionable. Moreover, many Black men erroneously believe that Black ladies are taking jobs reserved for them. In their eyes, being Black, female, and seemingly less threatening to Whites advantages Black ladies. Wahneema Lubiano points out how images of the welfare queen and the Black lady evolved in tandem with persistent efforts to cut social welfare spending for working-class Blacks and limit affirmative action opportunities for middle-class Blacks: "Whether by virtue of not achieving and thus passing on bad culture as welfare mothers, or by virtue of managing to achieve middle-class success . . . black women are responsible for the disadvantaged status of African Americans" (Lubiano 1992, 335). Thus, when taken together, the welfare queen and the Black lady constitute class-specific versions of a matriarchy thesis whose fundamental purpose is to discredit Black women's full exercise of citizenship rights. These interconnected images leave U.S. Black women between a rock and a hard place.

A final controlling image—the jezebel, whore, or "hoochie"—is central in this nexus of controlling images of Black womanhood. Because efforts to control Black women's sexuality lie at the heart of Black women's oppression, historical jezebels and contemporary "hoochies" represent a deviant Black female sexuality. The image of jezebel originated under slavery when Black women were portrayed as being, to use Jewelle Gomez's words, "sexually aggressive wet nurses" (Clarke et al. 1983, 99). Jezebel's function was to relegate all Black women to the category of sexually aggressive women, thus providing a powerful rationale for the widespread sexual assaults by White men typically reported by Black slave women (Davis 1981; D. White 1985). Jezebel served yet another function. If Black slave women could be portrayed as having excessive sexual appetites, then increased fertility should be the expected outcome. By suppressing the nurturing that African-American women might give their own children which would strengthen Black family networks, and by forcing Black women to work in the field, "wet nurse" White children, and emotionally nurture their White owners, slave owners effectively tied the controlling images of jezebel and mammy to the economic exploitation inherent in the institution of slavery.

Rooted in the historical legacy of jezebel, the contemporary "hoochie" seems to be cut from an entirely different cloth. For one, whereas images of Black women as sexually aggressive certainly pervade popular culture overall, the image of the hoochie seems to have permeated everyday Black culture in entirely new ways. For example, 2 Live Crew's song "Hoochie Mama" takes Black women bashing to new heights. In this song, the group opens with the rallying cry "big booty hoes hop wit it!" and proceeds to list characteristics of the "hoodrat hoochie mama." The singers are quite clear about the use of such women: "I don't need no confrontation," they sing. "All I want is an ejaculation cos I like them ghetto hoochies." The misogyny in "Hoochie Mama" makes prior portrayals of jezebel seem tame. For example, 2 Live Crew's remedy for "lyin" shows their disdain for women: "Keep runnin ya mouth and I'ma stick my dick in it," they threaten. And for those listeners who remain confused about the difference between good and bad women, 2 Live Crew is willing to help out:

> Mama just don't understand
> why I love your hoochie ass
> Sex is what I need you for
> I gotta good girl but I need a whore

In the United States, guarantees of free speech allow 2 Live Crew and similar groups to speak their minds about "hoochies" and anything else that will make them money. The issue here lies in African-American acceptance of such images. African-American men and women alike routinely do not challenge these and other portrayals of Black women as "hoochies" within Black popular culture. For example, despite the offensive nature of much of 2 Live Crew's music, some Blacks argued that such views, while unfortunate, had long been expressed in Black culture (Crenshaw 1993). Not only does such acceptance mask how such images provide financial benefits to both 2 Live Crew and White-controlled media, such tacit acceptance validates this image. The more it circulates among U.S. Blacks, the more credence it is given. The "hoochie" image certainly seems to have taken on a life of its own. For example, an informal poll of my friends, students, and colleagues revealed a complex taxonomy of "hoochies." Most agreed that one category consisted of "plain hoochies" or sexually assertive women who can be found across social classes. Women who wear sleazy clothes to clubs and dance in a "slutty" fashion constitute "club hoochies." These women aim to attract men with money for a one-night stand. In contrast, the ambition of "gold-digging hoochies" lies in establishing a long-term relationship with a man with money. These gold-digging hoochies often aim to snare a highly paid athlete and can do so by becoming pregnant. Finally, there is the "hoochie-mama" popularized by 2 Live Crew, an image that links the hoochie image to poverty. As 2 Live Crew points out, the "hoochie mama" is a "hoodrat," a "ghetto hoochie" whose main purpose is to provide them sexual favors. The fact that she is also a "mama" speaks to the numbers of Black women in poverty who are single parents whose exchange of sexual favors for money is motivated by their children's economic needs.

Within assumptions that normalize heterosexuality, the historical jezebel and her modern "hoochie" counterpart mark a series of boundaries. Heterosexuality itself is constructed via binary thinking that juxtaposes male and female sexuality, with male and female gender roles pivoting on perceptions of appropriate male and female sexual expression. Men are active, and women should be passive. In the context of U.S. society, these become racialized—White men are active, and White women should be passive. Black people and other racialized groups simultaneously stand outside these definitions of normality and mark their boundaries. In this context of a gender-specific, White, heterosexual normality, the jezebel or hoochie becomes a racialized, gendered symbol of deviant female sexuality. Normal female heterosexuality is expressed via the cult of true White womanhood, whereas deviant female heterosexuality is typified by the "hot mommas" of Black womanhood.

Within intersecting oppressions, Black women's allegedly deviant sexuality becomes constructed around jezebel's sexual desires. Jezebel may be a "pretty baby," but her actions as a "hot momma" indicate that she just can't get enough. Because jezebel or the hoochie is constructed as a woman whose sexual appetites are at best inappropriate and, at worst, insatiable, it becomes a short step to imagine her as a "freak." And if she is a freak, her sexual partners become similarly stigmatized. For example, the hypermasculinity often attributed to Black men reflects beliefs about Black men's excessive sexual appetite. Ironically, jezebel's excessive sexual appetite masculinizes her because she desires sex just as a man does. Moreover, jezebel can also be masculinized and once again deemed "freaky" if she desires sex with other women. 2 Live Crew had little difficulty making this conceptual leap when they sing: "Freaky shit is what I like and I love to see two bitches dyke." In a context where feminine women are those who remain submissive yet appropriately flirtatious toward men, women whose sexual aggression resembles that of men become stigmatized.

When it comes to women's sexuality, the controlling image of jezebel and her hoochie counterpart constitute one side of the normal/deviant binary. But broadening this binary thinking that underpins intersecting oppressions of race, class, gender, and sexuality reveals that heterosexuality is juxtaposed to homosexuality as its oppositional, different, and inferior "other." Within this wider oppositional difference, jezebel becomes the freak on the border demarking heterosexuality from homosexuality. Her insatiable sexual desire helps define the boundaries of normal sexuality. Just across the border stand lesbian, bisexual, and transgendered women who are deemed deviant in large part because of their choices of sexual partners. As a sexual freak, jezebel has one foot over the line. On this border, the hoochie participates in a cluster of "deviant female sexualities," some associated with the materialistic ambitions where she sells sex for money, others associated with so-called deviant sexual practices such as sleeping with other women, and still others attached to "freaky" sexual practices such as engaging in oral and anal sex.

Images of sexuality associated with jezebel and the hoochie not only mark the boundaries of deviant sexualities, they weave throughout prevailing conceptualizations of the mammy, matriarch, and the Janus-faced welfare queen/Black lady. Connecting all is the common theme of Black women's sexuality. Each image transmits distinctive messages about the proper links among female sexuality, desired levels of fertility for working-class and middle-class Black women, and U.S. Black women's placement in social class and citizenship hierarchies. For example, the mammy, one of two somewhat positive figures, is a desexed individual. The mammy is typically portrayed as overweight, dark, and with characteristically African features—in brief, as an unsuitable sexual partner for White men. She is asexual and therefore is free to become a surrogate mother to the children she acquired not through her own sexuality. The mammy represents the clearest example of the split between sexuality and motherhood present in Eurocentric masculinist thought. In contrast, both the matriarch and the welfare mother are sexual beings. But their sexuality is linked to their fertility, and this link forms one fundamental reason they are negative images. The matriarch represents the sexually aggressive woman, one who emasculates Black men because she will not permit them to assume roles as Black patriarchs. She refuses to be passive and thus is stigmatized. Similarly, the welfare mother represents a woman of low morals and uncontrolled sexuality, factors identified as the cause of her impoverished state. In both cases Black female control over sexuality and fertility is conceptualized as antithetical to elite White male interests. The Black lady completes the circle. Like mammy, her hard-earned, middle-class respectability is grounded in her seeming asexuality. Yet fertility is an issue here as well. Despite the fact that the middle-class Black lady is the woman deemed best suited to have children, in actuality, she remains the least likely to do so. She is told that she can reproduce, but no one except her is especially disturbed if she does not.

Taken together, these prevailing images of Black womanhood represent elite White male interests in defining Black women's sexuality and fertility. Moreover, by meshing smoothly with intersecting oppressions of race, class, gender, and sexuality, they help justify the social practices that characterize the matrix of domination in the United States.

Controlling Images and Social Institutions

Schools, the news media, and government agencies constitute important sites for reproducing these controlling images. Whereas schools and the scholarship produced and disseminated by their faculty historically have played an important part in generating these controlling images (Morton 1991), their current significance in reproducing these images is less often noted. Take, for example, how social science research on Black women's sexuality has been influenced by assumptions of the jezebel. Two topics, both deemed as social problems, take the lion's share—Black women's sexuality appears within AIDS research and within scholarship on adolescent pregnancy. Both reference two types of allegedly deviant sexuality with an eye toward altering Black women's behavior. In AIDS research, the focus is on risky sexual practices that might expose women, their unborn children, and their partners to HIV infection. Prostitutes and other sex workers are of special concern. The underlying reason for studying Black adolescent sexuality may lie in helping the girls, but an equally plausible stimulus lies in desires to get these girls off the public dole. Their sexuality is not that of risky sexual practices, but sexuality outside the confines of marriage. Embedding research on Black women's sexuality within social problems frameworks thus fosters its portrayal as a social problem.

The growing influence of television, radio, movies, videos, CDs, and the Internet constitute new ways of circulating controlling images. Popular culture has become increasingly important in promoting these images, especially with new global technologies that allow U.S. popular culture to be exported throughout the world. Within this new corporate structure, the misogyny in some strands of Black hip-hop music becomes especially troubling. Much of this music is produced by a Black culture industry in which African-American artists have little say in production. On the one hand, Black rap music can be seen as a creative response to racism by Black urban youth who have been written off by U.S. society (Rose 1994; Kelley 1997, 43–77). On the other hand, images of Black women as sexually available hoochies persist in Black music videos. As "freaks," U.S. Black women can now be seen "poppin' that coochie"—yet another term by 2 Live Crew that describes butt shaking—in global context.

Government agencies also play a part in legitimating these controlling images. Because legislative bodies and, in the case of 2 Live Crew's obscenity trial (see, e.g., Crenshaw 1993), courts determine which narratives are legitimated and which remain censured, government agencies decide which official interpretations of social reality prevail (Van Dijk 1993). The inordinate attention paid to Black adolescent pregnancy and parenting in scholarly research and the kinds of public policy initiatives that target Black girls illustrate the significance of government support for controlling images. Because assumptions of sexual hedonism are routinely applied to Black urban girls, they are more likely to be offered coercive birth control measures, such as Norplant and Depo Provera than their White, suburban, middle-class counterparts (Roberts 1997).

Confronting the controlling images forwarded by institutions external to African-American communities remains essential. But such efforts should not obscure the equally important issue of examining how African-American institutions also perpetuate these same controlling images. Although it may be painful to examine—especially in the context of a racially charged society always vigilant for signs of Black disunity—the question of how the organizations of Black civil society reproduce controlling images of Black womanhood and fail to take a stand against images developed elsewhere is equally important.

Since 1970, U.S. Black women have become increasingly vocal in criticizing sexism in Black civil society (Wallace 1978; E.F. White 1984; Cleage 1993; Crenshaw 1993). For example, Black feminist Pauline Terrelonge confronts the issue of the Black community's role in the subordination of African-American women by asking, "If there is much in the objective condition of black women that warrants the development of a black feminist consciousness, why have so many black women failed to recognize the patterns of sexism that directly impinge on their everyday lives?" (1984, 562). To answer this question, Terrelonge contends that a common view is that African-Americans have withstood the long line of abuses perpetuated against us mainly because of Black women's "fortitude, inner wisdom, and sheer ability to survive." Connected to this emphasis on the strength of Black women is the related argument that African-American women play critical roles in keeping Black families together and in supporting Black men. These activities have been important in preventing the potential annihilation of African-Americans as a "race." As a result, "many blacks regard the role of uniting all blacks to be the primary duty of the black woman, one that should supersede all other roles that she might want to perform, and certainly one that is essentially incompatible with her own individual liberation" (p. 557).

This analysis shifts our understanding of Black community organizations. Rather than seeing family, church, and Black civic organizations through a race-only lens of resisting racism, such institutions may be better understood as complex sites where dominant ideologies are simultaneously resisted and reproduced. Black community organizations can oppose racial oppression yet perpetuate gender oppression, can challenge class exploitation yet foster heterosexism. One might ask where within Black civil society African-American women can openly challenge the hoochie image and other equally controlling images. Institutions controlled by African-Americans can be seen as contradictory sites where Black women learn skills of independence and self-reliance that enable African-American families, churches, and civic organizations to endure. But these same institutions may also be places where Black women learn to subordinate our interests as women to the allegedly greater good of the larger African-American community.

Take, for example, historically Black colleges and universities. In their goal of dispelling the myths about African-American women and making Black women acceptable to wider society, some historically Black colleges may also foster Black women's subordination. In *Meridian* Alice Walker describes an elite college for Black women where "most of the students—timid, imitative, bright enough but never daring, were being ushered nearer to Ladyhood every day" (1976, 39). Confined to campus, Meridian, the heroine, had to leave to find the ordinary Black people who exhibited all of the qualities that her elite institution wished to eliminate. Walker's description of the fence surrounding the campus symbolizes how stultifying the cult of true womanhood was for Black students. But it also describes the problems that African-American institutions create for Black women when they embrace externally defined controlling images:

> The fence that surrounded the campus was hardly noticeable from the street and appeared, from the outside, to be more of an attempt at ornamentation than an effort to contain or exclude. Only the students who lived on campus learned, often painfully, that the beauty of a fence is no guarantee that it will not keep one penned in as securely as one that is ugly. (Walker 1976, 41)

Jacquelyn Grant (1982) identifies the church as one key institution whose centrality to Black community development may have come at the expense of many of the African-American women who constitute the bulk of its membership. Grant asserts, "it is often said that women are the 'backbone' of the church. On the surface, this may appear to be a compliment. . . . It has become apparent to me that most of the ministers who use this term are referring to location rather than function. What they really mean is that women are in the 'background' and should be kept there" (1982, 141). At the same time, Black churches have clearly been highly significant in Black political struggle, with U.S. Black women central to those efforts. Historically, Black women's participation in Black Baptist and other Black churches suggests that Black women have been the backbone yet have resisted staying totally in the "background" (Gilkes 1985; Higginbotham 1993). One wonders, however, if contemporary Black churches are equipped to grapple with the new questions raised by the global circulation of the hoochie and comparable images. Denouncing "hoochies" and all they represent from the pulpit with a cautionary warning "don't be one" simply is not enough.

African-American families form another contradictory location where the controlling images of Black womanhood become negotiated. Middle-class White feminists seemingly have had few qualms in criticizing how their families perpetuate women's subordination (see, for example, Chodorow 1978). Until recently, however, because Black families have been so pathologized by the traditional family ideal, Black women have been reluctant to analyze in public the potential culpability of families in Black women's oppression. Black women thinkers have been more uniformly positive when describing Black families, and much more reluctant to criticize Black family organization than their White counterparts. As a result, Black studies emphasizes material that, although it quite rightly demonstrates the strengths of U.S. Black families in a context of intersecting oppressions, skims over problems (see, e.g., Billingsley 1992). But this emphasis on strengths has often come at a cost, and that cost has far too often been paid by African-American women. Thus, within Black feminist scholarship, we are finally hearing not only the long-hidden stories of those strong Black women (Joseph 1981; Collins 1987), but those of women whose gendered family responsibilities cause them trouble (Ritchie 1996; Kaplan 1997).

Some Black feminist activists claim that relegating Black women to more submissive, supporting roles in African-American organizations has been an obstacle to Black political empowerment. Black nationalist philosophies, in particular, have come under attack for their ideas about Black women's place in political struggle (White 1990; Lubiano 1997; Williams 1997; Collins 1998a, 155–86). In describing the 1960s nationalist movement, Pauli Murray contends that many Black men misinterpreted Black women's qualities of self-reliance and independence by tacitly accepting the matriarchy thesis. Such a stance was and is highly problematic for Black women. Murray observes, "The black militant's cry for the retrieval of black manhood suggests an acceptance of this stereotype, an association of masculinity with male dominance and a tendency to treat the values of self-reliance and independence as purely masculine traits" (1970, 89). Echoing Murray, Sheila Radford-Hill (1986) sees Black women's subordination in African-American institutions as a continuing concern. For Radford-Hill the erosion of Black women's traditional power bases in African-American communities which followed nationalist movements is problematic in that "Black macho constituted a betrayal by black men; a psychosexual rejection of black women experienced as the capstone to our fall from cultural power. . . . Without the power to influence the purpose and direction of our collective experience, without the power to influence our culture from within, we are increasingly immobilized" (p. 168).

Color, Hair Texture, and Standards of Beauty

Like everyone else, African-American women come to understand the workings of intersecting oppressions without obvious teaching or conscious learning. The controlling images of Black women are not simply grafted onto existing social institutions but are so pervasive that even though the images themselves change in the popular imagination, Black women's portrayal as the Other persists. Particular meanings, stereotypes, and myths can change, but the overall ideology of domination itself seems to be an enduring feature of intersecting oppressions (Omi and Winant 1994).

African-American women encounter this ideology through a range of unquestioned daily experiences. But when the contradictions between Black women's self-definitions and everyday treatment are heightened, controlling images become increasingly visible. Karen Russell, the daughter of basketball great Bill Russell, describes how racial stereotypes affect her:

> How am I supposed to react to well-meaning, good, liberal white people who say things like: "You know, Karen, I don't understand what all the fuss is about. You're one of my good friends, and I never think of you as black." Implicit in such a remark is, "I think of you as white," or perhaps just, "I don't think of your race at all." (Russell 1987, 22)

Ms. Russell was perceptive enough to see that remarks intended to compliment her actually insulted African-Americans. As the Others, U.S. Blacks are assigned all of the negative characteristics opposite and inferior to those reserved for Whites. By claiming that Ms. Russell is not really "black," her friends unintentionally validate this system of racial meanings and encourage her to internalize those images.

Although most Black women typically resist being objectified as the Other, these controlling images remain powerful influences on our relationships with Whites, Black men, other racial/ethnic groups, and one another. Dealing with prevailing standards of beauty—particularly skin color, facial features, and hair texture—is one specific example of how controlling images derogate African-American women. A children's rhyme often sung in Black communities proclaims:

> Now, if you're white you're all right,
> If you're brown, stick around,
> But if you're black, Git back! Git back! Git back!

Prevailing standards of beauty claim that no matter how intelligent, educated, or "beautiful" a Black woman may be, those Black women whose features and skin color are most African must "git back." Within the binary thinking that underpins intersecting oppressions, blue-eyed, blond, thin White women could not be considered beautiful without the Other—Black women with African features of dark skin, broad noses, full lips, and kinky hair.

Race, gender, and sexuality converge on this issue of evaluating beauty. Black men's blackness penalizes them. But because they are not women, valuations of their self-worth do not depend as heavily on their physical attractiveness. In contrast, part of the objectification of all women lies in evaluating how they look. Within binary thinking, White and Black women as collectivities represent two opposing poles, with Latinas, Asian-American women, and Native American women jockeying for positions in between. Judging White women by their physical appearance and attractiveness to men objectifies them. But their White skin and straight hair simultaneously privilege them in a system that elevates whiteness over blackness. In contrast, African-American women experience the pain of never being able to live up to prevailing standards of beauty—standards used by White men, White women, Black men, and, most painfully, one another. Regardless of any individual woman's subjective reality, this is the system of ideas that she encounters. Because controlling images are hegemonic and taken for granted, they become virtually impossible to escape.

In her Preface to *Skin Deep: Women Writing on Color, Culture and Identity,* editor Elena Featherstone suggests that contrary to popular belief, "issues of race and color are *not* as simple as Black and white—or Red, Yellow, or Brown and white" (1994, vi). Featherstone is right, and volumes such as hers remain necessary. Yet at the same time, colorism in the U.S. context operates the way that it does because it is deeply embedded in a distinctly American form of racism grounded in Black/White oppositional differences. Other groups "of color" must negotiate the meanings attached to their "color." All must position themselves within a continually renegotiated color hierarchy where, because they define the top and the bottom, the meanings attached to Whiteness and Blackness change much less than we think. Linked in symbiotic relationship, White and Black gain meaning only in relation to one another. However well-meaning conversations among "women of color" concerning the meaning of color in the United States may be, such conversations require an analysis of how institutionalized racism produces color hierarchies among U.S. women. Without this attention to domination, such conversations can work to flatten bona fide differences in power among White women, Latinas, Asian-American women, Native women, and Black women. Even Featherstone recognizes the fact of Blackness, by pointing out, "color is the ultimate test of 'American-ness,' and black is the most un-American color of all" (1994, iii).

Since U.S. Black women have been most uniformly harmed by the colorism that is a by-product of U.S. racism, it is important to explore how prevailing standards of beauty affect U.S. Black women's treatment in everyday life. The long-standing attention of musicians, writers, and artists to this theme reveals African-American women's conflicted feelings concerning skin color, hair texture, and standards of beauty. In her autobiography, Maya Angelou records her painful realization that the only way she could become truly beautiful was to become white:

> Wouldn't they be surprised when one day I woke out of my black ugly dream, and my real hair, which was long and blond, would take the place of the kinky mass that Momma wouldn't let me straighten? . . . Then they would understand why I had never picked up a Southern accent, or spoke the common slang, and why I had to be forced to eat pigs' tails and snouts. Because I was really white and because a cruel fairy stepmother . . . had turned me into a too-big Negro girl, with nappy black hair. (Angelou 1969, 2)

Gwendolyn Brooks also explores the meaning of skin color and hair texture for U.S. Black women. During Brooks's childhood, having African features was so universally denigrated that she writes, "when I was a child, it did not occur to me even once, that the black in which I was encased . . . would be considered, one day, beautiful" (Brooks 1972, 37). Early on, Brooks learned that a clear pecking order existed among African-Americans, one based on one's closeness to Whiteness. As a member of the "Lesser Blacks," those furthest from White, Brooks saw firsthand the difference in treatment of her group and that of the "Brights":

> One of the first "world" truths revealed to me when I at last became a member of SCHOOL was that, to be socially successful, a little girl must be Bright (of skin). It was better if your hair was curly, too—or at least Good Grade (Good Grade implied, usually, no involvement with the Hot Comb)—but Bright you marvelously *needed* to be. (1972, 37)

This division of African-Americans into two categories—the "Brights" and the "Lesser Blacks"—affects dark-skinned and light-skinned women differently. Darker women face being judged inferior and receiving the treatment afforded "too-big Negro girls with nappy hair." Institutions controlled by Whites clearly show a preference for lighter-skinned Blacks, discriminating against darker ones or against any African-Americans who appear to reject White images of beauty. Sonia Sanchez reports, "Sisters tell me . . . that when they go out for jobs they straighten their hair because if they go in with their hair natural or braided, they probably won't get the job" (Tate 1983, 141).

Sometimes the pain most deeply felt is the pain that Black women inflict on one another. Marita Golden's mother told her not to play in the sun because "you gonna have to get a light husband anyway, for the sake of your children" (1983, 24). In *Color*, a short film exploring the impact of skin color on Black women's lives, the dark-skinned character's mother tries to get her to sit still for the hot comb, asking "don't you want your hair flowing like your friend Rebecca's?" We see the sadness of a young Black girl sitting in a kitchen, holding her ears so they won't get burned by the hot comb that will straighten her hair. Her mother cannot make her beautiful, only "presentable" for church. Marita Golden's description of a Black beauty salon depicts the internalized oppression that some African-American women feel about African features:

> Between customers, twirling in her chair, white-stockinged legs crossed, my beautician lamented to the hairdresser in the next stall, "I sure hope that Gloria Johnson don't come in here asking for me today. I swear 'fore God her hair is this long." She snapped her fingers to indicate the length. Contempt riding her words, she lit a cigarette and finished, "Barely enough to wash, let alone press and curl." (Golden 1983, 25)

African-American women who are members of the "Brights" fare little better, for they too receive special treatment because of their skin color and hair texture. Harriet Jacobs, an enslaved light-skinned woman, was sexually harassed because of her looks. Her straight hair and fair skin, her appearance as a dusky White woman, made her physically attractive to White men. But the fact that she was Black made her available to White men as no group of White women had been. In describing this situation, Jacobs notes, "if God has bestowed beauty upon her, it will prove her greatest curse. That which commands admiration in the white woman only hastens the degradation of the female slave" (Washington 1987, 17).

This different valuation and treatment of dark-skinned and light-skinned Black women influences the relationships among African-American women. Toni Morrison's (1970) novel *The Bluest Eye* explores this theme of the tension that can exist among Black women grappling with the meaning of prevailing standards of beauty. Frieda, a dark-skinned, "ordinary" Black girl, struggles with the meaning of these standards. She wonders why adults always got so upset when she rejected the White dolls they gave her and why light-skinned Maureen Peal, a child her own age whose two braids hung like "lynch-ropes down her back," got the love and attention of teachers, adults, and Black boys alike. Morrison explores Frieda's attempt not to blame Maureen for the benefits her light skin and long hair afforded her as part of Frieda's growing realization that the "Thing" to fear was not Maureen herself but the "Thing" that made Maureen beautiful.

Gwendolyn Brooks (1953) captures the anger and frustration experienced by dark-skinned women in dealing with the differential treatment they and their lighter-skinned sisters receive. In her novel *Maud Martha,* the dark-skinned heroine ponders actions she could take against a red-headed Black woman whom her husband found so attractive. "I could," considered Maud Martha, "go over there and scratch her upsweep down. I could spit on her back. I could scream. 'Listen,' I could scream, 'I'm making a baby for this man and I mean to do it in peace.' " (Washington 1987, 422). But Maud Martha rejects these actions, reasoning, "If the root was sour what business did she have up there hacking at a leaf?"

This "sour root" also creates issues in relationships between African-American women and men. Maude Martha explains:

> It's my color that makes him mad. I try to shut my eyes to that, but it's no good. What I am inside, what is really me, he likes okay. But he keeps looking at my color, which is like a wall. He has to jump over it in order to meet and touch what I've got for him. He has to jump away up high in order to see it. He gets awful tired of all that jumping. (Washington 1987, 421)

Her husband's attraction to light-skinned women hurt Maude Martha because his inability to "jump away up high" over the wall of color limited his ability to see her for who she truly was.

Black Women's Reactions to Controlling Images

In *Their Eyes Were Watching God,* Nanny eloquently expresses her perspective on Black womanhood: "Ah was born back in slavery so it wasn't for me to fulfill my dream of whut a woman oughta be and do. But nothing can't stop you from wishin! You can't beat nobody down so low till you can rob 'em of they will. Ah didn't want to be used for a work-ox and a brood-sow and Ah didn't want mah daughter used dat way neither" (Hurston 1937, 17). Like many African-American women, she resisted the controlling images of "work-ox" and "brood-sow," but her status as a slave prevented her fulfilling her "dreams of whut a woman oughta be and do." She saw the constraints on her own life but managed to keep the will to resist alive. Moreover, she tried to pass on that vision of freedom from controlling images to her granddaughter.

Given the ubiquitous nature of controlling images, it should not be surprising that exploring how Black women construct social realities is a recurring theme in Black feminist thought. Overall, despite the pervasiveness of controlling images, African-American women as a group have resisted these ideological justifications for our oppression (Holloway 1995). Unlike White women who "face the pitfall of being seduced into joining the oppressor under the pretense of sharing power," and for whom "there is a wider range of pretended choices and rewards for identifying with patriarchal power and its tools," Black women are offered fewer possibilities (Lorde 1984, 117–18). In this context, individual women and subgroups of women within the larger collectivity of U.S. Black women have demonstrated diverse reactions to their treatment. Understanding the contours of this heterogeneity generally, and how U.S. Black women can be better equipped to resist this negative treatment, constitutes one important task for U.S. Black feminist thought.

Historically, literature by U.S. Black women writers provides one comprehensive view of Black women's struggles to form positive self-definitions in the face of derogated images of Black womanhood. Portraying the range of ways that African-American women experience internalized oppression has been a prominent theme in Black women's writing. Mary Helen Washington's (1982) discussion of the theme of the suspended woman in Black women's literature describes one dimension of Black women's internalized oppression. Pain, violence, and death form the essential content of these women's lives. They are suspended in time and place; their life choices are so severely limited that the women themselves are often destroyed. Pecola Breedlove, an unloved, "ugly" 11-year-old Black girl in Toni Morrison's novel *The Bluest Eye* (1970), internalizes the negative images of African-American women and believes that the absence of blue eyes is central to her "ugliness." Pecola cannot value her Blackness—she longs to be White so that she can escape the pain of being Black, female, poor, and a child. Her mother, Pauline Breedlove, typifies the internalization of the mammy image. Pauline Breedlove neglects her own children, preferring to lavish her concern and attention on the White charges in her care. Only by accepting this subordinate role to White children could she, as a poor Black woman, see a positive place for herself.

U.S. Black women writers have chronicled other forms of Black women's attempts to escape from a world predicated upon derogated images of Black womanhood. Fictional African-American women characters use drugs, alcohol, excessive religion, and even retreat into madness in an attempt to create other worlds apart from the ones that produced such painful Black female realities. Pauline Breedlove in *The Bluest Eye* and Mrs. Hill in *Meridian* (Walker 1976) both demonstrate an attachment to religion that allows them to ignore their daughters. Eva Medina in Gayl Jones's *Eva's Man* (1976), Merle Kibona in Paule Marshall's *The Chosen Place, the Timeless People* (1969), and Velma Henry in Toni Cade Bambara's *The Salt Eaters* (1980) all experience madness as an escape from pain.

Denial is another characteristic response to the controlling images of Black womanhood and their accompanying conditions. By claiming that they are not like the rest, some African-American women reject connections to other Black women and demand special treatment for themselves. Mary Helen Washington (1982) refers to these characters as assimilated women. They are more aware of their condition than are suspended women, but despite their greater potential for shaping their lives, they still feel thwarted because they see themselves as misplaced by time and circumstances. Light-skinned, middle-class Cleo, a key figure in Dorothy West's novel *The Living Is Easy* (1948), typifies this response. In one scene strong-willed Cleo hustles her daughter past a playground filled with the children of newly arrived Southern Blacks, observing that "she wouldn't want her child to go to school with those niggers." Cleo clings to her social class position, one that she sees as separating her from other African-Americans, and tries to muffle the negative status attached to her Blackness by emphasizing her superior class position. Even though Cleo is more acceptable to the White world, the price she pays for her acceptance is the negation of her racial identity and separation from the sustenance that such an identity might offer.

U.S. Black women writers not only portray the range of responses that individual African-American women express concerning their objectification as the Other: they also document the process of personal growth toward positive self-definitions. The personal growth experienced by Renay, the heroine in Ann Allen Shockley's *Loving Her* (1974), illustrates the process of rejecting externally defined controlling images of Black womanhood. Shockley initially presents Renay as a suspended woman who is trapped in a heterosexual marriage to an abusive husband and who tries to deny her feelings for other women. Renay retreats into music and alcohol as temporary spaces where she can escape having her difference—in this case, her Blackness and lesbianism—judged as inferior and deviant. After taking a White woman lover, Renay is initially quite happy, but she grows to realize that she has replaced one set of controlling images—namely, those she experienced with her abusive husband—with another. She leaves her lover to pursue her own self-definition. By the novel's end Renay has begun to resist all external definitions of herself that stem from controlling images applied to Blacks, women, and lesbians.

Renay's experiences typify how Black women writers explore the theme of Black women's resistance to these controlling images, a resistance typified by the emergent woman in Black women's literature. Sherley Anne Williams's novel *Dessa Rose* (1986) describes a Black slave woman's emerging sense of power after she participates in a slave revolt, runs away, and eventually secures her own freedom. Dorine Davis, the heroine in Rosa Guy's *A Measure of Time* (1983), is raped at age 10 by her White employer, subsequently sleeps with men for money, yet retains a core of resistance. Bad things happen to Dorine, but Guy does not portray Dorine as a victim. In *The Bluest Eye* (1970), Toni Morrison presents the character of Claudia, a 10-year-old Black girl who, to the chagrin of grown-ups, destroys White dolls by tearing off their heads and who refuses to share her classmates' admiration of light-skinned, long-haired Maureen Peal. Claudia's growing awareness of the "Thing that made her [Maureen Peal] beautiful and us ugly" and her rejection of that Thing—racist images of Black women—represents yet another reaction to negative images of Black womanhood. Like Merle Kibona in Paule Marshall's *The Timeless Place, the Chosen People,* Vyry in Margaret Walker's *Jubilee* (1966), Janie Crawford in Zora Neale Hurston's *Their Eyes Were Watching God* (1937), or Meridian in Alice Walker's *Meridian* (1976), Claudia represents a young version of emergent Black women carving out new definitions of Black womanhood.

Independent Black women heroines populate U.S. Black women's fiction of the 1990s. Many of these Black female fictional characters express varying dimensions of the emergent woman thesis. Just as social class differences have become more prominent in Black women's controlling images overall, images of emergent women in Black women's literature also reflect social class diversity. Working-class women become emergent women by overcoming an array of hardships, many of them financial, that aim to keep them down. In Barbara Neely's novel *Blanche on the Lam* (1992) Blanche evades the law by hiding out as a domestic worker for a rich White family. Another working-class heroine is Valerie Wilson's fictional detective Tamara Hale. A single mother of a teenage son, Hale juggles issues of financial well-being and raising her son in the Newark metropolitan area. Interestingly, in both Neely and Wilson's fiction, working-class women spend little time bemoaning their unmarried, uncoupled status. Neither fictional heroine agonizes over the absence of a Black male husband or lover in their lives. In contrast, middle-class Black women become emergent women by changing their expectations about their femininity and Black men's expectations. Terry McMillan's two volumes, *Waiting to Exhale* (1992) and *How Stella Got Her Groove Back* (1996), can be read as companion pieces that advise Black middle-class women how to emerge. In *Waiting to Exhale,* four Black women friends struggle with issues of having satisfying relationships with Black men. By the end of the book, two of the women have found meaningful relationships with men.

More importantly, what they have all learned is that their friendship with one another is as important as their ties to men. In MacMillan's subsequent volume, Stella, a Black single mother who is a highly paid, successful professional, takes a trip to Jamaica by herself and meets Winston, a much younger man. By the end of the volume, Stella has shed the limitations of distinctly American controlling images, and decides that true love transcends differences of age and nationality. Whereas racism, sexism, and class exploitation do not preoccupy the emergent women created by Neely, Wilson, and McMillan, the social contexts in which these authors embed their characters are clearly structured by these oppressions.

The many documentaries and feature films where Black women appear as central characters constitute another arena where emergent Black women appear. Not only could Black women read about emergent Black women in Terry MacMillan's fiction, audiences could view images of Black women trying to "exhale" and "get their grove" on the big screen. This theme of U.S. Black women coming to know themselves, and often doing so in company of other Black women, wove throughout a cluster of films whose subject matter differed dramatically. Feature films made by Black women directors, such as Julie Dash's *Daughters of Dust*, Michelle Parkerson's *Gotta Make That Journey: Sweet Honey in the Rock,* and Ayoka Chenzira's *Alma's Rainbow* all illustrate the value Black women filmmakers place on Black women's emerging self-definitions.

Emergent women may have only recently made their appearance in Black women's fiction and film, but such women have long populated everyday lived experience. In her autobiography, Lorene Carey, a working-class African-American woman who helped desegregate a prestigious New England boarding school, tells of what happens when everyday Black women decide to "turn it out":

> My mother, and her mother, who had worked in a factory, and her mother, who had cleaned apartments in Manhattan, had been studying these people all their lives. . . . And I had studied them. I had studied my mother as she turned out elementary schools and department stores. I always saw it coming. Some white department-store manager would look at my mother and see no more than a modestly dressed young black woman making a tiresome complaint. He'd use that tone of voice they used when they had important work elsewhere. Uh-oh. Then he'd dismiss her with his eyes. I'd feel her body stiffen next to me, and I'd know that he'd set her off. And then it began in earnest, the turning out. She never moved back. It didn't matter how many people were in line. . . . Turning out, I learned, was not a matter of style; cold indignation worked as well as hot fury. Turning out had to do with will (Carey 1991, 58–59).

Emergent women have found that one way of surviving the everyday disrespect and outright assaults that accompany controlling images is to "turn it out." This is the moment when silence becomes speech, when stillness becomes action. As Karla Holloway says, "no one wins in that situation, but usually we feel better" (1995, 31).

5 THE POWER OF SELF- DEFINITION

"In order to survive, those of us for whom oppression is as American as apple pie have always had to be watchers," asserts Black feminist poet Audre Lorde (1984, 114). This "watching" generates a dual consciousness in African-American women, one in which Black women "become familiar with the language and manners of the oppressor, even sometimes adopting them for some illusion of protection" (p. 114), while hiding a self-defined standpoint from the prying eyes of dominant groups. Ella Surrey, an elderly Black woman domestic, eloquently summarizes the energy needed to maintain independent self-definitions: "We have always been the best actors in the world. . . . I think that we are much more clever than they are because we know that we have to play the game. We've always had to live two lives—one for them and one for ourselves" (Gwaltney 1980, 238, 240).[1]

Behind the mask of behavioral conformity imposed on African-American women, acts of resistance, both organized and anonymous, have long existed (Davis 1981, 1989; Terborg-Penn 1986; Hine 1989; Barnett 1993). Despite the strains connected with domestic work, Judith Rollins (1985) asserts that the domestic workers she interviewed appeared to have retained a "remarkable sense of self-worth." They "skillfully deflect these psychological attacks on their personhood, their adulthood, their dignity, these attempts to lure them into accepting employers' definitions of them as inferior" (p. 212). Bonnie Thornton Dill (1988a) found that the domestic workers in her study refused to let their employers push them around. As one respondent declared: "When I went out to work . . . my mother told me, 'Don't let anybody take advantage of you. Speak up for your rights, but do the work right. If they don't give you your rights, you demand that they treat you right. And if they don't, then you quit' " (p. 41). Jacqueline Bobo (1995) reports that the U.S. Black women in her study who viewed the film *The Color Purple* were not passive consumers of controlling images of Black womanhood. Instead, these women crafted identities designed to empower them. In 1905, a period of heightened racial repression, educator Fannie Barrier Williams viewed the African-American woman not as a defenseless victim but as a strong-willed resister: "As meanly as she is thought of, hindered as she is in all directions, she is always doing something of merit and credit that is not expected of her" (Williams 1987, 151). Williams saw the Black woman as "irrepressible. She is insulted, but she holds up her head; she is scorned, but she proudly demands respect. . . . The most interesting girl of this country is the colored girl" (p. 151).

Resisting by doing something that "is not expected" could not have occurred without Black women's long-standing rejection of mammies, matriarchs, and other controlling images. When combined, these individual acts of resistance suggest that a distinctive, collective Black women's consciousness exists. Such a consciousness was present in Maria Stewart's 1831 speech advising the "daughters of Africa" to "Awake! Arise! No longer sleep nor slumber, but distinguish yourselves. Show forth to the world that ye are endowed with noble and exalted faculties" (Richardson 1987, 30). Such a consciousness is present in the worldview of Johnny Mae Fields, a mill worker from North Carolina possessing few opportunities to resist. Ms. Fields wryly announces, "If they tell me something and I know I ain't going to do it, I don't tell them. I just go on and don't do it" (Byerly 1986, 141).

Silence is not to be interpreted as submission in this collective, self-defined Black women's consciousness. In 1925 author Marita Bonner cogently described how consciousness remained the one sphere of freedom available to her in the stifling confines of both her Black middle-class world and a racist White society:

> So—being a woman—you can wait. You must sit quietly without a chip. Not sodden—and weighted as if your feet were cast in the iron of your soul. Not wasting strength in enervating gestures as if two hundred years of bonds and whips had really tricked you into nervous uncertainty. But quiet; quiet. Like Buddha—who brown like I am—sat entirely at ease, entirely sure of himself; motionless and knowing. . . . Motionless on the outside. But inside? (Bonner 1987, 7)

U.S. Black women intellectuals have long explored this private, hidden space of Black women's consciousness, the "inside" ideas that allow Black women to cope with and, in many cases, transcend the confines of intersecting oppressions of race, class, gender, and sexuality. How have African-American women as a group found the strength to oppose our objectification as "de mule uh de world"? How do we account for the voices of resistance of Audre Lorde, Ella Surrey, Maria Stewart, Fannie Barrier Williams, and Marita Bonner? What foundation sustained Sojourner Truth so that she could ask, "Ain't I a woman?" The voices of these African-American women are not those of victims but of survivors. Their ideas and actions suggest that not only does a self-defined, group-derived Black women's standpoint exist, but that its presence has been essential to U.S. Black women's survival.

"A system of oppression," claims Black feminist activist Pauli Murray, "draws much of its strength from the acquiescence of its victims, who have accepted the dominant image of themselves and are paralyzed by a sense of helplessness" (1987, 106). U.S. Black women's ideas and actions force a rethinking of the concept of hegemony, the notion that Black women's objectification as the Other is so complete that we become willing participants in our own oppression. Most African-American women simply do not define themselves as mammies, matriarchs, welfare mothers, mules, or sexually denigrated women. The matrix of domination in which these controlling images are embedded is much less cohesive or uniform than imagined.

African-American women encounter these controlling images, not as disembodied symbolic messages but as ideas designed to provide meaning in our daily lives (Scott 1985). Black women's work and family experiences create the conditions whereby the contradictions between everyday experiences and the controlling images of Black womanhood become visible. Seeing the contradictions in the ideologies opens them up for demystification. Just as Sojourner Truth deconstructed the term *woman* by using her own lived experiences to challenge it, so in a variety of ways do everyday African-American women do the same thing. That fewer Maria Stewarts, Sojourner Truths, Ella Surreys, or Johnny Mae Fieldses are heard from may be less a statement about the existence of Black women's ideas than it is a reflection of the suppression of their ideas. As Nancy White, an inner-city resident points out, "I like to say what I think. But I don't do that much because most people don't care what I think" (Gwaltney 1980, 156). Like Marita Bonner, far too many Black women remain motionless on the outside . . . but inside?

Finding a Voice: Coming to Terms with Contradictions

"To be able to use the range of one's voice, to attempt to express the totality of self, is a recurring struggle in the tradition of [Black women] writers," maintains Black feminist literary critic Barbara Christian (1985, 172). African-American women have certainly expressed our individual voices. U.S. Black women have been described as generally outspoken and self-assertive speakers, a consequence of expectations that men and women both participate in Black civil society. But despite this tradition, the overarching theme of finding a voice to express a collective, self-defined Black women's standpoint remains a core theme in Black feminist thought.

Why this theme of self-definition should preoccupy African-American women is not surprising. Black women's lives are a series of negotiations that aim to reconcile the contradictions separating our own internally defined images of self as African-American women with our objectification as the Other. The struggle of living two lives, one for "them and one for ourselves" (Gwaltney 1980, 240) creates a peculiar tension to construct independent self-definitions within a context where Black womanhood remains routinely derogated. As Karla Holloway points out, "the reality of racism and sexism means that we must configure our private realities to include an awareness of what our public image might mean to others. This is not paranoia. It is preparedness" (Holloway 1995, 36).

Much of the best of Black feminist thought reflects this effort to find a collective, self-defined voice and express a fully articulated womanist standpoint (Collins 1998, 61–65). Audre Lorde observes that "within this country where racial difference creates a constant, if unspoken, distortion of vision, Black women have on the one hand always been highly visible, and so, on the other hand, have been rendered invisible through the depersonalization of racism" (1984, 42). Lorde also points out that the "visibility which makes us most vulnerable"—that which accompanies being Black—"is also the source of our greatest strength" (p. 42). The category of "Black woman" makes all U.S. Black women especially visible and open to the objectification of Black women as a category. This group treatment potentially renders each individual African-American woman invisible as fully human. But paradoxically, being treated as an invisible Other places U.S. Black women in an outsider-within position that has stimulated creativity in many.

For individual women, resolving contradictions of this magnitude takes considerable inner strength. In describing the development of her own racial identity, Pauli Murray remembers: "My own self-esteem was elusive and difficult to sustain. I was not entirely free from the prevalent idea that I must prove myself worthy of the rights that white individuals took for granted. This psychological conditioning along with fear had reduced my capacity for resistance to racial injustice" (1987, 106). Murray's quest was for constructed knowledge (Belenky et al. 1986), a type of knowledge essential to resolving contradictions. To learn to speak in a "unique and authentic voice, women must 'jump outside' the frames and systems authorities provide and create their own frame" (p. 134). Unlike the controlling images developed for middle-class White women, the controlling images applied to Black women are so uniformly negative that they almost necessitate resistance. For U.S. Black women, constructed knowledge of self emerges from the struggle to replace controlling images with self-defined knowledge deemed personally important, usually knowledge essential to Black women's survival.[2]

Safe Spaces and Coming to Voice

While domination may be inevitable as a social fact, it is unlikely to be hegemonic as an ideology within social spaces where Black women speak freely. This realm of relatively safe discourse, however narrow, is a necessary condition for

Black women's resistance. Extended families, churches, and African-American community organizations are important locations where safe discourse potentially can occur. Sondra O'Neale describes the workings of these Black women's spaces: "Beyond the mask, in the ghetto of the black women's community, in her family, and, more important, in her psyche, is and has always been another world, a world in which she functions—sometimes in sorrow but more often in genuine joy . . .—by doing the things that 'normal' black women do" (1986, 139). These spaces are not only safe—they form prime locations for resisting objectification as the Other. In these spaces Black women "observe the feminine images of the 'larger' culture, realize that these models are at best unsuitable and at worst destructive to them, and go about the business of fashioning themselves after the prevalent, historical black female role models in their own community" (O'Neale 1986, 139). By advancing Black women's empowerment through self-definition, these safe spaces help Black women resist the dominant ideology promulgated not only outside Black civil society but within African-American institutions.

These institutional sites where Black women construct independent self-definitions reflect the dialectical nature of oppression and activism. Schools, print and broadcast media, government agencies, and other institutions in the information business reproduce the controlling images of Black womanhood. In response, African-American women have traditionally used family networks and Black community institutions as sites for countering these images. On the one hand, these Black community institutions have been vitally important in developing strategies of resistance. In the context of deep-seated U.S. racial segregation that persisted through the 1960s, the vast majority of U.S. Black women lacked access to other forms of political organization.

On the other hand, many of these same institutions of Black civil society have also perpetuated racist, sexist, elitist, and homophobic ideologies. This same period of desegregation of U.S. society overall spurred a parallel desegregation *within* Black civil society where women, working-class folks, lesbians, gays, bisexuals and transgendered individuals, and other formerly subjugated subpopulations within Black civil society began to speak out.

As a result of this changing political context, the resulting reality is much more complex than one of an all-powerful White majority objectifying Black women with a unified U.S. Black community staunchly challenging these external assaults. No uniform, homogeneous culture of resistance ever existed among U.S. Blacks, and such a culture does not exist now. One can say, however, that U.S. Blacks have shared a common political agenda and culture, one that has been differently experienced and expressed by U.S. Blacks as a heterogeneous collectivity. Historically, survival depended on sticking together and in many ways aiming to minimize differences among African-Americans. More recently, in a changing political economy where survival for many U.S. Blacks seems less of an issue, space to express these differences now exists. Black feminism itself has been central in creating that space, in large part, via Black women's claims for self-definition. Overall, African-American women find ourselves in a web of crosscutting relationships, each presenting varying combinations of controlling images and Black women's self-definitions.

Thus, the historical complexity of these institutional arrangements of racial segregation and heterogeneous Black community politics profoundly affected Black women's consciousness and its articulation in a self-defined standpoint. Given this context, what have been some important safe spaces where Black women's consciousness has been nurtured? Where have individual African-American women spoken freely in contributing to a collective, self-defined standpoint? Moreover, how "safe" are these spaces now?

Black Women's Relationships with One Another

Traditionally, U.S. Black women's efforts to construct individual and collective voices have occurred in at least three safe spaces. One location involves Black women's relationships with one another. In some cases, such as friendships and family interactions, these relationships are informal, private dealings among individuals. In others, as was the case during slavery (D. White 1985), in Black churches (Gilkes 1985; Higginbotham 1993), or in Black women's organizations (Giddings 1988; Cole 1993; Guy-Sheftall 1993), more formal organizational ties have nurtured powerful Black women's communities. As mothers, daughters, sisters, and friends to one another, many African-American women affirm one another (Myers 1980).

The mother/daughter relationship is one fundamental relationship among Black women. Countless Black mothers have empowered their daughters by passing on the everyday knowledge essential to survival as African-American women (Joseph 1981; Collins 1987). Black daughters identify the profound influence that their mothers have had upon their lives (Bell-Scott et al. 1991). Mothers and mother figures emerge as central figures in autobiographies such as Maya Angelou's *I Know Why the Caged Bird Sings* (1969), Bebe Moore Campbell's *Sweet Summer* (1989), Mamie Garvin Fields and Karen Fields's *Lemon Swamp and Other Places* (1983), and Elaine Brown's *A Taste of Power* (1992). Alice Walker attributes the trust she has in herself to her mother. In describing this relationship, Mary Helen Washington points out that Walker "never doubted her powers of judgment because her mother assumed that they were sound; she never questioned her right to follow her intellectual bent, because her mother implicitly entitled her to it" (Washington 1984, 145). By giving her daughter a library card, Walker's mother showed she knew the value of a free mind.

In the comfort of daily conversations, through serious conversation and humor, African-American women as sisters and friends affirm one another's humanity, specialness, and right to exist. Black women's fiction, such as Toni

Cade Bambara's short story "The Johnson Girls" (1981) and Toni Morrison's novels *Sula* (1974), *The Bluest Eye* (1970), and *Beloved* (1987), as well as Terry McMillan's blockbuster novel *Waiting to Exhale* (1992), is one important location where Black women's friendships are taken seriously. In a dialogue with four other Black women, Evelynn Hammonds describes this special relationship that Black women can have with one another: "I think most of the time you have to be there to experience it. When I am with other black women I always laugh. I think our humor comes from a shared recognition of who we all are in the world" (Clarke et al. 1983, 114).

This shared recognition often operates among African-American women who do not know one another but who see the need to value Black womanhood. Marita Golden describes her efforts in 1968 to attend a college which was "nestled . . . in the comfortable upper reaches of northwest Washington, surrounded by . . . the manicured, sprawling lawns of the city's upper class." To enter this world, Golden caught the bus downtown with "black women domestic workers who rode to the end of the line to clean house for young and middle-aged white matrons." Golden describes her fellow travelers' reaction to her acquiring a college education:

> They gazed proudly at me, nodding at the books in my lap. . . . I accepted their encouragement and hated America for never allowing them to be selfish or greedy, to feel the steel-hard bite of ambition. . . . They had parlayed their anger, brilliantly shaped it into a soft armor of survival. The spirit of those women sat with me in every class I took. (Golden 1983, 21)

My decision to pursue my doctorate was stimulated by a similar experience. In 1978 I offered a seminar as part of a national summer institute for teachers and other school personnel. After my Chicago workshop, an older Black woman participant whispered to me, "Honey, I'm real proud of you. Some folks don't want to see you up there [in the front of the classroom], but you belong there. Go back to school and get your Ph.D., and then they won't be able to tell you nothing!" To this day, I thank her and try to do the same for others. In talking with other African-American women, I have discovered that many of us have had similar experiences.

This issue of Black women being the ones who really listen to one another is significant, particularly given the importance of voice in Black women's lives. Identifying the value of Black women's friendships, Karla Holloway describes how the women in her book club supported one another: "The events we shared among ourselves all had a similar trigger—it was when someone, a child's school principal or teacher, a store clerk, medical personnel, had treated us as if we had no sense of our own, no ability to filter through whatever nonsense they were feeding us, or no earned, adult power to make choices in our children's lives" (Holloway 1995, 31). These women described cathartic moments when, in creative ways, they responded to these assaults by "turning it out." Each knew that only another Black woman could fully understand how it felt to be treated that way and to respond in kind.

Audre Lorde describes the importance that the expression of individual voice within collective context of Black women's communities can have for self-affirmation: "Of course I am afraid, because the transformation of silence into language and action is an act of self-revelation, and that always seems fraught with danger" (1984, 42). One can write for a nameless, faceless audience, but the act of using one's voice requires a listener and thus establishes a connection. For African-American women the listener most able to pierce the invisibility created by Black women's objectification is another Black woman. This process of trusting one another can seem dangerous because only Black women know what it means to be Black women. But if we will not listen to one another, then who will?

Black women writers have led the way in recognizing the importance of Black women's relationships with one another. Mary Helen Washington points out that one distinguishing feature of Black women's literature is that it is about African-American women. Women talk to one another, and "their friendships with other women—mothers, sisters, grandmothers, friends, lovers—are vital to their growth and well-being" (1987, xxi). The significance placed on relationships among Black women transcends U.S. Black women's writings. For example, Ghanian author Ama Ata Aidoo's novel *Changes* (1991) uses the friendship between two African professional women to explore the challenges facing professional women in contemporary African societies. Within U.S. Black women's fiction, this emphasis on Black women's relationships has been so striking that novelist Gayl Jones suggests that women writers select different themes from those of their male counterparts. In the work of many Black male writers, the significant relationships are those that involve confrontation with individuals outside the family and community. But among Black women writers, relationships within family and community, between men and women, and among women are treated as complex and significant (Tate 1983, 92).

U.S. Black women writers and filmmakers have explored many themes affecting Black women's relationships. One concerns the difficulties that African-American women can have in affirming one another in a society that derogates Black women as a group. Albeit for different reasons, the inability of mothers to help their daughters come to understandings of Black womanhood characterize mother-daughter relationships in Toni Morrison's novel *The Bluest Eye* and in the film *Just Another Girl on the IRT*. Another theme concerns how Black women's relationships can support and renew. Relationships such as those between Celie and Shug in Alice Walker's novel *The Color Purple*, among sisters in the film *Soul Food*, among the four women in *Waiting to Exhale*, and among women in an extended family in the film *Daughters of Dust* all provide cases where Black women helped one another grow in some fashion. Another theme involves how relationships among Black women can control and repress. Audre Lorde's relationship with her mother in her autobiography *Zami* (1982) and Black adolescent Alma's relationship with her overbearing mother in the film *Alma's Rainbow* both illustrate ways in which Black women with some sort of power, in these examples that of the authority of motherhood, can suppress other women. Perhaps Ntozake Shange best summarizes the importance that Black women can have for one another in resisting oppressive conditions. Shange gives the following reason for why she writes: "When I die, I will not be guilty of having left a generation of girls behind thinking that anyone can tend to their emotional health other than themselves" (in Tate 1983, 162).

The Black Women's Blues Tradition

African-American music as art has provided a second location where Black women have come to voice (Jackson 1981). "Art is special because of its ability to influence feelings as well as knowledge," suggests Angela Davis (1989, 200). Davis contends that the dominant group failed to grasp the social function of music in general and particularly the central role music played in all aspects of life in West African society. As a result, "Black people were able to create with their music an aesthetic community of resistance, which in turn encouraged and nurtured a political community of active struggle for freedom" (1989, 201). Spirituals, blues, jazz, rhythm and blues, and progressive hip-hop all form part of a "continuum of struggle which is at once aesthetic and political" (p. 201).

African-derived communication patterns maintain the integrity of the individual and his or her personal voice, but do so in the context of group activity (Smitherman 1977; Kochman 1981; Asante 1987; Cannon 1988). In music one effect of this oral mode of discourse is that individuality, rather than being stifled by group activity or being equated with specialization, actually flourishes in a group context (Sidran 1971).[3] "There's something about music that is so penetrating that your soul gets the message. No matter what trouble comes to a person, music can help him face it," claims Mahalia Jackson (1985, 454). "A song must do something for me as well as for the people that hear it. I can't sing a song that doesn't have a message. If it doesn't have the strength it can't lift you" (p. 446).

The blues tradition is an essential part of African-American music.[4] Blues singer Alberta Hunter explains the importance of the blues as a way of dealing with pain: "To me, the blues are almost religious . . . almost sacred—when we sing the blues, we're singing out of our own hearts . . . our feelings" (Harrison 1978, 63). Black people's ability to cope with and even transcend trouble without ignoring it means that it will not destroy us (Cone 1972).

Traditionally, blues assumed a similar function in African-American oral culture to that played by print media for White, visually based culture. Blues was not just entertainment—it was a way of solidifying community and commenting on the social fabric of working-class Black life in America. Sherley Anne Williams contends that "the blues records of each decade explain something about the philosophical basis of our lives as black people. If we don't understand that as so-called intellectuals, then we don't really understand anything about ourselves" (in Tate 1983, 208). For African-American women, blues seemed to be every-where. Mahalia Jackson describes its pervasiveness during her childhood in New Orleans: "The famous white singers like Caruso—you might hear them when you went by a white folk's house, but in a colored house you heard blues. You couldn't help but hear blues—all through the thin partitions of the houses—through the open windows—up and down the street in the colored neighbor-hoods—everybody played it real loud" (1985, 447).

Black women have been central in maintaining, transforming, and re-creating the blues traditions of African-American culture (Harrison 1978, 1988; Russell 1982; Davis 1998). Michele Russell asserts, "Blues, first and last, are a familiar idiom for Black women, even a staple of life" (1982, 130). Blues has occupied a special place in Black women's music as a site of the expression of Black women's self-definitions. The blues singer strives to create an atmosphere in which analysis can take place, and yet this atmosphere is intensely personal and individualistic. When Black women sing the blues, we sing our own personalized, individualistic blues while simultaneously expressing the collective blues of African-American women.

Michele Russell's (1982) analysis of five Black women blues singers' music demonstrates how the texts of blues singers can be seen as expressions of a Black women's standpoint. Russell claims that the works of Bessie Smith, Bessie Jackson, Billie Holiday, Nina Simone, and Esther Phillips help Black women "own their past, present, and future." To Russell, these women are primary because "the content of their message, combined with the form of their delivery, make them so" (p. 130).

The music of the classic blues singers of the 1920s—almost exclusively women—marks the early written record of this dimension of U.S. Black oral cul-ture. The songs themselves were originally sung in small communities, where boundaries distinguishing singer from audience, call from response, and thought from action were fluid and permeable. Despite the control of White-run record companies, these records were made exclusively for the "race market" of African-Americans and thus targeted Black consumers. Because literacy was not possible for large numbers of Black women, these recordings represented the first permanent documents exploring a working-class Black women's standpoint that until then had been accessible to Black women in local settings. The songs can be seen as poetry, as expressions of ordinary Black women rearticulated through Black oral traditions.

The lyrics sung by many of the Black women blues singers challenge the externally defined controlling images used to justify Black women's objectifica-tion as the Other. The songs of Ma Rainey, dubbed "Queen of the Blues" and the first major female blues singer to be extensively recorded, validate Black feminist intellectual traditions expressed by working-class Black women. In contrast to the ingenues of most White popular music of the same period, Ma Rainey and her contemporaries sing of mature, sexual women. For example, Sara Martin's "Mean Tight Mama" rejects the cult of true womanhood and its confining images of beauty:

> Now my hair is nappy and I don't wear no clothes of silk
> Now my hair is nappy and I don't wear no clothes of silk
> But the cow that's black and ugly has often got the sweetest milk.
> (Harrison 1978, 69)

Bessie Smith's "Get It, Bring It, and Put It Right Here"—like the words of Maria Stewart—advises Black women to possess the spirit of independence. She sings of her man:

> I've had a man for fifteen years, give him his room and his board
> Once he was like a Cadillac, now he's like an old worn-out Ford.
> He never brought me a lousy dime, and put it in my hand
> Oh, there'll be some changes from now on, according to my plan.
> He's got to get it, bring it, and put it right here
> Or else he's gonna keep it out there.
> If he must steal it, beg it, or borrow it somewhere
> Long as he gets it, I don't care.
> (Russell 1982, 133)

Sometimes the texts of Black women blues singers take overtly political forms. Billie Holiday recorded "Strange Fruit" in 1939 at the end of a decade rife with racial unrest:

> Southern trees bear a strange fruit, blood on the leaves and blood at the root
> Black body swinging in the Southern breeze, strange fruit hanging from the poplar trees.
> Pastoral scene of the gallant South, the bulging eyes and the twisted mouth,
> Scent of magnolia sweet and fresh, and the sudden smell of burning flesh!
> Here is a fruit for the crows to pluck, for the rain to gather, for the wind to suck, for the sun to rot, for a tree to drop,
> Here is a strange and bitter crop.
> (*Billie Holiday Anthology* 1976, 111)

Through her powerful rendition of these lyrics, Billie Holiday demonstrated a direct connection to the antilynching political activism of Ida B. Wells-Barnett and other better-known Black feminists. Holiday's music reaches from the past to express themes that shed light on the present.

Despite the contributions of Black women's blues as one location where ordinary Black women found voice, Ann duCille (1993) cautions against a trend in contemporary Black cultural criticism of viewing the blues through idealized lenses. DuCille contends that while Black blues queens like Bessie Smith and Ma Rainey sang of sex and sexuality with a startling frankness for their times, they rarely could do so on their own terms. Despite the fact that at the peak of the classic blues era hundreds of women had the opportunity to record their work, they did so for White-male-controlled record companies. At the same time, middle-class Blacks who were engaged in a cultural Renaissance during the 1920s typically saw such music as antithetical to the aims of their cultural movement. Black women's blues was often designated as "low" culture (Davis 1998, xii–xiii). Thus, while it appears that the Black women blues singers of the 1920s sang freely of sexually explicit themes, they did so in a complicated context of race, class, and gender politics.

Moreover, duCille points out that identifying the blues as the "authentic" location for Black women's voice splits Black experience into two seemingly opposed groups, middle-class Black women "literati" and working-class Black women blues singers. Deeming the blues singers to be more "authentic" relegates Black women writers, and those who study them, to the category of a less authentic Blackness. DuCille explores how the fiction of two middle-class Black women writers, Jessie Fauset and Nella Lawson, offered a more complex critique of society than that forwarded by the blues singers. DuCille's argument is not with the singers themselves, but primarily with how such seemingly safe spaces of Black women's blues are viewed within contemporary Black cultural criticism. However, keeping her caveats in mind, it is important to remember that despite their contemporary appropriations, for the vast majority of Black working-class women, Black women's blues spaces have long been important and remain so today (Davis 1998). Where else could working-class Black women say in public the things they had long shared among one another in private?

The Voices of Black Women Writers

During the summer of 1944, recent law school graduate Pauli Murray returned to her California apartment and found the following anonymous note from the "South Crocker Street Property Owner's Association" tacked to her door: "We . . . wish to inform you the flat you now occupy . . . is restricted to the white or Caucasian race only. . . . We intend to uphold these restrictions, therefore we ask that you vacate the above mentioned flat . . . within seven days" (1987, 253). Murray's response was to write. She remembers: "I was learning that creative expression is an integral part of the equipment needed in the service of a compelling cause; it is another form of activism. Words poured from my typewriter" (p. 255).

Though a Black women's written tradition existed (Christian 1985; Carby 1987), it was available primarily to educated women. Denied the literacy that enabled them to read books and novels, as well as the time to do so, working-class Black women struggled to find a public voice. Hence the significance of the blues and other dimensions of Black oral traditions in their lives. In this class-segmented context, finding Black women's writing that transcends these divisions among written and oral traditions is noteworthy. In this regard, because it fits neither solely within the Black women's blues tradition nor within equally important traditions of Black women's writers, the work of Alice Childress (1956) remains exemplary. Childress created the character of Mildred, a fictional working-class, Black woman domestic worker. Through short monologues to her friend Marge, Mildred, a domestic worker, speaks out on a range of topics. Mildred's 62 monologues, each two or three pages in length, constitute provocative statements of Childress's Black feminist theory (Harris 1986). Take, for example, Mildred's rendition to Marge of what she said to her boss in response to hearing herself described to her boss's luncheon friends as a quasi-family member:

> I am *not* just like one of the family at all! The family eats in the dining room and I eat in the kitchen. Your mama borrows your lace tablecloth for her company and your son entertains his friends in your parlour, your daughter takes her afternoon nap on the living room couch and the puppy sleeps on your satin spread . . . so you can see I am not *just* like one of the family. (Childress 1956, 2).

In this passage, Childress creates a fictional version of what many Black women domestic workers have wanted to say at one time or another. She also advances a biting critique of how the mammy image has been used to justify Black women's bad treatment.

Foreshadowing Barbara Neely's creation of the character of Blanche, Mildred's ideas certainly ring true. But Childress's Mildred also illustrates a creative use of Black women's writing that is targeted not just to educated Black women, but to a wider Black women's community. The character of Mildred first appeared in a series of conversations that were originally published in Paul Robeson's newspaper, *Freedom,* under the title "Conversations from Life." They continued in the *Baltimore Afro-American* as "Here's Mildred." Since many of Childress's readers were themselves domestic workers, Mildred's bold assertions resonated with the silenced voices of many of these readers. Moreover, Mildred's identity as a Black working-class domestic and the form of publication of these fictionalized accounts illustrates an increasingly rare practice in Black intellectual production—a Black author writing to an African-American, working-class audience, using a medium controlled by Black people (Harris 1986).[5]

Since the 1970s, increased literacy among African-Americans has provided new opportunities for U.S. Black women to expand the use of scholarship and literature into more visible institutional sites of resistance. A community of Black women writers has emerged since 1970, one in which African-American women engage in dialogue among one another in order to explore formerly taboo subjects. Black feminist literary criticism has documented the intellectual and personal space created for African-American women in this emerging body of ideas (Washington 1980, 1982; Tate 1983; Evans 1984; Christian 1985; O'Neale 1986). Especially noteworthy are the ways in which many Black women writers build on former themes and approaches of the Black women's blues tradition (Williams 1979) and of earlier Black women writers (Cannon 1988).

How "Safe" Are Safe Spaces?

Historically, safe spaces were "safe" because they represented places where Black women could freely examine issues that concerned us. By definition, such spaces become less "safe" if shared with those who were not Black and female. Black women's safe spaces were never meant to be a way of life. Instead, they constitute one mechanism among many designed to foster Black women's empowerment and enhance our ability to participate in social justice projects. As strategies, safe spaces rely on exclusionary practices, but their overall purpose most certainly aims for a more inclusionary, just society. As the work of Black women blues singers and Black women writers suggests, many of the ideas generated in such spaces found a welcome reception outside Black women's communities. But how could Black women generate these understandings of Black women's realities without first talking to one another?

Since the 1970s, U.S. Black women have been unevenly incorporated into schools, jobs, neighborhoods, and other U.S. social institutions that historically have excluded us. As a result, African-American women have become more class stratified than at any period in the past. In these newly desegregated settings, one new challenge consists of building "safe spaces" that do not become stigmatized as "separatist." U.S. Black women who find ourselves integrating corporations and colleges encounter new forms of racism and sexism that require equally innovative responses. A new rhetoric of color-blindness that reproduces social inequalities by treating people the same (Crenshaw 1997) makes it more difficult to maintain safe spaces at all. Any group that organizes around its own self-interests runs the risk of being labeled "separatist," "essentialist," and anti-democratic. This protracted attack on so-called identity politics works to suppress historically oppressed groups that aim to craft independent political agendas around identities of race, gender, class, and/or sexuality.

Within this climate, African-American women are increasingly asked why we want to "separate" ourselves from Black men and why feminism cannot speak for all women, including us. In essence, these queries challenge the need for distinctive Black women's communities as *political* entities. Black women's organizations devoted to cooking, nails, where to find a good baby-sitter, and other apolitical topics garner little attention. But how do Black women as a collectivity resist intersecting oppressions as they affect us without organizing as a group? How do U.S. Black women identify the specific issues associated with controlling images of Black womanhood without safe spaces where we can talk freely?

One reason that safe spaces are so threatening to those who feel excluded, and so routinely castigated by them, is that safe spaces are free of surveillance by more powerful groups. Such spaces simultaneously remove Black women from surveillance and foster the conditions for Black women's independent self-definitions. When institutionalized, these self-definitions become foundational to politicized Black feminist standpoints. Thus, much more is at stake here than the simple expression of voice.

A broader climate that aims to suppress political speech among African-American women, among others, has affected the organization of historically safe spaces within Black civil society. Relationships among Black women, within families, and within Black community organizations all must contend with the new realities and rhetoric that characterize an unfulfilled racial and gender desegregation in the context of increasingly antagonistic class relationships.

The blues tradition in Black women's music also remains under assault under these new social conditions. Traditionally, Black women blues singers drew upon traditions of struggle in order to produce "progressive art." Such art was emancipatory because it fused thought, feeling, and action and helped Black women among others to see their world differently and act to change it. More recently, commodification of the blues and its transformation into marketable crossover music have virtually stripped it of its close ties to African-American oral traditions. Considerable controversy surrounds the issue of how to assess the diverse genres of contemporary Black music. As Angela Davis observes, "Some of the superstars of popular-musical culture today are unquestionably musical geniuses, but they have distorted the Black music tradition by brilliantly developing its form while ignoring its content of struggle and freedom" (1989, 208). Black literary critic Sondra O'Neale suggests that similar processes of depoliticization may be affecting Black women's writing. "Where are the Angela Davises, Ida B. Wellses, and Daisy Bateses of black feminist literature?" she asks (1986, 144).

Contemporary African-American musicians, writers, cultural critics, and intellectuals function in a dramatically different political economy than that of any prior generation. It remains to be seen whether the specialized thought generated by contemporary Black feminist thinkers in very different institutional locations is capable of creating safe spaces that will carry African-American women even further.

Consciousness as a Sphere of Freedom

Traditionally, when taken together, Black women's relationships with one another, the Black women's blues tradition, and the work of Black women writers provided the context for crafting alternatives to prevailing images of Black womanhood. These sites offered safe spaces that nurtured the everyday and specialized thought of African-American women. In them Black women intellectuals could construct ideas and experiences that infused daily life with new meaning. These new meanings offered African-American women potentially powerful tools to resist the controlling images of Black womanhood. Far from being a secondary concern in bringing about social change, challenging controlling images and replacing them with a Black women's standpoint constituted an essential component in resisting intersecting oppressions (Thompson-Cager 1989). What have been some of the important ideas that developed in these safe spaces? Moreover, how useful are these ideas in responding to the greatly changed social context that confronts U.S. Black women?

The Importance of Self-Definition

"Black groups digging on white philosophies ought to consider the source. Know who's playing the music before you dance," cautions poet Nikki Giovanni (1971, 126). Her advice is especially germane for African-American women. Giovanni suggests: "We Black women are the single group in the West intact. And anybody can see we're pretty shaky. We are . . . the only group that derives its identity from itself. I think it's been rather unconscious but we measure ourselves by ourselves, and I think that's a practice we can ill afford to lose" (1971, 144). When Black women's very survival is at stake, creating independent self-definitions becomes essential to that survival.

The issue of the journey from internalized oppression to the "free mind" of a self-defined, womanist consciousness has been a prominent theme in the works of U.S. Black women writers. Author Alexis DeVeaux notes that there is a "great exploration of the self in women's work. It's the self in relationship with an intimate other, with the community, the nation and the world" (in Tate 1983, 54). Far from being a narcissistic or trivial concern, this placement of self at the center of analysis is critical for understanding a host of other relationships. DeVeaux continues, "you have to understand what your place as an individual is and the place of the person who is close to you. You have to understand the space between you before you can understand more complex or larger groups" (p. 54).

Black women have also stressed the importance of self-definition as part of the journey from victimization to a free mind in their blues. Sherley Anne Williams's analysis of the affirmation of self in the blues make a critical contribution in understanding the blues as a Black women's text. In discussing the blues roots of Black literature, Williams notes, "The assertion of individuality and the implied assertion—as action, not mere verbal statement—of self is an important dimension of the blues" (1979, 130).

The assertion of self usually comes at the end of a song, after the description or analysis of the troublesome situation. This affirmation of self is often the only solution to that problem or situation. Nina Simone's (1985) classic blues song

"Four Women" illustrates this use of the blues to affirm self. Simone sings of three Black women whose experiences typify controlling images: Aunt Sarah, the mule, whose back is bent from a lifetime of hard work; Sweet Thing, the Black prostitute who will belong to anyone who has money to buy; and Saphronia, the mulatto whose Black mother was raped late one night. Simone explores Black women's objectification as the Other by invoking the pain these three women actually feel. But Peaches, the fourth woman, is an especially powerful figure, because Peaches is angry. "I'm awfully bitter these days," Peaches cries out, "because my parents were slaves." These words and the feelings they invoke demonstrate her growing awareness and self-definition of the situation she encountered. They offer to the listener not sadness and remorse, but an anger that leads to action. This is the type of individuality Williams means—not that of talk but self-definitions that foster action.

While the theme of the journey also appears in the work of Black men, African-American women writers and musicians explore this journey toward freedom in ways that are characteristically female (Thompson-Cager 1989). Black women's journeys, though at times embracing political and social issues, basically take personal and psychological forms and rarely reflect the freedom of movement of Black men who hop "trains," "hit the road," or in other ways physically travel in order to find that elusive sphere of freedom from racial oppression. Instead, Black women's journeys often involve "the transformation of silence into language and action" (Lorde 1984, 40). Typically tied to children and/or community, fictional Black women characters, especially those created prior to the 1990s, search for self-definition within close geographical boundaries. Even though physical limitations confine the Black heroine's quest to a specific area, "forming complex personal relationships adds depth to her identity quest in lieu of geographical breadth" (Tate 1983, xxi). In their search for self-definition and the power of a free mind, Black heroines may remain "motionless on the outside . . . but inside?"

Given the physical limitations on Black women's mobility, the conceptualization of self that has been part of Black women's self-definitions is distinctive. Self is not defined as the increased autonomy gained by separating oneself from others. Instead, self is found in the context of family and community—as Paule Marshall describes it, "the ability to recognize one's continuity with the larger community" (Washington 1984, 159). By being accountable to others, African-American women develop more fully human, less objectified selves. Sonia Sanchez points to this version of self by stating, "We must move past always focusing on the 'personal self' because there's a larger self. There's a 'self' of black people" (Tate 1983, 134). Rather than defining self in opposition to others, the connectedness among individuals provides Black women deeper, more meaningful self-definitions.[6]

This journey toward self-definition has political significance. As Mary Helen Washington observes, Black women who struggle to "forge an identity larger than the one society would force upon them . . . are aware and conscious, and that very consciousness is potent" (1980, xv). Identity is not the goal but rather the point of departure in the process of self-definition. In this process Black women journey toward an understanding of how our personal lives have been fundamentally shaped by intersecting oppressions of race, gender, sexuality, and class. Peaches's statement, "I'm awfully bitter these days because my parents were slaves," illustrates this transformation.

This particular expression of the journey toward self-definition offers a powerful challenge to the externally defined, controlling images of African-American women. Replacing negative images with positive ones can be equally problematic if the function of stereotypes as controlling images remains unrecognized. John Gwaltney's (1980) interview with Nancy White, a 73-year-old Black woman, suggests that ordinary Black women can be acutely aware of the power of these controlling images. To Nancy White the difference between the controlling images applied to African-American and White women is one of degree, not of kind:

> My mother used to say that the black woman is the white man's mule and the white woman is his dog. Now, she said that to say this: we do the heavy work and get beat whether we do it well or not. But the white woman is closer to the master and he pats them on the head and lets them sleep in the house, but he ain't gon' treat neither one like he was dealing with a person. (p. 148)

Although both groups are objectified, albeit in different ways, the images function to dehumanize and control both groups. Seen in this light, it makes little sense in the long run for Black women to exchange one set of controlling images for another even if positive stereotypes bring better treatment in the short run.

The insistence on Black women's self-definitions reframes the entire dialogue from one of protesting the technical accuracy of an image—namely, refuting the Black matriarchy thesis—to one stressing the power dynamics underlying the very process of definition itself. By insisting on self-definition, Black women question not only what has been said about African-American women but the credibility and the intentions of those possessing the power to define. When Black women define ourselves, we clearly reject the assumption that those in positions granting them the authority to interpret our reality are entitled to do so. Regardless of the actual content of Black women's self-definitions, the act of insisting on Black female self-definition validates Black women's power as human subjects.

Self-Valuation and Respect

Self-definition speaks to the power dynamics involved in rejecting externally defined, controlling images of Black womanhood. In contrast, the theme of Black women's self-valuation addresses the actual content of these self-definitions. Many of the controlling images applied to African-American women are actually distorted renderings of those aspects of our behavior that threaten existing power arrangements (Gilkes 1983a; D. White 1985). For example, strong mothers are threatening because they contradict prevailing definitions of femininity. To ridicule strong, assertive Black mothers by labeling them matriarchs reflects an effort to control a dimension of Black women's behavior that threatens the status quo. African-American women who value those aspects of Black womanhood that are stereotyped, ridiculed, and maligned in scholarship and the popular media challenge some of the basic ideas inherent in an ideology of domination.

The emphasis that Black feminist thinkers have placed on respect illustrates the significance of self-valuation. In a society in which no one is obligated to respect African-American women, we have long admonished one another to have self-respect and to demand the respect of others. Black women's voices from a variety of sources reflect this demand for respect. Katie G. Cannon (1988) suggests that Black womanist ethics embraces three basic dimensions: "invisible dignity," "quiet grace," and "unstated courage," all qualities essential for self-valuation and self-respect. Black feminist critic Claudia Tate (1983) reports that the issue of self-esteem is so primary in the writing of Black women that it deserves special attention. Tate claims that what the writers seem to be saying is, "Women must assume responsibility for strengthening their self-esteem by learning to love and appreciate themselves" (p. xxiii). Her analysis is certainly borne out in Alice Walker's comments to an audience of women. Walker cautioned, "Please remember, especially in these times of group-think and the right-on chorus, that no person is your friend (or kin) who demands your silence, or denies your right to grow and be perceived as fully blossomed as you were intended. Or who belittles in any fashion the gifts you labor so to bring into the world" (Walker 1983, 36). The right to be Black *and* female *and* respected pervades everyday conversations among African-American women. In describing the importance self-respect has for her, elderly domestic worker Sara Brooks notes, "I may not have as much as you, I may not have the education you got, but still, if I conduct myself as a decent person, I'm just as good as anybody" (Simonsen 1986, 132).

Respect from others—especially from Black men—has been a recurring theme in Black women's writing. In describing the things a woman wants out of life, middle-class Marita Bonner lists "a career as fixed and as calmly brilliant as the North Star. The one real thing that money buys. Time. . . . And of course, a husband you can look up to without looking down on yourself" (Bonner 1987, 3). Black women's belief in respect also emerges in the works of a variety of Black women blues singers. One of the best-known popular statements of Black women's demand for self-respect and the respect of others is found in Aretha Franklin's (1967) rendition of the Otis Redding song "Respect." Aretha sings to her man:

> What you want? Baby I got it.
> What you need? You know I got it.
> All I'm asking for is a little respect when you come home.

Even though the lyrics can be sung by anyone, they take on special meaning when sung by Aretha in the way that she sings them. On one level the song functions as a metaphor for the condition of African-Americans in a racist society. But Aretha's being a Black *woman* enables the song to tap a deeper meaning. Within the blues tradition, the listening audience of African-American women assumes "we" Black women, even though Aretha as the blues singer sings "I." Sherley Anne Williams describes the power of Aretha's blues: "Aretha was right on time, but there was also something about the way Aretha characterized respect as something given with force and great effort and cost. And when she even went so far as to spell the word 'respect,' we just knew that this sister wasn't playing around about getting Respect and keeping it" (Williams 1979, 124).

June Jordan suggests that this emphasis on respect is tied to a distinctive Black feminist politic. For Jordan, a "morally defensible Black feminism" is verified in the ways U.S. Black women present ourselves to others, and in the ways Black women treat people different from ourselves. While self-respect is essential, respect for others is key. "As a Black feminist," claims Jordan, "I cannot be expected to respect what somebody else calls self-love if that concept of self-love requires my suicide to any degree" (1981, 144).

Self-Reliance and Independence

In her 1831 essay Black feminist thinker Maria Stewart not only encouraged Black women's self-definition and self-valuations but linked Black women's self-reliance with issues of survival:

> We have never had an opportunity of displaying our talents; therefore the world thinks we know nothing. . . . Possess the spirit of independence. The Americans do, and why should not you? Possess the spirit of men, bold and enterprising, fearless and undaunted: Sue for your rights and privileges. . . . You can but die if you make the attempt; and we shall certainly die if you do not. (Richardson 1987, 38)

Whether by choice or circumstance, African-American women have "possessed the spirit of independence," have been self-reliant, and have encouraged one another to value this vision of womanhood that clearly challenges prevailing notions of femininity (Steady 1987). These beliefs have found wide support among African-American women. For example, when asked what they admired about their mothers, the women in Gloria Joseph's (1981) study of Black mother/daughter relationships recounted their mothers' independence and ability to provide in the face of difficulties. Participants in Lena Wright Myers's (1980) study of Black women's coping skills respected women who were resourceful and self-reliant. Black women's autobiographies, such as Shirley Chisholm's *Unbought and Unbossed* (1970) and Maya Angelou's *I Know Why the Caged Bird Sings* (1969), typify Black women's self-valuation of self-reliance. As elderly domestic worker Nancy White cogently explains, "Most black women can be their own boss, so that's what they be" (Gwaltney 1980, 149).

The works of prominent Black women blues singers also counsel the importance of self-reliance and independence for African-American women. In her classic ballad "God Bless the Child That Got His Own," Billie Holiday sings:

> The strong gets more, while the weak ones fade,
> Empty pockets don't ever make the grade;
> Mama may have, Papa may have,
> But God bless the child that got his own!
> (*Billie Holiday Anthology* 1976, 12)

In this mournful song Billie Holiday offers an insightful analysis of the need for autonomy and self-reliance. "Money, you got lots of friends, crowdin' 'round the door," she proclaims. But "when you're gone and spendin' ends they don't come no more." In these passages Holiday admonishes Black women to become financially independent because having one's "own" allows women to choose their relationships.

The linking of economic self-sufficiency as one critical dimension of self-reliance with the demand for respect permeates Black feminist thought. For example, in "Respect" when Aretha sings, "Your kisses sweeter than honey, but guess what, so is my money," she demands respect on the basis of her economic self-reliance. Perhaps this connection between respect, self-reliance, and assertiveness is best summarized by Nancy White, who declares, "There is a very few black women that their husbands can pocketbook to death because we can do for ourselves and will do so in a minute!" (Gwaltney 1980, 149).

Self, Change, and Personal Empowerment

"The master's tools will never dismantle the master's house. They may allow us temporarily to beat him at his own game, but they will never enable us to bring about genuine change" (Lorde 1984, 112). In this passage Audre Lorde explores how independent self-definitions empower Black women to bring about social change. By struggling for self-defined womanist perspectives that reject the "master's" images, African-American women change ourselves. A critical mass of individuals with a changed consciousness can in turn foster Black women's collective empowerment. A changed consciousness encourages people to change the conditions of their lives.

Nikki Giovanni illuminates these connections among self, change, and personal empowerment. She admonishes that people are rarely powerless, no matter how stringent the restrictions on our lives: "We've got to live in the real world. If we don't like the world we're living in, change it. And if we can't change it, we change ourselves. We can do something" (in Tate 1983, 68). Giovanni recognizes that effective change occurs through action. The multiple strategies of resistance that Black women have employed, such as withdrawing from postemancipation agricultural work in order to return their labor to their families, ostensibly conforming to the deference rituals of domestic work, protesting male bias in African-American organizations, or creating the progressive art of Black women's blues all represent actions designed to bring about change. Here is the connected self and the individual empowerment that comes from change in the context of community.

But change can also occur in the private, personal space of an individual woman's consciousness. Equally fundamental, this type of change is also personally empowering. Any individual Black woman who is forced to remain "motionless on the outside," can develop the "inside" of a changed consciousness as a sphere of freedom. Becoming personally empowered through self-knowledge, even within conditions that severely limit one's ability to act, is essential. In Black women's literature

> this type of change . . . occurs because the heroine recognizes, and more importantly respects her inability to alter a situation. . . . This is not to imply that she is completely circumscribed by her limitations. On the contrary, she learns to exceed former boundaries but only as a direct result of knowing where they lie. In this regard, she teaches her readers a great deal about constructing a meaningful life in the midst of chaos and contingencies, armed with nothing more than her intellect and emotions. (Tate 1983, xxiv)

In this passage Claudia Tate demonstrates the significance of rearticulation, namely, redefining social realities by combining familiar ideas in new ways (Omi and Winant 1994, 163). But rearticulation does not mean reconciling womanist ethics with typically opposed Eurocentric masculinist ones. Instead, as Chezia Thompson-Cager contends, rearticulation "confronts them in the tradition of 'naming as power' by revealing them very carefully" (1989, 590). Naming daily life by applying language to everyday experience infuses it with the new meaning of a womanist consciousness. Naming becomes a way of transcending the limitations of intersecting oppressions.

Black women's literature contains many examples of how individual Black women become personally empowered by a changed consciousness. Barbara Christian maintains that the heroines of 1940s Black women's literature, such as Lutie Johnson in Ann Petry's *The Street* (1946) and Cleo Judson in Dorothy West's *The Living Is Easy* (1948), are defeated not only by social reality but by their "lack of self-knowledge." In contrast, the heroines from the 1950s to the present represent a significant shift toward self-knowledge as a sphere of freedom. Christian dates the shift from Gwendolyn Brooks's *Maud Martha* (1953) and claims, "Because Maud Martha constructs her own standards, she manages to transform that 'little life' into so much more despite the limits set on her. . . . [She] emerges neither crushed nor triumphant" (1985, 176).

According to many African-American women writers, no matter how oppressed an individual woman may be, the power to save the self lies within the self. Other Black women may assist a Black woman in this journey toward personal empowerment, but the ultimate responsibility for self-definitions and self-valuations lies within the individual woman herself. An individual woman may use multiple strategies in her quest for the constructed knowledge of an independent voice. Like Celie in Alice Walker's *The Color Purple,* some women write themselves free. Sexually, physically, and emotionally abused, Celie writes letters to God when no one else will listen. The act of acquiring a voice through writing, of breaking silence with language, eventually moves her to the action of talking with others. Other women talk themselves free. In *Their Eyes Were Watching God,* Janie tells her story to a good friend, a prime example of the rearticulation process essential for Black feminist thought (Hurston 1937). Ntozake Shange's *For Colored Girls* (1975) also captures this journey toward self-definition, self-valuation, and an empowered self. At the end of the play the women gather around one woman who speaks of the pain she experienced at seeing her children killed. They listen until she says, "I found God in myself and I loved her fiercely." These words, expressing her ability to define herself as worthwhile, draw them together. They touch one another as part of a Black women's community that heals the member in pain, but only after she has taken the first step of wanting to be healed, of wanting to make the journey toward finding the voice of empowerment.

Does Black Women's Consciousness Still Matter?

Despite the persistence of these four ideas about consciousness—the importance of self-definition, the significance of self-valuation and respect, the necessity of self-reliance and independence, and the centrality of a changed self to personal empowerment—these themes do not find a prominent place in much U.S. Black feminist thought within academia. Sadly, Black women intellectuals in the academy find themselves pressured to write for academic audiences, most of which remain resistant to including U.S. Black women as students, faculty, and administrators. However interested highly educated, middle-class, White male and female academic audiences may be in Black women's intellectual production, their concerns differ markedly from those of the majority of U.S. Black women.

Despite this context, many Black women intellectuals within academia still explore this theme of consciousness, but do so in new and often highly important ways. Take, for example, criminologist Beth Richie's (1996) book *Compelled to Crime: The Gender Entrapment of Battered Black Women.* Through interviews with women who were being detained in jail, Richie advances the innovative thesis that those Black women who had been self-reliant and independent as children and thus imagined themselves as strong Black women were *more* likely

to be battered than those who did not. Upon first glance, this is a curious combination—the more self-reliant simultaneously value themselves less. Richie's
explanation is revealing. The strong Black women saw themselves as personal failures if they sought help. In contrast, those women who did not carry the burden
of this seemingly positive image of Black womanhood found it easier to ask for
help. Richie's study points to the significance of external definitions of all types.
By attending to heterogeneity among Black women, her work creates space for
new self-valuations to appear that need not be attached to images of strong Black
women.

The increased scholarly attention to Black adolescent girls should reveal new
reactions to intersecting oppressions among a population that has come of age
under new social conditions. Within this tradition, *Sugar in the Raw* (1997),
Rebecca Carroll's 15 published interviews from more than 50 that she conducted
among U.S. Black girls provides a glimpse into the consciousness of contemporary Black girls. Despite elements of Black popular culture that bombard them
with images of sexualized women and the plethora of "hoochies" populating
music videos, many of the girls display an impressive maturity. Take, for example, 18-year-old Kristen's reflections on her struggles for self-valuation brought
on by her crush on a Black boy who seemed unaware that she existed:

> It was obvious and evident that most if not all of the black boys in my
> school wanted nothing to do with black girls, which was sort of trauma-
> tizing. You can't really come away from an experience like that without
> feeling like there is something wrong with you. In the final analysis, I
> ended up feeling that there was something wrong with him, but it was
> hell getting there. (Carroll 1997, 131–32)

The increased attention in Black feminist-influenced scholarship paid to Black
women's pain in abusive relationships of all sorts, and to the special concerns of
Black adolescent girls both seem designed to create new intellectual and political space for the "hellish" journeys that many Black women still encounter. At
least at this historic moment, the need to put up a united front seems less
important than exploring the various ways that individual Black women are personally empowered and disempowered, even within allegedly safe spaces.
Consciousness still matters, but it becomes one that acknowledges the complexities of crosscutting relations of race, gender, class, and sexuality.

Weaving throughout these historic and contemporary efforts at self-definition is the quest to move from silence to language to individual and group action.
In this quest, persistence is a fundamental requirement for this journey. Black
women's persistence is fostered by the strong belief that to be Black and female
is valuable and worthy of respect. In the song "A Change Is Gonna Come," Aretha
Franklin (1967) expresses this feeling of enduring despite the odds. She sings
that there were times that she thought that she would not last for long. She sings
of how it has been an "uphill journey all the way" to find the strength to carry

on. But despite the difficulties, Aretha "knows" that "a change is gonna come."

Whether individual struggles to develop a changed consciousness or the group persistence needed to transform social institutions, actions that bring about changes empower African-American women. By persisting in the journey toward self-definition, as individuals, we are changed. When linked to group action, our individual struggles gain new meaning. Because our actions as individuals change the world from one in which we merely exist to one over which we have some control, they enable us to see everyday life as being in process and therefore amenable to change. Perhaps that is why so many African-American women have managed to persist and "make a way out of no way." Perhaps they knew the power of self-definition.

6 THE SEXUAL POLITICS OF BLACK WOMANHOOD

Even I found it almost impossible to let her say what had happened to her as *she* perceived it . . . And why? Because once you strip away the lie that rape is pleasant, that children are not permanently damaged by sexual pain, that violence done to them is washed away by fear, silence, and time, you are left with the positive horror of the lives of thousands of children . . . who have been sexually abused and who have never been permitted their own language to tell about it.
—Alice Walker 1988, 57

In *The Color Purple* Alice Walker creates the character of Celie, a Black adolescent girl who is sexually abused by her step-father. Writing letters to God and forming supportive relationships with other Black women help Celie find her own voice, and her voice enables her to transcend the fear and silence of her childhood. By creating Celie and giving her the language to tell of her sexual abuse, Walker adds Celie's voice to muted yet growing discussions of the sexual politics of Black womanhood. But when it comes to other important issues concerning Black women's sexuality, U.S. Black women have found it almost impossible to say what has happened.

As Evelynn Hammonds points out, "Black women's sexuality is often described in metaphors of speechlessness, space, or vision; as a 'void' or empty space that is simultaneously ever-visible (exposed) and invisible, where black women's bodies are already colonized" (1997, 171). In response to this portrayal, Black women have been silent. One important factor that contributes to these long-standing silences both among African-American women and within Black feminist thought lies in Black women's lack of access to positions of power in U.S. social institutions. Those who control the schools, news media, churches, and government suppress Black women's collective voice. Dominant groups are the ones who construct Black women as "the embodiment of sex and the attendant invisibility of black women as the unvoiced, unseen—everything that is not white" (Hammonds 1997, 171).

Critical scholarship also has approached Black women's sexuality through its own set of assumptions. Within U.S. Black intellectual communities generally and Black studies scholarship in particular, Black women's sexuality is either ignored or included primarily in relation to African-American men's issues. In Black critical contexts where Black women struggle to get gender oppression recognized as important, theoretical analyses of Black sexuality remain sparse (Collins 1993b; 1998a, 155–83). Women's studies scholarship demonstrates a predilection for placing Black women in comparative frameworks. Interested in building coalitions among women across differences of race, theorists typically add Black women into preexisting feminist frameworks, often to illustrate how Black women "have it worse." Everyone has spoken for Black women, making it difficult for us to speak for ourselves.

But suppression does not fully explain African-American women's persistent silences about sexuality. U.S. Black women have been discouraged from analyzing and speaking out about a host of topics. Why does this one remain so difficult? In response, Paula Giddings identifies another important factor, namely, the "last taboo" of disclosing "not only a gender but a sexual discourse, unmediated by the question of racism" (Giddings 1992, 442). Within this taboo, to talk of White racist constructions of Black women's sexuality is acceptable. But developing analyses of sexuality that implicate Black men is not —it violates norms of racial solidarity that counsel Black women always to put our own needs second. Even within these racial boundaries, some topics are more acceptable than others— White men's rape of Black women during slavery can be discussed whereas Black men's rape of Black women today cannot. In her essay "Remembering Anita Hill and Clarence Thomas: What Really Happened When One Black Woman Spoke Out," Nellie McKay explains why Black women have remained silent concerning issues of sexuality:

> In all of their lives in America . . . black women have felt torn between the loyalties that bind them to race on one hand, and sex on the other. Choosing one or the other, of course, means taking sides against the self, yet they have almost always chosen race over the other: a sacrifice of their self-hood as women and of full humanity, in favor of the race (McKay 1992, 277–78).

"Taking sides against the self" requires that certain elements of Black women's sexuality can be examined, namely, those that do not challenge a race discourse that historically has privileged the experiences of African-American men. The cost is that other elements remain off-limits. Rape, incest, misogyny in Black cultural practices, and other painful topics that might implicate Black men remain taboo.

Yet another factor influencing Black women's silences concerns the potential benefits of remaining silent. For example, during the early-twentieth-century club movement, White women were much more successful in advancing analyses of intraracial gender relations and sexuality than were Black women. In a context of virulent racism, public disclosure could leave Black men and women vulnerable to increased sexual violence at the hands of White men. White women who forwarded a gendered analysis faced no such fears. In situations such as these, where regulating Black women's bodies benefited systems of race, class, and gender alike, protecting the safe spaces for Black women's self-definitions often required public silences about seemingly provocative topics. This secrecy was especially important within a U.S. culture that routinely accused Black women of being sexually immoral, promiscuous jezebels. In a climate where one's sexuality is on public display, holding fast to privacy and trying to shut the closet door becomes paramount. Hine refers to this strategy as a culture of dissemblance, one where Black women appeared to outgoing and public, while using this facade to hide a secret world within. As Hine suggests, "only with secrecy, thus achieving a self-imposed invisibility, could ordinary black women accrue the psychic space and harness the resources needed to hold their own in the often one-sided and mismatched resistance struggle" (Hine 1995, 382). In contexts of violence where internal self-censorship was seen as protection, silence made sense.

The convergence of all of these factors—the suppression of Black women's voice by dominant groups, Black women's struggles to work within the confines of norms of racial solidarity, and the seeming protections offered by a culture of dissemblance—influences yet another factor shaping patterns of silence. In general, U.S. Black women have been reluctant to acknowledge the valuable contributions of Black lesbian feminist theory in reconceptualizing Black women's sexuality. Since the early 1980s, Black lesbian theorists and activists have identified homophobia and the toll it takes on African-American women as an important topic for Black feminist thought. "The oppression that affects Black gay people, female and male, is pervasive, constant, and not abstract. Some of us die from it," argues Barbara Smith (1983, xlvii). Despite the increasing visibility of Black lesbians as parents (Lorde 1984, 72–80; Williams 1997), as academics (Davenport 1996), as activists (Gomez and Smith 1994), within lesbian history (Kennedy and Davis 1993, 113–31), and who have publicly come out (Moore 1997), African-Americans have tried to ignore homosexuality generally and have avoided serious analysis of homophobia within African-American communities.

In this context, Black lesbian theorizing about sexuality has been marginalized, albeit in different ways, both within Black intellectual communities and women's studies scholarship. As a result, Black feminist thought has not yet taken full advantage of this important source of Black feminist theory. As a group, heterosexual African-American women have been strangely silent on the issue of Black lesbianism. Barbara Smith suggests one compelling reason: "Heterosexual privilege is usually the only privilege that Black women have. None of us have racial or sexual privilege, almost none of us have class privilege, maintaining 'straightness' is our last resort" (1982b, 171). In the same way that White feminists identify with their victimization as women yet ignore the privilege that racism grants them, and that Black men decry racism yet see sexism as being less objectionable, heterosexual African-American women may perceive their own race and gender oppression yet victimize lesbians, gays, and bisexuals. Barbara Smith raises a critical point that can best be seen through the outsider-within standpoint available to Black lesbians—namely, that intersecting oppressions of sexuality, race, gender, and class produce neither absolute oppressors nor pure victims.

The widely publicized 1992 Supreme Court Justice confirmation hearings of Clarence Thomas shattered this multifaceted silence. During the hearings, Anita Hill, a lawyer and former employee of Thomas during his years of heading up the Equal Employment Opportunity Commission, accused Thomas of sexually harassing her. For days, the U.S. public remained riveted to their television sets, listening to the details of Hill's accusations concerning Thomas's alleged abuse of power, and Thomas's ingenious rebuttals. The hearings were remarkable in several ways—their highly public, televised format, the similar race/class backgrounds and politically conservative ideologies shared by Thomas and Hill, and the public disclosure of sexually explicit material. By putting questions of race, gender, class, and sexuality on public display, the hearings served as a powerful catalyst to break long-standing silences.

The reactions to the hearings highlighted significant differences among White women and Black men that left African-American women scrambling to find ways to avoid "taking sides against the self" (Crenshaw 1992). White American women routinely viewed the hearings as a landmark event that placed the largely hidden issue of sexual harassment on the national agenda. Seeing a shared sisterhood around issues of sexual harassment in the workplace, they regarded Anita Hill's race as of little concern. Instead, her Blackness operated as an unearned bonus—it buttressed claims that regardless of skin color and other markers of difference, all women needed to rally together to fight sexual harassment. In contrast, U.S. Blacks viewed the event through the lens of racial solidarity whereby Hill's testimony violated Black "family secrets" about abusive Black men. For many African-American men and women, the integrity of Hill's claim became erased by her transgression of airing "dirty laundry" in public. Even if Thomas was a sexual harasser, some argued, out of solidarity with Black men Hill should have kept her mouth shut. Cultural critic Lisa Jones describes a common reaction: "What happened to Hill sent a more forceful message than her face on the tube: Speaking out doesn't pay. A harassed woman is still a double victim, and a vocal, critical black woman is still a traitor to the race" (Jones 1994, 120).

African-American women found themselves caught in the middle, with issues of sexuality on public display. For many, Anita Hill's dilemma had a familiar ring. For one, images of a row of affluent White men sitting in judgment of both Anita Hill's and Clarence Thomas's sexual narratives smacked of pervasive silencing by dominant groups. Throwing in her lot with White women seemed foolish, because discourses of gender had long ignored the special circumstances of Black women. Because she had to live with the consequences of sexual harassment, the code of silence mandated by racial solidarity also had not served Anita Hill well. No place appeared to exist for Anita Hill's story, because long-standing silences on Black women's sexuality had failed to provide one.

Much has been written about the 1992 hearings, much of it by U.S. Black women (see, e.g., Morrison 1992; Smitherman 1995). Within this discourse lies a new readiness to explore how social constructions of Black women's sexualities must become more central to Black feminist thought. Following patterns established by Black feminist-influenced studies of work, family, controlling images, and other core themes of Black feminism, much of this work contextualizes analyses of Black women's sexualities within structural power relations. Treating race, class, gender, and sexuality less as personal attributes and more as systems of domination in which individuals construct unique identities, Black feminist analyses routinely identify multiple oppressions as important to the study of Black women's sexualities. For example, Black feminist thinkers have investigated how rape as a specific form of sexual violence is embedded in intersecting oppressions of race, gender, and class (Davis 1978, 1981, 1989; Crenshaw 1991). Reproductive rights issues such as access to information on sexuality and birth control, the struggles for abortion rights, and patterns of forced sterilization require attention to how nation-state policies affect U.S. Black women (Davis 1981; Roberts 1997; Collins 1999b). Black lesbians' work on homophobia investigates how heterosexism's impact on African-American women remains embedded in larger social structures (Lorde 1982, 1984; C. Clarke 1983; Shockley 1983; Barbara Smith 1983, 1998b). This contextualization in power relations generates a particular kind of social constructionist argument, one that views Black women's sexualities as being constructed within an historically specific matrix of domination characterized by intersecting oppressions. In understanding these Black feminist contextualizations, it may be more appropriate to speak of the *sexual politics of Black womanhood,* namely, how sexuality and power become linked in constructing Black women's sexualities.

Black Women, Intersecting Oppressions, and Sexual Politics

Due in large part to the politicized nature of definitions themselves, questions of sexuality and the sexual politics in which they participate raise special concerns. What is sexuality? What is power? Both of these questions generate widespread debate. Moreover, analyzing questions of sexuality and power within an interpretive framework that takes intersecting oppressions into account can appear to be a daunting task.

Whereas sexuality is part of intersecting oppressions, the ways in which it can be conceptualized differ. Sexuality can be analyzed as a freestanding system of oppression similar to oppressions of race, class, and gender. This approach views heterosexism as a system of power that victimizes Black women in particular ways. Within heterosexism as a system of oppression, African-American women find that their distinctive group placement within hierarchies of race, class, and gender shape the experiences of Black women as a collectivity as well as the sexual histories of individual Black women.

A second approach examines how sexualities become manipulated *within* class, race, nation, and gender as distinctive systems of oppression and draw upon heterosexist assumptions to do so. Regulating Black women's sexualities emerges as a distinctive feature of social class exploitation, of institutionalized racism, of U.S. nation-state policies, and of gender oppression. In essence, this approach suggests that both the sexual meanings assigned to Black women's bodies as well as the social practices justified by sexual ideologies reappears across seemingly separate systems of oppression.

Yet another approach views sexuality as a specific site of intersectionality where intersecting oppressions meet. Studying Black women's sexualities reveals how sexuality constitutes one important site where heterosexism, class, race, nation, and gender as systems of oppression converge. For Black women, ceding control over self-definitions of Black women's sexualities upholds multiple oppressions. This is because all systems of oppression rely on harnessing the power of the erotic. In contrast, when self-defined by Black women ourselves, Black women's sexualities can become an important place of resistance. Just as harnessing the power of the erotic is important for domination, reclaiming and self-defining that same eroticism may constitute one path toward Black women's empowerment.

Heterosexism as a System of Power

One important outcome of social movements advanced by lesbians, gays, bisexuals, and transgendered individuals has been the recognition of heterosexism as a system of power. In essence, the political and intellectual space carved out by these movements challenged the assumed normality of heterosexuality (Jackson 1996; Richardson 1996). These challenges fostered a shift from seeing sexuality as residing in individual biological makeup, to analyzing heterosexism as a system of power. Similar to oppressions of race or gender that mark bodies with social meanings, heterosexism marks bodies with sexual meanings. Within this logic, *heterosexism* can be defined as the belief in the inherent superiority of one form of sexual expression over another and thereby the right to dominate.

When it comes to thinking about Black women's sexualities, what is needed is a framework that not only analyzes heterosexism as a system of oppression, but also conceptualizes its links to race, class, and gender as comparable systems of oppression. Such a framework might emphasize two interdependent dimensions of heterosexism, namely, its symbolic and structural dimensions. The symbolic dimension refers to the sexual meanings used to represent and evaluate Black women's sexualities. For example, via the "hoochie" image, Black women's sexualities are seen as unnatural, dirty, sick, and sinful. In contrast, the structural dimension encompasses how social institutions are organized to reproduce heterosexism, primarily through laws and social customs. For example, refusing to prosecute Black women's rapists because the women are viewed as sexual "freaks" constitutes a social practice that reinforces and shapes these symbolic structures. While analytically distinct, in actuality, these two dimensions work together.

In the United States, assumptions of heterosexuality operate as a hegemonic or taken-for-granted ideology—to be heterosexual is considered normal, to be anything else is to become suspect. The system of sexual meanings associated with heterosexism becomes normalized to such a degree that they are often unquestioned. For example, the use of the term *sexuality* itself references *hetero-sexuality* as normal, natural, and normative.

The ideological dimension of heterosexism is embedded in binary thinking that deems heterosexuality as normal and other sexualities as deviant. Such thinking divides sexuality into two categories, namely, "normal" and "deviant" sexuality, and has great implications for understanding Black women's sexualities. Within assumptions of normalized heterosexuality, two important categories of "deviant" sexuality emerge. First, *African* or *Black* sexuality becomes constructed as an abnormal or pathologized heterosexuality. Long-standing ideas concerning the excessive sexual appetite of people of African descent conjured up in White imaginations generate gender-specific controlling images of the Black male rapist and the Black female jezebel, and they also rely on myths of Black hypersexuality. Within assumptions of normalized heterosexuality, regardless of individual behavior, being White marks the normal category of heterosexuality. In contrast, being Black signals the wild, out-of-control hyperheterosexuality of excessive sexual appetite.

Within assumptions of normalized heterosexuality, *homosexuality* emerges as a second important category of "deviant" sexuality. In this case, homosexuality constitutes an abnormal sexuality that becomes pathologized as heterosexuality's opposite. Whereas the problem of African or Black sexual deviancy is thought to lie in Black hyperheterosexuality, the problem of homosexuality lies not in an excess of heterosexual desire, but in the seeming absence of it. Women who lack interest in men as sexual partners become pathologized as "frigid" if they claim heterosexuality and stigmatized as lesbians if they do not.

Under Eurocentric ideologies, normalized heterosexuality thus becomes constructed in contrast to two allegedly deviant sexualities, namely, those attributed to people of African descent and those applied to lesbians and gays, among others. The binary fundamental to heterosexism, namely, that dividing alleged normal sexuality from its deviant other dovetails with binaries that underlie other systems of oppression. The important binaries introduced in Chapter 3's discussion of Black women's objectification—white/black, male/female, reason/emotion, and mind/body—now become joined by a series of sexual binaries: madonna/whore, real woman/dyke, real man/faggot, and stud/sissy. These sexual binaries in turn receive justification via medical theories (normal/sick), religious beliefs (saved/sinner), and state regulation (legal/illegal).

All of this influences the actual system of sexual regulation in the United States, where ideas about normalized heterosexuality permeate a range of social institutions. Despite the similarities that characterize constructions of African/Black sexuality and homosexuality, these sexualities differ in their characteristic modes of regulation. Black people experience a highly visible *sexualized racism,* one where the visibility of Black bodies themselves reinscribes the hypervisibility of Black men and women's alleged sexual deviancy. Because U.S. understandings of race rely on biological categories that, while renegotiated, cannot be changed—skin color is permanent—Black hypersexuality is conceptualized as being intergenerational and resistant to change.

The seeming intractability of the stigma of Blackness in turn shapes possible responses to this socially constructed yet highly visible deviancy.[1] Because biological traits are conceptualized as permanent, reformist strategies are unlikely to work. In this context, containment strategies of all sorts rise in importance. For example, racial segregation in housing, schools, employment, and public facilities not only benefit some groups of Whites economically— they also keep allegedly hypersexual Blacks separated from Whites. Maintaining physical distance need not be the sole strategy. Blacks have long worked in close proximity to Whites, but Blacks and Whites alike were discouraged from seeing one another as friends, neighbors, lovers, and, most important, legal sexual partners. In a context where Black bodies signal sexual deviancy, laws against intermarriage and other components of racial segregation ensured that the deviancy could be simultaneously exploited yet contained.

Because the nature of the threat is deemed different, forms of control for lesbians, gays, and other sexually stigmatized groups differ from those of sexualized racism. *Homophobia* flourishes in a context where the invisibility of the alleged deviancy is perceived to be the problem. Whereas the fears associated with racism lie in ideas projected upon highly visible, objectified Black bodies, the fears underlying homophobia emerge from the understanding that *anyone* could be gay or lesbian. Reminiscent of the proximate racism of anti-Semitism, one where, for example, Nazi scientists spent considerable time trying to find ways to identify Jewishness, homophobia constitutes a proximate fear that anyone could at any time reveal himself or herself as gay or lesbian.

The panoply of responses to the alleged deviancy of homosexuality also match the nature of the perceived threat. Containment also operates, but differently. For example, the medical profession has been assigned the reformist strategy of counseling gays and lesbians to better cope with normalized heterosexuality. Hate crimes punish individuals, but such crimes make an example of a visible homosexuality in order to drive the rest back into the closet. Recognizing that homosexuality most likely cannot be eliminated, the intended effect is to remove it from public and thereby legitimated space. Laws forbidding gay and lesbian marriages coupled with resistance to gays and lesbians having and raising children seem designed to stop the "spread" of homosexuality. Within this logic of the proximate threat, efforts to keep gays, lesbians, and other sexual minorities "in the closet" and "hidden" seem designed to contain the threat within.

Making heterosexism as a system of oppression more central to thinking through Black women's sexualities suggests two significant features. First, different groups remain differentially placed within heterosexism as an overarching structure of power. As I discuss later in this chapter and the next, African-American women's group history becomes crafted in the context of the specificity of the U.S. matrix of domination. Black women's particular group history within heterosexism intersects with that of other groups. For example, constructions of Black male and female sexuality are linked—they are similar yet different. Similarly, middle-class White women's sexuality could not be constructed as it is without corresponding controlling images applied to U.S. Black women. Moreover, this collective U.S. Black women's history does not eliminate further specification of group histories within the larger collectivity of African-American women, e.g., Black lesbians, adolescent Black women, older Black women, Black women who must rely on social welfare programs, and so on. Instead, it specifies the contours of sexual meanings that have been attributed to Black women. Considerable diversity exists among U.S. Black women as to how the symbolic and structural dimensions of heterosexism will be experienced and responded to.

A second significant feature concerns the space created for Black women's individual agency. Because African-American women express a range of sexualities, including celibate, heterosexual, lesbian, and bisexual, with varying forms of sexual expression changing throughout an individual's life course, Black women's self-definitions become essential. It is important to stress that both the symbolic and structural dimensions of heterosexism are always contested. Individual African-American women construct sexual meanings and practices within this overarching structure of heterosexual power relations. Thus, the individual agency of any one U.S. Black woman emerges in the context of larger institutional structures and particular group histories that affect many others. For individual Black women, the struggle lies in rejecting externally defined ideas and practices, and claiming the erotic as a mechanism for empowerment.

Sexuality within Distinctive Systems of Class, Race, Gender, and Nation

Analyzing how heterosexism as a system of oppression victimizes Black women constitutes one major approach to examining sexuality. A second approach explores how sexualities constructed in conjunction with an unquestioned heterosexism become manipulated within class, race, gender, and nation as distinctive systems of oppression. For example, the controlling image of jezebel reappears across several systems of oppression. For class oppression, the jezebel image fosters the sexual exploitation of Black women's bodies through prostitution. The jezebel image reinforces racial oppression by justifying sexual assaults against Black women. Gender ideology also draws upon the jezebel image—a devalued jezebel makes pure White womanhood possible. Overseeing these relationships are nation-state policies that because they implicitly see Black women as jezebels, deny Black women equal treatment under the law. Unmarried Black mothers have struggled to gain social welfare benefits long available to White women (Amott 1990), Black adolescents are more likely than White women to receive Norplant and other contraceptive methods that assume they cannot control their sexual libidos (Roberts 1997, 104–49), and as Anita Hill found out, Black women's claims of being sexually harassed and raped are often discounted. Thus, each system has a vested interest in regulating sexuality and relies on symbolic and structural practices to do so.

Examining how regulating Black women's sexuality functions to support each system constitutes one way of investigating these relationships. Controlling Black women's bodies has been especially important for capitalist class relations in the United States. When it comes to U.S. Black women's experiences, two features of capitalism remain noteworthy. First, Black women's bodies have been objectified and commodified under U.S. capitalist class relations. The objectification of Black women discussed in Chapter 4 and the subsequent commodification of those objectified bodies are closely linked—objectifying Black women's bodies turns them into commodities that can be sold or exchanged on the open market. Commodified bodies of all sorts become markers of status within class hierarchies that rely on race and gender. For example, healthy White babies are hot commodities in the U.S. adoption market, while healthy Black babies often languish in foster care. A second feature of U.S. capitalist class relations concerns how Black women's bodies have been exploited. Via mechanisms such as employment discrimination, maintaining images of Black women that construct them as mules or objects of pleasure, and encouraging or discouraging Black women's reproduction via state intervention, Black women's labor, sexuality, and fertility all have been exploited.

Not only are commodification and exploitation linked, patterns of exploiting Black women's sexuality have taken many forms. In some cases, the entire body itself became commodified. For example, slave auctions brokered the commodified bodies of both Black women and men—bodies could be bought and sold on the open market. In other cases, parts of the body could be commodified and sold for profitability. Barbara Omolade introduces this notion of specialized commodification where "every part of the black woman" was used by the White master. "To him she was a fragmented commodity whose feelings and choices were rarely considered: her head and her heart were separated from her back and her hands and divided from her womb and vagina" (Omolade 1994, 7). Black women's sexuality could be reduced to gaining control over an objectified vagina that could then be commodified and sold. The long-standing interest in Black women's genitalia within Western science seems apt here in that reducing Black women to commodified genitalia and vaginas effectively treats Black women as potential prostitutes. Similarly, current portrayals of Black women in popular culture—reducing Black women to butts—works to reinscribe these commodified body parts. Commodifying and exploiting Black women's wombs may be next. When a California judge rejected African-American Anna Johnson's claim that the White baby she had carried in her womb entitled her to some rights of motherhood, the message seemed clear—storage lockers and wombs constitute rental property (Hartouni 1997).

Regulating Black women's sexuality has certainly been significant within racist discourse and practice. In the United States, because race has been constructed as a biological category that is rooted in the body, controlling Black sexuality has long been important in preserving racial boundaries. U.S. notions of racial purity, such as the rule claiming that one drop of Black "blood " determines racial identity, required strict control over the sexuality and subsequent fertility of Black women, White women, and Black men. Although explicitly a means to prevent Blacks and Whites from associating in public accommodations, racial segregation in the South rested upon a deep-seated fear that "social mixing would lead to sexual mixing" (d'Emilio and Freedman 1988, 106). These mechanisms of control affected diverse population groups differently. Affluent White men typically enjoyed access to the bodies of all women and removed other men from sexual competition. The creation of a class of "angry White men" in the aftermath of social reforms of the 1960s and 1970s reflects, in part, the deterioration of White supremacist practices that gave White men such power (Ferber 1998). Wealthy White women were valued for a premarital virginity that when "lost" in the context of heterosexual marriage, ensured that all children would be biologically "White." Regardless of social class, Whites were encouraged to fear racial amalgamation, believing that it would debase them to the status of other races (d'Emilio and Freedman 1988, 86). In this context, Black men were constructed as sexually violent beasts, a view that not only justified their persecution by the state (Berry 1994), but was used to deny them access to White women's bodies. Black women's sexuality found no protections. Thus, notions of White supremacy relied on a notion of racial difference where "difference would be largely based on perceptions of sexual difference, and . . . the foundation of sexual difference lay in attitudes about black women" (Giddings 1995, 417).

Regulating Black women's sexuality also constituted a part of gender oppression. Dividing women into two categories—the asexual, moral women to be protected by marriage and their sexual, immoral counterparts—served as a gender template for constructing ideas about masculinity and femininity. The major archetypal symbols of women in Western thought construct women's sexuality via a tightly interwoven series of binaries. Collectively, these binaries create a sexual hierarchy with approved sexual expression installed at the top and forbidden sexualities relegated to the bottom. Assumptions of normal and deviant sexuality work to label women as good girls or bad girls, resulting in two categories of female sexuality. Virgins are the women who remain celibate before marriage, and who gain license to engage in heterosexual sexual practices after marriage. In contrast, whores are the unmarried women who are willingly "screwed." Whether a woman is an actual virgin or not is of lesser concern than whether she can socially construct herself as a "good" girl within this logic. Racializing this gender ideology by assigning all Black women, regardless of actual behavior, to the category of "bad" girls simplifies the management of this system.

It is important to remember that what appear to be natural and normal ideas and practices concerning sexuality are in fact carefully manufactured and promoted by schools, organized religions, the news media, and, most importantly, government policies. The local, state, and federal branches of the U.S. government may appear to be removed from issues of sexuality, but via their taxation, social welfare, and other policies, the U.S. nation-state in effect regulates which sexualities are deemed legitimate and which are not. For example, U.S. nation-state policies shape understandings of which citizens shall be afforded privacy. Affluent families living in suburban gated communities are provided with far more privacy and government protection than are poor families who live in urban public housing, where police intrude on family privacy more often than they protect it. In a similar fashion, Black women's sexuality has been constructed by law as public property—Black women have no rights of privacy that Whites must observe. As Barbara Omolade suggests, "White men used their power in the public sphere to construct a private sphere that would meet their needs and their desire for black women, which if publicly admitted would have undermined the false construct of race they needed to maintain public power. Therefore, the history of black women in America reflects the juncture where the private and public spheres and personal and political oppression meet" (Omolade 1994, 17).

Regulating Black Women's Bodies

Sexuality can be conceptualized as a freestanding system of oppression similar to oppressions of race, class, nation, and gender, as well as part of each of these distinctive systems of oppression. A third approach views sexuality as one important social location that joins these distinctive systems of oppression. This conceptualization views sexuality as conceptual glue that binds intersecting oppressions together. Stated differently, intersecting oppressions share certain core features. Manipulating and regulating the sexualities of diverse groups constitutes one such shared feature or site of intersectionality.

In this context, investigating efforts to regulate Black women's bodies can illuminate the larger question of how sexuality operates as a site of intersectionality. Within this larger endeavor, Black women's experiences with pornography, prostitution, and rape constitute specific cases of how more powerful groups have aimed to regulate Black women's bodies. These cases emphasize the connections between sexual ideologies developed to justify actual social practices and the use of force to maintain the social order. As such, these themes provide a useful lens for examining how intersecting oppressions rely on sexuality to mutually construct one another.

Pornography and Black Women's Bodies

> For centuries the black woman has served as the primary pornographic "outlet" for White men in Europe and America. We need only think of the black women used as breeders, raped for the pleasure and profit of their owners. We need only think of the license the "master" of the slave women enjoyed. But, most telling of all, we need only study the old slave societies of the South to note the sadistic treatment—at the hands of white "gentlemen"—of "beautiful young quadroons and octoroons" who became increasingly (and were deliberately bred to become) indistinguishable from white women, and were the more highly prized as slave mistresses because of this. (Walker 1981, 42)

Alice Walker's description of the rape of enslaved African women for the "pleasure and profit of their owners" encapsulates several elements of contemporary pornography. First, Black women were used as sex objects for the pleasure of White men. This objectification of African-American women parallels the portrayal of women in pornography as sex objects whose sexuality is available for men (McNall 1983). Exploiting Black women as breeders objectified them as less than human because only animals can be bred against their will. In contemporary pornography women are objectified through being portrayed as pieces of meat, as sexual animals awaiting conquest. Second, African-American women were raped, a form of sexual violence. Violence is typically an implicit or explicit theme in pornography. Moreover, the rape of Black women linked sexuality and violence, another characteristic feature of pornography (Eisenstein 1983). Third, rape and other forms of sexual violence act to strip victims of their will to resist and make them passive and submissive to the will of the rapist. Female passivity, the fact that women have things done to them, is a theme repeated over and over in contemporary pornography (McNall 1983). Fourth, the profitability of Black women's sexual exploitation for White "gentlemen" parallels pornography's financially lucrative benefits for pornographers (Dines 1998). Finally, the actual breeding of "quadroons and octoroons" not only reinforces the themes of Black women's passivity, objectification, and malleability to male control but reveals pornography's grounding in racism and sexism. The fates of both Black and White women were intertwined in this breeding process. The ideal African-American woman as a pornographic object was indistinguishable from a White woman and thus resembled the images of beauty, asexuality, and chastity forced on White women. But inside was a highly sexual whore, a "slave mistress" ready to cater to her owner's pleasure.[2]

Contemporary pornography consists of a series of icons or representations that focus the viewer's attention on the relationship between the portrayed individual and the general qualities ascribed to that class of individuals. Pornographic images are iconographic in that they represent realities in a manner determined by the historical position of the observers and by their relationship to their own time and to the history of the conventions which they employ (Gilman 1985). The treatment of Black women's bodies in nineteenth-century Europe and the United States may be the foundation upon which contemporary pornography as the representation of women's objectification, domination, and control is based. Icons about the sexuality of Black women's bodies emerged in these contexts. Moreover, as race and gender-specific representations, these icons have implications for the treatment of both African-American and White women in contemporary pornography.

I suggest that African-American women were not included in pornography as an afterthought but instead form a key pillar on which contemporary pornography itself rests. As Alice Walker points out, "The more ancient roots of modern pornography are to be found in the almost always pornographic treatment of black women who, from the moment they entered slavery . . . were subjected to rape as the 'logical' convergence of sex and violence. Conquest, in short" (1981, 42).

One key feature about the treatment of Black women in the nineteenth century was how their bodies were objects of display. In the antebellum American South, White men did not have to look at pornographic pictures of women because they could become voyeurs of Black women on the auction block. A chilling example of this objectification of the Black female body is provided by the exhibition, in early-nineteenth-century Europe, of Sarah Bartmann, the so-called Hottentot Venus. Her display formed one of the original icons for Black female sexuality. An African women, Sarah Bartmann was often exhibited at fashionable parties in Paris, generally wearing little clothing, to provide entertainment. To her audience she represented deviant sexuality. At the time European audiences thought that Africans had deviant sexual practices and searched for physiological differences, such as enlarged penises and malformed female genitalia, as indications of this deviant sexuality. Sarah Bartmann's exhibition stimulated these racist and sexist beliefs. After her death in 1815, she was dissected, with her genitalia and buttocks placed on display (Gilman 1985).

Sander Gilman explains the impact that Sarah Bartmann's exhibition had on Victorian audiences:

> It is important to note that Sarah Bartmann was exhibited not to show her genitalia—but rather to present another anomaly which the European audience . . . found riveting. This was the steatopygia, or protruding buttocks, the other physical characteristic of the Hottentot female which captured the eye of early European travelers. . . . The figure of Sarah Bartmann was reduced to her sexual parts. The audience which had paid to see her buttocks and had fantasized about the uniqueness of her genitalia when she was alive could, after her death and dissection, examine both. (1985, 213)

In this passage Gilman unwittingly describes how Bartmann was used as a pornographic object similar to how women are represented in contemporary pornography. She was reduced to her sexual parts, and these parts came to represent a dominant icon applied to Black women throughout the nineteenth century. Moreover, the fact that Sarah Bartmann was both African and a woman underscores the importance of gender in maintaining notions of racial purity. In this case Bartmann symbolized Blacks as a "race." Her display also served to buttress notions of European nations as "civilized" as opposed to the backward colonies that were incapable of development (Fausto-Sterling 1995). In the creation of the icon applied to Black women, notions of gender, race, nation, and sexuality were linked in overarching structures of political domination and economic exploitation.

The pornographic treatment of the bodies of enslaved African women and of women like Sarah Bartmann has since developed into a full-scale industry. Within pornography, all women are objectified differently by racial/ethnic category. Contemporary portrayals of Black women in pornography represent the continuation of the historical treatment of their actual bodies (Forna 1992). African-American women are usually depicted in a situation of bondage and slavery, typically in a submissive posture, and often with two White men. A study of fifty-four videos found that Black women more often were portrayed as being subjected to aggressive acts and as submitting after initial resistance to a sexual encounter. Compared with White women, Black women were shown performing fellatio on their knees more often (Cowan and Campbell 1994). Russell (1993, 45–49) reports that Black women are equated with snakes, as engaging in sex with animals, as incestuous, and as lovers of rape, especially by White men. As Bell observes, these settings remind us of "the trappings of slavery: chains, whips, neck braces, wrist clasps" (1987, 59). White women and women of color have different pornographic images applied to them. The image of Black women in pornography is almost consistently one featuring them breaking from chains. The image of Asian women in pornography is almost consistently one of being tortured (Bell 1987, 161).

The pornographic treatment of Black women's bodies challenges prevailing assumptions that since images of White women prevail in pornography, racism has been grafted onto pornography. African-American women's experiences suggest that Black women were not added into a preexisting pornography, but rather that pornography itself must be reconceptualized as a shift from the objectification of Black women's bodies in order to dominate and exploit them, to one of media representations of all women that perform the same purpose. Notions of biological determinism claiming that people of African descent and women possess immutable biological characteristics marking their inferiority to elite White men lie at the heart of both racism and sexism (Halpin 1989; Fausto-Sterling 1992). In pornography these racist and sexist beliefs are sexualized. Moreover, African-American women's pornographic treatment has not been timeless and universal but emerged in conjunction with European colonization and American slavery (Torgovnick 1990; McClintock 1995). The profitability of pornography thus serves capitalist class relations.

This linking of views of the body, social constructions of race and gender, pornography's profitability, and conceptualizations of sexuality that inform Black women's treatment as pornographic objects promises to have significant implications for how we assess contemporary pornography. Pornography's significance as a site of intersecting oppressions promises new insights toward understanding social injustice.

Investigating racial patterns in pornography offers one route for such an analysis. Black women have often claimed that images of White women's sexuality were intertwined with the controlling image of the sexually derogated Black woman: "In the United States, the fear and fascination of female sexuality was projected onto black women; the passionless lady arose in symbiosis with the primitively sexual slave" (Hall 1983, 333). Comparable linkages exist in pornography (Gardner 1980). Alice Walker provides a fictional account of a Black man's growing awareness of the different ways that African-American and White women are objectified in pornography: "What he has refused to see—because to see it would reveal yet another area in which he is unable to protect or defend black women—is that where white women are depicted in pornography as 'objects,' black women are depicted as animals. Where white women are depicted as human bodies if not beings, black women are depicted as shit" (Walker 1981, 52).

Walker's distinction between "objects" and "animals" is crucial in untangling gender, race, and class dynamics in pornography. Within the mind/body, culture/nature, male/female binaries in Western social thought, objects occupy an uncertain interim position. As objects, White women become creations of culture—in this case, the mind of White men—using the materials of nature—in this case, uncontrolled female sexuality. In contrast, as animals, Black women receive no such redeeming dose of culture and remain open to the type of exploitation visited on nature overall. Black women's portrayal in pornography as caged, chained, and naked creatures who possess "panther-like," savage, and exotic sexual qualities (Forna 1992) reinforces this theme of Black women's "wildness" as symbolic of an unbridled female sexuality. In a context where Whiteness as symbolic of both civilization and culture is used to separate objects from animals, racial difference constructed on the bedrock of sexuality becomes the distinguishing feature in determining the type of objectification women will encounter.

While the sexual and racial dimensions of being treated like an animal are important, the economic foundation underlying this treatment is critical. Under capitalist class relations, animals can be worked, sold, killed, and consumed, all for profit. As "mules," African-American women become susceptible to such treatment. The political economy of pornography meshes with this overarching value system that objectifies, commodifies, and markets products, ideas, images, and actual people. Pornography is pivotal in mediating contradictions in changing societies (McNall 1983). It is no accident that racist biology, religious justifications for slavery and women's subordination, and other explanations for nineteenth-century racism and sexism arose during a period of profound political and economic change. Symbolic means of domination become particularly important in mediating contradictions in changing political economies. The exhibition of Sarah Bartmann and Black women on the auction block were not benign intellectual exercises—these practices defended real material and political interests. Current transformations in international capitalism require similar ideological justifications. Contemporary pornography meshes with late-twentieth-century global transformations of postcolonialism in a fashion reminiscent of global changes associated with nineteenth-century colonialism (Dines 1998).

Publicly exhibiting Black women may have been central to objectifying Black women as animals and to creating the icon of Black women as animals. Yi-Fu Tuan (1984) offers an innovative argument about similarities in efforts to control nature—especially plant life—the domestication of animals, and the domination of certain groups of humans. Tuan suggests that displaying humans alongside animals implies that such humans are more like monkeys and bears than they are like "normal" people. This same juxtaposition leads spectators to view the captive animals in a special way. Animals acquire definitions of being like humans, only more openly carnal and sexual, an aspect of animals that forms a major source of attraction for visitors to modern zoos. In discussing the popularity of monkeys in zoos, Tuan notes: "Some visitors are especially attracted by the easy sexual behavior of the monkeys. Voyeurism is forbidden except when applied to subhumans" (1984, 82). Tuan's analysis suggests that the public display of Sarah Bartmann and of the countless enslaved African women on the auction blocks of the antebellum American South—especially in proximity to animals—fostered their image as animalistic.

This linking of Black women and animals is evident in nineteenth-century scientific literature. The equation of women, Blacks, and animals is revealed in the following description of an African woman published in an 1878 anthropology text:

> She had a way of pouting her lips exactly like what we have observed in the orangutan. Her movements had something abrupt and fantastical about them, reminding one of those of the ape. Her ear was like that of many apes. . . . These are animal characters. I have never seen a human head more like an ape than that of this woman. (Halpin 1989, 287)

In a climate such as this, it is not surprising that one prominent European physician even stated that Black women's "animal-like sexual appetite went so far as to lead black women to copulate with apes" (Gilman 1985, 212). Late-twentieth-century science has had difficulty shedding itself of these deep-seated beliefs. The association of Africa, animals, and seemingly deviant sexualities within AIDS discourse speaks to the persistence of these ideas (Hammonds 1986; Watney 1990). As Paula Giddings suggests, the fact that "respectable journals would make connections between green monkeys and African women, for example, or trace the origin of AIDS to African prostitutes—the polluted sexual organs of black women—reveals our continued vulnerability to racist ideology" (Giddings 1992, 458).

The treatment of all women in contemporary pornography has strong ties to the portrayal of Black women as animals. In pornography women become non-people and are often represented as the sum of their fragmented body parts. Scott McNall observes:

> This fragmentation of women relates to the predominance of rear-entry position photographs. . . . All of these kinds of photographs reduce the woman to her reproductive system, and, furthermore, make her open, willing, and available—not in control. . . . The other thing rear-entry position photographs tell us about women is that they are animals. They are animals because they are the same as dogs—bitches in heat who can't control themselves. (McNall 1983, 197–98)

This linking of animals and women within pornography becomes feasible when grounded in the earlier debasement of Black women as animals.

Developing a comprehensive analysis of Black women's placement in pornography and of pornography itself as a site of intersecting oppressions offers possibilities for change. Those Black feminist intellectuals investigating sexual politics imply that the situation is much more complicated than that advanced within Western feminism in which "men oppress women" because they are men. Such approaches implicitly assume biologically deterministic views of gender and sexuality and offer few possibilities for change. In contrast, the willingness of Black feminist analyses of sexual politics to embrace intersectional paradigms provides space for human agency. Women are not hard-wired as victims of pornography, nor are men destined uncritically to consume it. In the short story "Coming Apart," Alice Walker describes one Black man's growing realization that his enjoyment of pornography, whether of White women as "objects" or Black women as "animals," degraded him:

> He begins to feel sick. For he realizes that he has bought some of the advertisements about women, black and white. And further, inevitably, he has bought the advertisements about himself. In pornography the black man is portrayed as being capable of fucking anything . . . even a piece of shit. He is defined solely by the size, readiness and unselectivity of his cock. (Walker 1981, 52)

Walker conceptualizes pornography as a mechanism within intersecting oppressions that entraps everyone. But by exploring an African-American *man's* struggle to understand his participation in pornography, Walker suggests that a changed consciousness is essential to social change. If Black men can understand how pornography affects them, then other groups enmeshed in the same system are equally capable of similar shifts in consciousness and action.

Because pornography as a way of thinking is so deeply ingrained in Western culture, it is difficult to achieve this changed consciousness and action. Reacting to the same catalyst of the Anita Hill hearings, Black feminist theorist Patricia Williams was intrigued by Clarence Thomas's claims that he admired Malcolm X. A friend's comment that Malcolm X wasn't just a role model but had become the "ultimate pornographic object" sent Williams to the library in search of work on pornography. Her subsequent description of pornography shows it to be a way of thinking that, she argues, has no necessary connection to sex. Williams came to see pornography as "a habit of thinking" that replays relationships of dominance and submission. For Williams, pornography:

> permits the imagination of the voyeur to indulge in auto-sensation that obliterates the subjectivity of the observed. A habit of thinking that allows that self-generated sensation to substitute for interaction with a whole other human being, to substitute for listening or conversing or caring . . . the object is pacified, a malleable "thing" upon which to project. (Williams 1995, 123)

Sadly, this "way of thinking" persists even among self-proclaimed progressive thinkers. I have seen three public uses of Sarah Bartmann's image. The first was by a White feminist scholar who refused to show the images without adequately preparing her audience. She knew that graphic images of Black women's objectification and debasement, whether on the auction block as the object of a voyeuristic nineteenth-century science, or within contemporary pornography, would be upsetting to some audience members. Initially, I found her concern admirable yet overly cautious. Then I saw the reactions of young Black women who saw images of Sarah Bartmann for the first time. Even though the speaker tried to prepare them, these young women cried. They saw and felt the connections among the women exhibited on the auction block, the voyeuristic treatment of Sarah Bartmann, the depiction of Black women in pornography, and their own daily experiences of being under sexual surveillance. I quickly changed my opinion of my colleague's concern—she was right.

The remaining two uses of Sarah Bartmann's image illustrate the contradictions and ironies in contemporary scholarship. A prominent White male scholar who has done much to challenge scientific racism apparently felt few qualms at using a slide of Sarah Bartmann as part of his PowerPoint presentation. Leaving her image on screen for several minutes with a panel of speakers that included Black women seated on stage in front of the slide, this scholar told jokes about the seeming sexual interests of the White voyeurs of the nineteenth century. He seemed incapable of grasping how his own twentieth-century use of this image, as well as his invitation that audience members become voyeurs along with him, reinscribed Sarah Bartmann as an "object. . . . a malleable 'thing' " upon which he projected his own agenda. When I questioned him about his pornographic use of the slide, his response was telling. Just as pornographers hide behind the protections of "free speech," so did this prominent scholar. He defended his "right" to use public domain material any way he saw fit, even if it routinely offended Black women and contributed to their continued objectification.

The final use illustrates yet another limitation of failing to see pornography via the lens of intersecting oppressions. In this case, I attended a conference on race and ethnicity where a prominent Black male scholar presented his analysis of the significance of the changing size of Black bodies portrayed in racist iconography. Once again, the slide show began, and there she was again. Sarah Bartmann's body appeared on the screen, not to provide a humorous interlude, but as the body chosen to represent the nineteenth-century "raced" body. Again, the audience was allowed a lengthy, voyeuristic peek at Bartmann, all the while listening to how this particular "raced" body illustrated my colleague's latest insight about body size. Despite the fact that we stared at a half-naked Black woman, he made no mention of gender, let alone how this particular "raced" and "gendered" body has been central to the pornographic treatment of Black women. As much as I hated to violate the unspoken norm of racial solidarity, during the discussion period, I questioned these omissions. After a brief and disapproving silence, he dismissed my question. In a derisive tone suggesting that I had somehow missed the profundity of his argument, this arrogant individual replied, "I'm concerned about race here, not gender!"

Sadly, both my White male colleague and his Black male counterpart had apparently developed "habits of thinking" that allowed them to use their imaginations "to indulge in auto-sensation that obliterates the subjectivity of the observed." Certainly Black women's subjectivity, both Sarah Bartmann's and my own, were obliterated by how these two men used her image. Instead, I was invited to objectify myself in order to develop the objectivity that would allow me to participate in her objectification. I could become either a laughing voyeur of Bartmann's debasement or a voyeur of her "raced" yet ungendered body, but a voyeur all the same. Apparently, among some thinkers, some habits of thinking are extremely hard to break.

Prostitution and the Exploitation of Black Women's Bodies

In *To Be Young, Gifted and Black,* Lorraine Hansberry creates three characters: a young domestic worker; a chic, professional, middle-aged woman; and a mother in her thirties. Each speaks a variant of the following:

> In these streets out there, any little white boy from Long Island or Westchester sees me and leans out of his car and yells—"Hey there, *hot chocolate!* Say there, Jezebel! Hey you—'Hundred Dollar Misunderstanding'! YOU! Bet you know where there's a good time tonight . . ." Follow me sometimes and see if I lie. I can be coming from eight hours on an assembly line or fourteen hours in Mrs. Halsey's kitchen. I can be all filled up that day with three hundred years of rage so that my eyes are flashing and my flesh is trembling—and the white boys in the streets, they look at me and think of sex. They look at me and that's all they think. . . . Baby, you could be Jesus in drag—but if you're brown they're sure you're selling! (Hansberry 1969, 98)

Like the characters in Hansberry's fiction, all Black women are affected by the widespread controlling image that African-American women are sexually promiscuous. The pervasiveness of this image is vividly recounted in Black activist lawyer Pauli Murray's description of an incident she experienced while defending two women from Spanish Harlem who had been arrested for prostitution: "The first witness, a white man from New Jersey, testified on the details of the sexual transaction and his payment of money. When asked to identify the woman with whom he had engaged in sexual intercourse, he unhesitatingly pointed directly at me, seated beside my two clients at the defense table!" (Murray 1987, 274). Murray's clients were nonetheless convicted.

Not just White men, but Black men have been involved in finding ways to profit from Black women's bodies. During an interview with Brother Marquis from the group 2 Live Crew, Black cultural critic Lisa Jones realizes that "hoochie mama" and other songs by this group actually constitute "soft porn." Jones's interview with Brother Marquis reveals the important links among pornography, the marketing of Black women's images, and the exploitation of Black women's bodies. In defending the misogynist lyrics of 2 Live Crew's music, Brother Marquis states:

> I'm not gonna try to disrespect you and call you all those names like I do on those records. I would never do that to a young lady, especially a sister. I'm degrading you to try to get me some money. . . . And besides, you let

me do that. You got pimps out here who are making you sell your body. Just let me talk about you for a little while, you know what I'm saying? And make me a little money. (Jones 1994, 243)

Brother's Marquis's explanation displays familiar rationalizations. He divided women into two categories of good girls and "hoochies." In his mind, if Black women are devalued within prostitution already, what harm can it do to *talk* about debasing Black women, especially if he can profit from such talk?

Within Brother Marquis's logic, images of Black women as jezebels and "hoochies" do little harm. Yet this controlling image has been vital in justifying the negative treatment that Black women encounter with intersecting oppressions. Exploring how the image of the African-American woman as prostitute has been used by selected systems of oppression illustrates how sexuality links the three systems. But Black women's treatment also demonstrates how prostitution operates as a site of intersectionality.

Yi-Fu Tuan (1984) suggests that power as domination involves reducing humans to animate nature in order to exploit them economically or to treat them condescendingly as pets. Domination may be either cruel and exploitative with no affection or may be exploitative yet coexist with affection. The former produces the victim—in this case, the Black woman as "mule" whose labor has been exploited. In contrast, the combination of dominance and affection produces the pet, the individual who is subordinate and whose survival depends on the whims of the more powerful. The "beautiful young quadroons and octoroons" described by Alice Walker were bred to be pets—enslaved Black mistresses whose existence required that they retain the affection of their owners. The treatment afforded these women illustrates a process that affects all African-American women: their portrayal as actual or potential victims and pets of elite White males.[3]

African-American women simultaneously embody the coexistence of the victim and the pet, with survival often linked to the ability to be appropriately subordinate. Black women's experiences as unpaid and paid workers demonstrate the harsh lives victims are forced to lead. While the life of the victim is difficult, pets experience a distinctive form of exploitation. Zora Neale Hurston's 1943 essay, "The 'Pet' Negro System," speaks contemptuously of this ostensibly benign situation that combines domination with affection. Writing in a Black oratorical style, Hurston notes, "Brother and Sisters, I take my text this morning from the Book of Dixie. . . . Now it says here, 'And every white man shall be allowed to pet himself a Negro. Yea, he shall take a black man unto himself to pet and cherish, and this same Negro shall be perfect in his sight' " (Walker 1979a, 156). Pets are treated as exceptions and live with the constant threat that they will no longer be "perfect in his sight," that their owners will tire of them and relegate them to the unenviable role of victim.

Prostitution represents the fusion of exploitation for an economic purpose—namely, the commodification of Black women's sexuality—with the demeaning treatment afforded pets. Sex becomes commodified not merely in the sense that it can be purchased—the dimension of economic exploitation—but also in the sense that one is dealing with a totally alienated being who is separated from and who seemingly does not control her body: the dimension of power as domination (McNall 1983). Commodified sex can then be appropriated by the powerful. When the "white boys from Long Island" look at Black women and *all* they think about is sex, they believe that they can appropriate Black women's bodies. When they yell, "Bet you know where there's a good time tonight," they expect commodified sex with Black women as "animals" to be better than sex with White women as "objects." Both pornography and prostitution commodify sexuality and imply to the "white boys" that all African-American women can be bought.

Prostitution under European and American capitalism thus exists within a complex web of political and economic relationships. Gilman's (1985) analysis of the exhibition of Sarah Bartmann as the "Hottentot Venus" suggests another intriguing connection between race, gender, and sexuality in nineteenth-century Europe—the linking of the icon of the Black woman with the icon of the White prostitute. While the Hottentot woman stood for the essence of Africans as a race, the White prostitute symbolized the sexualized woman. The prostitute represented the embodiment of sexuality and all that European society associated with it: disease as well as passion. As Gilman points out, "It is this uncleanliness, this disease, which forms the final link between two images of women, the black and the prostitute. Just as the genitalia of the Hottentot were perceived as parallel to the diseased genitalia of the prostitute, so . . . : the power of the idea of corruption links both images" (1985, 237). These connections between the icons of Black women and White prostitutes demonstrate the interdependence of race, gender, and sexuality in shaping European understandings of social class.

In the American antebellum South both of these images were fused in the forced prostitution of enslaved African women. The prostitution of Black women allowed White women to be the opposite; Black "whores" make White "virgins" possible. This race/gender nexus fostered a situation whereby White men could then differentiate between the sexualized woman-as-body who is dominated and "screwed" and the asexual woman-as-pure-spirit who is idealized and brought home to mother (Hoch 1979, 70). The sexually denigrated woman, whether she was made a victim through her rape or a pet through her seduction, could be used as the yardstick against which the cult of true womanhood was measured. Moreover, this entire situation was profitable.

The image of the lesbian can also be linked with that of the prostitute and with images of Black women as the embodiment of the Black "race." Christian notes that Black women writers broadened the physical image of lesbians: "The stereotypical body type of a black lesbian was that she looked mannish; . . . she was not so much a woman as much as she was a defective man, a description that has sometimes been applied to any Negroid-looking or uppity-acting black woman" (1985, 191). Note Christian's analysis of the links among gender, race, and sexuality. Lesbianism, an allegedly deviant sexual practice, becomes linked to biological markers of race and looking "mannish." These links also reinforce constructions of Black women's sexualities as deviant—the co-joining of Black heterosexual women's sexual deviancy as lying in their excess sexual appetite with the perceived deviancy of Black lesbians as lying in their rejection of what makes women feminine, namely, heterosexual contact with men.

Rape and Sexual Violence

Force was important in creating African-American women's centrality to American images of the sexualized woman and in shaping their experiences with both pornography and prostitution. Black women did not willingly submit to their exhibition on Southern auction blocks—they were forced to do so. Enslaved African women could not choose whether to work—they were beaten and often killed if they refused. Black domestics who resisted the sexual advances of their employers often found themselves looking for work where none was to be found. Both the reality and the threat of violence have acted as a form of social control for African-American women (Collins 1998d).

Rape has been one fundamental tool of sexual violence directed against African-American women. Challenging the pervasiveness of Black women's rape and sexual extortion by White men has long formed a prominent theme in Black women's writings. Autobiographies such as Maya Angelou's *I Know Why the Caged Bird Sings* (1970) and Harriet Jacobs's "The Perils of a Slave Woman's Life" (1860/1987) from *Incidents in the Life of a Slave Girl* record examples of actual and threatened sexual assault. The effects of rape on African-American women is a prominent theme in Black women's fiction. Gayl Jones's *Corregidora* (1975) and Rosa Guy's *A Measure of Time* (1983) both explore interracial rape of Black women. Toni Morrison's *The Bluest Eye* (1970), Alice Walker's *The Color Purple* (1982), and Gloria Naylor's *The Women of Brewster Place* (1980) all examine rape within African-American families and communities. Elizabeth Clark-Lewis's (1985) study of domestic workers found that mothers, aunts, and community othermothers warned young Black women about the threat of rape. One respondent in Clark-Lewis's study, an 87-year-old North Carolina Black domestic worker, remembers, "nobody was sent out before you was told to be careful of the white man or his sons" (Clark-Lewis 1985, 15).

Rape and other acts of overt violence that Black women have experienced, such as physical assault during slavery, domestic abuse, incest, and sexual extortion, accompany Black women's subordination in intersecting oppressions. These violent acts are the visible dimensions of a more generalized, routinized system of oppression. Violence against Black women tends to be legitimated and therefore condoned while the same acts visited on other groups may remain nonlegitimated and non-excusable. Historically, this violence has garnered the backing and control of the state (James 1996). Specific acts of sexual violence visited on African-American women reflect a broader process by which violence is socially constructed in a race- and gender-specific manner. Thus Black women, Black men, and White women experience distinctive forms of sexual violence. As Angela Davis points out, "It would be a mistake to regard the institutionalized pattern of rape during slavery as an expression of white men's sexual urges. . . . Rape was a weapon of domination, a weapon of repression, whose covert goal was to extinguish slave women's will to resist, and in the process, to demoralize their men" (1981, 23).

Angela Davis's work (1978, 1981, 1989) illustrates this effort to conceptualize sexual violence against African-American women as a site of intersecting oppressions. Davis suggests that depicting African-American men as sexually charged beasts who desired White women created the myth of the Black rapist. Lynching emerged as the specific form of sexual violence visited on Black men, with the myth of the Black rapist as its ideological justification. The significance of this myth is that it "has been methodically conjured up when recurrent waves of violence and terror against the black community required a convincing explanation" (Davis 1978, 25). Black women experienced a parallel form of race- and gender-specific sexual violence. Treating African-American women as pornographic objects and portraying them as sexualized animals, as prostitutes, created the controlling image of jezebel. Rape became the specific act of sexual violence forced on Black women, with the myth of the Black prostitute as its ideological justification.

Lynching and rape, two race/gender-specific forms of sexual violence, merged with their ideological justifications of the rapist and prostitute in order to provide an effective system of social control over African-Americans. Davis asserts that the controlling image of Black men as rapists has always "strengthened its inseparable companion: the image of the black woman as chronically promiscuous. And with good reason, for once the notion is accepted that black men harbor irresistible, animal-like sexual urges, the entire race is invested with bestiality" (1978, 27). A race of "animals" can be treated as such—as victims or pets. "The mythical rapist implies the mythical whore—and a race of rapists and whores deserves punishment and nothing more" (Davis 1978, 28).

Black women continue to deal with this legacy of the sexual violence visited on African-Americans generally and with our history as collective rape victims. One effect lies in the treatment of rape victims. Such women are twice victimized, first by the actual rape, in this case the collective rape under slavery. But they are victimized again by family members, community residents, and social institutions such as criminal justice systems which somehow believe that rape victims are responsible for their own victimization. Even though current statistics indicate that Black women are more likely to be victimized than White women, Black women are less likely to report their rapes, less likely to have their cases come to trial, less likely to have their trials result in convictions, and, most disturbing, less likely to seek counseling and other support services.

Another effect of this legacy of sexual violence concerns the significance of Black women's continued silences concerning rape. But Black women's silence about rape obscures an important issue: Most Black women are raped by Black men. While the historical legacy of the triad of pornography, prostitution, and the institutionalized rape of Black women may have created the larger social context within which all African-Americans reside, the unfortunate current reality is that many Black men have internalized the controlling images applied to Black women. Like Brother Marquis, they feel that if they as individuals do not rape women, they contribute little to the overall cultural climate that condones sexual violence. These beliefs allow them to ignore Black women's rape by other Black men, their own culpability in fostering Black women's objectification as pornographic objects, and, in some cases, their own behavior as rapists. For example, Black women and men often disagree as to whether Nola Darling, the sexually liberated heroine in Spike Lee's acclaimed film *She's Gotta Have It,* was raped. Men disbelieve Nola's protestations and see her protest as serving to heighten the sexual pleasure of her male partner. In contrast, many women see her reaction as typical for those of a rape victim. Recognizing that it is useless to protest, Nola Darling submits. Was Nola Darling raped? Do the sexual politcs of Black womanhood that construct jezebels and "hoochies" have any grounding in reality? The answers to both questions may lie in who has the power to define.

7 BLACK WOMEN'S LOVE RELATIONSHIPS

In Toni Morrison's *Beloved* (1987), Sethe tells her friend Paul D how she felt after escaping from slavery:

> It was a kind of selfishness I never knew nothing about before. It felt good. Good and right. I was big, Paul D, and deep and wide and when I stretched out my arms all my children could get in between. I was that wide. Look like I loved em more after I got here. Or maybe I couldn't love em proper in Kentucky because they wasn't mine to love. But when I got here, when I jumped down off that wagon—there wasn't nobody in the world I couldn't love if I wanted to. You know what I mean? (Morrison 1987, 162)

By distorting Sethe's ability to love her children "proper," slavery annexed Sethe's power as energy for its own ends. Her words touch a deep chord in Paul D, for he too remembers how slavery felt. His unspoken response to Sethe expresses the mechanisms used by systems of domination such as slavery in harnessing potential sources of power in a subordinated group:

> So you protected yourself and loved small. Picked the tiniest stars out of the sky to own; lay down with head twisted in order to see the loved one over the rim of the trench before you slept. Stole shy glances at her between the trees at chain-up. Grass blades, salamanders, spiders, woodpeckers, beetles, a kingdom of ants. Anything bigger wouldn't do. A woman, a child, a brother—a big love like that would split you wide open in Alfred, Georgia. He knew exactly what she meant: to get to a place where you could love anything you chose—not to need permission for desire—well, now, *that* was freedom. (Morrison 1987, 162)

Sethe and Paul D's words suggest that in order to perpetuate itself, slavery corrupts and distorts those sources of power within oppressed groups that provide energy for change. To them, freedom from slavery meant not only the absence of capricious masters and endless work but regaining the power to "love anything you chose." Both Sethe and Paul D understood how slavery inhibited their ability to have "a big love," whether for children, for friends, for each other, or for principles such as justice. Both saw that systems of oppression often succeed because they control the "permission for desire"—in other words, they harness the power of deep feelings to the exigencies of domination.

This type of power that flows from "a big love" flies in the face of Western epistemologies that often see emotions and rationality as different and competing concerns (Collins 1998a, 243–45). Described by Black feminist poet Audre Lorde (1984) as the power of the erotic, deep feelings that arouse people to action constitute an important source of power. In her groundbreaking essay, "Uses of the Erotic: The Erotic as Power," Audre Lorde explores this fundamental link between deep feelings and power and provides a road map for an oppositional sexual politics:

> There are many kinds of power, used and unused, acknowledged or otherwise. The erotic is a resource within each of us that lies in a deeply female and spiritual plane, firmly rooted in the power of our unexpressed or unrecognized feeling. In order to perpetuate itself, every oppression must corrupt or distort those various sources of power within the culture of the oppressed that can provide energy for change. For women, this has meant a suppression of the erotic as a considered source of power and information in our lives. (Lorde 1984, 53)

For Lorde sexuality is a component of the erotic as a source of power in women. Lorde's notion is one of power as energy, as something people possess that must be annexed in order for larger systems of oppression to function.[1]

Lorde suggests that this erotic power resides in women, but men too can experience these deep feelings. Divergent expressions of deep feelings may lie less in biologically based gender differences than in social structures that associate this type of passion with femininity and weakness. Sadly, within capitalist marketplace relations, this erotic power is so often sexualized that not only is it routinely misunderstood, but the strength of deeply felt love is even feared.

African-American women's experiences with pornography, prostitution, and rape demonstrate how erotic power becomes commodified and exploited by social institutions. Equally important is how Black women hold fast to this source of individual empowerment and use it in crafting fully human love relationships. When people "protect themselves and love small" by seeing certain groups of people as worthy of love and deeming others less deserving, potential sources of power as energy that can flow from love relationships are attenuated. But when people reject the world offered by intersecting oppressions, the power as energy that can flow from a range of love relationships becomes possible.

All love relationships potentially tap the energy associated with deep feelings, but not all love relationships are the same. Such relationships can be arranged on a continuum from caring yet asexual love relationships, to sexualized love relationships—those where deep feelings find sexual expression—to those that reflect the "just sex" commodity relations of the capitalist marketplace.

This chapter examines selected Black women's love relationships that tap deep feelings, whether or not they find sexual expression. The deep love that African-American women feel for our parents, children, and siblings constitute spiritual, deeply felt love relationships that are not considered sexual. Conversely, love relationships that encompass sexual expression constitute sexualized love relationships. Loving friendships of all sorts remain arrayed in between, with some of the most contested relationships occurring when people do not know where to draw the sexual line. In some cases, sexuality itself clouds the boundaries. For example, for many heterosexual Black men and Black women, dominant constructions of Black male and Black female sexuality often limit the ability to form nonsexualized, loving friendships. In other cases, loving a forbidden other becomes the source of contention. Love across the color line, where individuals of different "races" fall in love, or across social class categories muddy the waters between asexual friendships and sexualized love relationships. In still other cases, the fear lies in loving too deeply elements of oneself found in the other. As Black lesbians point out, much homophobia expressed by heterosexual African-American women stems from the fear that their love of Black women might find sexual expression.

The intersecting oppressions that produce systems of domination such as slavery aim to thwart the power as energy available to subordinate groups. The sexual politics that constrains Black womanhood constitutes an effective system of domination because it intrudes on people's daily lives at the point of consciousness. Exactly how do the sexual politics of Black womanhood influence Black women's interpersonal love relationships? More important, how might an increased understanding of these relationships enable African-American women to tap sources of power as energy and thus become more empowered?

Black Women, Black Men, and the Love and Trouble Tradition

In her groundbreaking essay, "On the Issue of Roles," Toni Cade Bambara remarks, "Now it doesn't take any particular expertise to observe that one of the most characteristic features of our community is the antagonism between our men and our women" (Bambara 1970a, 106). Exploring the tensions between African-American men and women has been a long-standing theme in U.S. Black feminist thought. In an 1833 speech, Maria Stewart boldly challenged what she saw as Black men's lackluster response to racism: "Talk, without effort, is nothing; you are abundantly capable, gentlemen, of making yourselves men of distinction; and this gross neglect, on your part, causes my blood to boil within me" (Richardson 1987, 58). Ma Rainey, Bessie Smith, and other classic

Black women blues singers offer rich advice to Black women on how to deal with unfaithful and unreliable men (Harrison 1978, 1988; Russell 1982; Davis 1998). More recently, Black women's troubles with Black men have generated anger and, from that anger, self-reflection: "We have been and are angry some-times," suggests Bonnie Daniels, "not for what men have done, but for what we've allowed ourselves to become, again and again in my past, in my mother's past, in my centuries of womanhood passed over, for the 'sake' of men, whose manhood we've helped undermine" (1979, 62).

Juxtaposed against this tradition of trouble is another long-standing theme—namely, the great love Black women feel for Black men. African-American slave narratives contain countless examples of newly emancipated Black women who spent years trying to locate their lost children, spouses, fathers, and other male loved ones (Gutman 1976). Black women writers express love for their sons and fears about their futures (Angelou 1969; Golden 1995). Love poems written to Black men permeate Black women's poetry. Black women's music is similarly replete with songs about sexualized love. Whether the playful voice of Alberta Hunter proclaiming that her "man is a handy man," the mourn-ful cries of Billie Holiday singing "My Man," the sadness Nina Simone evokes in "I Loves You Porgy" at being forced to leave her man, or the powerful voice of Jennifer Holliday, who cries out, "You're gonna love me," Black vocalists identify Black women's relationships with Black men as a source of strength, sup-port, and sustenance (Harrison 1978, 1988; Russell 1982). As U.S. Black feminists point out, many Black women reject feminism because they see it as being antifamily and against Black men. They do not want to give up men—they want Black men to change. Black activist Fannie Lou Hamer succinctly captures what a good love relationship between a Black woman and man can be: "You know, I'm not hung up on this about liberating myself from the black man, I'm not going to try that thing. I got a black husband, six feet three, two hundred and forty pounds, with a 14 shoe, that I don't want to be liberated from" (Lerner 1972, 612).

African-American women have long commented on this "love and trouble" tradition in Black women's relationships with Black men. Novelist Gayl Jones explains: "The relationships between the men and the women I'm dealing with are blues relationships. So they're out of a tradition of 'love and trouble.' . . . Blues talks about the simultaneity of good and bad, as feeling, as something felt. . . . Blues acknowledges all different kinds of feelings at once" (Harper 1979, 360). Both the tensions between African-American women and men and the strong attachment that we feel for one another represent a rejection of binary thinking and an acceptance of the both/and conceptual stance in Black feminist thought.

Understanding this love and trouble tradition requires assessing the influ-ence of heterosexist, Eurocentric gender ideology—particularly ideas about men and women advanced by the traditional family ideal—on African-American women and men. Definitions of appropriate gender behavior for Black women,

Black men, and members of other racial/ethnic groups not only affect social institutions such as schools and labor markets, they also shape daily interactions. Analyses claiming that African-Americans would be just like Whites if offered comparable opportunities implicitly support prevailing sexual politics. Such thinking offers hegemonic gender ideologies of White masculinity and White femininity as models for African-Americans to emulate. Similarly, those proclaiming that Black men experience a more severe form of racial oppression than Black women routinely counsel African-American women to subjugate our needs to those of Black men (see, e.g., Staples 1979). However, advising Black women to unquestioningly support sexual harassment, domestic violence, and other forms of sexism done by U.S. Black men buttresses a form of sexual politics that differently controls everyone. As Audre Lorde queries, "If society ascribes roles to black men which they are not allowed to fulfill, is it black women who must bend and alter our lives to compensate, or is it society that needs changing?" (1984, 61). Bonnie Daniels provides an answer: "I've learned . . . that being less than what I am capable of being to boost someone else's ego *does not help either of us* for real" (1979, 61).

Black women intellectuals directly challenge not only the derogation of African-American women within prevailing sexual politics—for example, the controlling images of mammy, the matriarch, the welfare mother, and the jezebel—but often base this rejection on a more general critique of Eurocentric heterosexism itself. Sojourner Truth's 1851 query, "I could work as much and eat as much as a man—when I could get it—and bear the lash as well! And ain't I a woman?" confronts the premises of the cult of true womanhood that "real" women were fragile and ornamental. Toni Cade Bambara contends that Eurocentric understandings of gender derived from White, middle-class experience are not only troublesome for African-Americans but damaging: "I have always, I think, opposed the stereotypical definitions of 'masculine' and 'feminine,' . . . because I always found the either/or implicit in those definitions antithetical to what I was all about—and what revolution for self is all about—the whole person" (Bambara 1970a, 101).

As many U.S. Black feminist activists point out, the sexual politics of Black womanhood limits the development of transformative social justice projects within Black civil society. Black activist Frances Beale identifies the negative effects that sexism within the Black community had on Black political activism in the 1960s:

> Unfortunately, there seems to be some confusion in the Movement today as to who has been oppressing whom. Since the advent of Black power, the Black male has exerted a more prominent leadership role in our struggle for justice in this country. He sees the system for what it really is for the most part, but where he rejects its values and mores on many issues, when it comes to women, he seems to take his guidelines from the pages of the *Ladies' Home Journal*. (Beale 1970, 92)

Mainstream social science also seems overly preoccupied with Black men's issues. Sociologist William Julius Wilson's (1987; 1996) groundbreaking work on joblessness and poverty among U.S. Blacks pays more attention to men's issues than women's. From Black conservatism to Black nationalism, regardless of Black political perspective, an implicit male bias persists. The inordinate emphasis placed on providing more Black male role models for Black boys in contemporary Black political theory and practice often occurs by neglecting the needs of girls. This masculinist bias spurred two Black feminist thinkers to observe: "The struggle is defined as one to reclaim and redefine Black manhood. Ironically, this is also the point at which the politics and positions of some cultural nationalists, liberals and right-wing conservatives seem to converge" (Ransby and Matthews, 1993, 60).

While some African-American women criticize the sexual politics that accompanies intersecting oppressions, even fewer have directly challenged Black men who accept prevailing notions of both Black and White masculinity (Wallace 1978). Until the watershed event of Anita Hill's 1992 public testimony against Clarence Thomas, the blues tradition provided the most consistent and long-standing text of Black women who demand that Black men "change their ways." Both then and now, songs often encourage Black men to define new types of relationships. In "Do Right Woman—Do Right Man," when Aretha Franklin (1967) sings that a woman is only human and is not a plaything but is flesh and blood just like a man, she echoes Sojourner Truth's claim that women and men are equally human. Aretha sings about knowing that she's living in a "man's world" but she encourages her man not to "prove" that he's a man by using or abusing her. As long as she and her man are together, she wants him to show some "respect" for her. Her position is clear—if he wants a "do right, all night woman," he's got to be a "do right, all night man." Aretha challenges African-American men to reject the prevailing sexual politics that posit "it's a man's world" in order to be a "do right man." By showing Black women respect and being an "all night" man—one who is faithful, financially reliable, and sexually expressive—Black men can have a relationship with a "do right woman."

Within the corpus of their works, some Black women hip-hop artists echo Aretha's challenge. In her song "Unity," Queen Latifah asks for a man who knows how to respect a woman. For those who need more details, Salt 'n' Pepa's anthem "Whatta Man" on *Very Necessary* (1993) identifies the qualities of a "mighty good man." Recognizing that "good men are hard to find," the song aspires to "give respect to the men who made a difference." The list of qualities is clear. A good man is one who makes a woman laugh, does not run around with other women, has a good body, is a good lover, can hold a decent conversation, and "spends time with his kids when he can." He always has his woman's "back" when she needs him, and he's "never disrespectful 'cause his momma taught him that."

Many Black men have not taken kindly to these requests. Black men's response to the publications of Black women writers illustrate these reactions. Apparently forgetting the norms of racial solidarity that they long expected Black women to show for Black men's achievements, many men resented the success of Black women's writers. Explaining this situation, Black literary critic Calvin Hernton describes how this antagonistic posture stems from Black men's acceptance of prevailing sexual politics:

> Too often Black men have a philosophy of manhood that relegates women to the back burner. Therefore it is perceived as an offense for black women to struggle on their own, let alone achieve something independently. Thus, no matter how original, beautiful, and formidable the works of black women writers might be, black men become "offended" if such works bear the slightest criticism of them, or if the women receive recognition from other women, especially from the white literary establishment. They do not behave as though something of value has been added to the annals of black literature. Rather, they behave as though something has been subtracted, not only from the literature, but from the entire race, and specifically, from *them*. (Hernton 1985, 6)

Whereas some men merely grumble at no longer having their perceived needs always come first, other men interpret Black women's success as a direct attack on them. If the sexual politics that foster these reactions remain unexamined, as Lisa Jones succinctly states, the potential damage done to both Black women and Black men is great: "Between rappers turning 'ho' into a national chant and [the movie *Waiting to*] *Exhale* telling African Americans that our real problem is the shortage of brothers who are both well hung and well paid, I'm getting to think that all we can offer each other as black women and men is genitalia and the paycheck" (Jones 1994, 267).

Avoiding being reduced to the "genitalia and the paycheck" requires developing a comprehensive analysis of how prevailing sexual politics influences Black heterosexual love relationships. In developing this analysis, however, it is equally important to keep in mind the analytical distinction between the interpersonal domain of power where men and women as individuals interact, and how broader overarching structures of power operate to encourage these individual outcomes. For example, womanist thinker Geneva Smitherman maintains this distinction when pressed to describe some Black men's treatment of Black women. In responding to claims that Black men are sexist, she contends, "This is not to argue that Black men don't display sexist attitudes. Of course. Such attitudes are in the very fiber of American society; they have infected us all—including women. However, the practice of patriarchy, the subordination of women—and men—requires power, on a grand scale, and control over the nation's institutions. Sorry, but the Brothers ain't there" (Smitherman 1996, 105). Black men may not be in corporate boardrooms, and thus cannot be blamed for actions aimed at protecting the privileges associated with White masculinity (Ferber 1998). But at the same time the "Brothers" most certainly are in Black women's homes. They *can* be held accountable, no matter how badly treated they may be under racial oppression, for how they treat Black women, children, and each other.

The antagonism that many African-American women and men feel and express toward one another reflects the contradictions characterizing Black masculinity and Black femininity within prevailing U.S. sexual politics. Racialized heterosexism objectifies both Black men and Black women. Thus, when African-American men see Black women as little more than mammies, matriarchs, or "hoochies," or even if they insist on placing African-American women on the same queenly pedestal reserved for White women, they objectify not only Black women but themselves (Gardner 1980). Conversely, when Black women demand of their partners, "Show me the money," they not only reduce Black men to a measure of their financial worth, but reinscribe controlling images of themselves as materialistic "bitches." The challenge lies in disrupting Eurocentric scripts of Black masculinity and Black femininity, not just to receive better treatment for oneself, but to undermine and change prevailing sexual politics.

In her article "Sensuous Sapphires: A Study of the Social Construction of Black Female Sexuality," Annecka Marshall (1994) explores how Black women perceived the controlling images applied to them and how they negotiated those images in shaping their sexual selves. The women in her study saw the limitations of Eurocentric scripts of Black femininity concerning sexuality, and reported diverse strategies in dealing with them. While some women reject all of the stereotypes, they see no way of avoiding them. Some feel that they must choose between being seen as asexual mothers or hypersexual whores. Others recognize the power that being seen as "sensuous sapphires" has in how others see them, and try to exempt themselves from the category. By claiming that it's the other Black women who are "sapphires," not them, they may receive individual relief, but they leave the images themselves intact. Marshall also reports a range of coping strategies where women aim to challenge the very foundations of the images themselves.

Until recently, many heterosexual Black men have remained either unable to challenge controlling images of Black masculinity or have been unwilling to try.[2] Sadly, believing in dominant notions of Black masculinity and Black femininity, they engage in controlling behaviors that often go unrecognized as such. U.S. Black men encounter contradictory expectations concerning Black manhood. On the one hand, Black men have been constructed as sexually violent rapists, as brutes, and as irresponsible boys who fail to marry the mothers of their children and financially support their children. Whereas Black men under slavery knew that they were not these things, their powerlessness denied them the trappings of manhood as defined by White propertied men. Emancipation brought with it Black male outrage at the treatment of Black women under slavery. A good deal of Black male energy went into protecting Black women from both economic and sexual exploitation. Given this history, efforts by Black men to protect Black women become valued. Many Black women want protection. Sonsyrea Tate, who was raised within the Nation of Islam, ultimately rejected the strict gender norms that routinely elevated boys above girls. But Tate also describes how protected she felt within the Nation: "While I was growing up, the Fruit of Islam, the security unit of the Nation of Islam, had made me, a small black child, feel safer than I felt at any other time in America" (Tate 1997, 4–5).

Barbara Omolade argues that "protecting black women was the most significant measure of black manhood and the central aspect of black male patriarchy" (1994, 13). If Omolade is correct, then this important choice to protect Black women, for many men, became harnessed to ideologies of Black masculinity in such a way that Black manhood became dependent on Black women's willingness to accept protection. Within this version of masculinity, a slippery slope emerges between *protecting* Black women and *controlling* them. This control is often masked, all in defense of widespread beliefs that Black men must be in charge in order to regain their lost manhood. As Paula Giddings points out, "It is men, not women, who control the sociosexual and professional relationships in the black community. Among other notions that must be dispensed with is the weak male/strong female patriarchal paradigm that clouds so much of our thinking about ourselves" (Giddings 1992, 463).

This general climate fosters a situation where some Black women feel that they must subordinate their needs to those of Black men in order to help Black men regain and retain their manhood. Yet at the same time, Black women's daily struggles for survival encourage patterns of self-reliance and self-valuation that benefit not just Black women, but men and children as well. As Barbara Omolade points out, "A black woman could not be completely controlled and defined by her own men, for she had already learned to manage and resist the advances of white men" (1994, 16). Tensions characterizing Black women's necessary self-reliance joined with our bona fide need for protection, as well as those characterizing Black men's desire to protect Black women juxtaposed to their admiration and resentment of Black women's assertiveness and independence, result in a complicated love and trouble tradition.

Failure to challenge an overall climate that not only defines Black masculinity in terms of Black men's ability to "own" and "control" their women, and Black femininity in terms of Black women's ability to help U.S. Black men feel like men, can foster African-American women's abuse. Black men who feel that they cannot be men unless they are in charge can be highly threatened by assertive Black women, especially those in their own households. In *The Color Purple*, Alice Walker's portrayal of Mister, a Black man who abuses his wife, Celie, explores the coexistence of love and trouble in African-American communities generally, and in Black men specifically:

> At the root of the denial of easily observable and heavily documented sexist brutality in the black community—the assertion that black men don't act like Mister, and if they do, they're justified by the pressure they're

under as black men in a white society—is our deep, painful refusal to accept the fact that we are not only descendants of slaves, but we are also the descendants of slave *owners*. And that just as we have had to struggle to rid ourselves of slavish behaviors we must as ruthlessly eradicate any desire to be mistress or "master." (1989, 80)

Those Black men who wish to become "master" by fulfilling traditional definitions of masculinity—White, prosperous, and in charge—and who are blocked from doing so can become dangerous to those closest to them (Asbury 1987).

Rethinking relationships such as these has garnered increasing attention in Black feminist thought (E. White 1985). Refusing to reduce Black men's abuse to individualistic, psychological flaws, Black feminist analyses are characterized by careful attention to how intersecting oppressions of race, gender, class, and sexuality provide the backdrop for Black heterosexual love relationships (White 1985). Angela Davis contends, "We cannot grasp the true nature of sexual assault without situating it within its larger sociopolitical context" (1989, 37). Author Gayl Jones concurs: "It's important for me to clarify . . . relationships in *situation*, rather than to have some theory of the way men are with women" (Harper 1979, 356). In Toni Morrison's *The Bluest Eye* (1970), Pecola Breedlove is a study in emotional abuse. Morrison portrays the internalized oppression that can affect a child who experiences daily assaults on her sense of self. Pecola's family is the immediate source of her pain, but Morrison also exposes the role of the larger community in condoning Pecola's victimization. In her choreopoem *For Colored Girls Who Have Considered Suicide*, Ntozake Shange (1975) creates the character Beau Willie Brown, a man who abuses his lover, Crystal, and who kills their two young children. Rather than blaming Beau Willie Brown as the source of Crystal's oppression, Shange considers how the situation of "no air"—in this case, the lack of opportunities for both individuals—stifles the humanity of both Crystal and Beau Willie Brown.

Investigating the problems caused by abusive Black men often exposes Black women intellectuals to criticism. Alice Walker's treatment of male violence in works such as *The Third Life of Grange Copeland* (1970) and *The Color Purple* (1982) attracted censure. Even though Ntozake Shange's choreopoem is about Black women, one criticism leveled at her work is its purportedly negative portrayal of Black men (Staples 1979). Particularly troubling to some critics is the depiction of Beau Willie Brown. In an interview, Claudia Tate asked Ntozake Shange, "Why did you have to tell about Beau Willie Brown?" In this question Tate invokes the bond of family secrecy that often pervades dysfunctional families because she wants to know why Shange violated the African-American community's collective family "secret." Shange's answer is revealing: "I refuse to be a part of this conspiracy of silence. I will not do it. So that's why I wrote about Beau Willie Brown. I'm tired of living lies" (Tate 1983, 158–59).

This "conspiracy of silence" about Black men's physical and emotional abuse of Black women parallels Black women's silences about the politics of sexuality in general. Both silences stem from a larger system of legitimated, routinized violence targeted toward Black women and, via silence, both work to reinscribe social hierarchies (Richie 1996; Collins 1998d). Because hegemonic ideologies make everyday violence against Black women appear so routine, some women perceive neither themselves nor those around them as victims. Sara Brooks's husband first assaulted her when she was pregnant, once threw her out of a window, and often called her his "Goddam knock box." Despite his excessive violence, she considered his behavior routine: "If I tried to talk to him he'd hit me so hard with his hands till I'd see stars. Slap me, and what he slap me for, I don't know. . . . My husband would slap me and then go off to his woman's house. That's the way life was" (Simonsen 1986, 162). Ostensibly positive images of Black women make some women more likely to accept domestic violence as routine (E. White 1985). Many African-American women have had to exhibit independence and self-reliance to ensure their own survival and that of their loved ones. But this image of the self-reliant Black woman can be troublesome for women in violent relationships. When an abused woman like Sara Brooks believes that "strength and independence are expected of her, she may be more reluctant to call attention to her situation, feeling that she should be able to handle it on her own; she may deny the seriousness of her situation" (Asbury 1987, 101).

Abused women, particularly those bearing the invisible scars of emotional abuse, are often silenced by the image of the "superstrong" Black woman (Richie 1996). But according to Audre Lorde, sexual violence against Black women is "a disease striking the heart of Black nationhood, and silence will not make it disappear" (1984, 120). To Lorde, such violence is exacerbated by racism and powerlessness such that "violence against Black women and children often becomes a standard within our communities, one by which manliness can be measured. But these woman-hating acts are rarely discussed as crimes against Black women" (p. 120). By making visible the pain the survivors feel, Black feminist intellectuals like Alice Walker, Audre Lorde, and Ntozake Shange challenge the alleged "rationality" of this particular system of control and rearticulate it as violence.

One of the best Black feminist analyses of domestic violence is found in Zora Neale Hurston's *Their Eyes Were Watching God* (1937). In the following passage Hurston recounts how Tea Cake responded to a threat that another man would win the affections of Janie:

> Before the week was over he had whipped Janie. Not because her behavior justified his jealousy, but it relieved that awful fear inside him. Being able to whip her reassured him in possession. "Tea Cake, you sho is a lucky man," Sop-de-Bottom told him. "Uh person can see every place you hit her. Ah bet she never raised her hand tuh hit yuh back, neither. Take some uh dese ol' rusty black women and dey would fight yuh all night long and next day nobody couldn't tell you ever hit 'em. . . . Lawd! wouldn't Ah love tuh whip uh tender woman lak Janie! Ah bet she don't even holler. She jus' cries, eh Tea Cake?" (Hurston 1937, 121)

Hurston's work can be read as a Black feminist analysis of the sexualized vio-lence that many Black women encounter in their deepest love relationships. Tea Cake and Sop-de-Bottom see women as commodities, property that they can whip to "reassure their possession." Janie is not a person; she is objectified as something owned by Tea Cake. Even if a man loves a woman, as is clearly the case of Tea Cake and Janie, the threat of competition from another male is enough to develop an "awful fear" that Janie will choose another man and thus deem him less manly than his competitors. Whipping Janie reassured Tea Cake that she was his. The conversation between the two men is also revealing. Images of color and beauty pervade their conversation. Sop-de-Bottom is envious because he can "see every place" that Tea Cake hit her and that she was passive and did not resist like the rest of the "rusty black women." Tea Cake and Sop-de-Bottom have accepted Eurocentric gender ideology concerning masculinity and femininity and have used force to maintain it. Furthermore, Janie's transgres-sion was the potential to become unfaithful, the possibility to be sexually promiscuous, to become a whore. Finally, the violence occurs in an intimate relationship where love is present. This incident shows the process by which power as domination—in this case gender oppression structured through Eurocentric gender ideology and class oppression reflected in the objectifica-tion and commodification of Janie—has managed to annex the basic power of the erotic in Janie and Tea Cake's relationship. Tea Cake does not want to beat Janie, but he does because he *feels*, not thinks, he must.[3] Their relationship rep-resents the linking of sexuality and power, the potential for domination with-in sexualized love relationships, and the potential for using the erotic, their love for each other, as a catalyst for change.

Black Women Alone

Many Black women want loving sexual relationships with Black men, but instead end up alone. Black men may be the closest to Black women, and thus receive the lion's share of the blame for all the daily ways that Black women are caused to feel less worthy, yet this societal judgment and rejection of Black women permeates the entire culture. As Karla Holloway points out, "the tragic loneliness black women consistently face as we stand before judgmental oth-ers—sometimes white, but sometimes black; sometimes male, but sometimes female—demands that we have some wisdom, experience, and some passion with which to combat this abuse" (1995, 38). For African-American women, rejection by Whites is one thing—rejection by Black men is entirely another. In coping with the loneliness of not finding Black male partners, "wisdom, expe-rience, and some passion" become important weapons.

This aloneness, the sense that one is at the bottom of the scale of desirability, fosters divergent reactions among African-American women. Many continue to express hope that one day they will be married to a good Black man and go on with their lives. Some pour their energies into Black motherhood, a respected and important part of Black civil society. Black single mothers are not as looked down upon in Black civil society, because most African-American women know that Black men are hard to find. The intensity of their ties with their children meshes with long-standing belief systems that value motherhood. However, despite the importance of this choice, for many, it can substitute for the lack of steady, sexualized love relationships in their lives. The character of Gloria in Terry McMillan's *Waiting to Exhale* (1992) typifies this choice of giving up hope that one will ever be lovable enough to find Salt 'n' Pepa's (1993) "mighty good man." Gloria pours all of her energies into raising her son. She cooks for him, gains weight, and never dates for fear of compromising the respectability she has carved out within the stigma attached to unmarried Black mothers. Yet Gloria confronts a crisis when her son becomes sexually active and is old enough to leave home. He is becoming a man and can no longer be "her man." MacMillan provides a storybook resolution to Gloria's situation. A widower moves in across the street, becomes captivated with Gloria, and helps her learn to love herself as a sexual being. Real life is rarely this forgiving.

Dealing with the reality that Black men reject them leads other Black women to become devoted to careers. Eventually, these women become the middle-class, respectable, often childless Black ladies that Wahneema Lubiano (1992) argues Anita Hill symbolizes. Despite the often remarkable achievement of middle-class Black women, the pain many experience on the way to middle-class respectability, while masked by achievement, is no less real. Gloria Wade-Gayles describes the anger and frustration of the Black women college students in her classes when they realize the breadth of rejection. Many of her students spend all four years of their college lives without a single romantic relationship, Wade-Gayles observes. Conversations about this loneliness reveal the anger, sadness, and sorrow that many young Black women feel when living through rejection of this magnitude. In a nutshell, Black men pick non-Black women over them, and for many, it hurts. Wade-Gayles reaches back into her own experiences to try to understand this situation: "The pain we experience as black teenagers follows many of us into adulthood, and, if we are professional black women, it follows with a vengeance. As a colleague in an eastern school explained our situation, 'Black men don't want us as mates because we are independent; white men, because we are black'" (Wade-Gayles 1996, 106)

In this context, heterosexual Black women become competitors, most searching for the elusive Black male, with many resenting the White women who naively claim them. These efforts to grapple with societal rejection that emerge from these sexual politics cut across age and class. As Wade-Gayles points out, "Teenagers know about athletes and entertainers; we know about politicians and scholars. Teenagers see faces; we see symbols that, in our opinion, spin the image of white women to the rhythm of symphonic chords" (Wade-Gayles 1996, 106–107).

In this context of what is perceived as widespread rejection by Black men, often in favor of White women, African-American women's relationships with Whites take on a certain intensity. On the one hand, antagonism can characterize relationships between Black and White women, especially those who appear blissfully unaware of the sexual politics that privileges White skin. Despite claims of shared sisterhood, heterosexual women remain competitors in a competition that many White women do not even know they have entered. "White men use different forms of enforcing oppression of white women and of women of Color," argues Chicana scholar Aida Hurtado. "As a consequence, these groups of women have different political responses and skills, and at times these differences cause the two groups to clash" (1989, 843). On the other hand, given the culpability of White men in creating and maintaining these sexual politics, Black women remain reluctant to love White men. Constrained by social norms that deem us unworthy of White men and norms of Black civil society that identify Black women who cross the color line as traitors to the race, many Black women remain alone.

This speaks to the double standard within Black civil society concerning interracial, heterosexual love relationships. For Black women the historical relationship with White men has been one of legal but not sexual rejection: Propertied White men have exploited, objectified, and refused to marry African-American women and have held out trappings of power to their poorer brothers who endorse this ideology. The relationships between Black women and White men have long been constrained by the legacy of Black women's sexual abuse by White men and the unresolved tensions this creates. Traditionally, freedom for Black women has meant freedom *from* White men, not the freedom to choose White men as lovers and friends. Black women who have willingly chosen White male friends and lovers have been severely chastised in African-American communities for selling out the "race." Or they are accused of being like prostitutes, demeaning themselves by willingly using White men for their own financial or social gain.

Given the history of sexual abuse of Black women by White men, individual Black women who choose White partners become reminders of a difficult history for Black women as a collectivity. Such individual liaisons aggravate a collective sore spot because they recall historical master/slave relationships. Any sexual encounters between two parties where one has so much control over the other could never be fully consensual, even if the slave appeared to agree. Structural power differences of this magnitude limit the subordinate's power to give free consent or refusal. Controlling images such as jezebel are created to mask just this power differential and provide the illusion of consent. At the same time, even under slavery, to characterize interracial sex purely in terms of the victimization of Black women would be a distortion, because such depictions strip Black women of agency. Many Black women successfully resisted sexual assault while others cut bargains with their masters. More difficult to deal with, however, is the fact that even within these power differentials, genuine affection characterized some sexual relationships between Black women and White men (d'Emilio and Freedman 1988, 100–104).

This history of sexual abuse contributes to a contemporary double standard where Black women who date and marry White men are often accused of losing their Black identity. Within this context, Black women who do engage in relationships with White men encounter Black community norms that question their commitment to Blackness. A 20-year-old student participant in Annecka Marshall's (1994) study of how British Black women construct sexuality describes her own experiences with "mixed race" relationships as positive. But she also recognizes the double standard that is often applied to crossing the color line: "It's more acceptable in the Black community for Black men to go out with white women than for Black women to go out with white men. It's all about control and power. A Black man is seen as the one who controls the relationship and so his 'race' isn't being downtrodden and trampled. But if a Black women does the same thing she is being submissive" (p. 119).

Relationships among U.S. Black women and U.S. White women demonstrate a similar complexity. Because White men have not married Black women, in large part due to laws against miscegenation designed to render the children of unions between White men and Black women propertyless (d'Emilio and Freedman 1988, 106), few delusions of enjoying the privileges attached to White male power have existed among Black women. In contrast, White women have been offered a share of White male power, but at the cost of participating in their own subordination. "Sometimes I really feel more sorrier for the white woman than I feel for ourselves because she been caught up in this thing, caught up feeling very special," observes Fannie Lou Hamer (Lerner 1972, 610). Thus even though "white women, as a group, are subordinated through seduction, women of Color, as a group, through rejection" (Hurtado 1989, 844), many White women appear unwilling to relinquish the benefits they accrue. This is the view of Tina, a Black woman in Minneapolis, whose White coworker routinely shared the details of her many sexual liaisons with Black men. Unconvinced that her coworker could be so ignorant of Black women's issues in finding men to date and marry, Tina rejected the view that White women are "racial innocents." She asked, "What stake would she have in dismantling a pecking order of femininity that puts her at the top?" (Jones 1994, 255).

This historical legacy of rejection and seduction frames relationships between Black and White women. Black women often express anger and bitterness against White women for their history of excusing the transgressions of their sons, husbands, and fathers. In her diary a slaveholder described White women's widespread predilection to ignore White men's actions:

> Under slavery, we live surrounded by prostitutes. . . . Who thinks any
> worse of a negro or mulatto woman for being a thing we can't name? God
> forgive us, but ours is a monstrous system. . . . Like the patriarchs of old,

> our men live all in one house with their wives and their concubines; and
> the mulattoes one sees in every family partly resemble the white children.
> Any lady is ready to tell you who is the father of all the mulatto children
> in everybody's household but her own. Those, she seems to think drop
> from the clouds. (Lerner 1972, 51)

If White women under slavery could ignore transgressions of this magnitude,
contemporary White women can more easily do the same.

For many African-American women, far too few White women are willing
to acknowledge—let alone challenge—the actions of White men because they
have benefited from them. Fannie Lou Hamer analyzes White women's culpability in Black women's subordination: "You've been caught up in this thing
because, you know, you worked my grandmother, and after that you worked my
mother, and then finally you got hold of me. And you really thought . . . you
thought that you was *more* because you was a woman, and especially a white
woman, you had this kind of angel feeling that you were untouchable" (Lerner
1972, 610). White women's inability to acknowledge how racism privileges
them reflects the relationship that they have to White male power. "I think whites
are carefully taught not to recognize white privilege," argues feminist scholar
Peggy McIntosh, "just as males are taught not to recognize male privilege"
(1988, 1). McIntosh describes her own struggles with learning to see how she
had been privileged: "I have come to see white privilege as an invisible package
of unearned assets which I can count on cashing in each day, but about which I
was 'meant' to remain oblivious" (p. 1).

One manifestation of White women's privilege is the seeming naiveté many
heterosexual White women have concerning how Black women perceive White
women's sexualized love relationships with Black men. In *Dessa Rose*, Nathan,
a Black slave, and Rufel, a White woman on whose land they both live, have
sexual relations. Even though Dessa, a Black woman, is not romantically attracted
to Nathan, she deeply resents his behavior:

> White folks had taken everything in the world from me except my baby
> and my life and they had tried to take them. And to see him, who had
> helped to save me, had friended with me through so much of it, laying
> up, wallowing in what had hurt me so—I didn't feel that nothing I could
> say would tell him what that pain was like. And I didn't feel like it was on
> me to splain why he shouldn't be messing with no white woman; I
> thought it was on him to say why he was doing it. (Williams 1986, 186)

Like many African-American women, Dessa sees Black male admiration for
White women as a rejection of her. She asks, "Had he really wanted me to be
like Mistress, I wondered, like Miz Ruint, that doughy skin and slippery hair?
Was *that* what they wanted?" (Williams 1986, 199).

The numbers of U.S. Black men who "want" White women has risen since
the 1960s, in the context of two developments. For one, the elimination of de

jure (but not de facto) racial segregation has brought Blacks and Whites in close contact in schools and job sites, often as equals. In particular, the laws against miscegenation that forbade interracial marriage passed by Southern states during the 1860s were abolished. When it comes to Black men and White women, legally at least, the *Driving Miss Daisy* days are done. At the same time, changes in sexual attitudes challenged long-standing arrangements where, according to Paula Giddings, "sex was the principle around which wholesale segregation and discrimination was organized with the ultimate objective of preventing intermarriage. The sexual revolution . . . separated sexuality from reproduction, and so diluted the ideas about purity—moral, racial, and physical" (Giddings 1995, 424). These changing social conditions allowed Black male desire for White women as well as White female desire for Black men to be expressed without the censure afforded Nathan and Rufel's relationship.

The birth of biracial or mixed-race children speaks to the reality of these sexualized love relationships between Black men and White women. Historically, mixed-race children were accepted into a segregated Black civil society because everyone knew that such children should not be held accountable for the circumstances of their conception and birth. More often though, biracial and mixed-race children were the offspring of Black mothers and, as such, participated in Black civil society much as their mothers did. Currently, however, the birth of biracial and mixed-race children to so many White mothers raises new questions for African-American women. Even in the face of rejection by Black men that leaves so many without partners, ironically, Black women remain called upon to accept and love the mixed-race children born to their brothers, friends, and relatives. By being the Black mothers that these children do not have, these women are expected to help raise biracial children who at the same time often represent tangible reminders of their own rejection.

Currently, much more is known about how White women negotiate these new relationships with their biracial children than we do about either Black men's participation in being a parent to these children or the Black women who are so often called upon to help White mothers raise them. What does appear in accounts of children are reports of how important their Black relatives can be in helping them understand and cope with racism (see, e.g., Jones 1994).

Biracial Black women who recognize these contradictions struggle with this situation. On the one hand, the biracial girlchild's White mother positions her closer to Whiteness, and this physical beauty often makes her more attractive to many Black men. But on the other, she joins the ranks of Black women and thus inherits the history of rejection. In her essay titled "Mamas White," Lisa Jones describes her reactions to seeing White female and Black male couples and thus taps some of the complexities that accompany these new relationships: "Clearly I was saying that these duos tangle up my emotions; I look at them as a child of an interracial marriage, but also as a black woman who has witnessed the market value put on white femininity" (Jones 1994, 30). Rejecting yet another form of seduction, the seeming benefits of a mixed-race identity as a haven within a society that derogates Blackness, Jones recognizes the difficulties if not impossibility of stepping outside racial categories by pretending that they simply don't apply. Putting brackets around the term "Black woman" and pointing out its socially constructed nature does not erase the fact of living as a Black woman and all that entails. By simultaneously problematizing and accepting these relationships, Jones points the way toward a new analysis.

No matter how much in love Black men and White women may be, such couples will continue to attract Black women's attention. Gloria Wade-Gayles describes the power that the reality of these couples has for many African-American women:

> We see them, and we feel abandoned. We feel abandoned because we have been abandoned in so many ways, by so many people, and for so many centuries. We are the group of women furthest removed from the concept of beauty and femininity which invades every spot on the planet, and, as a result, we are taught not to like ourselves, or, as my student said, not to believe that we can ever do enough or be enough to be loved and desired. The truth is we experience a pain unique to us as a group when black men marry white women and even when they don't. It is a pain our mothers knew and their mothers before them. A pain passed on from generation to generation because the circumstances that create the pain have remained unchanged (Wade-Gayles 1996, 110).

Moving through this pain requires more than blaming White women for allegedly taking Black men, or Black men for rejecting us. It demands changing the "circumstances that create the pain."

Black Women and Erotic Autonomy

Changing the circumstances that create the pain requires developing an analysis of Black women's deep love relationships of all sorts. As Evelynn Hammonds points out, "mirroring as a way of negating a legacy of silence needs to be explored in much greater depth than it has been to date by black feminist theorists" (1997, 179). Karla Holloway suggests that one important first step occurs at an "essential moment when black women must acknowledge the powerful impact of our physical appearance. How we look is a factor in what happens to us" (1995, 36). Holloway argues that via constructions of Black women's sexuality, systems of oppression hold up distorted mirrors of a "public image" through which Black women learn to view ourselves. Holloway counsels Black women to disable "mirrored reflection of a prejudicial gaze" via a "reflexive, self-mediated vision of our bodies" (45). When Black women learn to hold up new "mirrors" to one another that enable us to see and love one another for who we really are, new possibilities for empowerment via deep love can emerge.

Theoretically, this sounds good, but practically, Black women learning to provide mirrors for one another that enable us to love one another comes face to face with the possible eroticization of such love. When it comes to issues of sexuality, mirroring reveals how the sharing required to support and love one another can find erotic expression. If sexuality constitutes a dimension of expressed love, then, for many Black women, loving Black women means loving them sexually. This recognition that loving oneself and loving Black women may find erotic or sexual expression can be threatening. The stigmatization of lesbian relationships seems designed to contain this threat.

In this sense, Black lesbian relationships are not only threatening to intersecting systems of oppression, they can be highly threatening to heterosexual African-American women's already assaulted sense of self. Certainly the homophobia expressed by many Black heterosexual women is influenced, in part, by accepting societal beliefs about lesbians. For Black women who have already been labeled the Other by virtue of race and gender, the threat of being labeled a lesbian can have a chilling effect on Black women's ideas and on our relationships with one another. In speculating about why so many competent Black women writers and reviewers have avoided examining lesbianism, Ann Allen Shockley suggests that "the fear of being labeled a Lesbian, whether they were one or not" (1983, 84), has been a major deterrent.

The issues, however, may go much deeper. "I think the reason that Black women are so homophobic," suggests Barbara Smith, "is that attraction-repulsion thing. They have to speak out vociferously against lesbianism because if they don't they may have to deal with their own deep feelings for women" (Smith and Smith 1981, 124). Shockley agrees: "Most black women feared and abhorred Lesbians more than rape—perhaps because of the fear bred from their deep inward potentiality for Lesbianism" (1974, 31–32). In the same sense that men who accept Eurocentric notions of masculinity fear and deny the dimensions of themselves that they associate with femininity—for example, interpreting male expressiveness as being weak and unmanly (Hoch 1979)—avowedly heterosexual Black women may suppress their own strong feelings for other Black women for fear of being stigmatized as lesbians. Similarly, in the way that male domination of women embodies men's fears about their own masculinity, Black heterosexual women's treatment of Black lesbians reflects fears that all African-American women are essentially the same. Yet, as Audre Lorde points out, "in the same way that the existence of the self-defined Black woman is no threat to the self-defined Black man, the Black lesbian is an emotional threat only to those Black women whose feelings of kinship and love for other Black women are problematic in some way" (1984, 49).

Black lesbian relationships pose little threat to "self-defined" Black men and women secure in their sexualities. But loving relationships among Black women do pose a tremendous threat to systems of intersecting oppressions. How dare these women love one another in a context that deems Black women as a collectivity so unlovable and devalued? The treatment of Black lesbians reveals how the sexual expression of all Black women becomes regulated within intersecting systems of oppression. As a specific site of intersectionality, Black lesbian relationships constitute relationships among the ultimate Other. Black lesbians are not White, male, or heterosexual and generally are not affluent. As such they represent the antithesis of Audre Lorde's "mythical norm" and become the standard by which other groups measure their own so-called normality and self-worth. Sexual politics functions smoothly only if sexual nonconformity is kept invisible or is punished if it becomes visible. "By being sexually independent of men, lesbians, by their very existence, call into question society's definition of woman at its deepest level," observes Barbara Christian (1985, 199). Visible Black lesbians challenge the mythical norm that the best people are White, male, rich, and heterosexual. In doing so lesbians generate anxiety, discomfort, and a challenge to the dominant group's control of power and sexuality on the interpersonal level (Vance 1984).

For African-American women, taking seriously the idea of generating loving "mirrors" for one another requires taking on all of the "isms" that keep Black women down, including heterosexism. It means moving beyond the stigmatization of Black heterosexual women as jezebels—the sexual deviants *inside* an assumed heterosexuality—and of Black lesbians, whose homosexuality labels them sexual deviants *outside* heterosexuality. In crafting such an argument, Evelynn Hammonds is one of many who argues for a "different level of engagement between black heterosexual and black lesbian women as the basis for the development of a black feminist praxis that articulates the ways in which invisibility, otherness, and stigma are produced and re-produced on black women's bodies" (Hammonds 1997, 181–82). Examining these connections in order to explore what M. Jacqui Alexander (1997) describes as *erotic autonomy* may provide space to think and do something new.

Alexander suggests that women's sexual agency or erotic autonomy has been threatening to a series of social institutions. In particular, the prostitute and the lesbian have historically functioned as the major symbols of threat. Both sets of women reject the heterosexual nuclear family upon which so many social institutions rely for meaning. As a result, "the categories lesbian and prostitute now function together . . . as outlaw, operating outside the boundaries of law and, therefore, poised to be disciplined and punished within it" (Alexander 1997, 65). Alexander examines how this erotic autonomy becomes suppressed within the Bahamian state. Yet her arguments contain important insights for U.S. Black women where the need exists to develop an erotic autonomy that does three things.

First, it must help U.S. Black women reject the dual stigma applied to Black heterosexual women as "hoochies" and to Black lesbians as sexual deviants. Recognizing how heterosexual and lesbian sexualities are both stigmatized within an overarching heterosexism and how this dual stigmatization has long been important in shoring up intersecting oppressions should help identify practices within Black civil society that are harmful to Black women as a collectivity. Evelynn Hammonds suggests that within the historical legacy of silences concerning Black women's sexuality, certain expressions of Black female sexuality will be rendered as dangerous, for individuals and for the group. Within this logic, a culture of dissemblance that counsels a self-imposed silence concerning Black women's sexuality makes it acceptable for some heterosexual Black women to cast both openly sensual heterosexual Black women and Black lesbians as "traitors" to the race. This censure operates in much the same way as Anita Hill's testimony against Clarence Thomas did. The continuation of a culture of dissemblance explains why Black heterosexual women who take control of their sexuality in public are often censured. When they sing of Black women's sensuality and erotic desires in public, the Black blues women of the 1920s and hip-hop group Salt 'N' Pepa's music both become cast as inappropriate public expressions of Black female sexuality. This culture of dissemblance might also explain why Black lesbians, "whose 'deviant' sexuality is framed within an already existing deviant sexuality—have been wary of embracing the status of 'traitor,' and the potential loss of community such an embrace engenders" (Hammonds 1997, 181).

A second component of moving toward erotic autonomy involves redefining beauty in ways that include Black women. New understandings of beauty would necessarily alter the types of mirrors held up to Black women to judge Black women's beauty. Redefining beauty requires learning to see African-American women who have Black African features as being capable of beauty. Proclaiming Black women "beautiful" and White women "ugly" merely replaces one set of controlling images with another and fails to challenge Eurocentric masculinist aesthetics. This is simply binary thinking in reverse: In order for one individual to be judged beautiful, another individual—the Other—must be deemed ugly. Dessa Rose's view of Miz Ruint as having "doughy skin and slippery hair" illustrates one Black woman's attempt to protect herself from a derogated Blackness by reversing the categories of beauty. Creating an alternative Black feminist aesthetic involves, instead, rejecting binary thinking altogether.

In this endeavor, African-American women can draw on African-derived aesthetics (Gayle 1971; Walton 1971) that potentially free women from standards of ornamental beauty.[4] Though such aesthetics are present in music (Sidran 1971; Cone 1972), dance (Asante 1990), and language (Smitherman 1977; Kochman 1981), quilt making offers a suggestive model for a Black feminist aesthetic that might move Black women and others toward erotic autonomy. African-American women quilt makers do not seem interested in a uniform color scheme but use several methods of playing with colors to create unpredictability and movement (Wahlman and Scully 1983 in Brown 1989, 922). For example, a strong color may be juxtaposed with another strong color, or with a weak one. Contrast is used to structure or organize. Overall, the symmetry in

African-American quilts does not come from uniformity as it does in Euro-American quilts. Rather, symmetry comes through diversity. Nikki Giovanni points out that quilts are traditionally formed from scraps. "Quilters teach there is no such thing as waste," she observes, "only that for which we currently see no purpose" (1988, 89).

This dual emphasis on beauty occurring via individual uniqueness juxtaposed in a community setting and on the importance of creating functional beauty from the scraps of everyday life offers a powerful alternative to Eurocentric aesthetics. African-derived notions of diversity in community and functional beauty potentially heal many of the binaries that underlie Western social thought. From African-influenced perspectives, women's beauty is not based solely on physical criteria because mind, spirit, and body are not conceptualized as separate, oppositional spheres. Instead, all are central in aesthetic assessments of individuals and their creations. Beauty is functional in that it has no meaning independent of the group. Deviating from the group "norm" is not rewarded as "beauty." Instead, participating in the group and being a functioning individual who strives for harmony is key to assessing an individual's beauty (Asante 1987). Moreover, participation is not based on conformity but instead is seen as individual uniqueness that enhances the overall "beauty" of the group. With such criteria, no individual is inherently beautiful because beauty is not a state of being. Instead beauty is a state of becoming. Just as all African-American women as well as all humans become capable of beauty, all can move toward erotic autonomy.

A final component of developing African-American women's erotic autonomy requires finding ways to stress that African-American women learn to see expressing love for one another as fundamental to resisting oppression. This component politicizes love and reclaims it from the individualized and trivialized place that it now occupies. Self-defined and publicly expressed Black women's love relationships, whether such relationships find sexual expression or not, constitute resistance. If members of the group on the bottom love one another and affirm one another's worth, then the entire system that assigns that group to the bottom becomes suspect.

Many Black women understand the power that maternal love has had in empowering them as individuals. Yet this power of deep love remains circumscribed in biological motherhood, biological sisterhood, sorority ties, and other similar socially approved relationships. As the next two chapters explore, this legitimated maternal love has spurred many Black women into more activist arenas and can be seen as an important dimension of U.S. Black feminism. Broadening the spectrum of Black women's loving relationships with one another, including those that find sexual expression, may move Black womanhood closer to reclaiming the power of deep love.

Love and Empowerment

"In order to perpetuate itself, every oppression must corrupt or distort those various sources of power within the culture of the oppressed that can provide energy for change" (Lorde 1984, 53). The ability of social practices such as pornography, prostitution, and rape to distort the private domain of Black women's love relationships with Black men, with Whites, and with one another typifies this process. The parallels between distortions of deep human feelings in racial oppression and of the distortions of the erotic in sexual oppression are striking. Analysts of the interpersonal dynamics of racism point out that Whites fear in Blacks those qualities they project onto Blacks that they most fear in themselves. By labeling Blacks as sexually animalistic and by dominating Blacks, Whites aim to repress these dimensions of their own inner being. When men dominate women and accuse them of being sexually passive, the act of domination, from pressured sexual intercourse to rape, reduces male anxiety about male impotence, the ultimate sexual passivity (Hoch 1979). Similarly, the suppression of gays and lesbians symbolizes the repression of strong feelings for members of one's own gender, feelings U.S. culture has sexualized and stigmatized within heterosexism. All of these emotions—the fact that Whites know that Blacks are human, the fact that men love women, and the fact that women have deep feelings for one another—must be distorted on the emotional level of the erotic in order for oppressive systems to endure. Sexuality in the individual, interpersonal domain of power becomes annexed by intersecting oppressions in the structural domain of power in order to ensure the smooth operation of domination.

Recognizing that corrupting and distorting basic feelings human beings have for one another lies at the heart of multiple systems of oppression opens up new possibilities for transformation and change. June Jordan (1981) explores this connection between embracing feeling and human empowerment: "As I think about anyone or any thing—whether history or literature or my father or political organizations or a poem or a film—as I seek to evaluate the potentiality, the life-supportive commitment/possibilities of anyone or any thing, the decisive question is, always, *where is the love?*" (p. 141).

Jordan's question touches a deep nerve in African-American social and ethical thought. In her work *Black Womanist Ethics,* Katie G. Cannon (1988) suggests that love, community, and justice are deeply intertwined in African-American ethics. Cannon examines the work of two prominent Black male theorists—Howard Thurman and Martin Luther King, Jr.—and concludes that their ideas represent core values from which Black women draw strength. According to Thurman, love is the basis of community, and community is the arena for moral agency. Only love of self, love between individuals, and love of God can shape, empower, and sustain social change. Martin Luther King, Jr., gives greater significance in his ethics to the relationship of love and justice, suggesting that love is active, dynamic, and determined and generates the motive and drive for justice. For both Thurman and King, everything moves toward community and the expression of love within the context of community. It is this version of love and community, argues Cannon, that stimulates a distinctive Black womanist ethics.

For June Jordan love begins with self-love and self-respect, actions that propel African-American women toward the self-determination and political activism essential for social justice. By grappling with this simple yet profound question, "Where is the love?" Black women resist multiple types of oppression. This question encourages all groups embedded in systems of domination to move toward a place where, as Toni Morrison's Paul D expresses it, "You could love anything you chose—not to need permission for desire—well, now, *that* was freedom" (1987, 162).

8 BLACK WOMEN AND MOTHERHOOD

Just yesterday I stood for a few minutes at the top of the stairs leading to a white doctor's office in a white neighborhood. I watched one Black woman after another trudge to the corner, where she then waited to catch the bus home. These were Black women still cleaning somebody else's house or Black women still caring for somebody else's sick or elderly, before they came back to the frequently thankless chores of their own loneliness, their own families. And I felt angry and I felt ashamed. And I felt, once again, the kindling heat of my hope that we, the daughters of these Black women, will honor their sacrifice by giving them thanks. We will undertake, with pride, every transcendent dream of freedom made possible by the humility of their love.   —June Jordan 1985, 105

June Jordan's words poignantly express the need for African-American women to honor our mothers' sacrifices by developing self-defined analyses of Black motherhood. Until the growth of modern Black feminism in the 1970s, analyses of Black motherhood were largely the province of men, both White and Black, and male perspectives on Black mothers prevailed. Black mothers were accused of failing to discipline their children, of emasculating their sons, of defeminizing their daughters, and of retarding their children's academic achievement (Moynihan 1965). Citing high rates of divorce, female-headed households, and out-of-wedlock births, prevailing scholarship claimed that African-American mothers wielded unnatural power in allegedly deteriorating family structures (Zinn 1989; Dickerson 1995b). The African-American mothers observed by Jordan vanished from these accounts.

Feminist work on motherhood from the 1970s and 1980s produced a limited critique of these views. Reflecting White, middle-class women's angles of vision, feminist analyses typically lacked an adequate race and class analysis

(Collins 1994). Dedicated to demystifying the traditional family ideal, much work from this period confronted prevailing analyses of White, middle-class women's experiences as mothers. Such critiques remained less successful at challenging the controlling images let alone the practices they defended aimed at African-American women. Recognizing that much feminist scholarship from this period failed to include Black mothers "still cleaning somebody else's house or . . . caring for somebody else's sick or elderly," subsequent feminist scholarship by U.S. White women explicitly aimed to address differences among women based on race, class, sexuality, and citizenship status (Andersen 1991; Coontz 1992; Thorne 1992).

Ideas about Black motherhood emanating from African-American communities have been quite different. Historically, the concept of motherhood has been of central importance in the philosophies of people of African descent. In many African-American communities so much sanctification surrounds Black motherhood that "the idea that mothers should live lives of sacrifice has come to be seen as the norm" (Christian 1985, 234). In the context of this historical significance, many African-American thinkers tend to glorify Black motherhood. They refuse to acknowledge the issues faced by Black mothers who "came back to the frequently thankless chores of their own loneliness, their own families." This mother glorification is especially prominent in the works of U.S. Black men who routinely praise Black mothers, especially their own. However, by claiming that Black women are richly endowed with devotion, self-sacrifice, and unconditional love—the attributes associated with archetypal motherhood—U.S. Black men inadvertently foster a different albeit seemingly positive image for Black women. The controlling image of the "superstrong Black mother" praises Black women's resiliency in a society that routinely paints us as bad mothers. Yet, in order to remain on their pedestal, these same superstrong Black mothers must continue to place their needs behind those of everyone else, especially their sons. Even Black-nationalist-inspired critical social theory finds it difficult to move beyond images of strong Black mothers working on behalf of the new Black nation. Within Afrocentrism, for example, images persist of "authentic" Black women who hold fast to traditional African-derived values in the context of U.S. racism (Collins 1998a, 167–74).

Stepping out of the realm of Black discourse reveals that far too many Black men who praise their own mothers feel less accountable to the mothers of their daughters and sons. They allow their wives and girlfriends to support the growing numbers of African-American children living in poverty (Nightingale 1993, 16–22). Despite the alarming deterioration of economic and social supports for U.S. Black mothers, large numbers of young men hold fast to myths of Black male hypersexuality and encourage their unmarried teenage girlfriends to give birth to children whose futures are at risk (Ladner 1972; Ladner and Gourdine 1984). Even when they are aware of the poverty and struggles these women face, many Black men cannot get beyond powerful controlling images of matriarchs and superstrong Black mothers. As Michele Wallace points out, many African-American men fail to see the very real costs of mothering to African-American women:

> I remember once I was watching a news show with a black male friend of mine who had a Ph.D. in psychology and was the director of an out-patient clinic. We were looking at some footage of a black woman. . . . She was in bed wrapped in blankets, her numerous small, poorly clothed children huddled around her. Her apartment looked rat-infested, cramped, and dirty. She had not, she said, had heat and hot water for days. My friend, a solid member of the middle class now but surely no stranger to poverty in his childhood, felt obliged to comment . . . "That's a *strong* sister," as he bowed his head in reverence. (1978, 108–109)

In this overall context, the patterns of emphasis and omission characterizing Black feminist analyses of motherhood are not particularly surprising. Several factors within Black civil society contribute to these patterns. One reflects the self-imposed restrictions that accompany norms of racial solidarity. In a context of institutionalized racism where African-Americans have long aimed to present a united front to Whites, many U.S. Blacks learn to police one another (Lubiano 1997). Internal dissent is especially frowned upon when it comes to motherhood, the seeming core of family, culture, and community. Another factor concerns African-American women's reluctance to challenge African-American men *in public*. The vehement attacks sustained by Michele Wallace, Alice Walker, Ntozake Shange, and other Black feminist scholars accused of attacking Black men served as a lesson to others that speaking out can bring painful censure (see, for example, Staples 1979). As Anita Hill found out, whether true or not, criticisms aimed at a Black man in public are frowned upon by many African-Americans. For many U.S. Black women, much silence emanates from efforts to support Black men's well-intentioned efforts to defend and protect Black womanhood. Glorifying the strong Black mother represents Black men's attempts to replace negative White male interpretations with positive Black male ones.

Another set of factors influencing Black women's relative silences concerns the perceived Whiteness of U.S. feminism. Unfortunately, while feminism remains one of the few discourses advancing important analyses of motherhood, the combination of its perceived Whiteness and antifamily politics limits its effectiveness. In the context of a racially segregated society where White women historically and currently benefit from Black women's subordination, African-American women who remain suspicious of feminism are being neither unreasonable nor demonstrating a lack of feminist consciousness. Moreover, when combined with the perception of feminism as being antifamily and, by implication, antimotherhood, U.S. Black women's collective reluctance to advance critical analyses of Black motherhood becomes even more understandable.

No matter how sincere, externally defined definitions of Black womanhood—even those offered by sympathetic African-American men or well-meaning White feminists—are bound to come with their own set of problems. In the case of Black motherhood, the problems have been a stifling of dialogue among African-American women and the perpetuation of troublesome, controlling images, both negative and positive. As Renita Weems observes: "We have simply sat and nodded while others talked about the magnificent women who bore and raised them and who, along with God, made a way out of no way. . . . We paid to hear them lecture about the invincible strength and genius of the Black mother, knowing full well that the image can be as bogus as the one of the happy slave" (1984, 27). In general, African-American women need a revitalized Black feminist analysis of motherhood that debunks the image of "happy slave," whether the White-male-created "matriarch" or the Black-male-perpetuated "superstrong Black mother."

A Black Women's Standpoint on Mothering

The institution of Black motherhood consists of a series of constantly renegotiated relationships that African-American women experience with one another, with Black children, with the larger African-American community, and with self. These relationships occur in specific locations such as the individual households that make up African-American extended family networks, as well as in Black community institutions (Martin and Martin 1978; Sudarkasa 1981b). Moreover, just as U.S. Black women's work and family experiences varied during the transition from slavery to the post–World War II political economy, how Black women define, value, and shape Black motherhood as an institution shows comparable diversity.

Black motherhood as an institution is both dynamic and dialectical. Ongoing tensions characterize efforts to mold the institution of Black motherhood to benefit intersecting oppressions of race, gender, class, sexuality, and nation and efforts by African-American women to define and value our own experiences with motherhood. The controlling images of the mammy, the matriarch, and the welfare mother and the practices they justify are designed to oppress. In the context of a sexual politics that aims to control Black women's sexuality and fertility, African-American women struggle to be good mothers. In contrast, motherhood can serve as a site where Black women express and learn the power of self-definition, the importance of valuing and respecting ourselves, the necessity of self-reliance and independence, and a belief in Black women's empowerment. These tensions foster a continuum of responses. Some women view motherhood as a truly burdensome condition that stifles their creativity, exploits their labor, and makes them partners in their own oppression. Others see motherhood as providing a base for self-actualization, status in the Black community, and a catalyst for social activism. These alleged contradictions can exist side by side in African-

American communities and families and even within individual women.

Embedded in these changing relationships are five enduring themes that have characterized and, for many African-American women, continue to characterize a Black women's standpoint on Black motherhood. For any given historical moment, the particular form that Black women's relationships with one another, children, community, and self actually take depends on how this dialectical relationship between the severity of oppression facing African-American women and our actions in resisting that oppression is expressed. Despite the shared thematic content of this Black women's standpoint, considerable heterogeneity concerning its expression has always existed. It is in many ways easier to see the contours of a Black women's standpoint on motherhood in the pre–World War II era. The five enduring themes described below emerged in the context of and were sustained by specific social conditions associated with slavery, Southern rural life, and class-stratified, racially segregated neighborhoods of earlier periods of urban Black migration. These conditions fostered the appearance of a distinctive Black women's standpoint on mothering and gave clear reasons for its continuation. In contrast, because African-American family organization and Black civil society have both been markedly reorganized since World War II, one must question in what form and even whether these themes endure.

Rather than viewing the themes as "normative" and then evaluating how contemporary African-American women do not measure up to some sort of "essentialist" Black women's standpoint, a better use of these themes views them as culturally specific, resilient lifelines that can be continually refashioned in response to changing contexts. Just as culture itself is dynamic and changing, the enduring themes characterizing a Black women's standpoint become shaped in dialogue with actual social practices. Stated differently, these themes encompass a complex network of ideas *and* social practices engaged in dialogue with one another. Within this context, U.S. Black women's agency becomes important in determining what a Black women's standpoint on motherhood will be, which themes characterizing this standpoint will endure, and whether new, culturally specific, resilient lifelines must be created to ensure collective survival. In some cases, a lifeline may form the foundation for new ways of dealing with social problems of special concern to African-Americans. U.S. Black working mothers' needs for child care, the chronically poor education offered to Black children in underfunded, inner-city public schools, the disproportionate numbers of young Black men who have arrest records or are incarcerated, and the large numbers of African-American children currently in government-run foster care all constitute new versions of some old problems of special concern to African-American women. One might ask in what ways the enduring themes may be reconstructed to respond to these types of social concerns. Alternately, some themes may prove more beneficial in grappling with these issues, and other themes may have outlived their usefulness. Viewing the enduring themes in this fashion tests them against the challenges of actual social conditions. Moreover, because this approach remains grounded in Black women's agency, it emphasizes the significance of Black women's ideas and actions in using this standpoint to meet the specific political, economic, and social challenges of today.

Bloodmothers, Othermothers, and Women-Centered Networks

In many African-American communities, fluid and changing boundaries often distinguish biological mothers from other women who care for children. Biological mothers, or bloodmothers, are expected to care for their children. But African and African-American communities have also recognized that vesting one person with full responsibility for mothering a child may not be wise or possible. As a result, othermothers—women who assist bloodmothers by sharing mothering responsibilities—traditionally have been central to the institution of Black motherhood (Troester 1984).

The centrality of women in African-American extended families reflects both a continuation of African-derived cultural sensibilities and functional adaptations to intersecting oppressions of race, gender, class, and nation (Tanner 1974; Stack 1974; Martin and Martin 1978; Sudarkasa 1981b; Reagon 1987). Women's centrality is characterized less by the *absence* of husbands and fathers than by the significance of women. Though men may be physically present or have well-defined and culturally significant roles in the extended family, the kin unit tends to be woman-centered. Bebe Moore Campbell's (1989) parents separated when she was small. Even though she spent the school year in the North Philadelphia household maintained by her grandmother and mother, Campbell's father assumed an important role in her life. "My father took care of me," Campbell remembers. "Our separation didn't stunt me or condemn me to a lesser humanity. His absence never made me a fatherless child. I'm not fatherless now" (p. 271). In woman-centered kin units such as Campbell's—whether a mother-child household unit, a married couple household, or a larger unit extending over several households—the centrality of mothers is not predicated on male powerlessness (Tanner 1974, 133).

Organized, resilient, women-centered networks of bloodmothers and othermothers are key in understanding this centrality. Grandmothers, sisters, aunts, or cousins act as othermothers by taking on child-care responsibilities for one another's children. Historically, when needed, temporary child-care arrangements often turned into long-term care or informal adoption (Stack 1974; Gutman 1976). These practices continue in the face of changing social pressures. Andrea Hunter's (1997) research on Black grandmothers explores how Black parents rely on grandmothers for parenting support. This traditional source of support became even more needed in the 1980s and 1990s, when increasing numbers of Black mothers saw their teenage children fall victim to drugs and the crime associated with it. Many witnessed their sons killed or incarcerated, while their daughters became addicts. In many cases, these young men and women left behind children, who often ended up in foster care. Other children did not, primarily because their grandmothers took responsibility for raising them, often under less than optimal conditions.

In many African-American communities these women-centered networks of community-based child care have extended beyond the boundaries of biologically related individuals to include "fictive kin" (Stack 1974). Civil rights activist Ella Baker describes how informal adoption by othermothers functioned in the rural Southern community of her childhood:

> My aunt who had thirteen children of her own raised three more. She had become a midwife, and a child was born who was covered with sores. Nobody was particularly wanting the child, so she took the child and raised him . . . and another mother decided she didn't want to be bothered with two children. So my aunt took one and raised him . . . they were part of the family. (Cantarow 1980, 59)

Stanlie James recounts how othermother traditions work with notions of fictive kin within her own extended family. James notes that the death of her grandmother in 1988 reunited her family, described as a host of biological and fictive kin. James's rendition of how one female family member helped James's nine-year-old daughter deal with the loss of her great-grandmother illustrates the interactions among women-centered extended kin networks, fictive kin, and othermother traditions. The woman who helped James's daughter was not a blood relative but had been "othermothered" by James's grandmother and was a full member of the extended family. James's grandmother believed that because all children must be fed, clothed, and educated, if their biological parents could not discharge these obligations, then some other member of the community should accept that responsibility. As James points out, "This fictive kin who stepped in to counsel my daughter was upholding a family tradition that had been modeled by my grandmother some fifty years before" (James 1993, 44).

Even when relationships are not between kin or fictive kin, African-American community norms traditionally were such that neighbors cared for one another's children. Sara Brooks, a Southern domestic worker, describes the importance that the community-based child care a neighbor offered her daughter had for her: "She kept Vivian and she didn't charge me nothin either. You see, people used to look after each other, but now its not that way. I reckon its because we all was poor, and I guess they put theirself in the place of the person that they was helpin' " (Simonsen 1986, 181). Brooks's experiences demonstrate how the African-American cultural value placed on cooperative child care traditionally found institutional support in the adverse conditions under which so many Black women mothered.

Othermothers can be key not only in supporting children but also in helping bloodmothers who, for whatever reason, lack the preparation or desire for motherhood. In confronting racial oppression, maintaining community-based child care and respecting othermothers who assume child-care responsibilities can serve a critical function in African-American communities. Children orphaned by sale or death of their parents under slavery, children conceived through rape, children of young mothers, children born into extreme poverty or to alcoholic or drug-addicted mothers, or children who for other reasons cannot remain with their bloodmothers have all been supported by othermothers, who, like Ella Baker's aunt, take in additional children even when they have enough of their own.

Young women are often carefully groomed at an early age to become othermothers. As a 10-year-old, Ella Baker learned to be an othermother by caring for the children of a widowed neighbor: "Mama would say, 'You must take the clothes to Mr. Powell's house, and give so-and-so a bath.' The children were running wild. . . . The kids . . . would take off across the field. We'd chase them down, and bring them back, and put 'em in the tub, and wash 'em off, and change clothes, and carry the dirty ones home, and wash them. Those kind of things were routine" (Cantarow 1980, 59).

Many Black men also value community-based child care but historically have exercised these values to a lesser extent. During slavery, for example, Black children under age 10 experienced little division of labor. They were dressed alike and performed similar tasks. If the activities of work and play are any indication of the degree of gender role differentiation that existed among slave children, "then young girls probably grew up minimizing the difference between the sexes while learning far more about the differences between the races" (D. White 1985, 94). Because they are often left in charge of younger siblings, many young Black men learn how to care for children. Geoffrey Canada (1995) recounts how he had to learn how to fight in his urban neighborhood. The climate of violence that he and his two brothers encountered mandated developing caretaking skills, especially since his single mother had to work and could not offer them the protection that they needed. Thus, differences among Black men and women in behaviors concerning children may have more to do with male labor force patterns and similar factors. As Ella Baker observes, "My father took care of people too, but . . . my father had to work" (Cantarow 1980, 60).

Historically, within Black diasporic societies, community-based child care and the relationships among bloodmothers and othermothers in women-centered networks have taken diverse institutional forms. In some polygynous West African societies, the children of the same father but different mothers referred to one another as brothers and sisters. While a strong bond existed between the biological mother and her child—one so strong that, among the Ashanti for example, "to show disrespect towards one's mother is tantamount to sacrilege" (Fortes 1950, 263)—children could be disciplined by any of their "mothers."

Cross-culturally, the high status given to othermothers and the cooperative nature of child-care arrangements among bloodmothers and othermothers in Caribbean and other Black diasporic societies gives credence to the importance that people of African descent place on mothering (Sudarkasa 1981a).

Although the political economy of slavery brought profound changes to Africans enslaved in the United States, beliefs in the importance of motherhood and the value of cooperative approaches to child care continued. During slavery, while older women served as nurses and midwives, their most common occupation was caring for the children of parents who worked (D. White 1985). Informal adoption of orphaned children reinforced the importance of social motherhood in African-American communities (Gutman 1976). The relationship between bloodmothers and othermothers also survived the transition from a slave economy to post-emancipation Southern rural agriculture. Children in Southern rural communities were not solely the responsibility of their biological mothers. Aunts, grandmothers, and others who had time to supervise children served as othermothers (Dougherty 1978). The significant status that women enjoyed in family networks and in African-American communities continued to be linked to their bloodmother and othermother activities.

In the 1980s, the entire community structure of bloodmothers and othermothers came under assault. Racial desegregation as well as the emergence of class-stratified Black neighborhoods greatly altered the fabric of Black civil society. African-Americans of diverse social classes found themselves in new residential, school, and work settings that tested this enduring theme of bloodmothers, othermothers, and woman-centered networks. In many inner-city, working-class neighborhoods, the very fabric of African-American community life eroded when crack cocaine flooded the streets. African-American children and youth often formed the casualties of this expanding market for drugs, from the increasing numbers of Black children in foster care (Nightingale 1993), to children threatened by violence (Canada 1995), to those killed. Residents of Central Harlem interviewed by anthropologist Leith Mullings repeatedly expressed concern about losing the community's children, leading Mullings to observe, "The depth of worry about children growing up in these conditions is difficult to convey" (Mullings 1997, 93). Given this situation, it is remarkable that even in the most troubled communities, remnants of the othermother tradition endure. Bebe Moore Campbell's 1950s North Philadelphia neighborhood underwent startling changes in the 1980s. Increases in child abuse and parental neglect left many children without care. But some residents, such as Miss Nee, continued the othermother tradition. After raising her younger brothers and sisters and five children of her own, Miss Nee cared for three additional children whose families fell apart. Moreover, on any given night Miss Nee's house may have been filled by up to a dozen children because she had a reputation for never turning away a needy child ("Children of the Underclass" 1989).

Black middle-class women and their families found challenges from another direction. In some fundamental ways, moving into the middle class means adopting the values and lifestyles of White middle-class families. While the traditional family ideal is not the norm, the relative isolation of such families from others is noteworthy. U.S. middle-class family life is based on privatization—buying a big house so that one need not cooperate with one's neighbors, or even see them. American middle-class families participate in the privatization of everything, from schools and health care, to for-fee health clubs and private automobiles. Working-class African-Americans who experience social mobility thus may encounter a distinctly different value system. Not only are woman-centered networks of bloodmothers and othermothers much more difficult to sustain structurally—class-stratified residential and employment patterns mean that middle-class Black women often see working-class and poor Black women only as their employees or clients—such ideas are often anathema to the ethos of achievement. From the security firms that find ways to monitor nannies, to the gated-communities of suburbia, purchasing services appears to be the hallmark of American middle-class existence. In this context, stopping to help others to whom one is not related and doing it for free can be seen as rejecting the basic values of the capitalist market economy.

In this context, these relationships among bloodmothers and othermothers and the persistence of woman-centered networks may have greater theoretical importance than currently recognized. The traditional family ideal assigns mothers full responsibility for children and evaluates their performance based on their ability to procure the benefits of a nuclear family household. Within this capitalist marketplace model, those women who "catch" legal husbands, who live in single-family homes, who can afford private school and music lessons for their children, are deemed better mothers than those who do not. In this context, those African-American women who continue community-based child care challenge one fundamental assumption underlying the capitalist system itself: that children are "private property" and can be disposed of as such. Under the property model that accompanies the traditional family ideal, parents may not literally assert that their children are pieces of property, but their parenting may reflect assumptions analogous to those they make in connection with property. For example, the exclusive parental "right" to discipline children as parents see fit, even if discipline borders on abuse, parallels the widespread assumption that property owners may dispose of their property without consulting members of the larger community.

By seeing the larger *community* as responsible for children and by giving othermothers and other nonparents "rights" in child rearing, those African-Americans who endorse these values challenge prevailing capitalist property relations. In Harlem, for example, Black women are increasingly the breadwinners in their families, and rates of households maintained by single mothers remain high. These families are clearly under stress, yet to see the household formation itself as an indication of decline in Black family organization misreads a more complex situation. Leith Mullings suggests that many of these households participate in fluid, familylike networks that have different purposes. Women activate some networks for socialization, reproduction, and consumption, and others for emotional support, economic cooperation, and sexuality. The networks may overlap, but they are not coterminous (Mullings 1997, 74).

The resiliency of women-centered family networks and their willingness to take responsibility for Black children illustrates how African-influenced understandings of family have been continually reworked to help African-Americans as a collectivity cope with and resist oppression. Moreover, these understandings of woman-centered kin networks become critical in understanding broader African-American understandings of community. At the same time, the erosion of such networks in the face of the changing institutional fabric of Black civil society points to the need either to refashion these networks or develop some other way of supporting Black children. For far too many African-American children, assuming that a grandmother or "fictive kin" will care for them is no longer a reality.

Mothers, Daughters, and Socialization for Survival

U.S. Black mothers of daughters face a troubling dilemma. On one hand, to ensure their daughters' physical survival, mothers must teach them to fit into the sexual politics of Black womanhood. For example, as a young girl, Black activist Ann Moody questioned why she was paid so little for the domestic work she began at age nine, why Black women domestics were sexually harassed by their White male employers, and why Whites had so much more than Blacks. But her mother refused to answer her questions and actually chastised her for questioning the system and stepping out of her "place" (Moody 1968). Like Ann Moody, Black daughters learn to expect to work, to strive for an education so they can support themselves, and to anticipate carrying heavy responsibilities in their families and communities because these skills are essential to their own survival and those for whom they will eventually be responsible (Ladner 1972; Joseph 1981). New Yorker Michele Wallace recounts: "I can't remember when I first learned that my family expected me to work, to be able to take care of myself when I grew up. . . . It had been drilled into me that the best and only sure support was self-support" (1978, 89–90). Mothers also know that if their daughters uncritically accept the glorified "mammy work" and sexual politics offered Black women, they can become willing participants in their own subordination. Mothers may have ensured their daughters' physical survival, but at the high cost of their emotional destruction.

On the other hand, Black daughters with strong self-definitions and self-valuations who offer serious challenges to oppressive situations may not physically survive. When Ann Moody became active in the early 1960s in sit-ins and voter registration activities, her mother first begged her not to participate and then told her not to come home because she feared the Whites in Moody's hometown would kill her. Despite the dangers, mothers routinely encourage Black daughters to develop skills to confront oppressive conditions. Learning that they will work and that education is a vehicle for advancement can also be seen as ways of enhancing positive self-definitions and self-valuations in Black girls. Emotional strength is essential, but not at the cost of physical survival.

Historian Elsa Barkley Brown describes this delicate balance Black mothers negotiate by pointing out that her mother's behavior demonstrated the "need to teach me to live my life one way and, at the same time, to provide all the tools I would need to live it quite differently" (1989, 929). Black daughters must learn how to survive the sexual politics of intersecting oppressions while rejecting and transcending these same power relations. In order to develop these skills in their daughters, mothers demonstrate varying combinations of behaviors devoted to ensuring their daughters' survival—such as providing them with basic necessities and protecting them in dangerous environments—to helping their daughters go further than mothers themselves were allowed to go (Joseph 1981, 1984). They remain simultaneously visionary about what is possible, yet pragmatic about what it might take to get there (James and Busia 1993).

This visionary pragmatism of many U.S. Black mothers may grow from the nature of work women have done to ensure Black children's survival. Their work experiences provide many Black women with a unique angle of vision, a particular perspective on the world to be passed on to their daughters. As is the case for women in Black diaspora societies, African-American women have long integrated economic self-reliance and mothering. In contrast to the cult of true womanhood associated with the traditional family ideal, in which paid work is defined as being in opposition to and incompatible with motherhood, work for Black women has been an important and valued dimension of motherhood. Sara Brooks describes the powerful connections that economic self-reliance and mothering had in her childhood: "When I was about nine I was nursin my sister Sally—I'm about seven or eight years older than Sally. And when I would put her to sleep, instead of me goin somewhere and sit down and play, I'd get my little old hoe and get out there and work right in the field around the house" (in Simonsen 1986, 86).

Mothers who are domestic workers or who work in proximity to Whites may experience a unique relationship with the dominant group. For example, African-American women domestics are exposed to all the intimate details of the lives of their White employers. Working for Whites offers domestic workers a view from the inside and exposes them to ideas and resources that might aid in their children's upward mobility. In some cases domestic workers form close, long-lasting relationships with their employers. But domestic workers also encounter some of the harshest exploitation confronting U.S. racial/ethnic women. The work is low paid, has few benefits, and exposes women to the threat and reality of sexual harassment. Black domestics could see the dangers awaiting their daughters.

Willi Coleman's mother used a Saturday-night hair-combing ritual to impart her views on domestic work to her daughters:

> Except for special occasions mama came home from work early on Saturdays. She spent six days a week mopping, waxing and dusting other women's houses and keeping out of reach of other women's husbands. Saturday nights were reserved for "taking care of them girls" hair and the telling of stories. Some of which included a recitation of what she had endured and how she had triumphed over "folks that were lower than dirt" and "no-good snakes in the grass." She combed, patted, twisted and talked, saying things which would have embarrassed or shamed her at other times. (Coleman 1987, 34)

Bonnie Thornton Dill's (1980) study of the child-rearing goals of domestic workers illustrates how many African-American women see their work as both contributing to their children's survival and instilling values that will encourage their children to reject their "place" and strive for more. Providing a better chance for their children was a dominant theme among Black women. Domestic workers described themselves as "struggling to give their children the skills and training they did not have; and as praying that opportunities which had not been open to them would be open to their children" (p. 110). But the women also realized that although they wanted to communicate the value of their work as part of the ethics of caring and personal accountability, the work itself was undesirable. Bebe Moore Campbell's (1989) grandmother and college-educated mother stressed the importance of education. Campbell remembers, "[They] wanted me to Be Somebody, to be the second generation to live out my life as far away from a mop and scrub brush and Miss Ann's floors as possible" (p. 83).

Understanding this goal of balancing the need for the physical survival of their daughters with the vision of encouraging them to transcend the boundaries of the sexual politics of Black womanhood explains many apparent contradictions in Black mother-daughter relationships. U.S. Black mothers are often described as strong disciplinarians and overly protective; yet these same women manage to raise daughters who are self-reliant and assertive. To explain this apparent contradiction, Gloria Wade-Gayles suggests that Black mothers

> do not socialize their daughters to be "passive" or "irrational." Quite the contrary, they socialize their daughters to be independent, strong and self-confident. Black mothers are suffocatingly protective and domineering precisely because they are determined to mold their daughters into whole and self-actualizing persons in a society that devalues Black women. (1984, 12)

African-American mothers place a strong emphasis on protection, either by trying to shield their daughters as long as possible from the penalties attached to their derogated status or by teaching them skills of independence and self-reliance so that they will be able to protect themselves. Consider the following verse from a traditional blues song:

> I ain't good lookin' and ain't got waist-long hair
> I say I ain't good lookin' and ain't got waist-long hair
> But my mama gave me something that'll take me anywhere.
> (Washington 1984, 144)

Unlike White women, symbolized by "good looks" and "waist-long hair," Black women have been denied male protection. Under such conditions Black mothers aim to teach their daughters skills that will "take them anywhere."

Black women's autobiographies and fiction can be read as texts revealing the multiple ways that African-American mothers aim to shield their daughters from the demands of being Black women in U.S. sexual politics. Michele Wallace describes her growing understanding of how her mother viewed raising Black daughters in Harlem: "My mother has since explained to me that since it was obvious her attempt to protect me was going to prove a failure, she was determined to make me realize that as a black girl in white America I was going to find it an uphill climb to keep myself together" (1978, 98). In discussing the mother-daughter relationship in Paule Marshall's *Brown Girl, Brownstones,* Rosalie Troester catalogs the ways mothers have aimed to protect their daughters and the impact this may have on relationships themselves:

> Black mothers, particularly those with strong ties to their community, sometimes build high banks around their young daughters, isolating them from the dangers of the larger world until they are old and strong enough to function as autonomous women. Often these dikes are religious, but sometimes they are built with education, family, or the restrictions of a close-knit and homogeneous community. . . . This isolation causes the currents between Black mothers and daughters to run deep and the relationship to be fraught with an emotional intensity often missing from the lives of women with more freedom. (1984, 13)

Michele Wallace's mother built banks around her headstrong adolescent daughter by institutionalizing her in a Catholic home for troubled girls. Wallace went willingly: "I thought at the time that I would rather live in hell than be with my mother" (1978, 98). But years later Wallace's evaluation of her mother's decision changed: "Now that I know my mother better, I know that her sense of powerlessness made it all the more essential to her that she take radical action" (p. 98).

African-American mothers often try to protect their daughters from the dangers that lie ahead by offering them a sense of their own unique self-worth. Many contemporary Black women writers report the experience of being singled out, of being given at an early age a sense of specialness that encouraged them to develop their talents. My own mother marched me to the public library at age five, helped me get my first library card, and told me that I could do anything if I learned how to read. In discussing the works of Paule Marshall, Dorothy West, and Alice Walker, Mary Helen Washington observes that all three writers make special claims about the roles their mothers played in the development of their creativity: "The bond with their mothers is such a fundamental and powerful source that the term 'mothering the mind' might have been coined specifically to define their experiences as writers" (1984, 144).

Black women's efforts to provide a physical and psychic base for their children can affect mothering styles and the emotional intensity of Black mother-daughter relationships. As Gloria Wade-Gayles points out, "Mothers in Black women's fiction are strong and devoted . . . they are rarely affectionate" (1984, 10). For example, in Toni Morrison's *Sula* (1974), Eva Peace's husband ran off, leaving her with three small children and no money. Despite her feelings, "the demands of feeding her three children were so acute she had to postpone her anger for two years until she had both the time and energy for it" (p. 32). Later in the novel, Eva's daughter Hannah asks, "Mamma, did you ever love us?" (p. 67). Eva angrily replies, "What you talkin' bout did I love you girl I stayed alive for you" (p. 69). For far too many Black mothers, the demands of providing for children in intersecting oppressions are sometimes so demanding that they have neither the time nor the patience for affection. And yet most Black daughters love and admire their mothers and are convinced that their mothers truly love them (Joseph 1981).

Elaine Bell Kaplan's (1997) study of Black teenage pregnancy reveals much about the mothering styles and emotional intensity of Black mother-daughter relationships. Kaplan points out that the sociological literature makes two assumptions about Black teenage mothers and their mothers: first, that adult Black women are supportive of their daughter's pregnancies and encourage them to keep and raise the babies; and second, that this attitude is linked to the existence of an extended kin network. Kaplan's research refutes both assumptions. Teen mothers often defied their mothers' demands that they have abortions, and conflicts between the teen mothers and their mothers grew more intense after the birth of the babies. Many of the teen mothers said that their mothers "were tremendously angry at them and never forgave them" (Kaplan 1997, 52). The majority of the teen mothers in Kaplan's study who had left or were leaving their mothers' homes did so because of continual fights over their pregnancies. All of the adult mothers worked hard to support them, and were deeply disappointed with their daughters, but for different reasons. Lower-income mothers felt their pregnant daughters had failed them. Until the pregnancy, this group had hoped their daughters would do better with their lives than they had. Middle-income mothers felt cheated. They had worked hard, and their daughters had thrown it all away.

Black daughters raised by mothers grappling with hostile environments have to come to terms with their feelings about the difference between the idealized versions of maternal love extant in popular culture, whether the stay-at-home Mom of the traditional family ideas or the superstrong Black mother, and the often troubled mothers in their lives. For a daughter, growing up means developing a better understanding that even though she may desire more affection and greater freedom, her mother's physical care and protection are acts of maternal love. Ann Moody describes her growing awareness of the cost her mother paid as a domestic worker who was a single mother of three. Watching her mother sleep after the birth of another child, Moody remembers:

> For a long time I stood there looking at her. I didn't want to wake her up. I wanted to enjoy and preserve that calm, peaceful look on her face, I wanted to think she would always be that happy. . . . Adline and Junior were too young to feel the things I felt and know the things I knew about Mama. They couldn't remember when she and Daddy separated. They had never heard her cry at night as I had or worked and helped as I had done when we were starving. (1968, 57)

Moody initially sees her mother as a strict disciplinarian, a woman who tries to protect her daughter by withholding information. But as Moody matures and better understands the domains of power in her community, her ideas change. On one occasion Moody left school early the day after a Black family had been brutally murdered by local Whites. Moody's description of her mother's reaction reflects her deepening understanding: "When I walked in the house Mama didn't even ask me why I came home. She just looked at me. And for the first time I realized she understood what was going on within me or was trying to anyway" (1968, 136).

Another example of a daughter's efforts to understand her mother is offered in Renita Weems's account of coming to grips with maternal desertion. In the following passage Weems struggles with the difference between the stereotypical image of the superstrong Black mother and her own alcoholic mother's decision to leave her children: "My mother loved us. I must believe that. She worked all day in a department store bakery to buy shoes and school tablets, came home to curse out neighbors who wrongly accused her children of any impropriety (which in an apartment complex usually meant stealing), and kept her house cleaner than most sober women" (1984, 26). Weems concludes that her mother loved her because she provided for her to the best of her ability.

Othermothers often help to defuse the emotional intensity of relationships between bloodmothers and their daughters. In recounting how she dealt with the intensity of her relationship with her mother, Weems describes the women teachers, neighbors, friends, and othermothers she turned to—women who, she observes, "did not have the onus of providing for me, and so had the luxury of talking to me" (1984, 27). Cheryl West's household included her brother, her lesbian mother, and Jan, her mother's lover. Jan became an othermother to West: "Yellow-colored, rotund and short in stature, Jan was like a second mother. . . .

Jan braided my hair in the morning, mother worked two jobs and tucked me in at night. Loving, gentle, and fastidious in the domestic arena, Jan could be a rigid disciplinarian. . . . To the outside world . . . she was my 'aunt' who happened to live with us. But she was much more involved and nurturing than any of my 'real' aunts" (1987, 43). This may be changing. The pregnant teenagers in Elaine Bell Kaplan's study had few women teachers, neighbors, or Jans in their lives. They felt the full force of the erosion of woman-centered kin networks. Perceiving their bloodmothers as unsupportive during a crucial time in their lives, only four of the thirty-two teen mothers in Kaplan's study said they could rely on other family members for support. Instead, more than three-quarters said they counted on friends (Kaplan 1997, 59).

June Jordan offers an eloquent analysis of one daughter's realization of the high personal cost African-American women can pay in providing for their children. In the following passage Jordan offers a powerful testament of how she came to see that her mother's work was an act of love:

> As a child I noticed the sadness of my mother as she sat alone in the kitchen at night. . . . Her woman's work never won permanent victories of any kind. It never enlarged the universe of her imagination or her power to influence what happened beyond the front door of our house. Her woman's work never tickled her to laugh or shout or dance. But she did raise me to respect her way of offering love and to believe that hard work is often the irreducible factor for survival, not something to avoid. Her woman's work produced a reliable home base where I could pursue the privileges of books and music. Her woman's work invented the potential for a completely different kind of work for us, the next generation of Black women: huge, rewarding hard work demanded by the huge, new ambitions that her perfect confidence in us engendered. (1985, 105)

Community Othermothers and Political Activism

U.S. Black women's experiences as othermothers provide a foundation for conceptualizing Black women's political activism. Experiences both of being nurtured as children and being held responsible for siblings and fictive kin within kin networks can stimulate a more generalized ethic of caring and personal accountability among African-American women. These women not only feel accountable to their own kin, they experience a bond with all of the Black community's children. In her study of Black professional women workers during the Jim Crow era, historian Stephanie J. Shaw's *What a Woman Ought to Be and to Do* describes this bond as reflecting an ethic of socially responsible individualism. Within this ethic, families and community mentors imbued the highly educated Black women in her study with a determination to use their education in a socially responsible way. Consequently, "these women became not simply schoolteachers, nurses, social workers, and librarians; they became . . . political and social leaders" (Shaw 1996, 2).

Because factors such as social class differences among African-Americans, region of the country, and the degree of racial discrimination in housing, education, jobs, and public services all influence Black community organization, othermother traditions characterizing Black women's community work have taken various forms. One concerns how these ideas impact daily interaction among Black women, children, and youth. Historically, this notion of Black women as community othermothers for all Black children often allowed African-American women to treat biologically unrelated children as if they were members of their own families. For example, sociologist Karen Fields describes how her grandmother, Mamie Garvin Fields, draws on her power as a community othermother when dealing with unfamiliar children: "She will say to a child on the street who looks up to no good, picking out a name at random, 'Aren't you Miz Pinckney's boy?' in that same reproving tone. If the reply is, 'No, *ma'am*, my mother is Miz Gadsden,' whatever threat there was dissipates" (Fields and Fields 1983, xvii).

The use of family language in referring to members of the African-American community also illustrates the socially responsible individualism of Black women's community work. In the following passage, Mamie Garvin Fields describes how she became active in surveying substandard housing conditions among African-Americans in Charleston. Note her explanation of why she uses family language:

> I was one of the volunteers they got to make a survey of the places where we were paying extortious rents for indescribable property. I said "we," although it wasn't Bob and me. We had our own home, and so did many of the Federated Women. Yet we still felt like it really was "we" living in those terrible places, and it was up to us to do something about them. (Fields and Fields 1983, 195)

Black women frequently use family language to describe Black children. In recounting her increasingly successful efforts to teach a boy who had given other teachers problems, my daughter's kindergarten teacher stated, "You know how it can be—the majority of children in the learning disabled classes are *our children*. I know he didn't belong there, so I volunteered to take him." In their statements both women use family language to describe the ties that bind them as Black women to their responsibilities as members of African-American communities.

Black women writers also explore this theme of African-American community othermothers who, via their socially responsible individualism, engage in Black women's community work. One of the earliest examples is found in Frances Ellen Watkins Harper's 1892 novel, *Iola Leroy*. By rejecting an opportunity to marry a prestigious physician and disassociate herself from the Black community, nearly White Iola, the main character, chooses instead to serve the African-American community. Similarly, in Alice Walker's *Meridian* (1976), the main character rejects the controlling image of the "happy slave," the self-sacrificing Black mother, and chooses to become a community othermother. Giving up her biological child to the care of an othermother, Meridian gets an education, works in the civil rights movement, and eventually takes on responsibility for the children of a small Southern town. She engages in a "quest that will take her beyond the society's narrow meaning of the word *mother* as a physical state and expand its meaning to those who create, nurture, and save life in social and psychological as well as physical terms" (Christian 1985, 242).

Studying Black women leaders in a Northern, urban community, sociologist Cheryl Gilkes (1980, 1983b) suggests that community othermother relationships can be key in stimulating Black women's decisions to become social activists. Gilkes asserts that many of the Black women community activists in her study became involved in community organizing in response to the needs of their own children and of those in their neighborhoods. The following comment is typical of how many of the Black women in Gilkes's study relate to Black children: "There were alot of summer programs springing up for kids, but they were exclusive . . . and I found that most of *our kids* were excluded" (1980, 219). Nancy Naples's (1991, 1996) work on what she labels *activist mothering* by Black and Latina women in low-income urban neighborhoods identifies a similar ideology. Like the women in Gilkes's studies, the women in Naples's study also entered community politics in direct response to the needs of their children. But their very definitions of good mothering went beyond a simple measure of caring for their own biological children. Instead, they saw good mothering as comprising all actions, including social activism, that addressed the needs of their children and community (Naples 1996, 230). For Black women in both studies, what began as the daily expression of their obligations to their children and as community othermothers often developed into full-fledged actions as community leaders.

This community othermother tradition also explains the "mothering the mind" relationships that can develop between African-American women teachers and their Black female and male students. Unlike the traditional mentoring so widely reported in educational literature, this relationship goes far beyond that of providing students with either technical skills or a network of academic and professional contacts. Gloria Wade-Gayles describes this special bond that she cultivates with her students at Spelman College: "I was like a plant from which one takes cuttings. A piece for this one. A piece for that one. . . . Although there were times when I could feel the blade, I did not regret the cuttings. They strengthened my roots" (Wade-Gayles 1996, 32–33). Like the mother-daughter relationship, this "mothering the mind" among Black women seeks to move toward the mutuality of a shared sisterhood that binds African-American women as community othermothers.

Community othermothers have made important contributions in building a different type of community in often hostile political and economic surroundings (Reagon 1987). Community othermothers' participation in activist mothering ·demonstrates a clear rejection of separateness and individual interest as the basis of either community organization or individual self-actualization. Instead, the connectedness with others and common interest expressed by community othermothers model a very different value system, one whereby ethics of caring and personal accountability move communities forward.

Motherhood as a Symbol of Power

Motherhood—whether bloodmother, othermother, or community othermother—can be invoked as a symbol of power by African-American women engaged in Black women's community work. Certainly much of Black women's status within women-centered kin networks stems from their important contributions as bloodmothers and othermothers. Moreover, much of U.S. Black women's status in African-American communities stems from their activist mothering as community othermothers. Some of the most highly respected Black women in working-class Black neighborhoods are those who demonstrate an ethic of community service.

Black communities and neighborhoods have long had women who served as community othermothers. The existence of this tradition among middle-class Black women has been recognized and studied via attention to middle-class Black women's political traditions (see, e.g., Giddings 1988; Higginbotham 1993; Shaw 1996). However, the community othermother traditions of working-class and poor Black women such as those examined by Nancy Naples (1991, 1996) remain underemphasized within U.S. Black feminism. Instead, those community othermothers who do receive well-deserved recognition do so in large part because of the confluence of unusual circumstances and their *individual* characteristics. We know of Fannie Lou Hamer because she was both so exceptional and her actions on behalf of African-Americans occurred during an historic era that granted her media visibility. In contrast, most community othermothers simply work on behalf of the children, women, and men of their communities with little fanfare or recognition. While efforts on behalf of Black children often may catalyze their actions, working on behalf of the community means addressing the multifaceted issues within it. These women often remain nameless in scholarly texts, yet everyone in their neighborhoods knows their names.

Black women's involvement in community work forms one important basis for power within Black civil society. This is the type of power many African-Americans have in mind when they describe the "strong Black women" they hope will revitalize contemporary Black neighborhoods. Community othermothers work on behalf of the Black community by expressing ethics of caring and personal accountability. Such power is transformative in that Black women's relationships with children and other vulnerable community members are not intended to dominate or control. Rather, their purpose is to bring people along, to—in the words of late-nineteenth-century Black feminists—"uplift the race" so that vulnerable members of the community will be able to attain the self-reliance and independence essential for resistance.

When older African-American women invoke their power as community othermothers, the results can be quite striking. Sociologist Charles Johnson (1934/1979) describes the behavior of an elderly Black woman at a church service in rural 1930s Alabama. Even though she was not on the program, the woman stood up to speak. The master of ceremonies rang for her to sit down, but she refused to do so, saying, "I am the mother of this church, and I will say what I please" (p. 172). The master of ceremonies offered the following explanation to the congregation as to why he let the woman continue: "Brothers, I know you all honor Sister Moore. Course our time is short but she has acted as a mother to me. . . . Any time old folks get up I give way to them" (p. 173).

The activist mothering of Black women's community work (see, e.g, Naples 1991, 1996) and the power it often engenders remain misunderstood. Often called "maternal politics" within North American and European-influenced feminisms, patterns of Black women's political activism associated with community othermother traditions as well as the power and recognition offered such women by African-Americans become derogated. Take for example, Julia Wells's arguments in an article titled "Maternal Politics in Organizing Black South African Women." According to Wells, maternal politics refers to "political movements which are rooted in women's defense of their roles as mothers and protectors of their children" (Wells 1998, 251). Citing as examples the cases of the South African women's antipass campaigns of the 1960s and mothers of the Plaza de Mayo in Argentina starting in 1979, Wells suggests that such movements develop because many women view their maternal roles as the driving force behind public political actions. Wells then distinguishes between "maternal politics" and "feminism." I cite Wells at length because her ideas succinctly state beliefs that are more diffusely held.

> Maternal politics are clearly not to be confused with feminism. Women swept up in mother-centered movements are not fighting for their own personal rights as women but for their custodial rights as mothers. Since concepts of the sanctity of motherhood are so deeply entrenched in the social fabric of most societies, this strategy often proves effective where other attempts to generate social change fail. So potent has been the traditional discourse on motherhood that husbands, families, and government officials all tend to acknowledge and respect the heartrending claims of mothers, giving women an unusual amount of political space in which to organize. Significant allies are easily won over, strengthening the political clout of such movements. Nevertheless, these movements must be recognized as limited in scope, duration, and success in achieving their goals and, above all, should not be mistaken for political maturity. (Wells 1998, 253)

This type of thinking sets up a hierarchy of feminisms, assigns the type engaged in by U.S. Black women and women in Africa (see, e.g., Iweriebor 1998) a secondary status, and fails to recognize motherhood as a symbol of power. Instead, the activist mothering associated with Black women's community work becomes portrayed as a "politically immature" vehicle claimed by women who fail to develop a so-called radical analysis of the family as the site of oppression similar to that advanced within Western feminism.

Feminist claims that "maternal politics" represents an immature form of political activism certainly raise questions for motherhood as a symbol of power in African-American communities. Black women's community work can be understood via maternal rhetoric as a static system of ideas that can be evaluated using some externally derived allegedly feminist criteria. But another approach views Black women's understandings of motherhood as a symbol of power and the activist mothering it might engender as an enduring theme that *politicizes* Black women. Viewing motherhood as a symbol of power can catalyze Black women to take actions that they otherwise might not have considered. For example, when Mamie Till Bradley's 14-year-old son, Emmett Till, was brutally murdered in Mississippi in the summer of 1955, Ms. Bradley found herself in the center of a national controversy. This 33-year-old Chicago resident "wanted the whole world to see" what had happened to her son (Feldstein 1994). "She insisted that his battered body appear in an open casket at the funeral." Similarly, a Black mother approached me after a talk I gave at a Detroit-area college. With her two children in tow, a boy age ten, and a girl age five, she described the challenges of leaving a marriage and moving back to Detroit as a single parent. Describing the limitations of her children's new school, this mother shared the horrible story of how a classmate had held a gun to her son's head. Despite this situation, this woman said that she was not moving—she would stay and fight. Certainly her actions can be seen as fighting for her own children. But she clearly understood that motherhood could be a symbol of power in that setting. Motherhood politicized her.

Not just Black women but those who care about Black women can also access the potential power associated with activist mothering. Writer Lisa Jones describes the politicization of her White mother as she came to understand the obstacles confronting her mixed-race, Black daughter: "Motherhood has been more than a domestic chore or emotional bond for my mother. It's a political vocation—one she's taken seriously enough to go up against the world for" (Jones 1994, 34). Studies of White mothers of mixed-race children confirm this phenomenon of White mothers becoming politicized in fighting the battles confronting their Black children. Raising their Black children in racist environments fosters new views of motherhood for many of these women. This is an entirely different understanding of political activism and empowerment than fighting on one's own behalf. To label this type of socially responsible individualism as "politically immature" seems especially misguided.

The View from the Inside: The Personal
Meaning of Mothering

Within African-American communities, women's innovative and practical approaches to mothering under oppressive conditions often bring recognition and foster their empowerment. But this situation should not obscure the costs of motherhood to many U.S. Black women. Black motherhood is a fundamentally contradictory institution. African-American communities value motherhood, but Black mothers' ability to cope with intersecting oppressions of race, class, gender, sexuality, and nation should not be confused with transcending the injustices characterizing these oppressions. Black motherhood can be rewarding, but it can also extract high personal costs. The range of Black women's reactions to motherhood and the ambivalence that many Black women feel about mothering reflect motherhood's contradictory nature.

Certain dimensions of motherhood advanced both via the traditional family ideal and via Black community expectations are clearly problematic for Black women. Coping with unwanted pregnancies and being unable to care for one's children is oppressive. Sara Brooks remembers, "I had babies one after another because I never knew how to avoid having babies and I didn't ask nobody, so I didn't know nothin. . . . After I separated from my husband, I *still* didn't know nothin, so there come Vivian" (Simonsen 1986, 174). Brooks became pregnant again even though she was unmarried and had three children from her marriage whom she could not support. Brooks describes the strain placed on Black women who must mother under oppressive conditions: "I hated it. . . . I didn't want no other baby. I couldn't hardly take care of myself, and I had other kids I'da loved to have taken care of, and I couldn't do that" (p. 177). Like Brooks, many Black women have children they really do not want. When combined with Black community values claiming that good Black women always want their children, ignorance about reproductive issues leaves many Black women with unplanned pregnancies and the long-term responsibilities of parenting.

Ann Moody's mother also did not celebrate her repeated pregnancies. Moody remembers her mother's feelings when her mother started "getting fat" and her boyfriend stopped coming by: "Again Mama started crying every night. . . . When I heard Mama crying at night, I felt so bad. She wouldn't cry until we were all in bed and she thought we were sleeping. Every night I would lie awake for hours listening to her sobbing quietly in her pillow. The bigger she got the more she cried, and I did too" (Moody 1968, 46). To her children, Moody's mother may have appeared to be the stereotypical strong Black mother, but Ann Moody was able to see the cost her mother paid for living with this controlling image.

Dealing with an unwanted pregnancy can have tragic consequences. All Sara Brooks could think about was "doing away with this baby." She self-medicated herself and almost died. But she was luckier than her mother. As Brooks recalls, "My momma, she got pregnant too close behind me—it was an unwanted pregnancy—and so she taken turpentine and she taken too much, I guess, and she died. She bled to death and died" (Simonsen 1986, 160). She was not alone. Prior to the 1973 *Roe v. Wade* U.S. Supreme Court decision that a woman's right to personal privacy gave her the right to decide whether or not to have an abortion, large numbers of women who died from illegal abortions were Black. In New York, for example, during the several years preceding the decriminalization of abortions, 80 percent of the women who died from illegal abortions were Black or Puerto Rican (Davis 1981).

Strong pronatalist values in African-American communities often vest adult status on women who become biological mothers. For many, becoming a biological mother is often seen as a significant first step toward womanhood. Annie Amiker, an elderly Black woman, describes the situation in the rural Mississippi of her childhood. When asked if there were many girls with out-of-wedlock children, she replied, "There was some but not many—not many because when you run upon a girl who had a child the other girls wouldn't have nothing to do with her . . . she was counted as a grown person so she wasn't counted among the young people" (Parker 1979, 268). Joyce Ladner describes how this link between adult status and motherhood operates in low-income urban communities: "If there was one common standard for becoming a woman that was accepted by the majority of the people in the community, it was the time when girls gave birth to their first child. This line of demarcation was extremely clear and separated the *girls* from the *women*" (1972, 212).

Despite high personal costs, Ann Moody's mother, Sara Brooks, and an overwhelming majority of unmarried Black adolescent mothers choose to keep their children. In part, this may reflect strong pronatalist values. However, Black women's willingness to sacrifice for their children may stem from a deep-seated but largely unstated reliance on motherhood in the absence of committed love relationships with Black men. In a harsh environment where sexual politics leaves far too many U.S. Black women alone, children provide solace and love.

The pain of knowing what lies ahead for Black children while feeling powerless to protect them is another problematic dimension of Black mothering. Michele Wallace remembers, "I can understand why my mother felt desperate. No one else thought it would be particularly horrible if I got pregnant or got married before I had grown up, if I never completed college. I was a black girl" (1978, 98). In a 1904 letter, a Black mother in the South wrote to a national magazine:

> I dread to see my children grow. I know not their fate. Where the white girl has one temptation, mine will have many. Where the white boy has every opportunity and protection, mine will have few opportunities and no protection. It does not matter how good or wise my children may be, they are colored. When I have said that, all is said. Everything is forgiven in the South but color. (Lerner 1972, 158)

Protecting Black children remains a primary concern of African-American mothers. Black children are at risk for higher infant mortality, poor nutrition, inferior housing, environmental pollutants, AIDS, and a host of other social problems. Because it can strike at random, violence is of special concern to Black mothers. Anthropologist Leith Mullings reports that women in Harlem spend an "extraordinary amount of time escorting children, limiting their movement, and trying by any means to keep them away from the violence of the streets" (Mullings 1997, 93). Such women organize building-by-building and block-by-block struggles to rid their neighborhoods of drug dealers. Because drug-related income may be the primary source of income for many low-income families, these mothers' efforts are often unsuccessful. But still they try. One mother expresses this general concern for Black children:

> I turn my eyes on the little children, and keep on praying that one of them will grow up at the right second, when the schoolteachers have time to say hello and give him the lessons he needs, and when they get rid of the building here and let us have a place you can breathe in and not get bitten all the time, and when the men can find work—because they *can't* have children, and so they have to drink or get on drugs to find some happy moments, and some hope about things. (Lerner 1972, 315)

To this mother, even though her children are her hope, the conditions under which she must mother are intolerable.

Black mothers also pay the cost of giving up their own dreams of achieving full creative ability. "When," Alice Walker asks, "did my overworked mother have time to know or care about feeding the creative spirit?" (1983, 239). Historically, much of that creativity could be expressed through music, much of it within Black churches. Many Black women blues singers, poets, and artists manage to incorporate their art into their daily responsibilities as bloodmothers and other-mothers. But for far too many African-American women who are weighed down by the incessant responsibilities of mothering others, that creative spark never finds full expression.

Harriet Jacobs's autobiography gives a clear example of one mother's denial of her own self-actualization and illustrates the costs paid by Black mothers who assume the heavy responsibilities inherent in their bloodmother and othermother relationships. Jacobs desperately wanted to escape slavery but explains how having children created a particular dilemma:

> I could have made my escape alone; but it was more for my helpless children than for myself that I longed for freedom. Though the boon would have been precious to me, above all price, I would not have taken it at the expense of leaving them in slavery. Every trial I endured, every sacrifice I made for their sakes, drew them closer to my heart, and gave me fresh courage. (1860/1987, 59)

Black mothers like those of Ann Moody and June Jordan and women like Harriet Jacobs and Sara Brooks are examples of women who gave up their freedom for the sake of their children. Community othermothers like Mamie Fields and Miss Nee pay a similar cost, not for the sake of their own biological children but for the Black community's children.

Despite the obstacles and costs, motherhood remains a symbol of hope for many of even the poorest Black women. One anonymous mother describes how she feels about her children:

> To me, having a baby inside me is the only time I'm really alive. I know I can make something, do something, no matter what color my skin is, and what names people call me. . . . You can see the little one grow and get larger and start doing things, and you feel there must be some hope, some chance that things will get better; because there it is, right before you, a real, live, growing baby. . . . The baby is a good sign, or at least he's *some* sign. If we didn't have that, what would be the difference from death? (Lerner 1972, 314)

Given the harshness of this mother's environment, her children offer hope. They are all she has.

Mothering is an empowering experience for many African-American women. Gwendolyn Brooks (1953) explores this issue of reproductive power in her novel *Maud Martha*. Maud Martha is virtually silent until she gives birth to her daughter, when "pregnancy and the birth of a child connect Maud to some power in herself, some power to speak, to be heard, to articulate feelings" (Washington 1987, 395). Her child serves as a catalyst for her movement into self-definition, self-valuation, and individual empowerment. Marita Golden describes a similar experience that illustrates how the special relationship between mother and child can foster a changed definition of self and an accompanying empowerment:

> Now I belonged to me. No parents or husband claiming me. . . . There was only my child who consumed and replenished me . . . my son's love was unconditional and, as such, gave me more freedom than any love I had known. . . . I at last accepted mama as my name. Realized that it did not melt down any other designations. Discovered that it expanded them— and me. (1983, 240–41)

This special relationship that Black mothers have with their children can also foster a creativity, a mothering of the mind and soul, for all involved. It is this gift that Alice Walker alludes to when she notes, "And so our mothers and grand-mothers have, more often than not anonymously, handed on the creative spark, the seed of the flower they themselves never hoped to see" (1983, 240).

But what cannot be overlooked in work emphasizing mothers' influences on their children is how Black children affirm their mothers and how important that affirmation can be in a society plagued by the sexual politics of Black womanhood. In her essay "One Child of One's Own," Alice Walker offers a vision of what African-American mother-child relationships can be:

> It is not my child who tells me: I have no femaleness white women must affirm. Not my child who says: I have no rights black men must respect. It is not my child who has purged my face from history and herstory, and left mystory just that, a mystery; my child loves my face and would have it on every page, if she could, as I have loved my own parents' faces above all others. . . . We are together, my child and I. Mother and child, yes, but *sisters* really, against whatever denies us all that we are. (Walker 1979b, 75)

9 RETHINKING BLACK WOMEN'S ACTIVISM

The way I looked at it, a white person might be judgin me, but I'm judgin them, too. If they seem as if they was scornful of a colored person, at the same time that they was scornful of me, I'm the same way about them . . . if my place ain't good enough for you—[if] I ain't good enough to drink out of a glass that you got because I'm black, I don't want to do it. —Sara Brooks, in Simonsen 1986, 199

Sara Brooks is not typically seen as a political activist. Her long hours as a domestic worker left her little time to participate in unions, community groups, demonstrations, or other forms of organized political activity. Her lifelong struggle was not for political causes but to garner sufficient resources to reunite her children and provide a home for them. To outsiders Sara Brooks may appear to be an exploited domestic worker victimized by the racial politics of an unfair labor market and the sexual politics of having too many children. But when she states, "If they was scornful of me, I'm the same way about them," she taps a powerful yet overlooked part of U.S. Black women's activism. She has not only survived her experiences with intersecting oppressions, but she clearly rejects their ideological justifications. "If my place ain't good enough for you—[if] I ain't good enough to drink out of a glass that you got because I'm black, I don't want to do it," she proclaims. Self-definition, self-valuation, and movement toward self-reliance inform her worldview, beliefs that stem from her struggles to *survive*.

To Sara Brooks survival is a form of resistance, and her struggles to provide for the survival of her children represent the foundations of Black women's activism. Historically African-Americans' resistance to racial and class oppression could not have occurred without an accompanying struggle for group survival. Sara Brooks's contributions in caring for her children and in rejecting the controlling images of herself as mammy or mule represent the unacknowledged yet essential actions taken by countless U.S. Black women to ensure this group survival. Without this important part of Black women's activism, struggles to transform U.S. educational, economic, and political institutions could not have been sustained. Yet popular perspectives on Black political activism often fail to see how struggles for group survival are just as important as confrontations with institutional power.

Prevailing definitions of political activism and resistance misunderstand the meaning of these concepts in Black women's lives. Social science research typically focuses on public, official, visible political activity even though unofficial, private, and seemingly invisible spheres of social life and organization may be equally important. For example, some approaches to social class see labor unions and political parties—two modes of political activism dominated by White males—as fundamental mechanisms for working-class activism (Vanneman and Cannon 1987). African-American women have been excluded from both of these arenas, leaving these approaches bereft of a theoretical analysis of Black women's social class protest. Such approaches assess Black women's absence from both positions of formal authority and the membership rosters of political organizations as indicating low levels of Black women's activism. These definitional limitations also influence analyses of Black women's actions in resistance struggles. For example, historian Rosalyn Terborg-Penn defines resistance as "women's involvement in the organized struggle against slavery, peonage, and imperialism. Strategies included open and guerrilla warfare, maroonage, slave revolts, and peasant revolts" (1986, 190). Terborg-Penn uncovers important and much-needed information about these specific types of Black women's resistance. But the limits of her definition lead her to overlook less visible but equally important forms of Black women's political activity within African-American communities.

Different understandings of political activism and resistance pervade Black women's studies scholarship. On one hand, research on African-American women stresses the ways in which Black women experience the injustices associated with intersecting oppressions of race, class, gender, sexuality, and nation (Beale 1970; Davis 1981; Dill 1983). This work provides a more nuanced view of how Black women's treatment is important to distinctive systems of oppression as well as their intersection. For example, constructions of Black women's sexuality are important to maintaining distinctions between normal and deviant sexualities associated with heterosexism; to structuring capitalist commodity relations that sell Black women's bodies on the open market; to reproducing notions of racial purity required for biological racism; to installing racialized gender hierarchies that distinguish between good girls and bad girls; and to understanding U.S. nation-state policies that legitimate these arrangements. Thus, analyzing the sexual politics of Black womanhood that characterizes Black women's placement in intersecting oppressions sheds light on the more general process of how power as domination is organized and operates.

On the other hand, Black women's studies scholarship simultaneously explores Black women's strength and resiliency in the face of hardship and despair, features thought to characterize Black women's resistance to this multifaceted oppression (Davis 1981, 1989; Steady 1981; Terborg-Penn 1986). Black feminist works portray African-American women as individuals and as a group struggling toward empowerment within an overarching matrix of domination. If power as domination is organized and operates via intersecting oppressions, then resistance must show comparable complexity.

Domination encompasses structural, disciplinary, hegemonic, and interpersonal domains of power (see Chapter 12). These domains constitute specific sites where oppressions of race, class, gender, sexuality, and nation mutually construct one another. Understanding the complexity of Black women's activism requires understanding not only the need to address more than one form of oppression, but the significance of how singular and multiple forms of oppression are organized. To focus on the structural domain of power whose social institutions deny Black women education, jobs, and income, without attending to how ideas about Black womanhood advanced within the hegemonic domain of power justify this treatment misses the complexity of U.S. power relations. To emphasize keeping Black women under surveillance and similar techniques of control associated with the disciplinary domain of power without recognizing their effect on Black women's everyday interpersonal relationships also limits our understanding of power.

Because the structural, disciplinary, hegemonic, and interpersonal domains of power work together to produce particular patterns of domination, Black women's activism demonstrates a comparable complexity. It may be more useful to assess Black women's activism less by the ideological content of individual Black women's belief systems—whether they hold conservative, reformist, progressive, or radical ideologies based on some predetermined criteria—and more by Black women's collective actions within everyday life that challenge domination in these multifaceted domains. For example, a Black mother who may be unable to articulate her political ideology but who on a daily basis contests school policies harmful to her children may be more an "activist" than the most highly educated Black feminist who, while she can manipulate feminist, nationalist, postmodern, and other ideologies, produces no tangible political changes in anyone's life but her own. Rather than reducing Black women's activism to some "essentialist" core of "authentic" Black women's activism originating in Black feminist imaginations, this approach creates space for diverse African-American women to see how their current or potential everyday activities participate in Black women's activism.

Conceptualizing Black Women's Activism

Whether as individuals or as members of organized groups, U.S. Black women's activism has occurred in two primary dimensions. The first, struggles for group survival, consist of actions taken to create Black female spheres of influence within existing social structures. This dimension may not directly challenge oppressive structures because, in many cases, direct confrontation is neither preferred nor possible. Instead, women craft Black female spheres of influence that resist oppressive structures by undermining them. Struggles for group survival require institutions that equip Blacks to struggle. Recognizing that the path to individual and collective empowerment lies in the power of a free mind, these spheres of influence often rely on crafting independent and oppositional identities for African-American women. As such, they embrace a form of identity politics, a worldview that sees lived Black experiences as important to creating a critical Black consciousness and crafting political strategies.

The second dimension of Black women's activism consists of struggles for institutional transformation—namely, those efforts to change discriminatory policies and procedures of government, schools, the workplace, the media, stores, and other social institutions. Whether expressed by individuals or via organized groups, all actions that directly challenge the legal and customary rules governing African-American women's subordination constitute part of the struggle for institutional transformation. Participating in civil rights organizations, labor unions, feminist groups, boycotts, and revolts exemplify this dimension of Black women's activism. Because struggles for institutional transformation are rarely successful without allies, this dimension of Black women's activism relies on coalition-building strategies. For example, Black feminism as a social justice project has long supported or in many cases engaged in coalitions with other movements for social justice. Whereas the identity politics of the struggle for group survival references the distinctiveness of U.S. Black women's particular encounters with social injustice, the coalition politics associated with struggles for institutional transformation link Black women's issues with broader social agendas.

While conceptually distinct, these two dimensions of U.S. Black women's activism are actually interdependent (see, e.g., Avery 1994). For example, studies of Black domestic workers reveal that they often draw on both dimensions while appearing to be doing neither (Rollins 1985; Dill 1988a). The vast majority of Black women domestic workers neither organized for better working conditions nor confronted their employers by demanding better pay—actions representing the struggle for institutional transformation—because they needed their jobs. Ensuring their families' survival came first. Rather, Black domestic workers found other ways to resist.

Many women superficially adhere to the prevailing rules and thus appear to be endorsing them. Black women domestic workers report that they are often called by their White employers to play roles as deferent, contented servants grateful for handouts of old clothes in place of decent wages. But these women simultaneously resist these ongoing attempts to dehumanize them. The childlike, obedient servants they pretend to be masks a very different analysis and worldview. The women share stories of *acting* grateful for the handouts given them by their employers while throwing the things away as soon as they leave their jobs (Rollins 1985). They tell of deliberately altering their physical appearance to look worse than normal. One woman actually reports concealing her children's college attendance from her employer in order not to appear out of her "place." But had these women fully accepted their "place," they would not encourage their children to attend college, they would not improve their physical appearance when out of view of their employers, and they would be truly grateful to receive handouts instead of raises. The Black female sphere of influence created in this case was Black women's refusal to relinquish control over their self-definitions. While they pretend to be mules and mammies and thus appear to conform to institutional rules, they resist by creating their own self-definitions and self-valuations in the safe spaces they create among one another.

Sustaining an independent consciousness as a sphere of freedom enables African-American women to engage in additional forms of resistance. Bonnie Thornton Dill recounts numerous stories of how Black domestic workers undermine the rules governing their employment by creating Black female spheres of influence and control over the conditions of their work. The following case reveals one woman's strategies in resisting her employer's attempts to supervise her work too closely:

> She [the employer] told me what she wanted done and then she said, "My girl always scrubs the floor." Well, I noticed down in the basement that she had a mop, and she had taken the mop and hid it. So I cleaned the whole house and everything, but I didn't mop the floors. And when I got ready to go, I took the bucket, the brush, and the knee-pad and set them in the corner. When she came in she was very pleased. . . . She went into the kitchen and she looked and she said, "But you didn't scrub the floor." She had a daughter who was ten years old, and I know I'm not her girl, I'm just the lady who came to do the day's work. So I said, "Well, you said your girl cleans the floor, and I'm not your girl . . . and I don't scrub floors on my hands and knees." "Well," she said, "tomorrow I'll go out and buy a mop." So, I got my coat on and I said, "Why don't you just let me go down in the basement and bring the mop up?" (Dill 1988a, 40)

This domestic worker avoided direct actions to change the rules. She did not form a union, confront her employer about the power inequities involved in calling her "girl" and asking her to scrub floors on her knees when a mop was available, or engage in other forms of overt political resistance. Yet even though her actions were constrained by the need to ensure her family's economic survival, she did challenge the rules that governed her work. Her participation in a Black female sphere of influence gave her different tools to resist, and she stimulated institutional transformation by undermining the rules governing her work.

Black women's community work, with its duality of internal and external efforts, also incorporates these interdependent dimensions of Black women's activism. Dodson and Gilkes (1987) contend that Black women's centrality in African-American families and communities reflects the both/and conceptual orientation of Black feminist epistemology. Curiously, Black women's actions to maintain community integrity through the struggle for group survival is simultaneously conservative and radical. Bernice Johnson Reagon (1987) views Black women who worked for Black community development as "cultural workers," women who thwarted European and White American efforts to eliminate African-derived cultural frameworks. The survival of certain African-influenced ideas and practices was not an accident but instead resulted from "continual resistance" whereby the women in particular "took it upon themselves to preserve certain customs" (Thiam 1978, 123). Algerian feminist Awa Thiam asserts, "In refusing to allow Black African civilization to be destroyed, our mothers were revolutionary. Yet some people describe this attitude as conservative" (1978, 123). In the context of the proximate racism associated with U.S. institutionalized racism—settings where Whites directly rule Blacks—efforts to preserve "Blackness" become highly significant. This everyday racism is so routinized that it is often taken for granted by both U.S. Blacks and Whites (Essed 1991). Yet its purpose is to destroy not just actions that resist, but the very ideas that might stimulate such resistance. Moreover, an emphasis on conserving African-derived ideas and practices as a form of resistance is not confined to U.S. Black women's activism. Kenyan thinker Acola Pala describes similar resistance traditions in Black diasporic locations: "Travelling in the Americas, the Caribbean and the African continent itself, one is struck by the effect of post-colonial economic and cultural conditions that have attempted to dehumanize and destroy the social and economic bases of Black society. Yet paradoxically, the trauma of subjugation has not led to total despair. Instead it has produced an insistent interrogation and resistance by Black people all over the world" (Pala 1995, 9).

By conserving and re-creating African-influenced cultural production, U.S. Black women participate in this larger "interrogation and resistance" effort. This dimension of activism undermines oppressive institutions by rejecting the anti-Black and antifemale ideologies they promulgate. In the context of U.S. race relations organized via deeply entrenched racial segregation, having access to a Black women's standpoint, especially one dedicated to reproducing African-influenced, gender-specific resistance traditions, is essential. The Black feminist consciousness nurtured and articulated in this safe space may be all that stands between many U.S. Black women and internalized oppression. For example, the domestic workers in Judith Rollins's (1985) study retain their sense of self-worth by adhering to an alternative value system that "measures an individual's worth less by material success than by 'the kind of person you are.'" These women judge themselves "by the quality of one's interpersonal relationships and by one's standing in the community" (1985, 212). This ethical system is what gives domestics the strength to accept what is beneficial to them in their employers' treatment while not being profoundly damaged by the negative controlling images on which such treatment is based (Cannon 1988). The presence of an alternative, African-influenced value system allows Black women to live with the contradictions inherent in viewing themselves as worthwhile individuals in a devalued occupation.

At the same time that African-American women engage in cultural maintenance within Black civil society that, via its conservation of African-influenced ideas and practices, lays the foundation for political activism of diverse ideological persuasions, Black women's political struggles to transform racist and sexist institutions represent a more overtly radical political thrust. "Any description of the roles of Black women in their communities . . . must incorporate an understanding of this seeming contradiction," suggest Dodson and Gilkes (1987, 82). Black women cannot be content with merely nurturing their families and communities because the welfare of those families and communities is profoundly affected by the injustices that characterize U.S. political, economic, and social institutions. Because African-American women and men must function in schools and labor markets controlled by unsympathetic officials, Black women often find themselves working for institutional transformation. Katie Murray, a sheet-metal worker, only wanted to earn a decent wage so that she could be economically self-reliant. But she found herself increasingly described as a troublemaker because she refused to ignore an incident in which her White coworkers were invited to attend a three-day workshop with pay while she was never included: "It's sad; we're all out there workin' together, payin' our union dues just like the whites are except they haven't asked a black person to go. And whenever I bring up something like this, they say I'm trying to cause trouble. But it is not that I wanna cause trouble. It's just that I wanna be treated equally" (Schroedel 1985, 137).

These dual dimensions of Black women's activism offer a new model for examining African-American political activism overall. Philosophies of Black nationalism and racial integration, typically seen as opposing ideological positions in Black social and political thought (Cruse 1967), resemble struggles for group survival and institutional transformation. Just as struggles for group survival and institutional transformation might better be viewed as complementary and essential parts of the same process, so might broader Black political philosophies.

These dual dimensions of Black women's activism illustrate the necessity of both types of political action in bringing about social change. In a 1981 speech at a women's music festival, Bernice Johnson Reagon, a longtime activist in the Black civil rights and women's movements and a founding member of the musical group Sweet Honey in the Rock, describes the necessity of linking struggles for group survival with those of institutional transformation. Reagon compared building community institutions with being in a barred room offering nurturance and a safe space: "That space while it lasts should be a nurturing space where you sift out what people are saying about you and decide who you really are . . . in that little barred room where you check everybody at the door, you act out community. You pretend that your room is a world" (Reagon 1983, 358). But while the barred room of community is necessary and often may be the only form of resistance available, it cannot be sufficient to bring about fundamental social change. Reagon continues:

> The problem with the experiment is that there ain't nobody in there but folk like you. . . . Now that's nationalism . . . it's nurturing, but it is also nationalism. At a certain stage nationalism is crucial to a people if you are going to ever impact as a group in your own interest. Nationalism at another point becomes reactionary because it is totally inadequate for surviving in the world with many peoples. (Reagon 1983, 358)

To Reagon struggles for group survival are designed to foster autonomy, not separatism. Moreover, this autonomy provides the foundation for the principled coalitions with other groups that are essential for institutional transformation.

This approach to Black women's activism is also distinctive in challenging some fundamental gendered assumptions that underlie both Black nationalism and racial integration. Within U.S. Black politics, both ideologies advance beliefs concerning what constitutes gender-appropriate political behavior for African-American women and men. Within Black organizations espousing Black nationalist ideologies, women are often associated with the private sphere of family and community—conceptualized as a Black nation within a nation—with men expected to defend this Black community within the public sphere of U.S. social institutions (Collins 1998a, 155–83). Similarly, until recently, Black women participants in civil rights organizations routinely did not serve as leaders and spokespersons. In both cases, gender-specific norms associate Black men's political activism with *public* sphere actions outside the organization itself and Black women's activism with *private* sphere activities within the organization. These assumptions replicate prevailing beliefs that routinely grant the public-sphere activities of men more credence than the private-sphere activities of women. They also limit organizational efficacy in confronting social injustice.

An alternative view centered in Black women's lived experiences reveals the significance of motherwork (Collins 1994). In general, the combination of mobility among Black and White neighborhoods as culturally distinct entities, the type of work Black women performed in both settings, and the meaning attached to Black women's labor in both settings converged to produce a distinctive sensibility concerning political activism. Often called "maternal politics" and misunderstood within that framework (see, e.g., Wells 1998), Black women's motherwork reflects how political consciousness can emerge within everyday lived experience. In this case, Black women's participation in a constellation of mothering activities, collectively called motherwork, often fostered a distinctive political sensibility.[1] Viewing Black women as activists in both struggles for group survival and for institutional transformations not only challenges gender-specific assumptions of Black political theory and practice, it simultaneously questions basic definitions of public, private, and political.

Struggles for Group Survival

The external constraints of racism, sexism, and poverty have been so severe that, like Sara Brooks, the majority of African-American women have found it difficult to participate in organized political activities. Possessing neither the opportunity nor the resources to confront oppressive institutions directly, the majority of U.S. Black women have engaged in struggles for group survival. This neither means that Black women eschew more visible forms of political protest, nor that community development activities constitute gender-appropriate terrain for Black women's activism. Instead, strategies of everyday resistance have largely consisted of trying to create spheres of influence, authority, and power within institutions that traditionally have allowed African-Americans and women little formal authority or real power.

Ranging from the private, individual actions of Black mothers within their homes to the more organized group behavior of Black churchwomen and sorority sisters, Black women use a variety of strategies to undermine oppressive institutions (Steady 1981; Bush 1986; Fox-Genovese 1986). As bloodmothers and othermothers in women-centered family networks, women are vital to African-derived cultural production. Like Sara Brooks, many Black women confined to underpaid, demanding, menial jobs resist passing on to their children externally defined images of Black women as mules, mammies, matriarchs, and jezebels. Rather, they use their families as effective Black female spheres of influence to foster their children's self-valuation and self-reliance (Dill 1980). In some cases Black women's centrality in Black family networks leads them to exert their political power through existing family structures without appearing to do so. Anna Julia Cooper (1892) reported that even though nineteenth-century Black women were disenfranchised, they were not without political influence: "It is notorious that ignorant black women in the South have actually left their husband's homes and repudiated their support for what was understood by the wife to be race disloyalty, or 'voting away,' as she expresses it, the privileges of herself and little ones" (p. 139).

Traditionally women's activism within Black families meshed smoothly with activism as community othermothers in the wider Black community as "family." In both meanings of family, African-American women worked to create Black female spheres of influence, authority, and power that produced a worldview markedly different from that advanced by the dominant group. Within African-American communities Black women's activities as cultural workers are empowering (Reagon 1987). "The power of black women was the power to make culture, to transmit folkways, norms, and customs, as well as to build shared ways of seeing the world that insured our survival," observes Sheila Radford-Hill. "This power . . . was neither economic nor political; nor did it translate into female dominance" (1986, 168). This culture was essential to the struggle for group survival.

Examining one specific version of the community othermother role—namely, Black women's support for education—illustrates this important dimension of Black women's political activism. Education has long served as a powerful symbol for the important connections among self, change, and empowerment in African-American communities (Lerner 1972, 83–149; Webber 1978; Davis 1981; Neverdon-Morton 1989). The commitment to the value of education by prominent Black women such as Anna Julia Cooper, whose 1892 book, *A Voice from the South,* championed the cause of Black women's education; Mary McLeod Bethune, the founder of a college; Nannie Burroughs, a vigorous campaigner for Black women's education; and Johnetta Cole, the first Black woman president of Spelman College, goes far beyond the themes of gaining the technical skills essential to African-American employability, or mastering the social skills required for White acceptance (Barnett 1978). In describing the purpose of the education offered at the Institute for Colored Youth, a school founded to educate the children of emancipated African-Americans, principal Fanny Jackson Coppin was "not interested in producing 'mere scholars' at the Institute, but rather students who would be committed to race 'uplift' "(Perkins 1982, 190). Like their anonymous slave foremothers, these women saw the activist potential of education and skillfully used this Black female sphere of influence to foster a definition of education as a cornerstone of Black community development.

African-American women have long realized that ignorance doomed Black people to powerlessness. Under slavery it was illegal to teach African-Americans to read and write. Mastering these skills was an expression of political activism not because education allowed slaves to become better slaves but because it offered skills essential in challenging the very tenets of slavery itself. One elderly ex-slave recalls the importance that reading held for enslaved African-Americans:

> I couldn't read, but my uncle could. I was a waiting-maid, an' used to
> help missis to dress in the morning. If massa wanted to tell her some-
> thing he didn't want me to know, he used to spell it out. I could remem-
> ber the letters, an' as soon as I got away I ran to uncle an' spelled them
> over to him, an' he told me what they meant. (Lerner 1972, 29–30)

When she became a mother, this anonymous African-American woman
encouraged her children to become educated, and they were among the first
to enter freedman's schools during the Civil War. Holding high expectations
for her children, she was heard to comment about her son in particular, "Why,
if I had his chance, do you think I would not learn!" For this mother education was clearly a powerful tool for liberation. Denied the opportunity to read
and write, this Black woman resisted by remembering the letters and asking
her uncle what they meant. She thus appeared to be conforming to the rules
of slavery—she remained illiterate—while rejecting the rules themselves. Not
only did this mother resist slavery in this way, she passed on her conceptions
of resistance to her children through her role as educator.

Many Black mothers continue to take their roles as educators seriously.
After an evening talk that I gave at a Detroit college with a high enrollment of
Black women adult learners, one woman approached me with a question. She
wanted to know if I planned to write some of the ideas in *Black Feminist
Thought* in a format suitable for teenage girls. Even though she worked a full-
time job, this mother had decided to return to school after her husband left her
with eight children in her care. As she described it, her children wanted to
know what she was learning in school, and when they asked, "What you reading Mamma?" she would stop and read to them from her college assignments.
When her two teenage daughters saw her reading *Black Feminist Thought,* they
asked about it. She translated the ideas for them, but wished for something
similar that she could place directly into their hands. The actions taken by this
mother are certainly exceptional, but her belief in education as a tool of
empowerment is not. She saw her education not as a commodity only for herself, but as an entity to be shared.

The activities of prominent Black female educators rest on the foundation
established by the collective actions of Black women like anonymous slave
mothers and the mother from Detroit. It is no accident that many well-known
U.S. Black women activists were either teachers or somehow involved in struggling for educational opportunities for African-Americans of both sexes
(Perkins 1983; Neverdon-Morton 1989). Prior to the civil rights gains of the
1960s, limited professional opportunities pushed Black women together and
fostered a sense of collective vision. The power and status earned from
women's roles as cultural workers served to reinforce the importance of Black
women's roles as educators. Black men and women who were perceived by the
community as leaders of the struggle for group survival were described as
"educators." Working for race uplift and education became intertwined.

This belief in education for race uplift and in the special role of Black women in this struggle continued well into the twentieth century. In a 1938 article in the *Journal of Negro History*, Mary McLeod Bethune argued, "If our people are to fight their way up and out of bondage we must arm them with the sword and the shield . . . of pride—belief in themselves and their possibilities, based upon a sure knowledge of the achievements of the past" (Lerner 1972, 544). More recently that belief and pride have come through the struggle to secure our own educations. Struggles around educational issues have politicized Black women. A 23-year-old Black woman participant in the 1982 struggle for better education at the predominantly Black and female Medgar Evers College at the City College of New York taps this meaning of education in what was formerly called race uplift but what came to be known in the 1960s as Black community development:

> I learned so much—more than I could ever learn in the classroom! I learned that there's a whole lot more than getting a degree and getting ahead financially. You must do so with principle and dignity. You can't just sit back and watch all the atrocious things continue to happen, take your little class notes, read your books, and do nothing to change conditions. (Nicola-McLaughlin and Chandler 1988, 195)

Traditionally, being a teacher in segregated Black communities meant the kind of visibility that emerged as community leadership (Neverdon-Morton 1989). In describing her role as a teacher, Fanny Jackson Coppin observed how she had always taught two schools—the students of the Institute and the Black community (Perkins 1982, 190). Black women used their classrooms and status as educators to promote African-American community development. In comparing the letters of Black and White women applying to missionary societies to become teachers in the South after the Civil War, historian Linda Perkins (1983) uncovered some significant differences. Overwhelmingly single, upper- and middle-class, unemployed, and educated in New England colleges and at Oberlin, White women wrote of the "deep need to escape idleness and boredom" brought on by their placement in the cult of true womanhood. In contrast, the Black women who applied were employed and financially supported families, and their letters consistently reflected themes of duty and race uplift. While White women working in the South generally did so for two to three years, Black women expressed the desire to "devote their entire lives to their work." Perkins points out that most did. Formally educated Black women teachers in early-twentieth-century Washington, D.C., also believed that they had a special responsibility to their respective communities which they alone could fulfill (Harley 1982). Such women "often saw themselves more as 'uplifters' than as working women. . . . Educating the children of poor unlettered blacks was considered part of their moral and social obligations as educated women" (Harley 1982, 257). In describing the work of one of her teachers who expressed this type of political leadership, Alice Walker notes, "mostly she taught by the courage of her own life, which to me is the highest form of teaching" (1983, 38).

Black women's activities in churches have also been profoundly influenced by similar ideas concerning education, motherwork, and political activism. Dodson and Gilkes (1987) suggest, "If any one ministry could be identified as central to the black sacred cosmos of the twentieth century, it would be education. . . . Black people . . . defined education of the oppressed and the oppressors as central tasks of Christian mission" (p. 84). Black churches have supported a variety of social, economic, political, and ethical actions essential to Black community development (Sobel 1979; Mitchell and Lewter 1986). While men dominate positions of formal authority in church hierarchies, women make up a large percentage of the congregations, hold positions of authority, and generally exert an important influence on African-American church communities across denominations (Dodson and Gilkes 1987). The situation is far more complex than that proposed by traditional models arguing that female "followers" obey the orders of male "leaders." Rather, men and women appear to exert different types of leadership within Black church communities.

"It was biblical faith grounded in the prophetic tradition," declares Katie Cannon, that helped Black women "devise strategies and tactics to make Black people less susceptible to the indignities and proscriptions of an oppressive white social order" (1985, 35). Cheryl Gilkes's (1985) work on the turn-of-the-century Sanctified Church describes how African-American women used this prophetic tradition to create and maintain a sophisticated sisterhood. Gilkes contends that "women's concentration in educational roles . . . was not simply a form of female segregation: instead it was the basis for alternative structures of authority, career pathways, and spheres of influence" (1985, 689). During a time when dominant society derogated African-American women, Black women in the Sanctified Church referred to one another as "saints." In doing this they clearly rejected their societally defined "place" in favor of creating their own self-definitions. Their emphasis on biblical authority made learning "the Word" an important means for living a sanctified life and offered a powerful rationale for getting an education. During a time when educated African-American women were scarce, the women in the largely working-class congregations encouraged one another to become educated. As fund-raisers women made essential economic contributions to Sanctified churches. Strong Women's Departments retained control over the disbursement and allocation of their funds. The women "believed in economic cooperation with men, not in economic dependence on them" (Gilkes 1985, 690). By giving advice to their younger "sisters," older women taught less experienced women the skills necessary for their survival as African-American women. Sisterhood did not occur at the expense of Black men or children. Rather, it meshed with the needs of these groups so that the church practiced unity without uniformity.

A similar perspective on the importance of education, sisterhood, self-definitions, self-valuations, and economic self-reliance permeated other Black women's organizations. Through advocacy and education the turn-of-the-century Black women's club movement aimed to address a broad spectrum of Black women's issues (Neverdon-Morton 1989). The original departments of the National Association of Colored Women, the first national organization of Black women's organizations, included the following units: Woman Suffrage, Patriotism, Education, Conditions in Rural Life, Music, Literature and Art, Gainful Occupation and Business, Better Railroad Conditions, Mothers Meetings and Night Schools, Public Speaking, and Child Welfare (Lerner 1972, 445). Black sororities also listed as part of their mission attending to the special needs of Black women as a key part of the struggle for group survival (Giddings 1988).

Not all African-American women were welcomed as equal participants in middle-class Black women's organizations. While working on behalf of all Black women, members of the Black Women's Club Movement did not work with them as equals. The general thinking among many middle-class reformers "was that most uneducated, unskilled women were in need of social and moral uplift and, therefore, lacked the refinement . . . to join in the uplift process, at least as members of their organizations" (Harley 1982, 258). Early-twentieth-century Black churches were key locations where Black women who were less educated and less financially secure than the better-educated teachers who populated Black women's organizations could exert leadership. Working-class and poor Black women took up membership in church women's groups, female auxiliaries to fraternal orders, and benevolent societies. These organizations generally required less affluent lifestyles and less active public roles and had more practical benefits for their members than did predominantly middle-class reform organizations (Harley 1982).

Despite social class differences among Black women, this tradition of becoming educated for Black community development has permeated U.S. Black women's activism. One study of 25 Black women community leaders found that they rejected limited definitions of education. In assessing their own educational experiences, these Black women were highly critical of the functions of higher education as an agency of socialization into a White middle-class worldview. They perceived higher education in White-controlled institutions as a "form of pacification and mystification," education that "teaches you not to fight." These women rejected this form of education in favor of "focused educations" within the same White institutions that would allow them to continue the tradition of Black women working for race uplift (Gilkes 1983b).

Depending on their social class backgrounds, these women followed different routes to acquiring a focused education. For middle-class women social responsibility was stressed by their parents. These women were taught to adhere to the long tradition of educated Black women working on behalf of the race. In contrast, working-class women went to school for the credentials and information they felt they needed for specific community problems. One respondent from a working-class background recounts her reasons for returning to school:

> I heard people talking about how black parents were apathetic and I never believed that black parents were apathetic. . . . Parents had always had the feeling, and I was under the same impression until I became involved with the teachers, that teachers were always right because we (black people) always have this great respect for education. . . . I felt even though I worked with a parents' group that because I wasn't a teacher no one took my words very seriously. And I decided that I was going to become a teacher, not to work in the classroom, but to work with parents. (Gilkes 1983b, 121)

This woman's focused education empowered her by granting her the credentials she felt she needed to organize parents. Her education was designed to further African-Americans as a group, not solely for her own personal development.

In still other cases, Black nationalist ideology stimulates a focused education that enables working class Black women to work as social activists. Despite being widely overlooked in Black feminist scholarship, the Garvey Movement remains the largest mass movement of U.S. Blacks. A large part of the membership was working-class and, as work on Amy Jacques Garvey suggests (Adler 1992), Black women who were influenced by Garvey's Black nationalism saw their contributions as women as vitally important to Black community development. The long and highly distinguished career of Elma Lewis, founder of the Boston-based Elma Lewis School of Fine Arts and the National Center of Afro-American Artists, illustrates the convergence of themes that distinguish Black women's struggles for group survival. The daughter of West Indian immigrants, her father a day laborer, and her mother a domestic worker, Lewis learned from them the value of education, the arts, and Marcus Garvey. Taking Garvey's philosophy, "Up you mighty people, you can what you will," to heart, Elma Lewis began her school in 1950 with $300, two used pianos, two used folding tables, and two used chairs. As Ms. Lewis recalls, it never occurred to her that the school might not succeed because she believed in the creed that she instills in her school's pupils, "Glory in yourself. Anything is possible." Over the years, thousands of children have studied classical ballet, theater, voice, and African dance at the center. Although she was 77 years old in 1998, Ms. Lewis still presided over the 29th season of "Black Nativity," the Langston Hughes gospel play that celebrates Black culture. Ms. Lewis is a cultural worker of the kind described by Bernice Johnson Reagon (1987). Her socially responsible individualism grounded in education, culture, and Marcus Garvey allows her to persist. She notes, "We're always looking at what's lost. I have to look at what I have and where I can go" (Rimer 1998, A16).

Acquiring a focused education demonstrates the significance of self, change, and empowerment for Black women. A 38-year-old mother of five who participated in the struggle at Medgar Evers College describes the importance the struggle for an education had for her: "More than anything, I learned that I am a powerful person! You see, it's important to realize that no matter what your age or what you've been through, each person can make a contribution to changing the conditions of our people" (Nicola-McLaughlin and Chandler 1988, 194). Perhaps Black women's empowerment through education is best summarized by another participant in that same political movement. She asserts, "I was basically a shy and reserved person prior to the struggle at Medgar, but I found my voice—and I used it! Now, I will never lose my voice again!" (Nicola-McLaughlin and Chandler 1988, 195).

Struggles for Institutional Transformation

Actions taken to eliminate discrimination in housing, employment, education, public accommodations, and political representation represent activism aimed at changing the rules that circumscribe African-American women's lives. Traditionally, Black women have either been excluded from or assigned subordinate roles within civil rights, women's, labor, or other organizations devoted to institutional transformation (Terborg-Penn 1985; Davis 1981). For example, the male leadership of Black civil rights organizations found it difficult to see Black women as leaders in the civil rights movement (Barnett 1993). U.S. women's organizations also relegated African-American women to subordinate positions (Caraway 1991). Even radical Black organizations such as the Black Panther Party found it difficult to shake notions that women were unsuitable for leadership (Brown 1992). Patterns of U.S. Black women's activism thus reflect less about Black women's preferred political choices and more about existing opportunities.

Depending on historical time and place, African-American women employed a range of strategies in challenging the rules governing our subordination. In many cases Black women practiced individual protest against unfair rules and practices. Ruth Powell had her first encounter with Jim Crow in Washington, D.C.'s drugstore cafeterias when she was a law student at Howard University in the 1940s. The experience was devastating: "I sat there for about ten minutes watching the waitresses whizzing back and forth in front of me, when suddenly the awful truth dawned and I realized what was happening" (Murray 1987, 205). She left the store. She knew that "I, alone, couldn't do anything concrete to revolutionize conditions," but she also believed "I had to do something to preserve what remained of my self-respect" (p. 205). Ruth

Powell's "something" evolved into a one-woman campaign. She would enter cafeterias, politely ask for service, and, when refused, sit quietly, sometimes for hours at a time. During her sit-ins she would pick out a waiter and stare at him for perhaps an hour or more. "Whether I was finally served or not was unimportant," Powell explained. "What I believed was that all these little bits of agitation would go toward that vital . . . awakening process" (p. 205).

Powell's stance represents action taken to get the rules themselves changed. Black women have also protested by working within formal organizations and groups. Many African-American women's organizations that actively engaged in the struggle for group survival were tireless lobbyists for legal reforms. Black women have also seen the need for principled coalitions with groups affected by similar issues. The contributions of countless Black female rank-and-file activists in civil rights, feminist, and labor movements reflect strategies designed to change the rules of the system by working within reformist organizations (Giddings 1984). During the 1970s and 1980s, even though Black women remained underrepresented in elected public office relative to their proportion of the population, Black women made greater gains than White women in election to mayoral, state legislative, and congressional office (Darcy and Hadley 1988). Still other cases involve African-American women's involvement in violent resistance against slavery and other forms of political and legal oppression (Terborg-Penn 1986).

Being one of the few groups negatively affected by multiple forms of oppression, African-American women have been in a better position to see their interrelationships. Thus the diverse strategies employed in the struggle for institutional transformation have been paralleled by a similar diversity in the types of rules Black women have challenged. Black women have had an enduring interest not just in resisting racist and sexist laws and customs, but in changing a broad segment of the rules shaping American society. For example, despite the fact that Black women do not readily identify themselves as feminists, high levels of support for feminist issues exist among African-American women (King 1988).

Although African-American women may implicitly support a humanist vision for institutional transformation, Black women's political strategies may not explicitly address this vision. Many women begin their political activism as advocates for African-Americans, the poor, or, less frequently, women. But over time Black women activists come to see oppressions as interconnected and the need for broad-based political action. Rather than joining a range of organizations, each devoted to single-purpose issues, many Black women activists either start new organizations or work to transform the institutions in which they are situated. For example, Black women in the civil rights movement initially joined to address racial inequality but found themselves protesting gender inequality as well (Evans 1979). Faye Wattleton's astute leadership of Planned Parenthood, Gloria Scott's resourceful actions to make the

Girl Scouts of America more racially and economically inclusive, and Marian Wright Edelman's judicious leadership of the Children's Defense Fund all appear to tie these women to single-issue causes that are not race specific. But closer examination reveals that even though these women do not project themselves as being advocates for Black women, their organizational actions directly benefit Black women. Where many just talk about resistance, they deliver tangible results.

Black Women's Leadership and Institutional Transformation

U.S. Black women's long-standing participation in organized political activities fosters a rethinking of the ways in which many Black women conceptualize and use power. Black women's use of power seems to grow from distinctive conceptions of how people become empowered, how power can be structured and shared in organizational settings, and how organizations would look if people were to be fully empowered within them. Examining Black women's leadership in organizations whose mission is institutional change offers a route to examining these larger questions.

African-American women have been active in movements for Black civil rights such as the abolitionist movement, the antilynching struggles in the early twentieth century, and the more recent civil rights movement in the South (Giddings 1984). While Black women in such organizations rarely worked exclusively on behalf of Black women, the types of issues they championed and the ways in which they operated within these organizations suggest that they brought an understanding of Black women's concerns to their political activism.

Black women's organizational style within predominantly Black organizations reveals much about how many U.S. Black women exercise power. Understandings of empowerment gained as community othermothers and cultural workers shape Black women's political activities. Drawing on the model of education as empowerment, many Black women routinely reject models of authority based on unjust hierarchies. For example, Black activist Septima Clark disagreed with the style of leadership in the Southern Christian Leadership Conference during the civil rights movement. Ms. Clark said, "You can work behind the scenes all you want. . . . But don't come forth and try to lead. That's not the kind of thing they [Black men] want" (Brown 1986, 77). Ms. Clark tried to influence the male-dominated organization: "I sent a letter to Dr. King asking him not to lead all the marches himself, but instead to develop leaders who could lead their own marches. Dr. King read that letter before the staff. It just tickled them; they just laughed" (p. 77).

African-American women like Septima Clark carried distinctive notions of leadership and empowerment into the Black civil rights struggle, ideas whereby, according to Nikki Giovanni, "the purpose of any leadership is to build more leadership. The purpose of being a spokesperson is to speak until the people gain a voice" (1988, 135). Septima Clark's explanation of why she wished to develop a broad base of community leaders illustrates how the commitment to education as an empowering tool can operate in Black women's political activism: "I thought that you develop leaders as you go along, and as you develop these people let them show forth their development by leading" (p. 77).

Black women's style of activism also reflects a belief that teaching people how to be self-reliant fosters more empowerment than teaching them how to follow. Black civil rights activist Ella Baker, a major figure in the Southern Christian Leadership Conference who worked closely with students, recounts how she nurtured the empowerment of student civil rights workers: "I never intervened between the struggles if I could avoid it. Most of the youngsters had been trained to believe in or to follow adults if they could. I felt they ought to have a chance to learn to think things through and to make the decisions" (Cantarow 1980, 87). Drawing on both the community othermother model of relationships and education as a tool of empowerment, Ms. Baker did intervene, but only if she felt that the students were in danger. Her model of "participatory democracy" emerges from these understandings of empowerment (Mueller 1990).

"We must strive to 'lift as we climb.' . . . We must climb in such a way as to guarantee that all our sisters, regardless of social class, and indeed all of our brothers climb with us. This must be the essential dynamic of our quest for power," counsels Angela Davis (1989, 5). The models of leadership offered by both Septima Clark and Ella Baker speak to a distinctively Black female mode of political activism. Both women clearly could have been leaders in the traditional sense of being figureheads with formal authority. But studying their actual behavior reveals that they both wielded considerable power within their organizations which grew from their perspective on social change.[2]

The strategies employed by many African-American women within labor organizations reinforces this theme that traditional sources of Black women's empowerment influence Black women's organizational behavior. One intriguing case study of a protracted and eventually successful effort to organize secretaries at a hospital in a small Southern city illustrates how Black women draw on prevailing African-American understandings of family and community (Sacks 1984, 1988).[3] Community and kin ties drew Black women together across the hospital's bureaucratic units. These workplace networks in turn became the basis for organizing. People in the networks shared a family idiom by celebrating one another's family and life-cycle events and referring to themselves as "family."

Certain women in these overlapping community and workplace networks became "centerwomen." The skills centerwomen gained from their centrality in women-centered family networks enabled them to keep people together, ensure that obligations were fulfilled, and maintain group consensus. In the union-organizing drive, Black women's motherwork proved to be fundamental to this particular effort at institutional transformation (Collins 1994). The drive was successful because of the existence of two equally important dimensions of leadership: that offered by spokespersons who engaged in direct negotiations with management, and that provided by centerpersons who fostered group solidarity among the workers. While men and women are capable of exercising both types, in this particular case the functions were divided by gender. Men were spokespersons and women were centerpersons. Despite the success of this case of community organizing, its assumptions of complementarity remain questionable. Complementarity in and of itself need not result in inequality. However, as Leith Mullings points out, "assumptions about inferiority and superiority are usually implicit in frameworks of complementarity that operate within the context of a hierarchical society" (Mullings 1997, 139).

Research on Black women community leaders reinforces this notion that Black women work for institutional transformation in characteristic ways (Gilkes 1983b, 1988). In one study, Black women leaders used their positions as heads of social service agencies to change the rules by which those agencies operated. One agency director commented, "You will never eliminate discrimination through complaints. . . . The thing that you've got to do is to get into those institutions and work from top to bottom: how they set policies; who's setting policies; why this is the policy" (1983b, 129). Even though their agencies were funded and controlled by Whites, in the same way that Black women domestic workers used their positions to deliver material goods and skills to their children, these women used their institutions to empower African-Americans. They "saw the black community as a group of relatives and other friends whose interests should be advanced and promoted at all times, under all conditions, and by almost any means" (1983b, 117).

These women's work for institutional transformation often put their jobs in jeopardy. Because the work, and not the particular job, was their focus, they moved on when organizational limits combined with turning points in their self-development. By defining their jobs as institutional transformation versus trying to fit into the existing system, they gained a degree of "spiritual independence." Acquiring a focused education by moving through jobs enabled the women to see the bigger picture obscured by working only within one setting.

By fostering African-American autonomy through their institutions, these women expanded their web of affiliations to make alliances with one another. Despite ideological differences, the women participating in this web of community workers sat on one another's boards and generally helped to further the distinctive goals of their individual organizations. Gilkes assesses this strategic placement on agency boards:

> The affiliations are reflections of the locations and types of problems in the community. Although a community worker may have a well-articulated political ideology, her affiliations are not always a reflection of her choice between sides of an ideological debate such as integration versus separatism or radical political strategies versus traditional party politics. The women's affiliations with white-controlled institutions are a reflection of where they feel Black folks need to be in order to exert some control over their lives and futures. (Gilkes 1988, 68)

Nancy Naples's (1991, 1996) research on activist mothering traditions among Black and Puerto Rican women in low-income urban neighborhoods provides another angle of vision on how U.S. Black women work for institutional transformation. Whereas prevailing academic approaches fragment social life by separating paid work from social reproduction, activism from mothering, and family from community, the ideas and actions of Black women community workers challenge these arrangements. Many of the women initially became involved in community politics because of their children. But their subsequent political involvement grew beyond their own individual families as they saw how their personal troubles were politically constituted. Naples describes how one Black single mother became politicized. Lack of heat, water leaks, and mice and rats roaming her apartment all contributed to her determination to fight against poor housing. Sadly, her son's death from pneumonia served as a powerful catalyst:

> What had happened is wrong! All the little babies that were born that year died that winter in those houses, except one little boy. And we took the babies to Metropolitan Hospital, and they bathed the babies in alcohol and gave them some aspirin and told us to take them home. And I started fighting them, the Health Department, and others, to get heat in the house, and other things like that. I knew that it didn't have to be like that. There's no reason that my children or anybody else's had to live like that. So when my kids started school I tried to organize the parents. (Naples 1996, 231)

Both African-American women and men have been workers for Black community development. Although neither Gilkes nor Naples takes this position, their work suggests that Black women community workers are more likely than men to maintain strategic affiliations with individuals and groups engaged in similar social justice projects. The community leader engaged in working for better housing in Harlem certainly has a vested interest in developing as broad based a constituency as possible. In the immediacy of providing services for Black children, especially given the immediate risk to many, ideological squabbles over the relative merits of racial integration or Black nationalism seem unimportant. This does not mean that Black women lack ideology but, rather, that our experiences as mothers, centerwomen, and community othermothers foster a distinctive form of political activism based on negotiation and a higher degree of attention to context (Gilligan 1982; Belenky et al. 1986).

Black Women's Activism Revisited

As long as social justice remains elusive for African-American women, it is likely to evade U.S. society overall. Therefore, the need for Black women's activism most likely will persist. But while the dialectical relationship linking oppression and activism remains, the changing organization of intersecting oppressions as well as the contours of activism required for resistance demand a dynamic Black women's activism and an equally vigorous U.S. Black feminism.

Different historical eras provide new challenges and opportunities for U.S. Black women's activism. With hindsight, the connections between the shape of Black women's activism during prior periods and the particular challenges of those eras seem fairly straightforward: The "race uplift" ideology of Black club women targeted the installation of racial segregation during the Jim Crow era, whereas the demonstrations during the civil rights era aimed to breathe life into newly passed laws that outlawed this segregation. Historical analysis is always valuable, yet looking ahead remains more difficult. As Tiffany, an 11-year-old Black girl from Birmingham, Alabama, puts it, "I'm not as concerned with black history as I am with black present" (Carroll 1997, 137).

The litany of social problems that now face far too many U.S. Black women—poverty, violence, poor living conditions, inadequate health care, and reproductive concerns—are well known. These same issues also confront women of African descent transnationally (Aina 1998). Many of the causes of these social problems are also known—the growth of the global economy has produced gender-specific forms of integration into the workforce; an increasingly effective global media that, via its routine circulation of updated controlling images of Black women, reinscribes long-standing notions of Black women's sexuality; deeply entrenched racial segregation in housing, schooling, and employment that gives Black women's poverty a particularly harsh expression; and the emergence of a conservative political climate in the United States seemingly dedicated to limiting the protections of the social welfare state. Despite the unique form that these social problems now assume in the United States, they resemble those confronted by African-American women in earlier periods as well as those currently faced by women of African descent transnationally. In this context, both dimensions of Black women's activism are needed yet both must also be reconfigured in new ways. Presenting either struggles for group survival or struggles for institutional transformation as being more fundamental than the other seems shortsighted.

Take, for example, struggles for group survival. The type of self-defined,

Black-oriented community politics that has long sustained African-Americans has come under attack. Since African-American women have long engaged in motherwork designed to build strong Black identities capable of withstanding the assaults of White supremacist rhetoric and practice, abandoning identity politics of this sort may work against group survival. As critical legal theorist Patricia Williams points out, "Whereas segregation and group exclusion were once thought of as the stigma of inferiority, now it is the very identification of blacks and other racial minorities as groups that is stigmatizing—despite the fact that the project is inclusion" (1995, 103). Williams recounts her stint on an admissions committee that received applications from Blacks with phrases such as "Don't admit me if you have to lower your standards" on their applications. This shift from claiming group membership and using it as a political force for social justice to seeing one's group membership as a permanent stigma that retards achieving it seemed lost on the applicants. They seemed unable to counter long-standing racist logic that argues that the inclusion of Blacks means that the system has been undermined, and the exclusion of Blacks means that it is still fair.

The challenges for U.S. Black women across diverse social classes consists of revitalizing institutions of Black civil society so that they can counter situations such as these. If African-Americans ourselves cannot identify with Blackness, then why would anyone else value it? If U.S. Black women cannot put ourselves in the center of our own intellectual and political work and claim identities as Black women, then who else will? It appears that increasing numbers of Blacks are unprepared politically to recognize and deal with new forms that racism, sexism, and other kinds of oppression now take. Pearl Cleage describes the type of socialization she had as a child that allowed her to confront institutionalized racism. "I had an oppressed person's most potent weapons: information, analysis and positive group identity," claims Cleage (1993, 31). The collective efforts of Black women ranging from well-known clubwomen to anonymous Black mothers provided these weapons for Black children. Now, however, large numbers of Black children remain warehoused in inner-city schools, sadly, many of them taught by Black teachers who have little institutional memory of this type of activism. Gaining access to this dimension of Black women's activism is not likely to improve without some sort of intervention. More than 70 percent of Black college students attend predominantly White institutions, and, unlike the community leaders in Cheryl Gilkes's studies, many fail to see the importance of gaining focused educations for either group survival or institutional transformation.

Struggles for institutional transformation also remain needed. The legislative victories of the 1960s provided a new floor for struggle—they did not signal an end to institutionalized racism and sexism as so many people believe. In a provocative article titled "White Men Can't Count," Patricia Williams observes, "There is simply no data anywhere to show that minorities or women have taken over any part of any given institution in America" (Williams 1995, 98). Despite our repeated stigmatization, U.S. Black women do not control military weaponry, industries, colleges and universities, banks, government agencies, and media empires. African-Americans still struggle to acquire positions of power.

Both U.S. institutions and Black civil society are organized quite differently now, in large part because of domestic and global political changes that legally desegregated America and decolonized the globe, as well as economic changes that fostered an interdependent, global economy. The effects of these factors on Black civil society have been mixed and fostered the emergence of new problems. For one, the magnitude of drugs, violence, and Black street children left to raise themselves threaten to erode the social fabric not only of Black neighborhoods, but of the United States overall. How much more land can suburbs and exurbs safely pave over to build affluent White neighborhoods far from the inner city without huge environmental costs? For another, misogynist strains within Black popular culture have revitalized a masculinist politics that far too often demeans Black women. The work of some Afrocentric scholars, the lyrics of 2 Live Crew and similar male rappers, and the symbolic portrayal of Malcolm X as a "redemptive Black patriarch" (Ransby and Matthews 1993, 57) all can be seen as evidence for the increasing intolerance Black women confront *within* Black civil society. Yet another issue concerns the growing numbers of mixed-race children who seek new guidelines of how to negotiate Black political identities. Prior eras granted mulattos and light-skinned Blacks special favors, suggesting that a similar fate may await mixed-race and biracial children. Attending to the political well-being of these children raises entirely new issues for Black women. In large part, these are the children of White mothers, and their understandings of Blackness reflect the range of their White mothers' willingness to embrace social and political Blackness. Lisa Jones, a Black woman raised by her White mother, puts her finger on the political problem: "One thing I'm clear on: If we can't find a way to make *multi*ethnic stand for *anti*racism, then I'll pass on it" (Jones 1994, 203).

These issues do not erase the need for Black women's organizations that build on the base of the activist mothering of Black women's community work. Such work does not explicitly advocate for Black women but instead sees Black women's advancement occurring in the context of community. As a result, this politicized motherwork is alternately seen as being a "conservative" example of "women's work" or, at best, as a less-developed form of feminism.[4] However, Black women's struggles for group survival as well as those dedicated to institutional transformation are just as needed now as in the past. Nothing in either struggle precludes individual Black women or groups of African-American women from engaging in coalitions with other groups. This is not an exclusionary identity politics, merely a Black-women-centered one.

The humanist vision in Black feminist thought has deep historical roots in the political activism of African-American women such as Sara Brooks, anonymous slave mothers, turn-of-the-century Black women educators, countless Ruth Powells, the centerwomen in the hospital union, the community women workers in Gilkes's study, and the Black and Latina community activists in Nancy Naples's work. These Black women activists generally transcended their differences in order to create a powerful Black women's activist tradition. It remains to be seen whether African-American women's responses to contemporary challenges will follow their lead and create new ways to "lift as we climb."

10 U.S. BLACK FEMINISM IN TRANSNATIONAL CONTEXT

Black women scholars and professionals cannot afford to ignore the straits of our sisters who are acquainted with the immediacy of oppression in a way many of us are not. The process of empowerment cannot be simplistically defined in accordance with our own particular class interests. We must learn to lift as we climb.
—Angela Davis 1989, 9

Within U.S. Black feminism, race, class gender, and sexuality constitute mutually constructing systems of oppression (Davis 1981; Smith 1983; Lorde 1984; Crenshaw 1991). Intersectional paradigms make two important contributions to understanding the connections between knowledge and empowerment. For one, they stimulate new interpretations of African-American women's experiences. Much of the work on U.S. Black women reported in earlier chapters relies on intersectional paradigms of some sort. For example, African-American women's confinement to domestic work revealed how race and gender influenced Black women's social class experiences. Similarly, the sexual politics of Black womanhood that shaped Black women's experiences with pornography, prostitution, and rape relied upon racist, sexist, and heterosexist ideologies to construct Black women's sexualities as deviant. Not only do intersectional paradigms prove useful in explaining U.S. Black women's experiences, such paradigms suggest that intersecting oppressions also shape the experiences of other groups as well. Puerto Ricans, U.S. White men, Asian American gays and lesbians, U.S. White women, and other historically identifiable groups all have distinctive histories that reflect their unique placement in intersecting oppressions (Andersen and Collins 1998).

Intersectional paradigms make a second important contribution to untangling the relationships between knowledge and empowerment—they shed new light on how domination is organized. The term *matrix of domination* describes this overall social organization within which intersecting oppressions originate, develop, and are contained. In the United States, such domination has occurred through schools, housing, employment, government, and other social institutions that regulate the actual patterns of intersecting oppressions that Black women encounter. Just as intersecting oppressions take on historically specific forms that change in response to human actions—racial segregation persists, but not in the forms that it took in prior historical eras—so the shape of domination itself changes.

As the particular form assumed by intersecting oppressions in one social location, any matrix of domination can be seen as an historically specific organization of power in which social groups are embedded and which they aim to influence. When Maria Stewart asked, "How long shall the fair daughters of Africa be compelled to bury their minds and talents beneath a load of iron pots and kettles?" (Richardson 1987), her query focused on the dialectical relationship linking oppression and activism for one period of time, the early 1800s, and in one social location, the United States. When Angela Davis counsels that privileged Black women not "ignore the straits of our sisters who are acquainted with the immediacy of oppression in a way many of us are not," she stresses the need for new ways of conceptualizing oppression and activism that take class differences of a global matrix of domination into account. All contexts of domination incorporate some combination of intersecting oppressions, and considerable variability exists from one matrix of domination to the next as to how oppression and activism will be organized. For example, as Senegalese feminists (Imam et al. 1997), Black American feminists (Guy-Sheftall 1995b), and Black British feminists (Mirza 1997) all point out, social institutions in Senegal, the United States, and the United Kingdom reflect intersecting oppressions of race, class, gender, and sexuality. Yet social relations within these three nation-states differ: Domination is structured differently in Senegal, the United States, and the United Kingdom. Thus, regardless of how any given matrix is actually organized either across time or from society to society, the concept of a matrix of domination encapsulates the universality of intersecting oppressions as organized through diverse local realities.

Placing U.S. Black women's experiences in the center of analysis without privileging those experiences shows how intersectional paradigms can be especially important for rethinking the particular matrix of domination that characterizes U.S. society. Claims that systems of race, social class, gender, and sexuality form mutually constructing features of social organization foster a basic rethinking of U.S. social institutions. For example, using intersecting paradigms to investigate U.S. Black women's experiences challenges deeply held beliefs that work and family constitute separate spheres of social organization. Since U.S. Black women's experiences have never fit the logic of work in the public sphere juxtaposed to family obligations in the private sphere, these categories lose meaning. As the persistent racial discrimination in schooling, housing, jobs, and public services indicates, Black women's experiences certainly challenge U.S. class ideologies claiming that individual merit is all that matters in determining social rewards. The sexual politics of Black womanhood reveals the fallacy of assuming that gender affects all women in the same way—race and class matter greatly. U.S. Black women's activism, especially its dual commitment to struggles for group survival and to institutional transformation, suggests that understandings of the political should be rethought. Thus, by using intersectional paradigms to explain both the U.S. matrix of domination and Black women's individual and collective agency within it, Black feminist thought helps reconceptualize social relations of domination and resistance.

Nation and Nationalism

Despite these contributions, U.S. Black feminist thought must continue to develop even more complex analyses of intersecting oppressions—how such oppressions are organized, their effect on group composition and history, their influence on individual consciousness, and, most importantly, collective strategies of resistance. Moving from race, class, and gender to generate analyses that include heterosexism as a system of oppression certainly constitutes a step in the right direction. But U.S. Black feminism will remain hindered in its goal of fostering Black women's empowerment in a context of social justice unless it incorporates more comprehensive analyses of how nation can constitute another form of oppression (Anthias and Yuval-Davis 1992; Yuval-Davis 1997).

Race, class, gender, and sexuality all remain closely intertwined with nation. In exploring these connections, it is important to distinguish among the terms nation, nation-state, and nationalism. These terms are often used interchangeably, but they refer to different things. A *nation* consists of a collection of people who have come to believe that they have been shaped by a common past and are destined to share a common future. That belief is usually nurtured by common cultural characteristics, such as language and customs; a well-defined geographic territory; the belief in a common history or origin; the belief that closer ties exist among members of the nation than with outsiders; a sense of difference from groups around them; and a shared hostility toward outsider groups. *Nationalism* is a political ideology that is expressed by any group that self-defines as a distinctive people or nation. Nationalist ideologies strive to foster beliefs and practices which permit a people or nation to control its own destiny. When any one group acquires sufficient state power that allows it to realize its goals, it controls a *nation-state*.

In the United States, because affluent White men control government and industry, public policies usually benefit this group. In other words, despite the U.S. Constitution's stated commitment to equality of all American citizens, historically, the differential treatment of U.S. Blacks, women, the working class, and other subordinated groups meant that the United States operated as a nation-state that disproportionately benefited affluent White men. Because this group controls schools, the news media, and other social institutions that legitimate what counts as truth, it possesses the authority to obscure its own power and to redefine its own special interests as being national interests. In response to this situation, U.S. Blacks, Chicanos, Puerto Ricans, Native Americans, and other similar groups have often themselves embraced nationalist ideologies. Because such ideologies stress solidarity and resistance, such ideologies have effectively been used in challenging U.S. state policies.

Women are important within nationalist philosophies, whether the nationalism is forwarded by dominant groups who wield nation-state power, or by subordinated groups who use nationalist ideologies to challenge their oppression. Groups on both sides of state power view the women in their group in particular ways. Because women are capable of becoming mothers, women are central to three elements in nationalist thinking, namely, issues of sexuality and fertility, of motherhood, and of being symbols of the nation (Yuval-Davis 1997). In the United States, all women experience the peculiar situation of being responsible for reproducing the nation-state's population, passing on an American national culture, and accepting the role of being inscribed with that same national culture. But within the U.S. matrix of domination, this entire process is racialized, is organized in class-specific ways, and has varying impact on women of diverse sexualities. Women are differentially evaluated based on their perceived value to give birth to the right kind of children, pass on appropriate American family values, and become worthy symbols of the nation. Black women, White women, Latinas, Native American women, and Asian American women all occupy different positions within gender, class, race, and nation as intersecting systems of power.

Because American citizenship is so often taken for granted among U.S. Black women, we often have difficulty seeing not only how deeply nationalistic U.S. society actually is, but how its nationalisms affect us. African-American women encounter differential treatment based on our perceived value as giving birth to the wrong race of children, as unable to socialize them properly because we bring them into bad family structures, and as unworthy symbols for U.S. patriotism. This treatment is based, in part, on ideologies that view U.S. Black women as the Other, the mammies, matriarchs, welfare mothers, and jezebels who mark the boundaries of normality for American women overall. African-American women and many others typically have difficulty seeing the assumptions that underlie this situation because American nation-state policies obscure how American national interests in actuality are special interests. These same assumptions also limit understanding of how U.S. nationalism operates globally. In this context, working exclusively within prevailing nationalistic assumptions fosters views of the U.S. matrix of domination where the effects of nationalism become difficult to see, let alone resist, because they seem so everyday and taken for granted.

One important assumption that affects African-American women is how ideas about family influence understandings of American national identity. Just as ideas about sexuality permeate multiple systems of oppression (see Chapter 6), ideas about family perform a similar function (Collins 1998c).

Similarly, ideas about motherhood become especially important to American national identity. Whereas all women are assigned the duty of reproducing the national group's population, and of passing on a national culture while simultaneously being inscribed with that same national culture, in the United States, these ideas about race, class, motherhood, and citizenship influence public policies. For example, U.S. population policies broadly defined aim to discourage Black women from having children, claiming that Black women make poor mothers and that their children end up receiving handouts from the state (Roberts 1997). In contrast, middle-class White women are encouraged to increase their fertility, and are assisted by a dazzling array of new reproductive technologies in the quest for the healthy White baby (Hartouni 1997). Working-class White women are encouraged to deliver healthy White babies, but place them for adoption with more worthy middle-class families (Collins 1999a). The fertility of undocumented women of color is seen as a threat to the nation-state, especially if such women's children gain citizenship and apply for public services (Chang 1994). Women thus emerge as being much more important to U.S. nation-state policies than is popularly believed.

Despite the contributions of incorporating ideas about motherhood and nation within U.S. Black feminist thought, the emphasis remains on U.S. *domestic* policies. U.S. Black feminist thought contains considerable work that assesses how U.S. educational, employment, taxation, and social welfare policies affect African-American women's lives. This is important scholarship, yet in the absence of studies that examine U.S. Black women in a global context, such work can foster the assumption that U.S. *foreign* policy is not important for African-American women. Stopping analysis at the U.S. border thus functions to contain U.S. Black feminist thought to Black women's interactions with groups that are already in the United States—Black men, White women, other racial/ethnic populations—groups that already hold American citizenship or that aspire to attain it.

Shifting to a global analysis not only reveals new dimensions of U.S. Black women's experiences in the particular matrix of domination that characterizes U.S. society, but it also illuminates how a transnational matrix of domination presents certain challenges for women of African descent. Intersecting oppressions do not stop at U.S. borders. Intersecting oppressions of race, class, gender, sexuality, and nation constitute global phenomena that have a particular organization in the United States. Nested within this U.S. version are distinctive group histories characterized by a unique combination of factors. U.S. Black women's experiences constitute one such group history that can be seen in the context of the particular social movements within the United States, the domestic policies of varying levels of U.S. government, and a global matrix of domination affecting women of African descent in general. Black women in Nigeria, Trinidad and Tobago, the United Kingdom, Botswana, Brazil, and other nation-states are similarly located. They encounter the contours of local social movements, the policies of their nation-states, and the same global matrix of domination in which

U.S. Black women are situated. All of these groups of women thus are positioned with situations of domination that are characterized by intersecting oppressions, yet their angle of vision on domination will vary greatly.

Shifting to a transnational context also brings women's rights activities to the forefront of discussion (Lindsey 1980). In a transnational context, women in African, Latin American, and Asian nations have not sat idly by, waiting for middle-class, White women from North American and Western European nation-states to tell them what to do. Instead, using the United Nations as a vehicle, women from quite diverse backgrounds have identified gender oppression as a major theme affecting women transnationally (see, e.g., *Rights of Women* 1998). These women are not just "theorizing" about oppression; their theory emerges from within the practical terrain of activism.

Within this broad transnational context, women of African descent have a distinctive, shared legacy that in turn is part of a global women's movement. At the same time, due to the peculiar combination of the legacy of African cultures, a history of racial oppressions organized via slavery, colonialism, and imperialism, and an emerging global racism that, assisted by modern technology, moves across national borders with dizzying speed, women of African descent encounter particular issues. For example, just as African-American women constitute one of the poorest groups within the United States, so do Black women in Brazil. Similarly, in the context of global women's poverty, women in Africa remain among the poorest. In this sense, women of African descent share much with women's rights struggles globally, but do so through particular Black diasporic experiences characterized by substantial heterogeneity.

Despite the national barriers that separate women of African descent, Black women's experiences demonstrate marked similarities that "illustrate how the persistence of the legacy of colonialism with its racial/ethnic, sexist and class biases has resulted in a system of 'global gendered apartheid'—a global economic system characterized by the exploitation of the labour of women of colour everywhere" (Antrobus 1995, 55). In this context, as social theorist Obioma Nnaemeka points out, "as people of African descent, our attention should not be solely on how blacks in Africa and those in the African Diaspora are *related with* each another, but also on how they *relate to* each other" (1998b, 377). One task, then, lies in stimulating dialogue across the very real limitations of national boundaries, to develop new ways of relating to one another, in order to unpack the interconnectedness of Black women's experiences.

Black Women in Transnational Context

In 1981, U.S. Black feminist theorist Barbara Smith identified her definition of what it meant to be radical: "What *I* really feel is radical is trying to make coalitions with people who are different from you. I feel it is radical to be dealing with race and sex and class and sexual identity all at one time. I think *that* is really radical because it has never been done before" (Smith and Smith 1981, 126). Whereas U.S. Black feminism has traveled some distance toward Smith's vision of radicalism, coalitions among U.S. Black women and among women of African descent differentially placed in "gendered global apartheid" face some tough questions. Such coalitions must attend not only to different histories, they must be aware of the varying strengths and limitations that groups bring to social justice efforts. Women of African descent thus remain differentially placed within an overarching matrix of "global gendered apartheid" organized via a plethora of distinct nation-state politics. As a result, dialogues among Black women across national boundaries remain difficult. But they are necessary because they promise to shed light on current issues within U.S. Black feminism that now appear to be "American" yet may be better understood in transnational context.

Placing African-American women's experiences in a transnational context simultaneously provides a new angle of vision on U.S. Black feminism as a social justice project and decenters the White/Black binary that has long plagued U.S. feminism. Within the U.S. White/Black framework, U.S. Black feminism can be seen only as a derivative movement. African-American women who self-define as Black feminists can be accused of being "White" identified, as if no independent Black feminist consciousness is possible. Refracted through the lens of U.S. race relations that sees Blacks as sidekicks, followers, and dependent beings, this interpretation has surface validity. Within assumptions that one need not consider anything outside U.S. national borders, these Black/White dialogues become intensified and can work to drown out other issues. When these debates are taken to their logical extreme, U.S. feminism can become one huge discussion about identity—as Black and White women, why can't we get along?

Placing U.S. Black women's experiences in a transnational context shifts this understanding of U.S. Black feminism. Instead of being White feminism in black-face, the core themes of U.S. Black feminism resemble similar issues raised by women of African descent elsewhere. Issues that are of great concern to U.S. Black women explored in earlier chapters—work and family, negative controlling images, struggles for self-definition in cultural contexts that deny Black women agency, sexual politics that make Black women vulnerable to sex work, rape, and media objectification, and understandings of motherwork within Black women's politics—find different meanings in a transnational context. As Andree Nicola McLaughlin points out, "The proliferation of Black women's organizations in the last decade signals a global phenomenon. Such organized political activity on the part of self-identified 'Black women' reflects a burgeoning, intercontinental Black women's consciousness movement" (1995, 73). Rather than being a White-identified anomaly within U.S. Black community development efforts, U.S. Black feminism can better be seen as part of an "intercontinental Black women's consciousness movement" that addresses the common concerns of women of African descent.

If common concerns link women of African descent transnationally, why don't more U.S. Black women see them? Certainly U.S. school curricula dedicated to glorifying American history and culture as well as a U.S. media that substitute news entertainment for serious coverage of global issues leave all U.S. citizens, including African-American women, ignorant of major world issues. But another important factor concerns U.S. Black women's relationships with two groups most closely aligned with African-American women's interests. Via their control over U.S. feminism and Black intellectual discourse, respectively, White American women and Black American men constitute two groups with which and through which African-American women construct U.S. Black feminism. Both groups may be well meaning, and in fact may express deep-seated concern for Black women's issues. But both groups find it difficult to get out of the way and encourage a fully articulated, Black feminist agenda where Black women are in charge.

Some strands of White Western feminism have been tireless in raising women's issues in defense of women who remain suppressed and therefore unable to speak for themselves. This is important work and often leads to valuable coalitions among First and Third World women. Yet the kinds of coalitions among groups such as these can become problematic. Because the groups remain so unequal in power, this inequality can foster a pseudo-maternalism among White women reminiscent of how U.S. middle-class social workers approached working-class, immigrant women in prior eras. The much-bandied-about accusation of racism in the women's movement may be much less about the racial attitudes of individual White women than it is about the unwillingness or inability of some Western White feminists to share power. These conflicts remain muted when the power differences among women are vast—the case when the interests of poor, rural, non-American Black women are championed by Western feminists. Yet when the power differentials shrink—the case of Black American and White American women who are seemingly equal under U.S. law—relationships become much more contentious.

U.S. Black men exercise a different kind of control. Here discourses of Black nationalism with their implicit counsel of a racial solidarity built on unquestioned support of African-American men stifles dialogue. Whereas the majority of African-Americans would most likely not identify themselves as "Black nationalists," most do ascribe to many of the basic tenets of Black nationalist–influenced ideologies that counsel Black self-determination (Franklin 1992). The historical viciousness and deeply entrenched nature of White supremacy in the United States makes this a rational response. Blacks may be the ones who are accused of "holding" onto race, but it is White Americans who move out of neighborhoods when Blacks move in. White Americans are the ones who want affirmative action programs in higher education dismantled, even if such efforts effectively bar African-American access to elite colleges. It is White Americans whose failure to vote for Black candidates forces civil rights organizations to remain embroiled in legal battles to find ways of ensuring Black representation under the rubric of American democracy. In this context, Black nationalism is not irrational—it has been essential for Black progress. However, despite their contributions, not all Black nationalisms are the same. But they do seem to share one common feature, namely, a norm of racial solidarity based on Black women's unquestioned support of Black men without extracting a similar commitment on the part of Black men to Black women. In contrast to White women's maternalism, U.S. Black women are encouraged to embrace a Black paternalism, one where Black men reclaim their manhood because Black women "let them be men."

Not only are both of these political responses unacceptable, the energy required to deal with both White women and Black men leaves little left over to engage in dialogue with other groups, both within the United States and transnationally. But a U.S. Black feminism that does not do so runs the risk of quickly running out of steam. It is important to remember that just as African-American women are neither African nor American, neither is U.S. Black feminism. Instead, it occupies its own space that reflects the privileges of U.S. citizenship juxtaposed to the second-class nature of that citizenship. However, while U.S. Black feminism occupies this location between Americaness—the struggles with White feminists and with Black men—and women of African descent globally, the lion's share of its attention has been directed at American groups. As a result, U.S. Black feminism has been preoccupied with responding to the issues raised by American groups. The task now lies in fleshing out dialogues and coalitions with Black women who live elsewhere in the Black diaspora, keeping in mind that intersecting oppressions have left a path of common challenges that are differently organized and resisted.

In the context of a global gendered apartheid, women of African descent share many qualities. One concerns the similarities that characterize contemporary Black women's organizing, much of which has been influenced by Black nationalist ideologies. In the post–World War II era of national independence and liberation movements in Africa, Asia, Latin America, and the Pacific, Black women actively participated in these anticolonialist and antiracist struggles, many of which relied on nationalist philosophies. In the global context of antiracist struggles, Black women have participated in activist struggles of all sorts (Terborg-Penn 1986). Many Black-run nation-states of the postcolonial era could not have been formed without women's efforts. For example, Black women were prominent in protracted anticolonial struggles against the Portuguese in both Mozambique and Angola. Black South African women have long engaged in political activism, much of it confrontational, that resulted in the successful overthrow of apartheid. Whereas other anticolonial efforts were more peaceful, they nonetheless relied on Black women's actions. Within the United States, Black women's participation in civil rights and Black power movements of the 1950s and 1960s reflected similar patterns (Crawford et al. 1990). In the U.S. context, the goal was not to form an independent nation-state, but rather to reform the existing one. U.S. political institutions required transformation so that rights of American citizenship would be fully extended to Black women and other historically disenfranchised groups.

These initial emphases on anticolonialist and antiracist agendas have since given way to new sets of issues. In particular, this transnational Black women's consciousness movement remains focused on how Black women's poverty becomes reorganized in conjunction with new institutional power arrangements of neocolonialism (the transnational context) and racial resegregation (the U.S. context). For example, African women have engaged in diverse types of liberation struggles, many of which brought new constitutional guarantees and legal freedoms ensuring women's rights. Women in South Africa, for example, now enjoy some of the most comprehensive constitutional protections anywhere. Yet despite these protracted anticolonial struggles, women in South Africa remain disproportionately poor and often have difficulty exercising the rights that they have earned. Similarly, African-American women who participated in the civil rights and Black power movements stimulated newfound political protections for all U.S. Black women, with many developing a Black feminist consciousness in the process. Despite the legal protections provided under these new political arrangements, Black women in both South Africa and the United States remain disproportionately poor.

Placing U.S. Black feminism within the context of global gendered apartheid provides new insights into U.S. Black feminist practices and thought. Expanding the process of self-definition described in Chapter 5 beyond individual and group identity for African-American women suggests that the transnational context would greatly aid U.S. Black women's struggles for group survival and institutional transformation. Self-defined Black diasporic feminisms require links among U.S. Black feminism and feminisms expressed by women of African descent as well as ties with transnational women's rights activism.

Developing this Black diasporic perspective among African-American women can be more difficult than one thinks, especially given the limited contact with Black women from the United Kingdom, Senegal, Brazil, and other nation-states, as well as the historically insular view of the world that permeates U.S. society. The absence of strong transnational organizations among Black women means that this type of Black feminist agenda is at its early stages. For example, in her arguments that this Black diasporic feminism be called *Africana womanism,* Clenora Hudson-Weems (1998) rejects both *African feminism* and *Black feminism* by asserting that both terms remain aligned with White, middle-class feminism. White women remain at the center, she suggests, even in global discussions of Black women's concerns. In response, Obioma Nnaemeka places the blame not on the rhetorical strategies of naming, but on the actual politics that limit Black women's ability to generate such an agenda:

> One can argue that the deficiency of African feminism and Black feminism respectively in addressing the full range of black women's experience arises more from their relationship one to the other than their relationship to white, middle-class feminism. (Nnaemeka 1998a, 21)

Despite these difficulties, it is important to investigate the potential and actual connections among U.S. Black feminism, African feminisms, and other feminisms advanced by women of African descent. Since this is obviously a very large task, one way of approaching it lies in examining selected challenges that have been identified by women of African descent transnationally. Stated differently, despite differences in how Black women encounter and respond to these common challenges, certain themes serve as a common agenda that characterizes Black women's concerns.

Unfortunately, the many structural barriers that impede Black women's access to education, housing, employment, and health care make it difficult for many to express self-defined women's agendas. In this regard, films made by women of African descent remain important. For example, *Femmes Aux Yeux Ouverts (Women with Open Eyes),* a 1994 documentary from Togo, remains exemplary in how it highlights the sophisticated political analyses and actions taken by African women themselves. In this film, Togolese women speak of how their eyes had formerly been closed but how their political consciousness as women is changing. Similarly, *Everyone's Child,* a 1996 film made in Zimbabwe, examines the devastating effects of AIDS on one African adolescent girl. As one of four siblings orphaned by losing her mother to AIDS, the girl tries to hold the family together. Out of desperation, she is forced into sex work until family members recognize that she and other children in her situation belong to everyone. The strength of *Femmes Aux Yeux Ouverts, Everyone's Child,* and similar film projects lies in their ability to transcend the limits of literacy. The issues raised by both films speak not just to and for many African women, they also raise issues familiar to U.S. Black women as well.

More common, however, is a pattern where women of African descent throughout the diaspora often begin defining our feminism in opposition to that advanced by middle-class, White Western women. This approach reproduces yet another binary, yet gathering together these dissident statements can also help identify points of convergence. At the 1992 conference on Women in Africa and African Development held in Nigeria, Olabisi Aina, a Nigerian social scientist, shared her thoughts on what she perceived as being the differences distinguishing African women's feminism from that of the West:

> The African woman today is concerned not only with overcoming the problems of foreign domination/rule, but also with the specific, immediate needs of surviving famine, hunger, drought, disease, and war. To be empowered, African women, unlike their Western sisters, are struggling not just to attain political power but also to be empowered by gaining

access to a good education and the professions, among other things. Many
of the issues which are of concern to the African feminist are often left out
of the Western feminist agenda. (Aina 1998, 75)

Whereas Olabisi Aina cannot speak for all women in a nation-state as large as
Nigeria, let alone a continent as large and diverse as Africa, her effort to identify
some defining features of a common agenda of African women provides a starting point for discussion. In many ways, she describes the types of struggles that
preoccupy African-American women. For example, U.S. Black women are also
engaged in overcoming problems of foreign rule and war, but the "foreigners"
in the U.S. context are the police. This issue of misuse of police authority against
African-Americans, especially against Black men, reemerges as an important
concern of U.S. Black women (Davis 1997). The women interviewed by Leith
Mullings (1997) who feared for their children's lives in Harlem certainly feel as
though they live in a war zone. U.S. Black women's citizenship status that provides a safety net of social services is designed to protect African-American
women from the "immediate needs of surviving famine [and] hunger." There is
no famine, but as the growing numbers of families who visit soup kitchens suggest, there may be hunger. Efforts to dismantle the social welfare state whose
purpose has been to provide food, housing, education, and health care for those
who could not afford these services preoccupy Black feminist agendas (Lubiano
1992; Brewer 1994). Disease is also a factor, with African-American women's
health identified as an important issue among Black women activists (White
1994). Aina's list can be used to compare the situation of African-American
women with Nigerian women, but this is not its best use. Instead, her comments provide a useful starting point for developing an intercontinental Black
women's consciousness that identifies how women of African descent encounter
different configurations of common challenges such as these.

Common Differences

Positioning African-American women within a transnational context suggests
that U.S. Black women occupy a both/and status regarding U.S. feminism, Black
diasporic feminisms, and transnational women's rights activism. On some
dimensions, U.S. Black feminism resembles that of women within and from
Black diasporic societies, while on other dimensions, it remains distinctively
American. Collectively, these common areas of concern link the feminisms of
women of African descent within a broader transnational context. They also
provide a useful starting point for examining the common differences that characterize an intercontinental Black women's consciousness movement, one
responding to intersecting oppressions that are differently organized via a global
matrix of domination.

On the one hand, intersections of race and gender that frame the category

"Black women" generate a shared set of challenges for all women of African descent, however differentially placed in other social hierarchies we may be. For example, not all Black women are poor, but Black women as a collectivity remain disproportionately poor. On the other hand, differences among Black women reflecting our diverse histories suggest that experiences with poverty will be far more complex than currently imagined. African-American women may be disproportionately poor, but Black women's poverty in the United States is organized differently from that confronting women of African descent transnationally. Despite the similarity of concerns, Black women in Africa, the Caribbean, South America, Canada, and other places experience these concerns differently and, as a result, organize in response to them differently.

Transnationally, women's advocates have aimed to use existing human rights laws to develop a women's rights agenda. In a workbook designed to be used by women of varying levels of literacy, the International Women's Tribune Centre identifies six areas of human rights laws that can be used to protect women's rights: women and education; women and employment; women and marriage; women refugees; sexual exploitation and trafficking; and women and torture (*Rights of Women* 1998, 19–54). They then move on to redefine women's human rights as encompassing six areas of concern: violence against women; housing, land and property; reproductive rights; environmental rights; women with disabilities; and sexual orientation rights (55–76). Even a cursory glance at this list reveals that these issues deemed important for women are also significant for women of African descent. What is also noteworthy is how and why some issues receive greater attention within U.S. Black feminism, while others remain muted or even invisible. A fully developed analysis of all six areas of human rights as well as the six areas of women's rights is beyond the scope of this chapter. However, a brief discussion of two issues sheds light on how exploring patterns of common differences among women of African descent might benefit a transnational Black women's consciousness movement.

Black Women's Poverty

Understandings of Black women's poverty illustrate these interconnections of race, gender, class, and nation. Whereas Black women's poverty takes similar forms globally and ultimately stems from a common source, the specific causes of U.S. Black women's poverty and that of women of African descent who are citizens of other nation-states or who are in the United States but lack American citizenship demonstrate how issues of national citizenship and nation-state policies matter. For one, the interconnections of U.S. domestic and foreign policy contribute differently to Black women's poverty. Especially critical of the "development" model imposed upon the Third World, Canadian feminist Angela Miles claims that categories such as development obscure some important linkages among women in First World countries and those in Third World countries. As Miles points out:

> In the process it is becoming clear that what we call "development issues" in the "third world," such as housing, education, health, child care, and poverty, are called "social issues" in the "first world." These are not qualitatively different phenomena as "development" definitions imply, but shared political issues that constitute a potential basis for common political struggle. Global feminisms are the result of this common struggle grounded in diverse local realities. (Miles 1998, 169)

U.S. foreign and domestic policies of the 1980s illustrate how the interconnections between "development issues" and "social issues" represent two sides of the same coin. On the one hand, Black women in so-called developing areas of Africa, Latin America, and the Caribbean point to the effects of structural adjustment policies as a major cause of the growing poverty among Black women. Introduced in the 1980s to alleviate the debt crisis of Third World nation-states, these policies fostered cuts in public services and subsidies to basic goods (food and fuel); increases in the price of transportation, housing, water, electricity, and medicines; privatization of government assets; and trade liberalization and devaluation of the currency. In this sense, these policies can be seen as deeply "raced" because these restrictions were targeted toward people of color.

Structural adjustment policies had two main objectives that in turn had a special impact on women. First, via cuts in government expenditures on social services, these policies aimed to reduce consumption. These actions jeopardized jobs in sectors in which women predominate and assumed that women would fill the gaps created by these cuts. Second, the policies aimed to increase production. Based on assumptions about a ready supply of cheap female labor, the policies incorporated women into capitalist market relations in especially exploitative ways. Both of these objectives devalue women's work in the household as well as in the labor force (Antrobus 1995). In this regard, policies of structural adjustment are deeply gendered, based as they are on an assumption that justifies exploitation of women's time and labor, both in the household and in the workplace.

The consequences of structural adjustment policies have been devastating. For entire populations, they have led to increasing unemployment, poverty, social disintegration, and violence. The poor have suffered the most—and poor women, children, and elderly more than anyone else (Antrobus 1995, 57). These policies relied upon media images designed to mask the culpability of policymakers whose decisions brought about such results. One such image was the portrayal of Black women's poverty in fatalistic terms that suggested the problem was so immense that very little could be done to remedy it. African feminist Ama Ada Aidoo decries the ways in which African women's poverty is portrayed in the media:

> The image of the African woman in the mind of the world has been set: she is breeding too many children she cannot take care of, and for whom she should not expect other people to pick up the tab. She is hungry, and so are her children. In fact, it has become a cliché of Western photojournalism that the African woman is old beyond her years; she is half-naked; her drooped and withered breasts are well exposed; there are flies buzzing around the faces of her children; and she has a permanent begging bowl in her hand. (Aidoo 1998, 39)

This image constructs African women either as too far gone to be worthy of aid or as passive recipients of government handouts. Significantly, the one area of agency allowed Black women lies in their sexuality and reproductive capacities—if African women are in fact "breeding too many children," then it is perfectly acceptable for Western nation-states to refuse to "pick up the tab."

Aidoo's description might seem uncomfortably familiar to African-American women, for despite its culturally specific content—poor U.S. Black women are rarely portrayed as "half-naked" with "flies buzzing around the faces of her children"—they have been depicted in a similar fashion. During the same period when Black women in "developing" nations castigated structural adjustment policies, U.S. Black feminists blamed the social policies of the Reagan administration as a major factor in fostering African-American women's poverty (Brewer 1994). Domestic social welfare policies of the 1980s and into the 1990s painted African-American women as unworthy citizens and stripped them of entitlements by blaming African-American women for creating both their own poverty and that of African-Americans (Collins 1989).

Reminiscent of Aidoo's African woman with a "permanent begging bowl in her hand," U.S. Black women's depiction as "welfare queens" served a similar purpose (Lubiano 1992). In both cases, the poverty of Black children was traced back to the sexuality and reproductive capacities of their mothers. But whereas African women's poverty was deemed permanent and thus unresponsive to aid, African-American women were deemed unworthy recipients of aid that maintained their status as permanent beggars. In both cases, the best action was to let them starve.

Black Women and Mother-Child Families

Another important and related issue that links the feminisms of women of African descent concerns how to be effective mothers, especially in the context of changing work and family responsibilities. U.S. Black women's motherwork, particularly efforts to successfully combine bloodmother, othermother, and community othermother responsibilities with the need to generate independent income, resonates with similar struggles engaged in by women transnationally. More important, issues of motherhood, work, and family responsibilities remain closely bundled in explaining Black women's poverty globally. Describing the poverty of women in the Caribbean, Peggy Antrobus points to the significance that low-paid and unpaid work has in influencing Black women's economic position:

> Women's poverty has its foundation in the fact that much of the work of women in the household, in subsistence agriculture and in the community is either unwaged or poorly paid for . . . the large amount of unwaged work that working-class or poor women do condemns them to a cycle of poverty, be it in rural or urban areas. One cannot understand poverty and exploitation without considering the impact of women's unwaged work on the economic system. (Antrobus 1995, 56)

Antrobus's observations resonate with earlier discussions of how U.S. Black women challenge prevailing U.S. understandings of income-generating work, unpaid family labor, and Black women's motherwork. Black women's poverty across diverse societies remains associated with their responsibility for children, often without sufficient male support.

One outcome of Black women's efforts to negotiate work, family, and motherhood is the emergence of Black mother-child families as a growing global phenomenon. Situating mother-child families in the context of the global political economy highlights the significance of advanced capitalism for understanding mother-child families in transnational context (Mencher and Okongwu 1993). In particular, important connections characterize the stage of capitalist development encountered by any group of people and the patterns of family organization that emerge within that group. Massive global economic restructuring since World War II suggests that shifting patterns of industrial development, their accompanying race- and gender-segmented labor markets, and associated outcomes such as migration, urbanization, and ghettoization all affect families. This literature has been used to examine issues of African-American political economy overall (see, e.g., Squires 1994), yet, despite its significance, it remains underutilized in regard to distinctive patterns of U.S. Black family organization. Historically higher rates of U.S. Black mother-child families and the accelerated increase of African-American mother-child families in the 1960s and 1970s may be better explained by attending to industrial and labor market patterns than to attributes of Black culture (Billingsley 1992).

Placing mother-child families maintained by Black women in African, Caribbean, Latin America, North American, and European nation-states in the context of global capitalist development demonstrates that this household formation emerges within groups that face similar political and economic challenges (Mencher and Okongwu 1993). One such challenge concerns how to adapt to the race- and gender-segmented labor markets that result from agribusiness, industrial flight, mechanization, and other workplace changes. The effects of diverse industrial patterns on household and family organization in the

Caribbean provides one view of how the intersections of race and class foster specific patterns of family organization (see, e.g., Momsen 1993). In these cases, the industrial mix characterizing an island's employment base produces gender-segmented labor markets. For example, in locales characterized by heavy industries that rely on male labor (e.g., oil refineries), rates of female-headedness are likely to be lower than in places whose industrial base relies more heavily on female labor (e.g., the garment industry). When men cannot get jobs and women can, men migrate, leaving their wives, girlfriends, and children behind.

Gender-specific patterns of migration arise in response to the creation and/or flight of economic opportunities in home communities. Moreover, industrial policy works with national policies concerning immigration. Work and family patterns among Mexican men and women who migrated to Mexican/U.S. border towns in the early 1980s reveal the complex ways in which industrial and immigration policies foster female-headed family households. One striking feature of this migration stream is that families migrated as units when they could no longer subsist within the capitalist market economies that incorporated their villages. While family groups migrated as units, employers on the Mexican side of the border hired women but not men. As a result, women and children remained in Mexico while men migrated into the United States in search of work. Over time, many men failed to return to their families left at the borders, leaving an increase in mother-child families in towns housing these border industries. In this case, employment policies on both sides of the Mexican/U.S. border fostered the emergence of female-headed households among a population previously lacking this form of family organization (Fernandez-Kelly 1983).

In some cases, national policies are overtly tied to the industrial policies that in turn stimulate increasing numbers of single mothers. Patterns of household formation under apartheid among Black South Africans are revealing in this regard. South African labor policies prior to apartheid's formal end in 1990 routinely fostered family dissolution (Martin 1984). Men and women were explicitly recruited to race- and gender-segmented labor markets that relied on their separation for profitability. For example, men in mining were expected to leave their wives and children and live in dormitories. The pass laws that proved so unpopular with Black South Africans emerged in part to regulate where male workers could work and live. In contrast, women were either left behind in the so-called homelands or forced to migrate to cities in search of domestic work to supplement inadequate male incomes. Neglected in this harsh system of labor regulation were Black South African children. Often they were forced to live illegally with their mothers in cities, were left in the "homelands," or were in other ways legally separated from their mothers (Kuzwayo 1985).

These combinations of economic opportunity and gender-specific responsibilities for Black women often result in recurring patterns of poverty that bear remarkable similarity from one culture to the next. Peggy Antrobus describes the cycle of poverty as it operates in Caribbean settings:

> The majority of the poor are women. While many of them have large fam-
> ilies, they are not poor *because* they have many children. In fact, the reverse
> is true. They may have many children because they are poor, which means
> they have very limited options in terms of education, training and
> employment, and see children as a source of wealth, perhaps the only
> source of affirmation. For many, the cycle starts with early motherhood,
> while they are still at school. With the failure of the baby's father to sup-
> port their child, the women often turn for support to other men, who
> leave her with yet more children. And so the cycle is repeated. Serial mat-
> ing in the Caribbean has to be seen as a survival strategy. We have to thus
> consider women's poverty in the context of massive unemployment and
> the inability of many men to support their children. (Antrobus 1995, 56)

Descriptions of Black male-female relationships in many U.S. inner cities bear
close resemblance to Antrobus's rendition of Caribbean societies. For example,
rates of infant mortality in some Black inner-city neighborhoods match those of
developing countries. In this regard, poor U.S. Black women, especially those in
inner-city neighborhoods, may share more with women in the Caribbean and
other Third World nations than with middle-class White and Black women in the
United States (Brewer 1995).

These cases of how mother-child families respond to the race- and gender-
segmented labor markets created by advanced, global capitalist development suggest that these factors may be more important in explaining family household
structures in African-American communities than has commonly been believed to
be the case (Collins 1997). The rapid increase in U.S. Black mother-child families
in the 1960s and 1970s reflects industrial policies, labor market reorganization,
and government policies (Brewer 1988, 1994). William Julius Wilson's (1987,
1996) work remains exemplary in linking patterns of family organization to the
changing contours of economic opportunities in Black urban neighborhoods.
Whereas Wilson has been criticized for his seeming neglect of contemporary
institutionalized racism, his work highlights how growing joblessness among
Black men in the 1960s and 1970s correlates with (but does not necessarily
cause) increasing rates of African-American mother-child families. His work
documents how the emergence of mother-child families among working-class
African-Americans can be attributed in part to a changing political economy that
disadvantaged U.S. Blacks. Whereas Wilson assumes a background of capitalist
development and encourages greater attention to its effects, Rose Brewer (1995)
criticizes capitalist development itself. Claiming that U.S. Black workers and families are at the center of a global economic restructuring process that has race- and
gender-specific dimensions, Brewer points out, "There is not enough money
in central cities to sustain either growth or two-parent family formation (1995,
p. 167)."

Overall, the status of mother-child families in inner-city neighborhoods can
be seen as an advanced case of what happens when male joblessness within an

urban context becomes coupled with the absence of social welfare state supports or—the case for African-Americans—declining social welfare state supports. The myriad of social problems associated with Black women's poverty and Black women's responsibilities in caring for children—violence, drugs, adolescent pregnancy, and school dropout rates—transcend the U.S. context. Instead, U.S. Black women's experiences are an American version of an important transnational phenomenon.

Groups, Coalitions, and Transversal Politics

The complexities of African-American women's group experiences challenge simple hierarchies that routinely label affluent White men as global oppressors, poor Black women as powerless victims, with other groups arrayed in between. Instead, race, gender, class, citizenship status, sexuality, and age shape any group's social location in the transnational matrix of domination. These locations in turn frame group participation in a wide range of activities. Because groups occupying different positions display varying expressions of power, they have distinctive patterns of participation in shaping domination and resistance. Coming to terms with these diverse group histories provides a new foundation for developing a transversal politics.

Originally coined by Italian feminists, transversal politics emphasizes coalition building that takes into account the specific positions of "political actors." As Nira Yuval-Davis describes it, "Transversal dialogue should be based on the principles of rooting and shifting—that is, being centered in one's own experience while being empathetic to the differential positioning of the partners in the dialogue . . . the boundaries of the dialogue would be determined by the message rather than its messengers" (1997, 88). Within this framework, African-American women and other comparable groups constitute "political actors" or "messengers" aiming to craft a Black feminist "message." Within the assumptions of transversalism, participants bring with them a "rooting" in their own particular group histories, but at the same time realize that in order to engage in dialogue across multiple markers of difference, they must "shift" from their own centers.[1]

This recognition of how the experiences of Black women in Africa, the Caribbean, the United States, Europe, and Latin America demonstrate common differences generates several important issues concerning the contours and potential effectiveness of transversal politics. First, transversal politics requires a basic rethinking of cognitive frameworks used to understand the world and to change it. Transversal politics requires rejecting the binary thinking that has been so central to oppressions of race, class, gender, sexuality, and nation. Under such models, one must be one thing or the other—Black women are poor *either* because they are Black or because they are women. One is either a racist or an antiracist individual, a sexist person or not, an oppressor group or oppressed one. In contrast, transversal politics requires *both/and* thinking. In such frameworks, all individuals and groups possess varying amounts of penalty and privilege in one historically created system. Within U.S. history, for example, White women have been penalized by their gender but privileged by their race and citizenship status. Similarly, Black heterosexual women have been penalized by both race and gender yet privileged by their sexuality and citizenship status. In a transnational context, U.S. Black women are privileged by their citizenship yet disadvantaged by their gender. Depending on the context, individuals and groups may be alternately oppressors in some settings, oppressed in others, or simultaneously oppressing and oppressed in still others.

A second and related issue associated with transversal politics concerns definitions of how social groups are organized and maintained. Long-standing views of group organization see groups as fixed, unchanging, and with clear-cut boundaries. In contrast, the view advanced here retains historically constructed groups, but perceives these groups as being much more fluid. U.S. Black women's experiences illustrate this fluidity. Just as each individual African-American woman has a unique biography that reflects her experiences within intersecting oppressions, the experiences of U.S. Black women as a collectivity reflect a similar process.[2] Group boundaries are not fixed. Within the U.S. context, this more fluid notion of groups suggests that African-American women as a collectivity encounter a particular configuration of race, class, and gender politics that, while overlapping with those of some groups, resembling those of others, and differing from still others, remains distinctive to Black women. U.S. Black women's placement in a transnational context suggests a similar set of relationships. Thus, as an historically identifiable population, U.S. Black women are simultaneously privileged and penalized within a matrix of domination. Within any matrix of domination characterized by intersecting oppressions, any specific social location where such systems meet or intersect generates distinctive group histories.

A third requirement of transversal politics concerns the internal dynamics of groups. For U.S. Black women, engaging in processes of group self-definition requires confronting the entire constellation of our history, not just a selective reading of it. Via these internal dialogues, African-American women potentially take one important step toward transversal politics. These private conversations required for group self-definitions can be affirming. For example, the safe spaces that African-American women carve out for self-definitions has been designed to protect Black women from external assaults. The mirrors that Black women hold up to one another in such spaces can be affirming. But the existence of these spaces does not mean that ugliness does not occur in safe spaces. As Black lesbians point out, safe spaces are safer for some than for others.

Moreover, what quickly becomes apparent is that these internal processes of self-definition cannot continue indefinitely without engaging in relationships with other groups. Since groups are not hermetically sealed entities, coming to terms with a particular group history leads to the realization that groups can neither define themselves in isolation nor resist social injustice on their own. At best, each group possesses a partial perspective on its own experiences and on those of other groups. The critical self-reflection and community organizing accomplished via coming to terms with one's own group history builds the foundation for effective coalition. For example, it's not enough to see that "Nigerian and U.S. Black women have been victimized" and to build an alliance solely on the foundation of shared victimization. The reality is that while Black women's victimization in these two settings may be similar, it is not the same. Instead, coalitions are built via recognition of one's own group position and seeing how the social location of groups has been constructed in conjunction with one another. Empathy, not sympathy, becomes the basis of coalition.

This recognition stimulates a fourth issue associated with transversal politics, namely, recognizing that group histories are relational. It is important to remember that U.S. Black women's group history remains interdependent with those of other groups—patterns characterizing one group's experiences are intimately linked to those of other groups. For example, in the U.S. context, the social construction of U.S. White womanhood as pure, fragile, and in need of protection from the assaults of "violent" African-American men required the use of differential patterns of institutionalized sexual violence against both African-American women and men. The transnational context reveals similar contradictions. U.S. Black women may encounter state violence within the United States, but U.S. nation-state foreign policies inflict comparable violence upon women outside U.S. borders. Both domestically and transnationally, through threats of violence or actual violence, groups actively police each other to ensure that domination is maintained.

Examining these interdependent group histories often reveals painful contradictions. It becomes more difficult, for example, for U.S. White women to retain moral credibility as survivors of sexual violence without simultaneously condemning the benefits that accompany racial violence enacted on their behalf. Similarly, claims by some African-American men that racial oppression is more fundamental than gender oppression sound hollow in a context of shirked responsibility for their violence against African-American women. Both cases reflect how White women and African-American men *both* experience the victimization that can serve as a foundation for building empathy with other groups, *and* bear some responsibility for systemic violence targeted to other groups. These examples suggest that moral positions as survivors of one expression of systemic violence become eroded in the absence of accepting responsibility for other expressions of systemic violence.

This recognition of relational group histories leads to a fifth issue associated with transversal politics, namely, the acknowledgment that coalitions with some groups are not possible. This is because while group experiences are interdependent, they are not equivalent. Even though, for example, U.S. White men and

African-American women both have group histories that reflect patterns of privilege and oppression, these groups are far from equal in the transnational matrix of domination. Instead, each group reflects a distinctive constellation of victimization, access to positions of authority, unearned benefits, and traditions of resistance. While the histories of both groups reflect all dimensions, the patterns within each group will differ based on the overall placement of the group in relation to other race/gender groups, as well as variations within the group stemming from class, citizenship status, sexuality, and age.

In this sense, the histories of U.S. White men and African-American women are linked, socially construct each other, share certain features, but are not equivalent. White men clearly have power over African-American women, but the relationship between the groups is more complex than a simple hierarchy of White male privilege that victimizes African-American women. The relationship between the two groups is certainly this, but it is much more than simply this. Because of this complexity, coalitions with some groups of White men are necessary for some issues, but virtually impossible on others. Women of African descent from and within Black diasporic societies share comparable crosscutting relationships. In this model, there are no absolute oppressors or victims. Instead, historically constructed categories create intersecting and crosscutting group histories that provide changing patterns of group participation in domination and resistance to it.

This non-equivalency fosters a final important dimension of transversal politics—the dynamic nature of coalitions. Coalitions ebb and flow based on the perceived saliency of issues to group members. This non-equivalency of group experience means that groups find some oppressions more salient than others. Patterns of common differences among U.S. Black women and women within and from Black diasporic societies speak to the saliency of one form of oppression over another across different social settings. Race, class, and gender represent the three axes of oppression that African-American women routinely identify as being most important to them. But these systems and the economic, political, and ideological conditions that support them may not be seen as the most fundamental oppressions by women of African descent transnationally. This is one important feature of the matrix of domination—whereas all systems operate in framing the experiences of Black women transnationally, different configurations of such systems have saliency for Black women differently placed within them.

Overall, Black feminist knowledge and the transversal politics that might guide Black women's activism share important features. Both rely on paradigms of intersectionality to conceptualize intersecting oppressions and group behavior in resisting them. Both are collaboratively constructed, making it virtually impossible to extract either from actual power relations. Both exhibit moments of collaboration and confrontation necessary for constructing knowledge and building coalitions. Despite the tensions between sameness (race/gender intersections) and difference (class, citizenship, sexuality, and age) that distinguish the experiences of Black women in the Caribbean, the United States, Africa, Latin America, and Europe, it is important to recognize that women of African descent remain differentially placed within an overarching transnational context characterized by a global gendered apartheid. As a result, dialogues among African-American women and other historically identifiable oppressed groups should benefit from the multiple angles of vision that accompany multiple group standpoints. These dialogues not only promise to shed light on current issues within U.S. Black feminism, they potentially inform new directions for transversal politics.

11 BLACK FEMINIST EPISTEMOLOGY

A small girl and her mother passed a statue depicting a European man who had bare-handedly subdued a ferocious lion. The little girl stopped, looked puzzled and asked, "Mama, something's wrong with that statue. Everybody knows that a man can't whip a lion." "But darling," her mother replied, "you must remember that the man made the statue." —As told by Katie G. Cannon

As critical social theory, U.S. Black feminist thought reflects the interests and standpoint of its creators. Tracing the origin and diffusion of Black feminist thought or any comparable body of specialized knowledge reveals its affinity to the power of the group that created it (Mannheim 1936). Because elite White men control Western structures of knowledge validation, their interests pervade the themes, paradigms, and epistemologies of traditional scholarship. As a result, U.S. Black women's experiences as well as those of women of African descent transnationally have been routinely distorted within or excluded from what counts as knowledge.

U.S. Black feminist thought as specialized thought reflects the distinctive themes of African-American women's experiences. Black feminist thought's core themes of work, family, sexual politics, motherhood, and political activism rely on paradigms that emphasize the importance of intersecting oppressions in shaping the U.S. matrix of domination. But expressing these themes and paradigms has not been easy because Black women have had to struggle against White male interpretations of the world.

In this context, Black feminist thought can best be viewed as subjugated knowledge. Traditionally, the suppression of Black women's ideas within White-male-controlled social institutions led African-American women to use music, literature, daily conversations, and everyday behavior as important locations for constructing a Black feminist consciousness. More recently, higher education and the news media have emerged as increasingly important sites for Black feminist intellectual activity. Within these new social locations, Black feminist thought has often become highly visible, yet curiously, despite this visibility, it has become differently subjugated (Collins 1998a, 32–43).

Investigating the subjugated knowledge of subordinate groups—in this case a Black women's standpoint and Black feminist thought—requires more ingenuity than that needed to examine the standpoints and thought of dominant groups. I found my training as a social scientist inadequate to the task of studying the subjugated knowledge of a Black women's standpoint. This is because subordinate groups have long had to use alternative ways to create independent self-definitions and self-valuations and to rearticulate them through our own specialists. Like other subordinate groups, African-American women not only have developed a distinctive Black women's standpoint, but have done so by using alternative ways of producing and validating knowledge.

Epistemology constitutes an overarching theory of knowledge (Harding 1987). It investigates the standards used to assess knowledge or *why* we believe what we believe to be true. Far from being the apolitical study of truth, epistemology points to the ways in which power relations shape who is believed and why. For example, various descendants of Sally Hemmings, a Black woman owned by Thomas Jefferson, claimed repeatedly that Jefferson fathered her children. These accounts forwarded by Jefferson's African-American descendants were ignored in favor of accounts advanced by his White progeny. Hemmings's descendants were routinely disbelieved until their knowledge claims were validated by DNA testing.

Distinguishing among epistemologies, paradigms, and methodologies can prove to be useful in understanding the significance of competing epistemologies (Harding 1987). In contrast to epistemologies, *paradigms* encompass interpretive frameworks such as intersectionality that are used to explain social phenomena.[1] *Methodology* refers to the broad principles of how to conduct research and how interpretive paradigms are to be applied.[2] The level of epistemology is important because it determines which questions merit investigation, which interpretive frameworks will be used to analyze findings, and to what use any ensuing knowledge will be put.

In producing the specialized knowledge of U.S. Black feminist thought, Black women intellectuals often encounter two distinct epistemologies: one representing elite White male interests and the other expressing Black feminist concerns. Whereas many variations of these epistemologies exist, it is possible to distill some of their distinguishing features that transcend differences among the paradigms within them. Epistemological choices about whom to trust, what to believe, and why something is true are not benign academic issues. Instead, these concerns tap the fundamental question of which versions of truth will prevail.

Eurocentric Knowledge Validation Processes and U.S. Power Relations

In the United States, the social institutions that legitimate knowledge as well as the Western or Eurocentric epistemologies that they uphold constitute two inter-related parts of the dominant knowledge validation processes. In general, schol-ars, publishers, and other experts represent specific interests and credentialing processes, and their knowledge claims must satisfy the political and epistemo-logical criteria of the contexts in which they reside (Kuhn 1962; Mulkay 1979). Because this enterprise is controlled by elite White men, knowledge validation processes reflect this group's interests.[3] Although designed to represent and pro-tect the interests of powerful White men, neither schools, government, the media and other social institutions that house these processes nor the actual epistemologies that they promote need be managed by White men themselves. White women, African-American men and women, and other people of color may be enlisted to enforce these connections between power relations and what counts as truth. Moreover, not all White men accept these power relations that privilege Eurocentrism. Some have revolted and subverted social institutions and the ideas they promote.

Two political criteria influence knowledge validation processes. First, knowl-edge claims are evaluated by a group of experts whose members bring with them a host of sedimented experiences that reflect their group location in intersecting oppressions. No scholar can avoid cultural ideas and his or her placement in intersecting oppressions of race, gender, class, sexuality, and nation. In the United States, this means that a scholar making a knowledge claim typically must con-vince a scholarly community controlled by elite White avowedly heterosexual men holding U.S. citizenship that a given claim is justified. Second, each com-munity of experts must maintain its credibility as defined by the larger popula-tion in which it is situated and from which it draws its basic, taken-for-granted knowledge. This means that scholarly communities that challenge basic beliefs held in U.S. culture at large will be deemed less credible than those that support popular ideas. For example, if scholarly communities stray too far from widely held beliefs about Black womanhood, they run the risk of being discredited.

When elite White men or any other overly homogeneous group dominates knowledge validation processes, both of these political criteria can work to sup-press Black feminist thought. Given that the general U.S. culture shaping the taken-for-granted knowledge of the community of experts is permeated by widespread notions of Black female inferiority, new knowledge claims that seem to violate this fundamental assumption are likely to be viewed as anomalies (Kuhn 1962). Moreover, specialized thought challenging notions of Black female inferiority is unlikely to be generated from within White-male-controlled acad-emic settings because both the kinds of questions asked and the answers to them would necessarily reflect a basic lack of familiarity with Black women's realities. Even those who think they are familiar can reproduce stereotypes. Believing that they are already knowledgeable, many scholars staunchly defend controlling images of U.S. Black women as mammies, matriarchs, and jezebels, and allow these commonsense beliefs to permeate their scholarship.

The experiences of African-American women scholars illustrate how individuals who wish to rearticulate a Black women's standpoint through Black feminist thought can be suppressed by prevailing knowledge validation processes. Exclusion from basic literacy, quality educational experiences, and faculty and administrative positions has limited U.S. Black women's access to influential academic positions (Zinn et al. 1986; Moses 1989). Black women have long produced knowledge claims that contested those advanced by elite White men. But because Black women have been denied positions of authority, they often relied on alternative knowledge validation processes to generate competing knowledge claims. As a consequence, academic disciplines typically rejected such claims. Moreover, any credentials controlled by White male academicians could then be denied to Black women who used alternative standards on the grounds that Black women's work did not constitute credible research.

Black women with academic credentials who seek to exert the authority that our status grants us to propose new knowledge claims about African-American women face pressures to use our authority to help legitimate a system that devalues and excludes the majority of Black women. When an outsider group—in this case, African-American women—recognizes that the insider group—namely, elite White men—requires special privileges from the larger society, those in power must find ways of keeping the outsiders out and at the same time having them acknowledge the legitimacy of this procedure. Accepting a few "safe" outsiders addresses this legitimation problem (Berger and Luckmann 1966). One way of excluding the majority of Black women from the knowledge validation process is to permit a few Black women to acquire positions of authority in institutions that legitimate knowledge, and to encourage us to work within the taken-for-granted assumptions of Black female inferiority shared by the scholarly community and the culture at large. Those Black women who accept these assumptions are likely to be rewarded by their institutions. Those challenging the assumptions can be placed under surveillance and run the risk of being ostracized.

African-American women academicians who persist in trying to rearticulate a Black women's standpoint also face potential rejection of our knowledge claims on epistemological grounds. Just as the material realities of powerful and dominated groups produce separate standpoints, these groups may also deploy distinctive epistemologies or theories of knowledge. Black women scholars may know that something is true—at least, by standards widely accepted among African-American women—but be unwilling or unable to legitimate our claims using prevailing scholarly norms. For any discourse, new knowledge claims must be consistent with an existing body of knowledge that the group controlling the interpretive context accepts as true. Take, for example, the differences between how U.S. Black women interpret their experiences as single mothers and how prevailing social science research analyzes the same reality. Whereas Black women stress their struggles with job discrimination, inadequate child support, inferior housing, and street violence, far too much social science research seems mesmerized by images of lazy "welfare queens" content to stay on the dole. The methods used to validate knowledge claims must also be acceptable to the group controlling the knowledge validation process. Individual African-American women's narratives about being single mothers are often rendered invisible in quantitative research methodologies that erase individuality in favor of proving patterns of welfare abuse. Thus, one important issue facing Black women intellectuals is the question of what constitutes adequate justification that a given knowledge claim, such as a fact or theory, is true. Just as Hemmings's descendants were routinely disbelieved, so are many Black women not seen as credible witnesses for our own experiences. In this climate, Black women academics who choose to believe other Black women can become suspect.

Criteria for methodological adequacy associated with positivism illustrate the standards that Black women scholars, especially those in the social sciences, would have to satisfy in legitimating Black feminist thought. Though I describe Western or Eurocentric epistemologies as a single cluster, many interpretive frameworks or paradigms are subsumed under this category. Moreover, my focus on positivism should be interpreted neither to mean that all dimensions of positivism are inherently problematic for Black women nor that nonpositivist frameworks are better.

Positivist approaches aim to create scientific descriptions of reality by producing objective generalizations. Because researchers have widely differing values, experiences, and emotions, genuine science is thought to be unattainable unless all human characteristics except rationality are eliminated from the research process. By following strict methodological rules, scientists aim to distance themselves from the values, vested interests, and emotions generated by their class, race, sex, or unique situation. By decontextualizing themselves, they allegedly become detached observers and manipulators of nature (Jaggar 1983; Harding 1986).

Several requirements typify positivist methodological approaches. First, research methods generally require a distancing of the researcher from her or his "object" of study by defining the researcher as a "subject" with full human subjectivity and by objectifying the "object" of study (Keller 1985; Asante 1987). A second requirement is the absence of emotions from the research process (Jaggar 1983). Third, ethics and values are deemed inappropriate in the research process, either as the reason for scientific inquiry or as part of the research process itself (Richards 1980). Finally, adversarial debates, whether written or oral, become the preferred method of ascertaining truth: The arguments that can withstand the greatest assault and survive intact become the strongest truths (Moulton 1983).

Such criteria ask African-American women to objectify ourselves, devalue our emotional life, displace our motivations for furthering knowledge about Black women, and confront in an adversarial relationship those with more social, economic, and professional power. On the one hand, it seems unlikely that Black women would rely exclusively on positivist paradigms in rearticulating a Black women's standpoint. For example, Black women's experiences in sociology illustrate diverse responses to encountering an entrenched positivism. Given Black women's long-standing exclusion from sociology prior to 1970, the sociological knowledge about race and gender produced during their absence, and the symbolic importance of Black women's absence to sociological self-definitions as a science, African-American women acting as agents of knowledge faced a complex situation. In order to refute the history of Black women's unsuitability for science, they had to invoke the tools of sociology by using positivistic frameworks to demonstrate their capability as scientists. However, they simultaneously needed to challenge the same structure that granted them legitimacy. Their responses to this dilemma reflect the strategic use of the tools of positivism when needed, coupled with overt challenges to positivism when that seemed feasible (Collins 1998a, 95–123).

On the other hand, many Black women have had access to another epistemology that encompasses standards for assessing truth that are widely accepted among African-American women. An experiential, material base underlies a Black feminist epistemology, namely, collective experiences and accompanying worldviews that U.S. Black women sustained based on our particular history (see Chapter 3). The historical conditions of Black women's work, both in Black civil society and in paid employment, fostered a series of experiences that when shared and passed on become the collective wisdom of a Black women's standpoint. Moreover, a set of principles for assessing knowledge claims may be available to those having these shared experiences. These principles pass into a more general Black women's wisdom and, further, into what I call here a Black feminist epistemology.

This alternative epistemology uses different standards that are consistent with Black women's criteria for substantiated knowledge and with our criteria for methodological adequacy. Certainly this alternative Black feminist epistemology has been devalued by dominant knowledge validation processes and may not be claimed by many African-American women. But if such an epistemology exists, what are its contours? Moreover, what are its actual and potential contributions to Black feminist thought?

Lived Experience as a Criterion of Meaning

"My aunt used to say, 'A heap see, but a few know,'" remembers Carolyn Chase, a 31-year-old inner-city Black woman (Gwaltney 1980, 83). This saying depicts two types of knowing—knowledge and wisdom—and taps the first dimension of Black feminist epistemology. Living life as Black women requires wisdom because knowledge about the dynamics of intersecting oppressions has been essential to U.S. Black women's survival. African-American women give such wisdom high credence in assessing knowledge.

Allusions to these two types of knowing pervade the words of a range of African-American women. Zilpha Elaw, a preacher of the mid-1800s, explains the tenacity of racism: "The pride of a white skin is a bauble of great value with many in some parts of the United States, who readily sacrifice their intelligence to their prejudices, and possess more knowledge than wisdom" (Andrews 1986, 85). In describing differences separating African-American and White women, Nancy White invokes a similar rule: "When you come right down to it, white women just *think* they are free. Black women *know* they ain't free" (Gwaltney 1980, 147). Geneva Smitherman, a college professor specializing in African-American linguistics, suggests, "From a black perspective, written documents are limited in what they can teach about life and survival in the world. Blacks are quick to ridicule 'educated fools,' . . . they have 'book learning' but no 'mother wit,' knowledge, but not wisdom" (Smitherman 1977, 76). Mabel Lincoln eloquently summarizes the distinction between knowledge and wisdom: "To black people like me, a fool is funny—you know, people who love to break bad, people you can't tell anything to, folks that would take a shotgun to a roach" (Gwaltney 1980, 68).

African-American women need wisdom to know how to deal with the "educated fools" who would "take a shotgun to a roach." As members of a subordinate group, Black women cannot afford to be fools of any type, for our objectification as the Other denies us the protections that White skin, maleness, and wealth confer. This distinction between knowledge and wisdom, and the use of experience as the cutting edge dividing them, has been key to Black women's survival. In the context of intersecting oppressions, the distinction is essential. Knowledge without wisdom is adequate for the powerful, but wisdom is essential to the survival of the subordinate.

For most African-American women those individuals who have lived through the experiences about which they claim to be experts are more believable and credible than those who have merely read or thought about such experiences. Thus lived experience as a criterion for credibility frequently is invoked by U.S. Black women when making knowledge claims. For instance, Hannah Nelson describes the importance that personal experience has for her: "Our speech is most directly personal, and every black person assumes that every other black person has a right to a personal opinion. In speaking of grave matters, your personal experience is considered very good evidence. With us, distant statistics are certainly not as important as the actual experience of a sober person" (Gwaltney 1980, 7). Similarly, Ruth Shays uses her lived experiences to challenge the idea that formal education is the only route to knowledge: "I am the kind of person who doesn't have a lot of education, but both my mother and my father had good common sense. Now, I think that's all you need. I might not know how to use thirty-four words where three would do, but that does not mean that I don't know what I'm talking about. . . . I know what I'm talking about because I'm talking about myself. I'm talking about what I have lived" (Gwaltney 1980, 27, 33). Implicit in Ms. Shays's self-assessment is a critique of the type of knowledge that obscures the truth, the "thirty-four words" that cover up a truth that can be expressed in three.

Even after substantial mastery of dominant epistemologies, many Black women scholars invoke our own lived experiences and those of other African-American women in selecting topics for investigation and methodologies used. For example, Elsa Barkley Brown (1986) subtitles her essay on Black women's history "How My Mother Taught Me to Be an Historian in spite of My Academic Training." Similarly, Joyce Ladner (1972) maintains that growing up as a Black woman in the South gave her special insights in conducting her study of Black adolescent women.

Experience as a criterion of meaning with practical images as its symbolic vehicles is a fundamental epistemological tenet in African-American thought systems (Mitchell and Lewter 1986). "Look at my arm!" Sojourner Truth proclaimed: "I have ploughed, and planted, and gathered into barns, and no man could head me! And ain't I a woman?" (Loewenberg and Bogin 1976, 235). By invoking examples from her own life to symbolize new meanings, Truth deconstructed the prevailing notions of woman. Stories, narratives, and Bible principles are selected for their applicability to the lived experiences of African-Americans and become symbolic representations of a whole wealth of experience. Bible tales are often told for the wisdom they express about everyday life, so their interpretation involves no need for scientific historical verification. The narrative method requires that the story be told, not torn apart in analysis, and trusted as core belief, not "admired as science" (Mitchell and Lewter 1986, 8).

June Jordan's essay about her mother's suicide illustrates the multiple levels of meaning that can occur when lived experience becomes valued as a criterion of meaning. Jordan describes her mother, a woman who literally died trying to stand up, and the effect her mother's death had on her own work:

> I think all of this is really about women and work. Certainly this is all about me as a woman and my life work. I mean I am not sure my mother's suicide was something extraordinary. Perhaps most women must deal with a similar inheritance, the legacy of a woman whose death you cannot possibly pinpoint because she died so many, many times and because, even before she became your mother, the life of that woman was taken. . . .

> I came too late to help my mother to her feet. By way of everlasting thanks
> to all of the women who have helped me to stay alive I am working never
> to be late again. (Jordan 1985, 26)

While Jordan has knowledge about the concrete act of her mother's death, she
also strives for wisdom concerning the meaning of that death.

Some feminist scholars claim that women as a group are more likely than
men to use lived experiences in assessing knowledge claims. For example, a substantial number of the 135 women in a study of women's cognitive development
were "connected knowers" and were drawn to the sort of knowledge that
emerges from firsthand observation (Belenky et al. 1986). Such women felt that
because knowledge comes from experience, the best way of understanding
another person's ideas was to develop empathy and share the experiences that led
the person to form those ideas. In explaining these patterns, some feminist theorists suggest that women are socialized in complex relational nexuses where
contextual rules versus abstract principles govern behavior (Chodorow 1978;
Gilligan 1982). This socialization process is thought to stimulate characteristic
ways of knowing (Hartsock 1983a; Belenky et al. 1986). These theorists suggest
that women are more likely to experience two modes of knowing: one located
in the body and the space it occupies and the other passing beyond it. Through
multiple forms of mothering, women mediate these two modes and use the lived
experiences of their daily lives to assess more abstract knowledge claims (D.
Smith 1987). These forms of knowledge allow for subjectivity between the
knower and the known, rest in the women themselves (not in higher authorities), and are experienced directly in the world (not through abstractions).

African-American women's lives remain structured at the convergence of
several factors: Black community organizations reflecting principles of African-
influenced belief systems; activist mothering traditions that stimulate politicized
understandings of Black women's motherwork; and a social class system that relegates Black women as workers to the bottom of the social hierarchy. Amanda
King, a young African-American mother whose experiences illustrate this convergence, describes how she used lived experience to assess the abstract and
points out how difficult mediating these two modes of knowing can be:

> The leaders of the ROC [a labor union] lost their jobs too, but it just
> seemed like they were used to losing their jobs. . . . This was like a lifelong
> thing for them, to get out there and protest. They were like, what do you
> call them—intellectuals. . . . You got the ones that go to the university that
> are supposed to make all the speeches, they're the ones that are supposed
> to lead, you know, put this little revolution together, and then you got the
> little ones . . . that go to the factory everyday, they be the ones that have to
> fight. I had a child and I thought I don't have the time to be running
> around with these people. . . . I mean I understand some of that stuff they
> were talking about, like the bourgeoisie, the rich and the poor and all that,
> but I had surviving on my mind for me and my kid. (Byerly 1986, 198)

For Ms. King abstract ideals of class solidarity were mediated by her lived experiences as a mother and the connectedness it involved.

In traditional African-American communities Black women find considerable institutional support for valuing lived experience. Black women's centrality in families, churches, and other community organizations allows us to share with younger, less experienced sisters our concrete knowledge of what it takes to be self-defined Black women. "Sisterhood is not new to Black women," asserts Bonnie Thornton Dill, but "while Black women have fostered and encouraged sisterhood, we have not used it as the anvil to forge our political identities" (1983, 134). Though not expressed in explicitly political terms, this relationship of sisterhood among Black women can be seen as a model for a series of relationships African-American women have with one another (Gilkes 1985; Giddings 1988).

Given that Black churches and families are often woman-centered, African-influenced institutions, African-American women traditionally have found considerable institutional support for this dimension of Black feminist epistemology. While White women may value lived experience, it is questionable whether comparable support comes from White families—particularly middle-class families where privatization is so highly valued—and other social institutions controlled by Whites that advance similar values. Similarly, while Black men participate in the institutions of Black civil society, they cannot take part in Black women's sisterhood. In terms of Black women's relationships with one another, African-American women may find it easier than others to recognize connectedness as a primary way of knowing, simply because we have more opportunities to do so and must rely upon it more heavily than others.

The Use of Dialogue in Assessing Knowledge Claims

"Dialogue implies talk between two subjects, not the speech of subject and object. It is a humanizing speech, one that challenges and resists domination," asserts bell hooks (1989, 131). For Black women new knowledge claims are rarely worked out in isolation from other individuals and are usually developed through dialogues with other members of a community. A primary epistemological assumption underlying the use of dialogue in assessing knowledge claims is that connectedness rather than separation is an essential component of the knowledge validation process (Belenky et al. 1986, 18).

This belief in connectedness and the use of dialogue as one of its criteria for methodological adequacy has African roots. Whereas women typically remain subordinated to men within traditional African societies, these same societies have at the same time embraced holistic worldviews that seek harmony. "One must understand that to become human, to realize the promise of becoming human, is the only important task of the person," posits Molefi Asante (1987,

185). People become more human and empowered primarily in the context of a community, and only when they "become seekers of the type of connections, interactions, and meetings that lead to harmony" (p. 185). The power of the word generally, and dialogues specifically, allows this to happen.

Not to be confused with adversarial debate, the use of dialogue has deep roots in African-based oral traditions and in African-American culture (Sidran 1971; Smitherman 1977; Kochman 1981). Ruth Shays describes the importance of dialogue in the knowledge validation process of enslaved African-Americans:

> They would find a lie if it took them a year. . . . The foreparents found the truth because they listened and they made people tell their part many times. Most often you can hear a lie. . . . Those old people was everywhere and knew the truth of many disputes. They believed that a liar should suffer the pain of his lies, and they had all kinds of ways of bringing liars to judgment. (Gwaltney 1980, 32)

The widespread use of the call-and-response discourse mode among African-Americans illustrates the importance placed on dialogue. Composed of spontaneous verbal and nonverbal interaction between speaker and listener in which all of the speaker's statements, or "calls," are punctuated by expressions, or "responses," from the listener, this Black discourse mode pervades African-American culture. The fundamental requirement of this interactive network is active participation of all individuals (Smitherman 1977, 108). For ideas to be tested and validated, everyone in the group must participate. To refuse to join in, especially if one really disagrees with what has been said, is seen as "cheating" (Kochman 1981, 28).

June Jordan's analysis of Black English points to the significance of this dimension of an alternative epistemology:

> Our language is a system constructed by people constantly needing to insist that we exist. . . . Our language devolves from a culture that abhors all abstraction, or anything tending to obscure or delete the fact of the human being who is here and now/the truth of the person who is speaking or listening. Consequently, *there is no passive voice construction possible in Black English*. For example, you cannot say, "Black English is being eliminated." You must say, instead, "White people eliminating Black English." The assumption of the presence of life governs all of Black English . . . every sentence assumes the living and active participation of at least two human beings, the speaker and the listener. (Jordan 1985, 129)

Many Black women intellectuals invoke the relationships and connectedness provided by use of dialogue. When asked why she chose the themes she did, novelist Gayl Jones replied: "I was . . . interested . . . in oral traditions of storytelling—Afro-American and others, in which there is always the consciousness and importance of the hearer" (Tate 1983, 91). In describing the difference in the way male and female writers select significant events and relationships, Jones says "With many women writers, relationships within family, community, between men and women, and among women—from slave narratives by black women writers on—are treated as complex and significant relationships, whereas with many men the significant relationships are those that involve confrontations—relationships outside the family and community" (in Tate 1983, 92). Alice Walker's reaction to Zora Neale Hurston's book *Mules and Men* is another example of the use of dialogue in assessing knowledge claims. In *Mules and Men* Hurston chose not to become a detached observer of the stories and folktales she collected but instead, through extensive dialogues with the people in the communities she studied, placed herself in the center of her analysis. Using a similar process, Walker tests the truth of Hurston's knowledge claims:

> When I read *Mules and Men* I was delighted. Here was this perfect book! The "perfection" of which I immediately tested on my relatives, who are such typical Black Americans they are useful for every sort of political, cultural, or economic survey. Very regular people from the South, rapidly forgetting their Southern cultural inheritance in the suburbs and ghettos of Boston and New York, they sat around reading the book themselves, listening to me read the book, listening to each other read the book, and a kind of paradise was regained. (Walker 1977, xii)

Black women's centrality in families, churches, and other community organizations provides African-American women with a high degree of support for invoking dialogue as a dimension of Black feminist epistemology. However, when African-American women use dialogues in assessing knowledge claims, we might be invoking ways of knowing that are also more likely to be used by women. Feminist scholars contend that men and women are socialized to seek different types of autonomy—the former based on separation, the latter seeking connectedness—and that this variation in types of autonomy parallels the characteristic differences between how men and women understand ideas and experiences (Chodorow 1978; Keller 1985; Belenky et al. 1986). For instance, in contrast to the visual metaphors (such as equating knowledge with illumination, knowing with seeing, and truth with light) that scientists and philosophers typically use, women tend to ground their epistemological premises in metaphors suggesting finding a voice, speaking, and listening (Belenky et al. 1986).

The Ethics of Caring

"Ole white preachers used to talk wid dey tongues widdout sayin' nothin', but Jesus told us slaves to talk wid our hearts" (Webber 1978, 127). These words of an ex-slave suggest that ideas cannot be divorced from the individuals who create and share them. This theme of talking with the heart taps the ethic of caring, another dimension of an alternative epistemology used by African-American women. Just as the ex-slave used the wisdom in his heart to reject the ideas of the preachers who talked "wid dey tongues widdout sayin' nothin'," the ethic of caring suggests that personal expressiveness, emotions, and empathy are central to the knowledge validation process.

One of three interrelated components of the ethic of caring is the emphasis placed on individual uniqueness. Rooted in a tradition of African humanism, each individual is thought to be a unique expression of a common spirit, power, or energy inherent in all life.[4] When Alice Walker "never doubted her powers of judgment because her mother assumed they were sound," she invokes the sense of individual uniqueness taught to her by her mother (Washington 1984, 145). The polyrhythms in African-American music, in which no one main beat subordinates the others, is paralleled by the theme of individual expression in Black women's quilting. Black women quilters place strong color and patterns next to one another and see the individual differences not as detracting from each piece but as enriching the whole quilt (Brown 1989). This belief in individual uniqueness is illustrated by the value placed on personal expressiveness in African-American communities (Smitherman 1977; Kochman 1981; Mitchell and Lewter 1986). Johnetta Ray, an inner-city resident, describes this African-influenced emphasis on individual uniqueness: "No matter how hard we try, I don't think black people will ever develop much of a herd instinct. We are profound individualists with a passion for self-expression" (Gwaltney 1980, 228).

A second component of the ethic of caring concerns the appropriateness of emotions in dialogues. Emotion indicates that a speaker believes in the validity of an argument. Consider Ntozake Shange's description of one of the goals of her work: "Our [Western] society allows people to be absolutely neurotic and totally out of touch with their feelings and everyone else's feelings, and yet be very respectable. This, to me, is a travesty. . . . I'm trying to change the idea of seeing emotions and intellect as distinct faculties" (Tate 1983, 156). The Black women's blues tradition's history of personal expressiveness heals this binary that separates emotion from intellect. For example, in her rendition of "Strange Fruit," Billie Holiday's lyrics blend seamlessly with the emotion of her delivery to render a trenchant social commentary on Southern lynching. Without emotion, Aretha Franklin's (1967) cry for "respect" would be virtually meaningless.

A third component of the ethic of caring involves developing the capacity for empathy. Harriet Jones, a 16-year-old Black woman, explains to her interviewer why she chose to open up to him: "Some things in my life are so hard for me to bear, and it makes me feel better to know that you feel sorry about those things and would change them if you could" (Gwaltney 1980, 11). Without her belief in his empathy, she found it difficult to talk. Black women writers often explore the growth of empathy as part of an ethic of caring. For example, the growing respect that the Black slave woman Dessa and the White woman Rufel gain for each other in Sherley Anne Williams's *Dessa Rose* stems from their increased understanding of each other's positions. After watching Rufel fight off the advances of a White man, Dessa lay awake thinking: "The white woman was subject to the same ravisment as me; this the thought that kept me awake. I hadn't knowed white mens could use a white woman like that, just take her by force same as they could with us" (1986, 220). As a result of her newfound empathy, Dessa observed, "It was like we had a secret between us" (p. 220).

These components of the ethic of caring—the value placed on individual expressiveness, the appropriateness of emotions, and the capacity for empathy— reappear in varying combinations throughout Black civil society. One of the best examples of the interactive nature of the importance of dialogue and the ethic of caring in assessing knowledge claims occurs in the use of the call-and-response discourse mode in many Black church services. In such services both the minister and the congregation routinely use voice rhythm and vocal inflection to convey meaning. The sound of what is being said is just as important as the words themselves in what is, in a sense, a dialogue of reason and emotion. As a result it is nearly impossible to filter out the strictly linguistic-cognitive abstract meaning from the sociocultural psychoemotive meaning (Smitherman 1977, 135, 137). While the ideas presented by a speaker must have validity (i.e., agree with the general body of knowledge shared by the Black congregation), the group also appraises the way knowledge claims are presented.

The emphasis placed on expressiveness and emotion in African-American communities bears marked resemblance to feminist perspectives on the importance of personality in connected knowing. Belenky et al. (1986) point out that two contrasting orientations characterize knowing: one of separation based on impersonal procedures for establishing truth, and the other of connection in which truth emerges through care. While these ways of knowing are not gender specific, disproportionate numbers of women rely on connected knowing. Separate knowers try to subtract the personality of an individual from his or her ideas because they see personality as biasing those ideas. In contrast, connected knowers see personality as adding to an individual's ideas and feel that the personality of each group member enriches a group's understanding. The significance of individual uniqueness, personal expressiveness, and empathy in African-American communities thus resembles the importance that some feminist analyses place on women's "inner voice" (Belenky et al. 1986).

The convergence of African-influenced and feminist principles in the ethic of caring seems particularly acute. White women may have access to women's experiences that encourage emotion and expressiveness, but few White-controlled U.S. social institutions except the family validate this way of knowing. In contrast, Black women have long had the support of the Black church, an institution with deep roots in the African past and a philosophy that accepts and encourages expressiveness and an ethic of caring. Black men share in this Black cultural tradition. But they must resolve the contradictions that confront them in redefining Black masculinity in the face of abstract, unemotional notions of masculinity imposed on them (Hoch 1979). Thus, the differences distinguishing U.S.

Black women from other groups, even those close to them, lies less in Black women's race or gender identity than in access to social institutions that support an ethic of caring in their lives.

The Ethic of Personal Accountability

An ethic of personal accountability also characterizes Black feminist epistemology. Not only must individuals develop their knowledge claims through dialogue and present them in a style proving their concern for their ideas, but people are expected to be accountable for their knowledge claims. Zilpha Elaw's description of slavery reflects this notion that every idea has an owner and that the owner's identity matters: "Oh, the abominations of slavery! . . . Every case of slavery, however lenient its inflictions and mitigated its atrocities, indicates an oppressor, the oppressed, and oppression" (Andrews 1986, 98). For Elaw abstract definitions of slavery mesh with the personal identities of slavery's perpetrators and its victims. African-Americans consider it essential for individuals to have definite positions on issues and assume full responsibility for arguing their validity (Kochman 1981).

Assessments of an individual's knowledge claims simultaneously evaluate an individual's character, values, and ethics. Within this logic, many African-Americans reject prevailing beliefs that probing into an individual's personal viewpoint is outside the boundaries of discussion. Rather, all views expressed and actions taken are thought to derive from a central set of core beliefs that cannot be other than personal (Kochman 1981, 23). "Does Aretha really *believe* that Black women should get 'respect,' or is she just mouthing the words?" is a valid question in Black feminist epistemology. Knowledge claims made by individuals respected for their moral and ethical connections to their ideas will carry more weight than those offered by less respected figures.

An example drawn from an undergraduate class session where the students were all Black women illustrates the uniqueness of this portion of the knowledge validation process. During one class discussion I asked the students to evaluate a prominent Black male scholar's analysis of Black feminism. Instead of removing the scholar from his context in order to dissect the rationality of his thesis, my students demanded facts about the author's personal biography. They were especially interested in specific details of his life, such as his relationships with Black women, his marital status, and his social class background. By requesting data on dimensions of his personal life routinely excluded in positivist approaches to knowledge validation, they invoked lived experience as a criterion of meaning. They used this information to assess whether he really cared about his topic and drew on this ethic of caring in advancing their knowledge claims about his work. Furthermore, they refused to evaluate the rationality of his written ideas without some indication of his personal credibility as an ethical human being. The entire exchange could only have occurred as a dialogue among members of a group that had established a solid enough community to employ an alternative episte-mology in assessing knowledge claims.

Traditional Black church services also illustrate the interactive nature of all four dimensions of this alternative epistemology. The services represent more than dialogues between the rationality used in examining biblical texts and sto-ries and the emotion inherent in the use of reason for this purpose. The reason such dialogues exist is to examine lived experiences for the presence of an ethic of caring. Neither emotion nor ethics is subordinated to reason. Instead, emo-tion, ethics, and reason are used as interconnected, essential components in assessing knowledge claims. In this alternative epistemology, values lie at the heart of the knowledge validation process such that inquiry always has an ethi-cal aim. Moreover, when these four dimensions become politicized and attached to a social justice project, they can form a framework for Black feminist thought and practice.

Black Women as Agents of Knowledge

Social movements of the 1950s, 1960s, and 1970s stimulated a greatly changed intellectual and political climate in the United States. Compared to the past, many more U.S. Black women became legitimated agents of knowledge. No longer passive objects of knowledge manipulated within prevailing knowledge validation processes, African-American women aimed to speak for ourselves.

African-American women in the academy and other positions of authority who aim to advance Black feminist thought now encounter the often conflicting epistemological standards of three key groups. First, Black feminist thought must be validated by ordinary African-American women who, in the words of Hannah Nelson, grow to womanhood "in a world where the saner you are, the madder you are made to appear" (Gwaltney 1980, 7). To be credible in the eyes of this group, Black feminist intellectuals must be personal advocates for their material, be accountable for the consequences of their work, have lived or experienced their material in some fashion, and be willing to engage in dialogues about their findings with ordinary, everyday people.

Historically, living life as an African-American woman facilitated this endeav-or because knowledge validation processes controlled in part or in full by Black women occurred in particular organizational settings. When Black women were in charge of our own self-definitions, these four dimensions of Black feminist epistemology—lived experience as a criterion of meaning, the use of dialogue, the ethic of personal accountability, and the ethic of caring—came to the fore-front. When the core themes and interpretive frameworks of Black women's knowledge were informed by Black feminist epistemology, a rich tradition of Black feminist thought ensued.

Traditionally women engaged in this overarching intellectual and political project were blues singers, poets, autobiographers, storytellers, and orators. They became Black feminist intellectuals both by doing intellectual work and by being validated as such by everyday Black women. Black women in academia could not openly join their ranks without incurring a serious penalty. In racially segregated environments that routinely excluded the majority of African-American women, only a select few were able to defy prevailing norms and explicitly embrace Black feminist epistemology. Zora Neale Hurston was one such figure. Consider Alice Walker's description of Hurston:

> In my mind, Zora Neale Hurston, Billie Holiday, and Bessie Smith form a sort of unholy trinity. Zora *belongs* in the tradition of black women singers, rather than among "the literati." . . . Like Billie and Bessie she followed her own road, believed in her own gods, pursued her own dreams, and refused to separate herself from "common" people. (Walker 1977, xvii–xviii)

For her time, Zora Neale Hurston remains an exception, for prior to 1950, few African-American women earned advanced degrees, and most of those who did complied with prevailing knowledge validation processes.

The community of Black women scholars constitutes a second constituency whose epistemological standards must be met. As the number of Black women academics grows, this heterogeneous collectivity shares a similar social location in higher education, yet finds a new challenge in building group solidarities across differences. African-American women scholars place varying amounts of importance on furthering Black feminist scholarship. However, despite this new-found diversity, since more African-American women earn advanced degrees, the range of Black feminist scholarship has expanded. Historically, African-American women may have brought sensibilities gained from Black feminist epistemology to their scholarship. But gaining legitimacy often came with the cost of rejecting such an epistemology. Studying Black women's lives at all placed many careers at risk. More recently, increasing numbers of African-American women scholars have chosen to study Black women's experiences, and to do so by relying on elements of Black feminist epistemology in framing their work. For example, Valerie Lee's (1996) study of African-American midwives in the South deploys an innovative merger of Black women's fiction, ethnographic method, and personal narrative, to good effect.

A third group whose epistemological standards must be met consists of dominant groups who still control schools, graduate programs, tenure processes, publication outlets, and other mechanisms that legitimate knowledge. African-American women academics who aim to advance Black feminist thought typically must use dominant Eurocentric epistemologies for this group. The difficulties these Black women now face lie less in demonstrating that they could master White male epistemologies than in resisting the hegemonic nature of these patterns of thought in order to see, value, and use existing alternative Black feminist ways of knowing. For Black women who are agents of knowledge within academia, the marginality that accompanies outsider-within status can be the source of both frustration and creativity. In an attempt to minimize the differences between the cultural context of African-American communities and the expectations of mainstream social institutions, some women dichotomize their behavior and become two different people. Over time, the strain of doing this can be enormous. Others reject Black women's accumulated wisdom and work against their own best interests by enforcing the dominant group's specialized thought. Still others manage to inhabit both contexts but do so critically, using perspectives gained from their outsider-within social locations as a source of insights and ideas. But while such women can make substantial contributions as agents of knowledge, they rarely do so without substantial personal cost. "Eventually it comes to you," observes Lorraine Hansberry, "the thing that makes you exceptional, if you are at all, is inevitably that which must also make you lonely" (1969, 148).

Just as migrating between Black and White families raised special issues for Black women domestic workers, moving among different and competing interpretive communities raises similar epistemological concerns for Black feminist thinkers. The dilemma facing Black women scholars, in particular, engaged in creating Black feminist thought illustrates difficulties that can accompany grappling with multiple interpretive communities. A knowledge claim that meets the criteria of adequacy for one group and thus is judged to be acceptable may not be translatable into the terms of a different group. Using the example of Black English, June Jordan illustrates the difficulty of moving among epistemologies:

> You cannot "translate" instances of Standard English preoccupied with abstraction or with nothing/nobody evidently alive into Black English. That would warp the language into uses antithetical to the guiding perspective of its community of users. Rather you must first change those Standard English sentences, themselves, into ideas consistent with the person-centered assumptions of Black English. (Jordan 1985, 130)

Although both worldviews share a common vocabulary, the ideas themselves defy direct translation.

Once Black women scholars face the notion that on certain dimensions of a Black women's standpoint, it may be fruitless to try to translate into other frameworks truths validated by   Black feminist epistemology, then other choices emerge. Rather than trying to uncover universal knowledge claims that can withstand the translation from one epistemology to another (initially, at least), Black women intellectuals might find efforts to rearticulate a Black women's standpoint especially fruitful. Rearticulating a Black women's standpoint refashions the particular and reveals the more universal human dimensions of Black women's everyday lives. "I date all my work," notes Nikki Giovanni, "because I think poetry, or any writing, is but a reflection of the moment. The universal comes from the particular" (1988, 57). Lorraine Hansberry expresses a similar idea: "I believe that one of the most sound ideas in dramatic writing is that in order to create the universal, you must pay very great attention to the specific. Universality, I think, emerges from the truthful identity of what is" (1969, 128).

Toward Truth

The existence of Black feminist thought suggests another path to the universal truths that might accompany the "truthful identity of what is." In this volume I place Black women's subjectivity in the center of analysis and examine the interdependence of the everyday, taken-for-granted knowledge shared by African-American women as a group, the more specialized knowledge produced by Black women intellectuals, and the social conditions shaping both types of thought. This approach allows me to describe the creative tension linking how social conditions influenced a Black women's standpoint and how the power of the ideas themselves gave many African-American women the strength to shape those same social conditions. I approach Black feminist thought as situated in a context of domination and not as a system of ideas divorced from political and economic reality. Moreover, I present Black feminist thought as subjugated knowledge in that African-American women have long struggled to find alternative locations and epistemologies for validating our own self-definitions. In brief, I examined the situated, subjugated standpoint of African-American women in order to understand Black feminist thought as a partial perspective on domination.

Because U.S. Black women have access to the experiences that accrue to being both Black and female, an alternative epistemology used to rearticulate a Black women's standpoint should reflect the convergence of both sets of experiences. Race and gender may be analytically distinct, but in Black women's everyday lives, they work together. The search for the distinguishing features of an alternative epistemology used by African-American women reveals that some ideas that Africanist scholars identify as characteristically "Black" often bear remarkable resemblance to similar ideas claimed by feminist scholars as characteristically "female." This similarity suggests that the actual contours of intersecting oppressions can vary dramatically and yet generate some uniformity in the epistemologies used by subordinate groups. Just as U.S. Black women and African women encountered diverse patterns of intersecting oppressions yet generated similar agendas concerning what mattered in their feminisms, a similar process may be at work regarding the epistemologies of oppressed groups. Thus the significance of a Black feminist epistemology may lie in its ability to enrich our understanding of how subordinate groups create knowledge that fosters both their empowerment and social justice.

This approach to Black feminist thought allows African-American women to explore the epistemological implications of transversal politics.. Eventually this approach may get us to a point at which, claims Elsa Barkley Brown, "all people can learn to center in another experience, validate it, and judge it by its own standards without need of comparison or need to adopt that framework as their own" (1989, 922). In such politics, "one has no need to 'decenter' anyone in order to center someone else; one has only to constantly, appropriately, 'pivot the center'" (p. 922).

Rather than emphasizing how a Black women's standpoint and its accompanying epistemology differ from those of White women, Black men, and other collectivities, Black women's experiences serve as one specific social location for examining points of connection among multiple epistemologies. Viewing Black feminist epistemology in this way challenges additive analyses of oppression claiming that Black women have a more accurate view of oppression than do other groups. Such approaches suggest that oppression can be quantified and compared and that adding layers of oppression produces a potentially clearer standpoint (Spelman 1988). One implication of some uses of standpoint theory is that the more subordinated the group, the purer the vision available to them. This is an outcome of the origins of standpoint approaches in Marxist social theory, itself reflecting the binary thinking of its Western origins. Ironically, by quantifying and ranking human oppressions, standpoint theorists invoke criteria for methodological adequacy that resemble those of positivism. Although it is tempting to claim that Black women are more oppressed than everyone else and therefore have the best standpoint from which to understand the mechanisms, processes, and effects of oppression, this is not the case.

Instead, those ideas that are validated as true by African-American women, African-American men, Latina lesbians, Asian-American women, Puerto Rican men, and other groups with distinctive standpoints, with each group using the epistemological approaches growing from its unique standpoint, become the most "objective" truths. Each group speaks from its own standpoint and shares its own partial, situated knowledge. But because each group perceives its own truth as partial, its knowledge is unfinished. Each group becomes better able to consider other groups' standpoints without relinquishing the uniqueness of its own standpoint or suppressing other groups' partial perspectives. "What is always needed in the appreciation of art, or life," maintains Alice Walker, "is the larger perspective. Connections made, or at least attempted, where none existed before, the straining to encompass in one's glance at the varied world the common thread, the unifying theme through immense diversity" (1983, 5). Partiality, and not universality, is the condition of being heard; individuals and groups forwarding knowledge claims without owning their position are deemed less credible than those who do.

Alternative knowledge claims in and of themselves are rarely threatening to conventional knowledge. Such claims are routinely ignored, discredited, or simply absorbed and marginalized in existing paradigms. Much more threatening is the challenge that alternative epistemologies offer to the basic process used by the powerful to legitimate knowledge claims that in turn justify their right to rule. If the epistemology used to validate knowledge comes into question, then all prior knowledge claims validated under the dominant model become suspect. Alternative epistemologies challenge all certified knowledge and open up the question of whether what has been taken to be true can stand the test of alternative ways of validating truth. The existence of a self-defined Black women's standpoint using Black feminist epistemology calls into question the content of what currently passes as truth and simultaneously challenges the process of arriving at that truth.

12 TOWARD A POLITICS OF EMPOWERMENT

To make a difference in the lives of Brazilian Black women, we have more to
do than just hope for a better future. . . . What we have to do is to organize, and to
never stop questioning. What we have to do, as always, is plenty of work.
— Sueli Carneiro 1995, 17

Brazilian feminist Sueli Carneiro's
words identify the work facing Black Brazilian women in fostering their own
empowerment. Because U.S. Black feminism participates in this larger social justice project of Black diasporic feminisms, it too must "never stop questioning"
social injustices. Within this larger endeavor, U.S. Black feminist thought can
make a special contribution. By stressing how African-American women must
become self-defined and self-determining within intersecting oppressions,
Black feminist thought emphasizes the importance of knowledge for empowerment. Ideas matter, but doing "plenty of work" may matter even more.
Historically, U.S. Black women's activism demonstrates that becoming empowered requires more than changing the consciousness of individual Black women
via Black community development strategies. Empowerment also requires transforming unjust social institutions that African-Americans encounter from one
generation to the next.

As Chapters 10 and 11 suggest, Black feminist thought offers two important
contributions concerning the significance of knowledge for a politics of empowerment. First, Black feminist thought fosters a fundamental paradigmatic shift in
how we think about unjust power relations. By embracing a paradigm of intersecting oppressions of race, class, gender, sexuality, and nation, as well as Black
women's individual and collective agency within them, Black feminist thought
reconceptualizes the social relations of domination and resistance. Second, Black
feminist thought addresses ongoing epistemological debates concerning the
power dynamics that underlie what counts as knowledge. Offering U.S. Black

women new knowledge about our own experiences can be empowering. But activating epistemologies that criticize prevailing knowledge and that enable us to define our own realities *on our own terms* has far greater implications.

Despite their significance, these contributions can serve only as guidelines because what works in one setting may not work in others. Chapter 2's discussion of the distinguishing features of Black feminist thought provides directions for Black feminist activism. However, if U.S. Black feminist thought is to reach its full potential, especially in its efforts to contribute to an "intercontinental Black women's consciousness movement" (McLaughlin 1995, 73), then U.S. Black feminist thought must redefine power and empowerment. This can be a daunting task because power defies simple explanations. But how does one develop a politics of empowerment without understanding how power is organized and operates?

Thus far, this volume has synthesized two main approaches to power. One way of approaching power concerns the dialectical relationship linking oppression and activism, where groups with greater power oppress those with lesser amounts. Rather than seeing social change or lack of it as preordained and outside the realm of human action, the notion of a dialectical relationship suggests that change results from human agency. Because African-American women remain relegated to the bottom of the social hierarchy from one generation to the next, U.S. Black women have a vested interest in opposing oppression. This is not an intellectual issue for most African-American women—it is a lived reality. As long as Black women's oppression persists, so will the need for Black women's activism. Moreover, dialectical analyses of power point out that when it comes to social injustice, groups have competing interests that often generate conflict. Even when groups understand the need for the type of transversal politics discussed in Chapter 10, they often find themselves on opposite sides of social issues. Oppression and resistance remain intricately linked such that the shape of one influences that of the other. At the same time, this relationship is far more complex than a simple model of permanent oppressors and perpetual victims.

Another way of approaching power views it not as something that groups possess, but as an intangible entity that circulates within a particular matrix of domination and to which individuals stand in varying relationships. These approaches emphasize how individual subjectivity frames human actions within a matrix of domination. U.S. Black women's efforts to grapple with the effects of domination in everyday life are evident in our creation of safe spaces that enable us to resist oppression, and in our struggles to form fully human love relations with one another, and with children, fathers, and brothers, as well as with individuals who do not see Black women as worthwhile. Oppression is not simply understood in the mind—it is felt in the body in myriad ways. Moreover, because oppression is constantly changing, different aspects of an individual U.S. Black woman's self-definitions intermingle and become more salient: Her gender may be more prominent when she becomes a mother, her race when she searches for housing, her social class when she applies for credit, her sexual orientation when she is walking with her lover, and her citizenship status when she applies for a job. In all of these contexts, her position in relation to and within intersecting oppressions shifts.

As each individual African-American woman changes her ideas and actions, so does the overall shape of power itself change. In the absence of Black feminist thought and other comparable oppositional knowledges, these micro-changes may remain invisible to individual women. Yet collectively, they can have a profound impact. When my mother taught me to read, took me to the public library when I was five, and told me that if I learned to read, I could experience a form of freedom, neither she nor I saw the magnitude of that one action in my life and the lives that my work has subsequently touched. As people push against, step away from, and shift the terms of their participation in power relations, the shape of power relations changes for everyone. Like individual subjectivity, resistance strategies and power are always multiple and in constant states of change.

Together, these two approaches to power point to two important uses of knowledge for African-American women and other social groups engaged in social justice projects. Dialectical approaches emphasize the significance of knowledge in developing self-defined, group-based standpoints that, in turn, can foster the type of group solidarity necessary for resisting oppressions. In contrast, subjectivity approaches emphasize how domination and resistance shape and are shaped by individual agency. Issues of consciousness link the two. In the former, group-based consciousness emerges through developing oppositional knowledges such as Black feminist thought. In the latter, individual self-definitions and behaviors shift in tandem with a changed consciousness concerning everyday lived experience. Black feminist thought encompasses both meanings of consciousness—neither is sufficient without the other. Together, both approaches to power also highlight the significance of multiplicity in shaping consciousness. For example, viewing domination itself as encompassing intersecting oppressions of race, class, gender, sexuality, and nation points to the significance of these oppressions in shaping the overall organization of a particular matrix of domination. Similarly, personal identities constructed around individual understandings of race, class, gender, sexuality, and nation define each individual's unique biography.

Both of these approaches remain theoretically useful because they each provide partial and different perspectives on empowerment. Unfortunately, these two views are often presented as *competing* rather than potentially *complementary* approaches. As a result, each provides a useful starting point for thinking through African-American women's empowerment in the context of constantly changing power relations, but neither is sufficient. Black feminism and other social justice projects require a language of power that is grounded within yet transcends these approaches. Social justice projects need a common, functional vocabulary that furthers their understanding of the politics of empowerment.

Thus far, using African-American women's experiences as a lens, this volume has examined race, gender, class, sexuality, and nation as forms of oppression that work together in distinctive ways to produce a distinctive U.S. matrix of domination. But earlier chapters have said much less about *how* these and other oppressions are organized. In response, this chapter sketches out a preliminary vocabulary of power and empowerment that emerges from these seemingly competing approaches to power. Whether viewed through the lens of a single system of power, or through that of intersecting oppressions, any particular matrix of domination is organized via four interrelated domains of power, namely, the structural, disciplinary, hegemonic, and interpersonal domains. Each domain serves a particular purpose. The structural domain organizes oppression, whereas the disciplinary domain manages it. The hegemonic domain justifies oppression, and the interpersonal domain influences everyday lived experience and the individual consciousness that ensues.

It is important to remember that although the following argument is developed from the standpoint of U.S. Black women, its significance is much greater. Recall that Black feminist thought views Black women's struggles as part of a wider struggle for human dignity and social justice. When coupled with the Black feminist epistemological tenet that dialogue remain central to assessing knowledge claims, the domains-of-power argument presented here should serve to stimulate dialogues about empowerment.

In the United States the particular contours of each domain of power illustrates how intersecting oppressions of race, class, gender, sexuality, and nation are organized in unique ways. Black women are incorporated in each domain of power in particular ways that while exhibiting patterns of common differences with women of African descent transnationally, remain quintessentially American. For example, the structural domain regulates citizenship rights, and much of African-American women's struggles have centered on gaining rights routinely granted to other American citizens. U.S. Black women have long recognized that the absence of usable citizenship rights limited Black women's ability to oppose the mammy, matriarch, jezebel and other controlling images routinely advanced within the hegemonic domain. Citizenship rights enable African-American women to pursue focused educations and challenge these portrayals of U.S. Black women. These moves toward empowerment are important, yet they remain dependent on ideas about American citizenship and therefore American national identity.

At the same time, as individuals and as part of groups who oppose U.S. social injustices, African-American women's resistance strategies reflect their placement both within each domain and within the U.S. matrix of domination. For example, through its reliance on rules, the disciplinary domain manages domination. African-American women rule breakers and rule benders and, upon occasion, Black women who capture positions of authority so that they can change the rules themselves become empowered within the disciplinary domain. Thus, U.S.

Black women's experiences and ideas illustrate how these four domains of power shape domination. But they also illustrate how these same domains have been and can be used as sites of Black women's empowerment.

Structural Domain of Power

The structural domain of power encompasses how social institutions are organized to reproduce Black women's subordination over time. One characteristic feature of this domain is its emphasis on large-scale, interlocking social institutions. An impressive array of U.S. social institutions lies at the heart of the structural domain of power. Historically, in the United States, the policies and procedures of the U.S. legal system, labor markets, schools, the housing industry, banking, insurance, the news media, and other social institutions as interdependent entities have worked to disadvantage African-American women. For example, Black women's long-standing exclusion from the best jobs, schools, health care, and housing illustrates the broad array of social policies designed to exclude Black women from full citizenship rights.

These interlocking social institutions have relied on multiple forms of segregation—by race, class, and gender—to produce these unjust results. For African-American women, racial segregation has been paramount. Racial segregation rested on the "separate but equal" doctrine established under the 1896 ruling of *Plessy v. Ferguson* where the Supreme Court upheld the constitutionality of segregation of groups. This ruling paved the way for a rhetoric of color-blindness (Crenshaw 1997). Under the "separate but equal" doctrine, Blacks and Whites as *groups* could be segregated as long as the law was color-blind in affording each group equal treatment. Despite the supposed formal equality promised by "separate but equal," subsequent treatment certainly was separate, but it was anything but equal. As a result, policies and procedures with housing, education, industry, government, the media, and other major social institutions have worked together to *exclude* Black women from exercising full citizenship rights. Whether this social exclusion has taken the form of relegating Black women to inner-city neighborhoods poorly served by social services, to poorly funded and racially segregated public schools, or to a narrow cluster of jobs in the labor market, the intent was to exclude.

Within the structural domain of power, empowerment cannot accrue to individuals and groups without transforming U.S. social institutions that foster this exclusion. Because this domain is large-scale, systemwide, and has operated over a long period of time via interconnected social institutions, segregation of this magnitude cannot be changed overnight. Structural forms of injustice that permeate the entire society yield only grudgingly to change. Since they do so in part when confronted with wide-scale social movements, wars, and revolutions that threaten the social order overall, African-American women's rights have not been gained solely by gradual reformism. A civil war preceded the abolition of slavery when all efforts to negotiate a settlement failed. Southern states routinely ignored the citizenship rights of Blacks, and even when confronted with the 1954 *Brown v. Board of Education* Supreme Court decision that outlawed racial segregation, many dug in their heels and refused to uphold the law. Massive demonstrations, media exposure, and federal troops all were deployed to implement this fundamental policy change. The reemergence of White supremacist organizations in the 1990s, many of which recirculate troubling racist ideologies of prior eras, speaks to the deep-seated resentment attached to Black women, among others, working toward a more just U.S. society. Events such as these indicate how deeply woven into the very fabric of American society ideas about Black women's subordination appear to be.

In the United States, visible social protest of this magnitude, while often required to bring about change, remains more the exception than the rule. For U.S. Black women, social change has more often been gradual and reformist, punctuated by episodes of systemwide upheaval. Trying to change the policies and procedures themselves, typically through social reforms, constitutes an important cluster of strategies within the structural domain. Because the U.S. context contains a commitment to reformist change by changing the laws, Black women have used the legal system in their struggles for structural transformation. African-American women have aimed to challenge the laws that legitimate racial segregation. As Chapter 9's discussion of Black women's activism suggests, African-American women have used various strategies to get laws changed. Grassroots organizations, forming national advocacy organizations, and event-specific social protest such as boycotts and sit-ins have all been used, yet changing the laws and the terms of their implementation have formed the focus of change. Even the development of parallel social institutions such as Black churches and schools have aimed to prepare African-Americans for full participation in U.S. society when the laws were changed.

African-American women have experienced considerable success not only in getting laws changed, but in stimulating government action to redress past wrongs. The Voting Rights Act of 1964, the Civil Rights Act of 1965, and other important federal, state, and local legislation have outlawed discrimination by race, sex, national origin, age, or disability status. This changed legal climate granted African-American women some protection from the widespread discrimination that we faced in the past. At the same time, class-action lawsuits against discriminatory housing, educational, and employment policies have resulted in tangible benefits for many Black women.

While necessary, these legal victories may not be enough. Ironically, the same laws designed to protect African-American women from social exclusion have increasingly become used against Black women. In describing new models for equal treatment under the law, Black feminist legal scholar Kimberle Crenshaw argues that the rhetoric of color-blindness was not unseated by the 1954 *Brown v. Board of Education* ruling. Instead, the rhetoric of color-blindness was refor-mulated to refer to the equal treatment of *individuals* by not discriminating among them. Under this new rhetoric of color-blindness, equality meant treat-ing all individuals the same, regardless of differences they brought with them due to the effects of past discrimination or even discrimination in other venues. "Having determined, then, that everyone was equal in the sense that everyone had a skin color," observes Crenshaw, "symmetrical treatment was satisfied by a general rule that nobody's skin color should be taken into account in govern-mental decision-making" (Crenshaw 1997, 284). Within this logic, the path to equality lies in ignoring race, gender, and other markers of historical discrimi-nation that might account for any differences that individuals bring to schools and the workplace.

As a new rule that maintains long-standing hierarchies of race, class, and gender while appearing to provide equal treatment, this rhetoric of color-blind-ness has had some noteworthy effects. For one, observes Black feminist legal scholar Patricia Williams (1995), it fosters a certain kind of race thinking among Whites: Because the legal system has now formally equalized *individual* access to housing, schooling, and jobs, any unequal *group* results, such as those that char-acterize gaps between Blacks and Whites, must somehow lie within the individ-uals themselves or their culture.

When joined to its twin of gender neutrality, one claiming that no signifi-cant differences distinguish men from women, the rhetoric of color-blindness works to unseat one important strategy of Black women's resistance within the structural domain. Black women who make claims of discrimination and who demand that policies and procedures may not be as fair as they seem can more easily be dismissed as complainers who want special, unearned favors. Moreover, within a rhetoric of color-blindness that defends the theme of no inherent dif-ferences among races, or of gender-neutrality that claims no differences among genders, it becomes difficult to talk of racial and gender differences that stem from discriminatory treatment. The assumption is that the U.S. matrix of domi-nation now provides equal treatment because where it once overtly discriminated by race and gender, it now seemingly ignores them. Beliefs such as these thus allow Whites and men to support a host of punitive policies that reinscribe social heirarchies of race and gender. In her discussion of how racism now relies on encoded language Angela Davis identifies how this rhetoric of color-blindness can operate as a form of "camouflaged racism":

> Because race is ostracized from some of the most impassioned political debates of this period, their racialized character becomes increasingly dif-ficult to identify, especially by those who are unable—or do not want—to decipher the encoded language. This means that hidden racist argu-ments can be mobilized readily across racial boundaries and political alignments. Political positions once easily defined as conservative, liberal, and sometimes even radical therefore have a tendency to lose their dis-

tinctiveness in the face of the seductions of this camouflaged racism (Davis 1997, 264).

Americans can talk of "street crime" and "welfare mothers," all the while claiming that they are not discussing race at all. Despite the new challenges raised by the rhetoric of color-blindness and gender neutrality, it is important to remember that legal strategies have yielded and most probably will continue to produce victories for African-American women. Historically, much of Black women's resistance to the policies and procedures of the structural domain of power occurred *outside* powerful social institutions. Currently, however, African-American women are more often included in these same social institutions that long excluded us. Increasing numbers of African-American women have gained access to higher education, now hold good jobs, and might be considered middle-class if not elite. These women often occupy positions of authority *inside* schools, corporations, and government agencies. Achieving these results required changing U.S. laws.

On the one hand, this new inclusion provides new opportunities to work for equitable policies and procedures. Many of the women described in this volume who advance Black feminist thought do so from jobs held as bankers, college professors, corporate executives, news producers, teachers, social workers, physicians, and managers. Unlike Black women from prior eras who were confined to either agricultural or domestic work, these women hold positions of authority within major social institutions. On the other hand, this same inclusion raises new questions, primarily because the organizations they struggled so long to enter can look entirely different once they get inside.

The Disciplinary Domain of Power

Ordering schools, industries, hospitals, banks, and realtors to stop discriminating against Black women does not mean that these and other social institutions will comply. Laws may change, but the organizations that they regulate rarely change as rapidly. In the post–World War II period, African-American women have gotten good jobs and achieved other positions of authority in organizations that formerly excluded them outright. As these women gained new angles of vision on the many ways that organizations discriminate, organizations searched for new ways to suppress Black women. If you can no longer keep Black women outside, then how can they best be regulated once they are inside?

As a way of ruling that relies on bureaucratic hierarchies and techniques of surveillance, the disciplinary domain manages power relations. It does so not through social policies that are explicitly racist or sexist, but through the ways in which organizations are run (Foucault 1979). The disciplinary domain of power has increased in importance with the growing significance of bureaucracy as a mode of modern social organization. Bureaucracy, in turn, has become important in controlling populations, especially across race, gender, and other markers of difference. As an increasingly prevalent feature of modern, transnational social organization—capitalist and socialist countries alike depend on bureaucracies— this style of organization becomes highly efficient in both reproducing inter- secting oppressions and in masking their effects. Bureaucracies, regardless of the policies they promote, remain dedicated to disciplining and controlling their workforces and clientele. Whether the inner-city public schools that many Black girls attend, the low-paid jobs in the rapidly growing service sector that young Black women are increasingly forced to take, the culture of the social welfare bureaucracy that makes Black mothers and children wait for hours, or the "mam- mified" work assigned to Black women professionals, the goal is the same—cre- ating quiet, orderly, docile, and disciplined populations of Black women.

In this bureaucratic context, surveillance has emerged as an important fea- ture of the disciplinary domain of power. There is a marked difference between merely looking at Black women and keeping them under surveillance. Whether the treatment of Black women on the auction block, the voyeuristic treatment of Sarah Bartmann, or the portrayal of Black women within contemporary pornog- raphy, objectifying Black women's bodies has meant that members from more powerful groups have all felt entitled to watch Black women. Surveillance now constitutes a major mechanism of bureaucratic control. For example, within pris- ons, guards watch Black female inmates; within businesses, middle managers supervise Black women clerical staff; and within universities, professors train "their" Black female graduate students within academic "disciplines." The fact that prison guards, middle managers, and professors might themselves be Black women remains less important than the purpose of this surveillance. Ironically, Black women prison guards, middle managers, and professors may themselves be watched by wardens, business executives, and university deans. In these settings, discipline is ensured by keeping Black women as a mutually policing subordinate population under surveillance.

When it comes to the disciplinary domain of power, resistance from *inside* bureaucracies constitutes the overarching strategy. Ironically, just as organizations may keep Black women under surveillance, these same Black women have the capacity to keep organizations themselves under surveillance. On the one hand, Black women's success in gaining positions of authority has produced new opportunities to use bureaucratic resources toward humanistic ends. This insider resistance tries to capture positions of authority within social institutions in order to ensure that existing rules will be fairly administered and, if need be, to change existing policies. Once inside, many Black women realize much more than getting hired is required to bring about change. Black women find them- selves searching for innovative ways to foster bureaucratic change (see, e.g., Guy- Sheftall 1993). An African-American colleague of mine once referred to this process as one of viewing her university as an egg and her job as one of "work- ing the cracks." From a distance, each egg appears to be smooth and seamless, but, upon closer inspection, each egg's distinctive patterns of almost invisible cracks become visible. Her insider administrative position granted her a view of higher education not as a well-oiled bureaucracy that was impervious to change, but at a series of cracks and fissures that represented organizational weaknesses. As she described it, she was committed to "working the cracks" and changing her workplace by persistent use of her insider knowledge concerning its pressure points. Once inside, many Black women do make a difference in how bureaucracies operate. Without much fanfare, they push for policy changes that move their organizations closer to basic fairness. Rarely mentioning words such as "racism," "sexism," "discrimination," and the like, they find innovative ways to work the system so that it will become more fair.

On the other hand, capturing positions of authority can foster new and unanticipated forms of disciplinary control. With dismay, many Black women in the United States come to recognize that, whether intentional or not, different sets of rules may be applied to them that distinguish them from their counterparts. Whereas their diplomas and prior training may qualify them on paper, they may be treated as second-class citizens. U.S. Black women's reactions to these new forms of disciplinary control typically reflect comparable heterogeneity. In this sense, the experiences of former generations of Black women domestic workers provide a template for analyzing the reactions of Black women who now desegregate a variety of bureaucracies. The existence of a collective wisdom available to domestic workers did not negate the heterogeneous responses they had to their jobs. Within the group, many individual responses emerged, most shaped by the actual working conditions that individual women encountered. The relations within bureaucracies are much the same—how African-American women choose to deal with the changing forms of disciplinary power seems more the issue than the codification of this domain of power in large, impersonal bureaucracies.

U.S. Black feminism in the academy offers a provocative case of these cross-cutting relationships. Unlike Black diasporic feminisms where much of Black women's thought emerges in relation to women's activism (see, e.g., *Femmes Aux Yeux Ouverts* 1994), a good deal of U.S. Black feminist thought must adhere to the disciplinary procedures of the academy. Elevating Black feminist thought to the level of theory and devaluing Black women's activism as less theoretical are strategies that aim to contain them both. Moreover, such actions place U.S. Black feminist thought in the academy under surveillance.

Disciplinary pressures may explain, in part, the mismatch between issues that often most interest U.S. Black women academics and those of pressing concern to large numbers of African-American women. Ordinary, everyday women are often accused of either being "afraid" of feminism or being so downtrodden by daily obligations and the whims of their men that they cannot think about their own subordination. But another interpretation points to the lack of attention given within academic Black feminism to issues that affect African-American women's lives. Many African-American women may reject Black feminism because they cannot see clear connections between elite Black feminism's claims to be a progressive discourse and the actual conditions in their lives. For example, the entrenched patterns of poverty and its accompanying violence that affect so many African-American women's lives suggest that gendered analyses of Black political economy become more prominent in U.S. Black feminist thought. Such analyses should have implications for public policy, as well as what types of actions for community development are required to position U.S. Blacks to address poverty. Despite the presence of such themes in the scholarship of some U.S. Black feminists (see, e.g., Davis 1981; Brewer 1993, 1994; Mullings 1997), these thinkers typically remain unrecognized within the academy as "symbolic" of Black feminism. For example, the 30-year span of Angela Davis's intellectual work clearly demonstrates her leadership in shaping U.S. Black feminist thought. Yet Davis is less often described as a "Black feminist" than as a socialist. Davis may be deeply committed to Black feminist politics, but she may not be the kind of "Black feminist" that U.S. higher education wants.

Given the power of surveillance in the disciplinary domain, it is unrealistic to expect that any essentially radical Black feminist thought will emanate from within the academy, especially in times when marketplace ideologies have become so prominent. Black feminist academics who wrap themselves in the flag of radicalism, feminist or otherwise, and use their self-proclaimed radical identity to push for promotion to full professor are simply deluding themselves. Marketplace ideologies increasingly affect all aspects of life, including actual people and ideas about people in outsider-within locations. The numbers of U.S. Black women employed by the academy, whether they recognize their outsider-within locations or not, expand and shrink not just in relation to political advocacy by African-American women and other similarly disadvantaged groups, but in response to perceived marketplace needs. If an organization perceives that it needs outsiders within, it buys them.

In this context, Black feminist thought in the academy is likely to become less focused on its own activist agenda and more on surviving and perhaps transcending academic politics. Thus, it is much more reasonable to investigate the ways in which Black feminist thought uses its placement in the academy to foster social justice and the ways in which its use and placement reinscribes existing social hierarchies.

The Hegemonic Domain of Power

Tactics within the disciplinary domain of power can be only so effective. U.S. Black women's success in gaining and exercising citizenship rights means that new ways must be found to involve African-American women in supporting the very system that fosters their own subordination and that of many other groups.

Because the hegemonic domain of power deals with ideology, culture, and consciousness, it becomes important in addressing this need. The structural and disciplinary domains of power operate through systemwide social policies managed primarily by bureaucracies. In contrast, the hegemonic domain of power aims to justify practices in these domains of power. By manipulating ideology and culture, the hegemonic domain acts as a link between social institutions (structural domain), their organizational practices (disciplinary domain), and the level of everyday social interaction (interpersonal domain).

To maintain their power, dominant groups create and maintain a popular system of "commonsense" ideas that support their right to rule. In the United States, hegemonic ideologies concerning race, class, gender, sexuality, and nation are often so pervasive that it is difficult to conceptualize alternatives to them, let alone ways of resisting the social practices that they justify. For example, despite scant empirical research, beliefs about Black women's sexuality remain deeply held and widespread. Moreover, the sexual politics of Black womanhood reveals how important the controlling images applied to Black women's sexuality have been to the effective operation of domination overall.

School curricula, religious teachings, community cultures, and family histories have long been important social locations for manufacturing ideologies needed to maintain oppression. However, an increasingly important dimension of why hegemonic ideologies concerning race, class, gender, sexuality, and nation remain so deeply entrenched lies, in part, in the growing sophistication of mass media in regulating intersecting oppressions. It is one thing to encounter school curricula that routinely exclude Black women as bona fide subjects of study; religious teachings that preach equality yet are often used to justify Black women's submission to all men; Black community ideologies that counsel Black women to be more "feminine" so that Black men can reclaim their masculinity; and family histories that cover up patterns of physical and emotional abuse that blame Black women for their own victimization. It is quite another to see images of U.S. Black women as "hoochies" broadcast globally in seemingly infinite variation.

In the United States, one would think that the combination of a better-educated public and scholarship designed to shatter old myths would effectively challenge hegemonic ideologies. As the resurgence of White supremacist organizations with staunch beliefs about Black intellectual and moral inferiority suggest, this has not been the case. Instead, old ideas become recycled in new forms. Yesterday's welfare mother splits into social-class-specific images of the welfare queen and the Black lady. Yesterday's jezebel becomes today's "hoochie."

Racist and sexist ideologies, if they are disbelieved, lose their impact. Thus, an important feature of the hegemonic domain of power lies in the need to continually refashion images in order to solicit support for the U.S. matrix of domination. Not just elite group support, but the endorsement of subordinated groups is needed for hegemonic ideologies to function smoothly. Realizing that Black feminist demands for social justice threaten existing power hierarchies, organizations must find ways of appearing to include African-American women—reversing historical patterns of social exclusion associated with institutional discrimination—while disempowering us. Ideas become critical within this effort to absorb and weaken Black women's resistance. Regardless of their placement in social hierarchies, other groups also encounter these pressures. For example, White women are told that they become "race traitors" if they date Black men, a stigma that in effect asks them to calculate whether the gain of an interracial relationship is worth the loss of White privilege. Similarly, in the current reorganization of U.S. racial ideologies where Vietnamese, Cambodians, and other recent Asian immigrant groups jockey to find a racial identity between the fixed points of Blackness and Whiteness, Asians are encouraged to derogate Blacks. Taking one's place at the top of the "minority" ladder certainly provides better treatment than that dished out to the Blacks and Native Americans who are relegated to the bottom. Yet until the category of "Whiteness" is expanded to reclassify Asians as "White," becoming a "model minority" remains a hollow victory.

The significance of the hegemonic domain of power lies in its ability to shape consciousness via the manipulation of ideas, images, symbols, and ideologies. As Black women's struggles for self-definition suggest, in contexts such as these where ideas matter, reclaiming the "power of a free mind" constitutes an important area of resistance. Reversing this process whereby intersecting oppressions harness various dimensions of individual subjectivity for their own ends becomes a central purpose of resistance. Thus, the hegemonic domain becomes a critical site for not just fending off hegemonic ideas from dominant culture, but in crafting counter-hegemonic knowledge that fosters changed consciousness. Regardless of the actual social locations where this process occurs—families, community settings, schools, religious institutions, or mass media institutions—the power of reclaiming these spaces for "thinking and doing not what is expected of us" constitutes an important dimension of Black women's empowerment.

By emphasizing the power of self-definition and the necessity of a free mind, Black feminist thought speaks to the importance that African-American women thinkers place on consciousness as a sphere of freedom. Rather than viewing consciousness as a fixed entity, a more useful approach sees it as continually evolving and negotiated. A dynamic consciousness is vital to both individual and group agency. Based on their personal histories, individuals experience and resist domination differently. Each individual has a unique and continually evolving personal biography made up of concrete experiences, values, motivations, and emotions. No two individuals occupy the same social space; thus no two biographies are identical. Human ties can be freeing and empowering, as is the case with many Black women's heterosexual love relationships or in the power of motherhood in African-American families and communities. Human ties can also be confining and oppressive, as in cases of domestic violence or struggles to sustain mother-child families in inner-city neighborhoods. The same situation can look quite different depending on the consciousness one brings to interpret it.

The cultural context formed by those experiences and ideas that are shared with other members of a group or community give meaning to individual biographies. Each individual biography is rooted in several overlapping cultural contexts—for example, groups defined by race, social class, age, gender, religion, and sexual orientation. The most cohesive cultural contexts are those with identifiable histories, geographic locations, and social institutions. Some can be so tightly interwoven that they appear to be one cultural context, the situation of traditional societies with customs that are carried on across generations, or that of protracted racial segregation in the United States where Blacks saw a unity of interests that necessarily suppressed internal differences within the category "Black." Moreover, cultural contexts contribute, among other things, the concepts used in thinking and acting.

Subjugated knowledges, such as U.S. Black women's thought, develop in cultural contexts controlled by oppressed groups. Dominant groups aim to replace subjugated knowledge with their own specialized thought because they realize that gaining control over this dimension of subordinate groups' lives simplifies control. While efforts to influence this dimension of an oppressed group's experiences can be partially successful, this level is more difficult to control than dominant groups would have us believe. For example, adhering to externally derived standards of beauty leads many African-American women to dislike their skin color or hair texture. Similarly, internalizing prevailing gender ideology leads some Black men to abuse Black women. These are cases of the successful infusion of dominant ideologies into the everyday cultural context of African-Americans. But the long-standing existence of Black women's resistance traditions as expressed through Black women's relationships with one another, the Black women's blues tradition, and the voices of contemporary African-American women writers all attest to the difficulty of eliminating the cultural context as a fundamental site of resistance.

In their efforts to rearticulate the standpoint of African-American women as a group, Black feminist thinkers potentially offer individual African-American women the conceptual tools to resist oppression. Empowerment in this context is twofold. Gaining the critical consciousness to unpack hegemonic ideologies is empowering. Coming to recognize that one need not believe everything one is told and taught is freeing for many Black women. But while criticizing hegemonic ideologies remains necessary, such critiques are basically reactive (Collins 1998a, 187–96). Thus, the second dimension of empowerment within the hegemonic domain of power consists of constructing new knowledge. In this regard, the core themes, interpretive frameworks, and epistemological approaches of Black feminist thought can be highly empowering because they provide alternatives to the way things are supposed to be.

Interpersonal Domain of Power

African-American women have been victimized by intersecting oppressions. But portraying U.S. Black women solely as passive, unfortunate recipients of abuse stifles notions that Black women can actively work to change our circumstances and bring about changes in our lives. Similarly, presenting African-American women solely as heroic figures who easily engage in resisting oppression on all fronts minimizes the very real costs of oppression and can foster the perception that Black women need no help because we can "take it."

Domination operates by seducing, pressuring, or forcing African-American women, members of subordinated groups, and all individuals to replace individual and cultural ways of knowing with the dominant group's specialized thought—hegemonic ideologies that, in turn, justify practices of other domains of power. As a result, suggests Audre Lorde, "the true focus of revolutionary change is never merely the oppressive situations which we seek to escape, but that piece of the oppressor which is planted deep within each of us" (1984, 123). Or as Toni Cade Bambara succinctly states, "Revolution begins with the self, in the self" (1970a, 109).

Lorde and Bambara's suppositions raise an important issue for Black women and for all others working for social justice. Although most individuals have little difficulty identifying their own victimization within some major system of oppression—whether it be by race, social class, religion, physical ability, sexual orientation, ethnicity, age or gender—they typically fail to see how their thoughts and actions uphold someone else's subordination. Thus White feminists routinely point with confidence to their oppression as women but resist seeing how much their White skin privileges them. African-Americans who possess eloquent analyses of racism often persist in viewing poor White men as symbols of White power. The radical left fares little better. "If only people of color and women could see their true class interests," they argue, "class solidarity would eliminate racism and sexism." In essence, each group identifies the oppression with which it feels most comfortable as being fundamental and classifies all others as being of lesser importance. Oppression is filled with such contradictions because these approaches fail to recognize that a matrix of domination contains few pure victims or oppressors. Each individual derives varying amounts of penalty and privilege from the multiple systems of oppression which frame everyone's lives.

Individual biographies are situated within all domains of power and reflect their interconnections and contradictions. Whereas the structural domain of power organizes the macro-level of social organization with the disciplinary domain managing its operations, the interpersonal domain functions through routinized, day-to-day practices of how people treat one another (e.g., micro-level of social organization). Such practices are systematic, recurrent, and so familiar that they often go unnoticed. Because the interpersonal domain stresses the everyday, resistance strategies within this domain can take as many forms as there are individuals. When I ask my students for examples of how they respond to everyday racism, sexism, or other unfair treatment, the range of strategies they give surprises me. One Black woman student described how, when she is followed in a store, she fills her shopping cart to the brim with goods and then leaves it at the front, stopping by the service desk to complain about their surveillance policy. Two students, one African-American and the other White, told of how they switched names on their respective papers when they suspected that the Black student's lower grades reflected the professor's prejudice. To their chagrin, when the switched papers were returned to them, the Black student got her same old "C" whereas the White student received her "A," even though they had submitted each other's work! Coalition strategies such as these become especially important in integrated social settings where differential treatment is hard to detect.

When you look for it, people who are actively engaged in changing the terms of their everyday relationships with one another surface in surprising places. Certainly this book has shared many examples of prominent African-American women who try to change the ways in which they live their everyday lives. What remains less visible, however, are the myriad ways in which ordinary individuals from all walks of life work for social justice in small yet highly significant ways. One of my favorite examples concerns an invitation that my daughter received to visit a kindergarten playmate's house. Her classmate was a blue-eyed, blonde boy who was well mannered and friendly to her and me. However, because I did not know his parents very well, I wondered what type of reception our daughter would receive in his home. Ironically, my concerns were reduced when I saw the toy that his mother allowed him to bring to school. There was this little boy, blue-eyes, blond hair and all, carrying a Black, bald, male Cabbage Patch doll to school. This was not his only toy, but the fact that this toy was included in the repertoire of this small child's imagination astounded me. With this one, small act, this mother took a stand against racism, sexism, and heterosexism in a way that took courage for this region of the United States. To this day, I do not know why she did it. Her intentionality was far less important than the unspoken actions that she took. I share this story not to encourage people to give dolls to little blonde boys, unless, of course, they really wish to do so, but rather to illustrate one of many unobtrusive yet creative ways that all sorts of ordinary people work to change the world around them.

The Politics of Empowerment

Rethinking Black feminism as a social justice project involves developing a complex notion of empowerment. Shifting the analysis to investigating how the matrix of domination is structured along certain axes—race, gender, class, sexuality, and nation—as well as how it operates through interconnected domains of power—structural, interpersonal, disciplinary, and hegemonic—reveals that the dialectical relationship linking oppression and activism is far more complex than simple models of oppressors and oppressed would suggest. This inclusive perspective enables African-American women to avoid labeling one form of oppression as more important than others, or one expression of activism as more radical than another. It also creates conceptual space to identify some new linkages. Just as oppression is complex, so must resistance aimed at fostering empowerment demonstrate a similar complexity.

When it comes to power, the challenges raised by the synergistic relationship among domains of power generate new opportunities and constraints for African-American women who now desegregate schools and workplaces, as well as those who do not. On the one hand, entering places that denied access to our mothers provides new opportunities for fostering social justice. Depending on the setting, using the insights gained via outsider-within status can be a stimulus to creativity that helps both African-American women and our new organizational homes. On the other hand, the commodification of outsider-within status whereby African-American women's value to an organization lies solely in our ability to market a seemingly permanent marginal status can suppress Black women's empowerment. Being a permanent outsider within can never lead to power because the category, by definition, requires marginality. Each individual must find her own way, recognizing that her personal biography, while unique, is never as unique as she thinks.

When it comes to knowledge, Black women's empowerment involves rejecting the dimensions of knowledge that perpetuate objectification, commodification, and exploitation. African-American women and others like us become empowered when we understand and use those dimensions of our individual, group, and formal educational ways of knowing that foster our humanity. When Black women value our self-definitions, participate in Black women's domestic and transnational activist traditions, view the skills gained in schools as part of a focused education for Black community development, and invoke Black feminist epistemologies as central to our worldviews, we empower ourselves. C. Wright Mills's (1959) concept of the "sociological imagination" identifies its task and its promise as a way of knowing that enables individuals to grasp the relations between history and biography within society. Resembling the holistic epistemology required by Black feminism, using one's point of view to engage the sociological imagination can empower the individual. "My fullest concentration of energy is available to me," Audre Lorde maintains, "only when I integrate all the parts of who I am, openly, allowing power from particular sources of my living to flow back and forth freely through all my different selves, without the restriction of externally imposed definition" (1984, 120–21). Developing a Black women's standpoint to engage a collective Black feminist imagination can empower the group.

Black women's empowerment involves revitalizing U.S. Black feminism as a social justice project organized around the dual goals of empowering African-American women and fostering social justice in a transnational context. Black feminist thought's emphasis on the ongoing interplay between Black women's oppression and Black women's activism presents the matrix of domination and its interrelated domains of power as responsive to human agency. Such thought views the world as a dynamic place where the goal is not merely to survive or to fit in or to cope; rather, it becomes a place where we feel ownership and accountability. The existence of Black feminist thought suggests that there is always choice, and power to act, no matter how bleak the situation may appear to be. Viewing the world as one in the making raises the issue of individual responsibility for bringing about change. It also shows that while individual empowerment is key, only collective action can effectively generate the lasting institutional transformation required for social justice.

In 1831 Maria Stewart asked, "How long shall the fair daughters of Africa be compelled to bury their minds and talents beneath a load of iron pots and kettles?" (Richardson 1987, 38). Stewart's response speaks eloquently to the connections between knowledge, consciousness, and the politics of empowerment:

> Until union, knowledge and love begin to flow among us. How long shall a mean set of men flatter us with their smiles, and enrich themselves with our hard earnings; their wives' fingers sparkling with rings, and they themselves laughing at our folly? Until we begin to promote and patronize each other. . . . Do you ask, what can we do? Unite and build a store of your own. . . . Do you ask where is the money? We have spent more than enough for nonsense, to do what building we should want. (Richardson 1987, 38)

Notes

Chapter 1

1. Numerous Black women intellectuals have explored the core themes first articulated by Maria W. Stewart (see Hull et al. 1982). Sharon Harley and Rosalyn Terborg-Penn's (1978) groundbreaking collection of essays on Black women's history foreshadowed volumes on Black women's history such as those by Giddings (1984), and D. White (1985) and the important historical encyclopedia by Hine et al. (1993). A similar explosion in Black women's literary criticism has occurred, as evidenced by the publication of book-length studies of Black women writers such as those by Barbara Christian (1985), Hazel Carby (1987), and Ann duCille (1996).

2. My use of the term *subjugated knowledge* differs somewhat from Michel Foucault's (1980a) definition. According to Foucault, subjugated knowledges are "those blocs of historical knowledge which were present but disguised," namely, "a whole set of knowledges that have been disqualified as inadequate to their task or insufficiently elaborated: naive knowledges, located low down on the hierarchy, beneath the required level of cognition or scientificity" (p. 82). I suggest that Black feminist thought is not a "naive knowledge" but has been made to appear so by those controlling knowledge validation procedures. Moreover, Foucault argues that subjugated knowledge is "a particular, local, regional knowledge, a differential knowledge incapable of unanimity and which owes its force only to the harshness with which it is opposed by everything surrounding it" (p. 82). The component of Black feminist thought that analyzes Black women's oppression partially fits this definition, but the long-standing, independent, African-derived influences within Black women's thought are omitted from Foucault's analysis.

3. Sojourner Truth's actions exemplify Antonio Gramsci's (1971) contention that every social group creates one or more "strata of intellectuals which give it homogeneity and an awareness of its own function not only in the economic but also in the social and political fields" (p. 5). Academics are the intellectuals trained to represent the interests of groups in power. In contrast, "organic" intellectuals depend on common sense and represent the interests of their own group. Sojourner Truth typifies an "organic" or everyday intellectual, but she may not be certified as such by the dominant group because her intellectual activity threatens the prevailing social order. The outsider-within position of Black women academics encourages us to draw on the traditions of both our discipline of training and our experiences as Black women but to participate fully in neither (Collins 1986b).

4. Elizabeth Spelman (1988) rejects additive approaches to conceptualizing oppression that treat the oppression of a Black woman in a sexist and racist society as if it were a *further* burden than her oppression in a sexist but nonracist society, when, in fact, it is a *different* burden. Similarly, Brittan and Maynard (1984) argue that separate oppressions cannot be merged under one "grand theory of oppression." Omi and Winant (1986) warn against the tendency to subsume one type of oppression under another—for example, of seeing everything as stemming from class structure. For an incisive discussion of multiple jeopardy as an alternative model, see King (1988). The field of intersectionality developed considerably in the 1990s. For edited volumes using the frame of race, class, and gender studies, see Andersen and Collins (1998). For a useful analysis of the literature on intersecting oppressions, see Anthias and Yuval-Davis (1992).

Chapter 2

1. For discussions of the concept of standpoint, see Hartsock (1983a, 1983b), Jaggar (1983), and Smith (1987). Even though I use standpoint epistemologies as an organizing concept in this volume, they remain controversial. For a helpful critique of standpoint epistemologies, see Harding (1986). See my extended discussion of standpoint theory (Collins 1998a, 201–28). Canadian sociologist Dorothy Smith (1987) also views women's lived, everyday world as stimulating theory. But the everyday she examines is individual, a situation reflecting in part the isolation of White, middle-class women. In contrast, I contend that the collective values in U.S. Black neighborhoods, when combined with the working-class experiences of the majority of Black women, historically provided collective as well as individual everyday worlds. Thus, U.S. Black culture continually created via lived Black experience with racial segregation provided a social context for the emergence of a Black women's standpoint. Whereas the contexts in which this collective standpoint developed are changing, the purpose or need for it has not.

2. Scott (1985) defines consciousness as the symbols, norms, and ideological forms people create to give meaning to their acts. For de Lauretis (1986), consciousness is a process, a "particular configuration of subjectivity . . . produced at the intersection of meaning with experience. . . . Consciousness is grounded in personal history, and self and identity are understood within particular cultural contexts. Consciousness . . . is never fixed, never attained once and for all, because discursive boundaries change with historical conditions" (p. 8). It is important to distinguish between individual and group consciousness.

3. Certainly middle-class White women and all others who both recognize the significance of members of oppressed groups speaking for themselves and who share in Black feminist thought's overall mission can support Black feminist thought's development. Examples of such work already exists, much of it making important contributions to Black feminist thought. Many White women academics in the United States have done important scholarship on Black women. For example, historian Jacqueline Jones's (1985) history of Black women and work, Nancie Caraway's (1991) analysis of U.S. feminism, Nancy Naples's (1991, 1996) work on activist Black motherhood, biologist Anne Fausto-Sterling's (1995) analysis of the use of the Hottentot Venus, and scholarship on the social construction of Whiteness by Jessie Daniels (1997) and Abby Ferber (1998) all make significant contributions to Black feminist thought. What distinguishes their work is a basic understanding of the distinguishing features of Black feminism. They see the connections between knowledge and power, between the power to define knowledge and intersecting oppressions. These connections are not peripheral to their work. Instead, they are central.

4. My use of the term *humanist* grows from an African-derived historical context distinct from that criticized by Western feminists. I use the term to tap an African-centered humanism as cited by West (1977–78) and Asante (1987) and as part of Black theological

traditions (Mitchell and Lewter 1986; Cannon 1988). For discussions of African-American spirituality, see Richards (1990) and Paris (1995).

5. Walker's use of the term *womanism* contains contradictions that in turn influence varying approaches to Black feminism. For a discussion of Walker's use, see Collins (1998a, 61–65).

Chapter 3

1. By dislodging beliefs in the naturalness or normality of any one family form, feminist scholarship analyzes the centrality of specific notions of family to gender oppression (Andersen 1991; Thorne 1992). As Stephanie Coontz (1992) reports, this traditional family ideal never existed, even during the 1950s, which is often assumed to be the era of its realization. Coontz's analysis of the historical origins of each segment of the ideal provides a concise overview of how the values characterizing the traditional family ideal emerged in specific historical circumstances. Feminist anthropologists also challenge the traditional family ideal by demonstrating that the nuclear, heterosexual married couple form in the United States is neither "natural," universal, nor normative cross-culturally (Collier et al. 1989). Recent family scholarship suggests that large numbers of American families never experienced the traditional family ideal, and those who may have once achieved this form are now abandoning it (Coontz 1992).

2. The definition of social class that I use in this section derives from class conflict models, especially those based in labor market segmentation theory (Vanneman and Cannon 1987).

Chapter 4

1. Dona Richards (1980) offers an insightful analysis of the relationship between Christianity's contributions to an ideology of domination and the culture/nature binary. She notes that European Christianity is predicated on a worldview that sustains the exploitation of nature: "Christian thought provides a view of man, nature, and the universe which supports not only the ascendancy of science, but of the technical order, individualism, and relentless progress. Emphasis within this worldview is placed on humanity's dominance over *all* other beings, which become 'objects' in an 'objectified' universe. There is no emphasis on an awe-inspiring God or cosmos. Being 'made in God's image,' given the European ethos, translates into 'acting *as* God,' recreating the universe. Humanity is separated from nature" (p. 69). For works exploring the connections among Western thought, colonialism, and capitalism, see works by Marianna Torgovnick (1990), Rey Chow (1993), Edward Said (1993), and Anne McClintock (1995).

2. Brittan and Maynard (1984) note that ideology (1) is common sense and obvious; (2) appears natural, inevitable, and universal; (3) shapes lived experience and behavior; (4) is sedimented in people's consciousness; and (5) consists of a system of ideas embedded in the social system as a whole. This example captures all dimensions of how racism and sexism function ideologically. The status of Black woman as servant is so "common sense" that even a child knows it. That the child saw a Black female child as a baby maid speaks to the naturalization dimension and to the persistence of controlling images in individual consciousness and the social system overall.

Chapter 5

1. The theme of double consciousness has a long history in U.S. Black Studies. The proximate character of U.S. race relations where Blacks have routinely encountered Whites as subordinates has stimulated this theme. For a discussion of this theme, see Paul Gilroy's

(1993) analysis of William E.B. Du Bois. Interestingly, in his discussion of the first edition of *Black Feminist Thought,* Gilroy expresses surprise that I did not mention Du Bois, leaving Gilroy under the erroneous impression that I was unaware of Du Bois's significance for double consciousness.

2. Belenky et al. (1986) suggest that achieving constructed knowledge requires self-reflection about and distancing from familiar situations, whether psychological and/or physical. For Black women intellectuals, being outsiders within may provide the distance from and angle of vision on the familiar that can be used to "find a voice" or create constructed knowledge. Belenky et al. describe this process as affecting individuals. I suggest that a similar argument can be applied to Black women as a group. They also report that women repeatedly use the metaphor of voice to depict their intellectual and ethical development: "The tendency for women to ground their epistemological premises in metaphors suggesting speaking and listening is at odds with the visual metaphors (such as equating knowledge with illumination, knowing with seeing, and truth with light) that scientists and philosophers most often use to express their sense of mind" (p. 16). This emphasis on voice in women's culture parallels the importance of oral communication in African-American culture (Sidran 1971; Smitherman 1977). When applied to Black women's intellectual traditions, this metaphor of finding a voice remains useful in many settings. However, as a metaphor for Black women's empowerment, it remains flawed. I discuss this contradiction at length in *Fighting Words* (Collins 1998a, 44-76).

3. Sidran (1971) suggests that to get one's own "sound" or voice is a key part of vocalized Black music. Black theologian James Cone has also written about Black music as carrier of the values of African-American culture. Cone notes that Black music is "unity music. It unites the joy and the sorrow, the love and the hate, the hope and the despair of black people. . . . Black music is unifying because it confronts the individual with the truth of black existence and affirms that black being is possible only in a communal context. Black music is functional. Its purposes and aims are directly related to the consciousness of the black community" (1972, 5). Note the both/and orientation of Cone's description, an analysis rejecting the binary thinking of Western societies.

4. Black women have participated in all forms of Black music but have been especially central in vocal music such as spirituals, gospel, and the blues (Jackson 1981). I focus on the blues because of its association with the Black women's secular tradition and because of the attention it has garnered within Black feminist analysis (see, e.g., Davis 1998). Though a more recent phenomenon, gospel music is also "a Black feminine musical tradition" (Jackson 1981). With roots in the urban Black folk church, the text of gospel songs could also be examined.

5. Unfortunately, Alice Childress is one of many African-American women writers whose work remains unrecognized. Born in South Carolina in 1920, the great-granddaughter of a slave, Childress not only wrote books and short stories, but was active in New York Black theater. Although Mildred's conversations were first issued in book form in 1956 by a small publisher, this important collection of Alice Childress's work was virtually neglected for two decades. In 1986, literary critic Trudier Harris examined the collection and was able to have it reissued under the title *Like One of the Family,* also the title of the first piece in the volume.

6. U.S. Black scholarship has examined this conceptualization of the self in African and African-American communities. See Smitherman (1977), Asante (1987), and Brown (1989). For feminist analyses of women's development of self as a distinctive process, see especially Evelyn Keller's (1985) discussion of dynamic autonomy and how it relates to relationships of domination. A fascinating discussion of the fragmented self can be found in Gloria Wekker's (1997) analysis of Afro-Surinamese women's agency.

Chapter 6

1. The perceived deviancy of sexual outlaws has been addressed in characteristic ways: if possible, fix it (the reformist posture); if it cannot be fixed, at least contain it so that disease will not infect the so-called healthy population (ghettoization, segregation); and if reform and elimination fail, then eliminate it by stamping out the deviant practices if not the actual people themselves (the genocidal impulse).

2. Offering a similar argument about the relationship between race and masculinity, Paul Hoch (1979) suggests that the ideal White man is a hero who upholds honor. But inside lurks a "Black beast" of violence and sexuality, traits that the White hero deflects onto men of color.

3. Any group can be made into pets. Consider Tuan's (1984) discussion of the role that young Black boys played as exotic ornaments for wealthy White women from the 1500s to the early 1800s in England. Unlike other male servants, the boys were the favorite attendants of noble ladies and gained entry into their mistresses' drawing rooms, bedchambers, and theater boxes. Boys were often given fancy collars with padlocks to wear. "As they did with their pet dogs and monkeys, the ladies grew genuinely fond of their black boys" (p. 142). In addition, Nancy White's analysis in Chapter 5 of the differences between how White and Black women are treated by White men uses this victim/pet metaphor (Gwaltney 1980, 148).

Chapter 7

1. French philosopher Michel Foucault makes a similar point: "I believe that the political significance of the problem of sex is due to the fact that sex is located at the point of intersection of the discipline of the body and the control of the population" (1980b, 125). The erotic is something felt, a power than is embodied. Controlling sexuality harnesses that power for the needs of larger, hierarchical systems by controlling the body and hence the population.

2. There is a growing body of work in which Black men analyze Black masculinity (see, e.g., Awkward 1996; Dyson 1996). Because much of this work has been advanced by or about Black gay men, it has been slow to be taken up by Black heterosexual men. For an important Black feminist analysis of how Black masculinity has been shaped by intersecting oppressions of class, race, and gender, see Barbara Omolade's (1994) essay "Hearts of Darkness," especially pp. 12–15.

3. Michel Foucault refers to this phenomenon as a "network or circuit of bio-power, or somato-power, which acts as the formative matrix of sexuality itself" (1980a, 186). To Foucault, "Power relations can materially penetrate the body in depth, without depending even on the mediation of the subject's own representations. If power takes hold on the body, this isn't through its having first to be interiorized in people's consciousness" (p. 186). This particular dimension of power as domination is extremely effective precisely because it is felt and not conceptualized.

4. Studies of African art and culture indicate that behavior, individuals, and creations deemed "beautiful" from an African-centered perspective are valued for qualities other than their appearance and their value in an exchange-based marketplace (Gayle 1971; Asante 1990). For example, the Yoruba assess everything aesthetically, from the taste of food and the qualities of dress to the deportment of a woman or man. Beauty is seen in the mean—in something not too tall or short, not too beautiful (overly handsome people turn out to be skeletons in disguise in many folktales) or too ugly. Moreover, the Yoruba appreciate freshness and improvisation in the arts (Thompson 1983).

Chapter 9

1. Black women's motherwork contains economic significance, social functions, and political meaning. First, since Black women's paid employment was often essential for their families' survival, their identities as paid workers and mothers contradicted the assumed distinctions between work and family so central to definitions of masculinity and femininity. Next, because even though they worked hard both at home and on their jobs these women still remained poor, Black women saw U.S. social class hierarchies from the bottom up. Finally, the different political interpretations attached to motherwork within Black civil society, in particular community othermothering traditions that elevated motherhood as a symbol of power, potentially politicized Black women's motherwork.

2. Another suggested source of Black women's power within African-American communities concerns Black women's authority as spiritual leaders. Rosalyn Terborg-Penn (1986) suggests that in cases in which women lead community resistance movements, respected older women often became leaders. These women were revered generally because of "supernatural or spiritual powers, which their followers believed were strong enough to combat the oppressive forces against which their society was struggling" (1986, 190).

3. Karen Sacks's case study describes an atypical case of Black women's experiences in unions. For many years Black women have participated in and organized a variety of labor actions designed to improve working conditions, wages, and occupational mobility. But the segregation of Black women in private domestic work which left them largely outside of industry, the occupational discrimination within industry, and prejudice within the unions themselves all worked to shape Black women's behavior as unionists (Terborg-Penn 1985).

4. African feminist Obioma Nnaemeka's argument that African women consistently reject radical feminism's views on motherhood can just as easily be applied to African-American women. Distinguishing among different strands of feminism based in part on their views on motherhood, Nnaemeka contends, "African feminism neither demotes/ abandons motherhood nor dismisses maternal politics as non-feminist or unfeminist politics" (Nnaemeka 1998a, 6). In brief, while African-American women may reject a feminism that seems antimotherhood, developing a Black women's standpoint on motherwork within the larger context of Black feminism as a social justice project might receive a markedly different reception.

Chapter 10

1. I apply this concept of transversal politics to groups organized around historically constructed identities, in this case the identity of "Black woman." Groups, however, need not be formed around identity categories. The local group history can just as easily be constructed around an issue or an "affinity." Thus, the model of transversal politics advanced here concerns coalitions of all sorts, and can accommodate the contradictions that seemingly distinguish identity politics and affinity politics.

2. For a discussion of the similarities and differences of using the individual and the group as levels of analysis, see Collins (1998a), especially pages 203–11.

Chapter 11

1. Many scholars view positivism and postmodernism, for example, as competing epistemologies, each with their own theories of what counts as truth and why. In contrast, I view positivism and postmodernism as yet another binary whose opposition to each other unifies them within an overarching Western epistemology (Collins 1998a, 126–37). The prior discussion of intersecting oppressions of race, class, gender,

sexuality, and nation aims to sketch out an alternative paradigm that, as I discuss later in this chapter, may constitute an important part of Black feminist epistemology.

2. For example, qualitative and quantitative methodologies represent two important methodological approaches that are often associated with Western humanities and the sciences respectively. A particular methodology may become identified with an epistemological approach and its interpretive frameworks. Whereas methodology refers to a broader theory of how to do research, nothing in a research methodology is inherently White or Black, male or female. Certain methodologies can become coded as "white" and/or "male" and thus work to disadvantage Black women (Collins 1998a, 101–105). Particular techniques used in the course of research, for example, interviewing and survey analysis, constitute research *methods* or specific tools that need not be attached to any particular group's interests. Whereas patterns of using specific techniques may vary among groups— White men may work with large-scale data sets whereas Black women may rely more on one-on-one interviewing—methods can be used for a variety of purposes.

3. Sandra Harding provides a useful definition of Eurocentrism that parallels my use here (Harding 1998, 12–15). Western or Eurocentric social and political thought contains three interrelated approaches to ascertaining "truth" that are routinely portrayed as competing epistemologies. The first, reflected in positivist science, has long claimed that absolute truths exist and that the task of scholarship is to develop objective, unbiased tools of science to measure these truths. But many social theories have challenged the concepts and epistemology of this version of science as representing the vested interests of elite White men and therefore as being less valid when applied to experiences of other groups and, more recently, to White male recounting of their own exploits. The second approach, earlier versions of standpoint theories that were themselves rooted in a Marxist positivism, essentially reversed positivist science's assumptions concerning whose truth would prevail. These approaches suggest that the oppressed allegedly have a clearer view of "truth" than their oppressors because they lack the blinders created by the dominant group's ideology. But this version of standpoint theory basically duplicates the positivist belief in one "true" interpretation of reality and, like positivist science, comes with its own set of problems. Postmodernism, the third approach, has been forwarded as the antithesis of and inevitable outcome of rejecting a positivist science. Within postmodern logic, groups themselves become suspect as well as any specialized thought. In extreme postmodern discourse, each group's thought is equally valid. No group can claim to have a better interpretation of the "truth" than another. In a sense, postmodernism represents the opposite of scientific ideologies of objectivity (Collins 1998a, 124–154).

4. In discussing the West African Sacred Cosmos, Mechal Sobel notes that *Nyam*, a root word in many West African languages, connotes an enduring spirit, power, or energy possessed by all life. Despite the pervasiveness of this important concept in African humanism (see Jahn 1961, for example), its definition remains elusive. Sobel observes, "Every individual analyzing the various Sacred Cosmos of West Africans has recognized the reality of this force, but no one has yet adequately translated this concept into Western terms" (1979, 13). For comprehensive discussions of African spirituality, see Richards (1990) and Paris (1995). Many African-American theologians, especially women, use this African-derived notion of spirituality to guide their work. For work within womanist traditions, see that done by Grant (1989) and Sanders (1995).

Glossary

agency: an individual or social group's will to be self-defining and self-determining.

binary thinking: a way of conceptualizing realities that divides concepts into two, mutually exclusive categories, e.g., white/black, man/woman, reason/emotion, and heterosexual/homosexual.

Black community: a set of institutions, communication networks, and practices that help African-Americans respond to social, economic, and political challenges confronting them. Also known as the Black public sphere or Black civil society.

Black nationalism: a political philosophy based on the belief that Black people constitute a people or nation with a common history and destiny.

capitalism: an economic system based on the private ownership of the means of production. Capitalism is typically characterized by extreme distributions of wealth and large differences between the rich and the poor.

commodification: in capitalist political economies, land, products, services, and ideas are assigned economic values and are bought and sold in marketplaces as commodities.

critical social theory: bodies of knowledge and sets of institutional practices that actively grapple with the central questions facing groups of people. These groups are differently placed in specific political, social, and historic contexts characterized by injustice. What makes critical social theory "critical" is its commitment to justice, for one's own group and/or for that of other groups.

disciplinary domain of power: a way of ruling that relies on bureaucratic hierarchies and techniques of surveillance.

epistemology: standards used to assess knowledge or why we believe what we believe to be true.

essentialism: belief that individuals or groups have inherent, unchanging characteristics rooted in biology or a self-contained culture that explain their status. When linked to oppressions of race, gender, and sexuality, binary thinking constructs "essential" group differences.

Eurocentrism: an ideology that presents the ideas and experiences of Whites as normal, normative, and ideal. Also known as white racism or white supremacy.

hegemonic domain of power: a form or mode of social organization that uses ideas and ideology to absorb and thereby depoliticize oppressed groups' dissent. Alternatively, the diffusion of power throughout the social system where multiple groups police one another and suppress one another's dissent.

identity politics: a way of knowing that sees lived experiences as important to creating knowledge and crafting group-based political strategies. Also, a form of political resistance where an oppressed group rejects its devalued status.

ideology: a body of ideas reflecting the interests of a particular social group. Scientific racism and sexism constitute ideologies that support domination. Black nationalism and feminism constitute counter-ideologies that oppose such domination.

interpersonal domain of power: discriminatory practices of everyday lived experience that because they are so routine typically go unnoticed or remain unidentified. Strategies of everyday racism and everyday resistance occur in this domain.

intersectionality: analysis claiming that systems of race, social class, gender, sexuality, ethnicity, nation, and age form mutually constructing features of social organization, which shape Black women's experiences and, in turn, are shaped by Black women.

matrix of domination: the overall organization of hierarchical power relations for any society. Any specific matrix of domination has (1) a particular arrangement of intersecting systems of oppression, e.g., race, social class, gender, sexuality, citizenship status, ethnicity and age; and (2) a particular organization of its domains of power, e.g., structural, disciplinary, hegemonic, and interpersonal.

oppositional knowledge: a type of knowledge developed by, for, and/or in defense of an oppressed group's interests. Ideally, it fosters the group's self-definition and self-determination.

oppression: an unjust situation where, systematically and over a long period of time, one group denies another group access to the resources of society. Race, gender, class, sexuality, nation, age, and ethnicity constitute major forms of oppression.

outsider-within locations: social locations or border spaces marking the boundaries between groups of unequal power. Individuals acquire identities as "outsiders within" by their placement in these social locations.

paradigm: an interpretive framework used to explain social phenomena.

public and private spheres: two areas of social organization with the public sphere of work and government typically juxtaposed to the private sphere of home and family.

racial segregation: a constellation of policies that separate groups by race based on the belief that proximity to the group deemed to be inferior will harm the allegedly superior group. Though currently forbidden by law in the United States, racially segregated neighborhoods, schools, occupational categories, and access to public facilities persist.

racial solidarity: the belief that members of a racial group have common interests and should support one another above the interests of members of other racial groups.

racism: a system of unequal power and privilege where humans are divided into groups or "races" with social rewards unevenly distributed to groups based on their racial classification. Variations of racism include institutionalized racism, scientific racism, and everyday racism. In the United States, racial segregation constitutes a fundamental principle of how racism is organized.

rhetoric of color-blindness: a view of the world that resists talking of race because to do so is believed to perpetuate racism.

scientific racism: a specific body of knowledge about Blacks, Asians, Native Americans, Whites, and Latinos produced within biology, anthropology, psychology, sociology, and other academic disciplines. Scientific racism was designed to prove the inferiority of people of color.

self-definition: the power to name one's own reality.

self-determination: the power to decide one's own destiny.

social class: in its most general sense, social groups differentiated from one another by economic status, cultural forms, practices, or ways of life. Social class refers to a group of people who share a common placement in a political economy.

social justice project: an organized, long-term effort to eliminate oppression and empower individuals and groups within a just society.

standpoint theory: a social theory arguing that group location in hierarchical power relations produces common challenges for individuals in those groups. Moreover, shared experiences can foster similar angles of vision leading to group knowledge or standpoint deemed essential for informed political action.

structural domain of power: a constellation of organized practices in employment, government, education, law, business, and housing that work to maintain an unequal and unjust distribution of social resources. Unlike bias and prejudice, which are characteristics of individuals, the structural domain of power operates through the laws and policies of social institutions.

subjugated knowledge: the secret knowledges generated by oppressed groups. Such knowledge typically remains hidden because revealing it weakens its purpose of assisting them in dealing with oppression. Subjugated knowledges that aim to resist oppression constitute oppositional knowledges.

transnationalism: a view of the world that sees certain interests as going beyond the borders of individual nation-states. Whereas internationalism emphasizes the relationship among nation-states, transnationalism takes a global perspective.

References

Adler, Karen S. 1992. " 'Always Leading Our Men in Service and Sacrifice': Amy Jacques Garvey, Feminist Black Nationalist." *Gender and Society* 6 (3): 346–75.

Aidoo, Ama Ata. 1991. *Changes: A Love Story.* New York: Feminist Press.

———. 1998. "The African Woman Today." In *Sisterhood, Feminisms, and Power: From Africa to the Diaspora,* ed. Obioma Nnaemeka, 39–50. Trenton, NJ: Africa World Press.

Aina, Olabisi. 1998. "African Women at the Grassroots: The Silent Partners of the Women's Movement." In *Sisterhood, Feminisms, and Power: From Africa to the Diaspora,* ed. Obioma Nnaemeka, 65–88. Trenton, NJ: Africa World Press.

Alexander, M. Jacqui. "Erotic Autonomy as a Politics of Decolonization: An Anatomy of Feminist and State Practice in the Bahamas Tourist Industry." In *Feminist Genealogies, Colonial Legacies, Democratic Futures,* ed. M. Jacqui Alexander and Chandra Talpade Mohanty, 63–100. New York: Routledge.

———, and Chandra Talpade Mohanty, eds. 1997. *Feminist Genealogies, Colonial Legacies, Democratic Futures.* New York: Routledge.

Alma's Rainbow. 1994. Written and directed by Ayoka Chenzira. Crossgrain Pictures.

Amott, Teresa L. 1990. "Black Women and AFDC: Making Entitlement Out of Necessity." In *Women, the State, and Welfare,* ed. Linda Gordon, 280–98. Madison: University of Wisconsin Press.

———, and Julie Matthaei. 1991. *Race, Gender, and Work: A Multicultural Economic History of Women in the United States.* Boston: South End Press.

Andersen, Margaret L. 1991. "Feminism and the American Family Ideal." *Journal of Comparative Family Studies* 22 (2) Summer: 235–46.

———, and Patricia Hill Collins, eds. 1998. *Race, Class, and Gender: An Anthology, Third Edition.* Belmont, CA: Wadsworth Press.

Andrews, William L. 1986. *Sisters of the Spirit: Three Black Women's Autobiographies of the Nineteenth Century.* Bloomington: Indiana University Press.

Angelou, Maya. 1969. *I Know Why the Caged Bird Sings.* New York: Bantam.

Anthias, Floya, and Nira Yuval-Davis. 1992. *Racialized Boundaries: Race, Nation,*

Gender, Colour and Class in the Anti-Racist Struggle. New York: Routledge.

Antrobus, Peggy. 1995. "Women in the Caribbean: The Quadruple Burden of Gender, Race, Class and Imperialism." In *Connecting Across Cultures and Continents: Black Women Speak Out on Identity, Race and Development,* ed. Achola O. Pala, 53–60. New York: United Nations Development Fund for Women.

Asante, Kariamu W. 1990. "Commonalities in African Dance: An Aesthetic Foundation." In *African Culture: The Rhythms of Unity,* ed. Molefi Asante and Kariamu W. Asante, 71–82. Trenton, NJ: Africa World Press.

Asante, Molefi Kete. 1987. *The Afrocentric Idea*. Philadelphia: Temple University Press.

Asbury, Jo-Ellen. 1987. "African-American Women in Violent Relationships: An Exploration of Cultural Differences." In *Violence in the Black Family: Correlates and Consequences,* ed. Robert L. Hampton, 89–105. Lexington, MA: Lexington Books.

Avery, Byliye Y. 1994. "Breathing Life into Ourselves: The Evolution of the National Black Women's Health Project." In *The Black Women's Health Book: Speaking for Ourselves,* ed. Evelyn C. White, 4–10. Seattle: Seal Press.

Awkward, Michael. 1996. "A Black Man's Place(s) in Black Feminist Criticism." In *Representing Black Men,* ed. Marcellus Blount and George P. Cunningham, 3–26. New York: Routledge.

Baloyi, Danisa E. 1995. "Apartheid and Identity: Black Women in South Africa." In *Connecting Across Cultures and Continents: Black Women Speak Out on Identity, Race and Development,* ed. Achola O. Pala, 39–46. New York: United Nations Development Fund for Women.

(Bambara), Toni Cade. 1970a. "On the Issue of Roles." In *The Black Woman: An Anthology,* ed. Toni Cade (Bambara), 101–10. New York: Signet.

———, ed. 1970b. *The Black Woman: An Anthology*. New York: Signet.

———. 1980. *The Salt Eaters*. New York: Vintage.

———. 1981. *Gorilla, My Love*. New York: Vintage.

Bannerji, Himani. 1995. *Thinking Through: Essays on Feminism, Marxism, and Anti-Racism*. Toronto: Women's Press.

Barnett, Bernice McNair. 1993. "Invisible Southern Black Women Leaders in the Civil Rights Movement: The Triple Constraints of Gender, Race, and Class." *Gender and Society* 7 (2): 162–82.

Beale, Frances. 1970. "Double Jeopardy: To Be Black and Female." In *The Black Woman: An Anthology,* ed. Toni Cade (Bambara), 90–100. New York: Signet.

Belenky, Mary Field, Blythe McVicker Clinchy, Nancy Rule Goldberger, and Jill Mattuck Tarule. 1986. *Women's Ways of Knowing*. New York: Basic Books.

Bell, Laurie, ed. 1987. *Good Girls/Bad Girls: Feminists and Sex Trade Workers Face to Face*. Toronto: Seal Press.

Bell-Scott, Patricia, Beverly Guy-Sheftall, Jacqueline Jones Royster, Janet Sims-Wood, Miriam DeCosta-Willis, and Lucie Fultz, eds. 1991. *Double Stitch: Black Women Write About Mothers and Daughters*. Boston: Beacon.

Berger, Peter L., and Thomas Luckmann. 1966. *The Social Construction of Reality*. New York: Doubleday.

Berry, Mary Frances. [1971] 1994. *Black Resistance, White Law: A History of Constitutional Racism in America.* New York: Penguin.

Billie Holiday Anthology/Lady Sings the Blues. 1976. Ojai, CA: Creative Concepts Publishing.

Billingsley, Andrew. 1992. *Black Families in White America.* Englewood Cliffs, NJ: Prentice Hall.

Bobo, Jacqueline. 1995. *Black Women as Cultural Readers.* New York: Columbia University Press.

Bonner, Marita O. 1987. "On Being Young—A Woman—and Colored." In *Frye Street and Environs: The Collected Works of Marita Bonner,* ed. Joyce Flynn and Joyce Occomy Stricklin, 3–8. Boston: Beacon.

Brewer, Rose. 1988. "Black Women in Poverty: Some Comments on Female-Headed Families." *Signs* 13(2): 331–39.

———. 1993. "Theorizing Race, Class and Gender: The New Scholarship of Black Feminist Intellectuals and Black Women's Labor." In *Theorizing Black Feminisms: The Visionary Pragmatism of Black Women,* ed. Stanlie M. James and Abena P.A. Busia, 13–30. New York: Routledge.

———. 1994. "Race, Class, Gender and US State Welfare Policy: The Nexus of Inequality for African American Families." In *Color, Class and Country: Experiences of Gender,* ed. Gay Young and Bette J. Dickerson, 115–27. London: Zed Books.

———. 1995. "Gender, Poverty, Culture, and Economy: Theorizing Female-Led Families." In *African American Single Mothers: Understanding Their Lives and Families,* ed. Bette Dickerson, 146–63. Thousand Oaks, CA: Sage.

Brittan, Arthur, and Mary Maynard. 1984. *Sexism, Racism and Oppression.* New York: Basil Blackwell.

Brooks, Gwendolyn. 1953. *Maud Martha.* Boston: Atlantic Press.

———. 1972. *Report from Part One: The Autobiography of Gwendolyn Brooks.* Detroit: Broadside Press.

Brown, Cynthia Stokes, ed. 1986. *Ready from Within: Septima Clark and the Civil Rights Movement.* Navarro, CA: Wild Trees Press.

Brown, Elaine. 1992. *A Taste of Power: A Black Woman's Story.* New York: Pantheon.

Brown, Elsa Barkley. 1986. *Hearing Our Mothers' Lives.* Atlanta: Fifteenth Anniversary of African-American and African Studies, Emory University (unpublished).

———. 1989. "African-American Women's Quilting: A Framework for Conceptualizing and Teaching African-American Women's History." *Signs* 14 (4): 921–29.

———. 1994. "Negotiating and Transforming the Public Sphere: African American Political Life in the Transition from Slavery to Freedom." *Public Culture* 7 (1): 107–46.

Brown-Collins, Alice, and Deborah Ridley Sussewell. 1986. "The Afro-American Woman's Emerging Selves." *Journal of Black Psychology* 13 (1): 1–11.

Burnham, Linda. 1985. "Has Poverty Been Feminized in Black America?" *Black Scholar* 16 (2): 14–24.

Burnham, Margaret A. 1987. "An Impossible Marriage: Slave Law and Family Law." *Law and Inequality* 5: 187–225.

Byerly, Victoria. 1986. *Hard Times Cotton Mills Girls*. Ithaca, NY: Cornell University Press.

Campbell, Bebe Moore. 1989. *Sweet Summer: Growing Up with and without My Dad*. New York: Putnam.

Canada, Geoffrey. 1995. *Fist Stick Knife Gun: A Personal History of Violence in America*. Boston: Beacon.

Cannon, Katie G. 1985. "The Emergence of a Black Feminist Consciousness." In *Feminist Interpretations of the Bible*, ed. Letty M. Russell, 30–40. Philadelphia: Westminster Press.

————. 1988. *Black Womanist Ethics*. Atlanta: Scholars Press.

Cantarow, Ellen. 1980. *Moving the Mountain: Women Working for Social Change*. Old Westbury, NY: Feminist Press.

Caraway, Nancie. 1991. *Segregated Sisterhood: Racism and the Politics of American Feminism*. Knoxville: University of Tennessee Press.

Carby, Hazel. 1987. *Reconstructing Womanhood: The Emergence of the Afro-American Woman Novelist*. New York: Oxford University Press.

————. 1992. "The Multicultural Wars." In *Black Popular Culture*, ed. Michele Wallace and Gina Dent, 187–199. Seattle: Bay Press.

Carneiro, Sueli. 1995. "Defining Black Feminism." In *Connecting Across Cultures and Continents: Black Women Speak Out on Identity, Race and Development*, ed. Achola O. Pala, 11–18. New York: United Nations Development Fund for Women.

Carroll, Rebecca. 1997. *Sugar in the Raw: Voices of Young Black Girls in America*. New York: Crown Trade.

Cary, Lorene. 1991. *Black Ice*. New York: Knopf.

Chang, Grace. 1994. "Undocumented Latinas: The New 'Employable Mothers.' " In *Mothering: Ideology, Experience, and Agency*, ed. Evelyn Nakano Glenn, Grace Chang, and Linda Rennie Forcey, 259–86. New York: Routledge.

"Children of the Underclass." 1989. *Newsweek*. September 11, 16–27.

Childress, Alice. [1956] 1986. *Like One of the Family: Conversations from a Domestic's Life*. Boston: Beacon.

Chisholm, Shirley. 1970. *Unbought and Unbossed*. New York: Avon.

Chodorow, Nancy. 1978. *The Reproduction of Mothering*. Berkeley: University of California Press.

Chow, Rey. 1993. *Writing Diaspora: Tactics of Intervention in Contemporary Cultural Studies*. Bloomington: Indiana University Press.

Christian, Barbara. 1985. *Black Feminist Criticism, Perspectives on Black Women Writers*. New York: Pergamon.

————. 1989. "But Who Do You Really Belong to—Black Studies or Women's Studies?" *Women's Studies* 17 (1–2): 17–23.

————. 1994. "Diminishing Returns: Can Black Feminism(s) Survive the Academy?" In *Multiculturalism: A Critical Reader*, ed. David Theo Goldberg, 168–79. Cambridge: Basil Blackwell.

Clarke, Cheryl. 1983. "The Failure to Transform: Homophobia in the Black

Community." In *Home Girls: A Black Feminist Anthology,* ed. Barbara Smith, 197–208. New York: Kitchen Table Press.

———, Jewell L. Gomez, Evelyn Hammonds, Bonnie Johnson, and Linda Powell. 1983. "Conversations and Questions: Black Women on Black Women Writers." *Conditions: Nine* 3 (3): 88–137.

Clark-Lewis, Elizabeth. 1985. *"This Work Had a' End": The Transition from Live–In to Day Work.* Southern Women: The Intersection of Race, Class and Gender. Working Paper #2. Memphis, TN: Center for Research on Women, Memphis State University.

Cleage, Pearl. 1993. *Deals With the Devil and Other Reasons to Riot.* New York: Ballantine.

Cole, Johnetta B. 1993. *Conversations: Straight Talk with America's Sister President.* New York: Anchor.

Coleman, Willi. 1987. "Closets and Keepsakes." *Sage: A Scholarly Journal on Black Women* 4 (2): 34–35.

Collier, Jane, Michelle Z. Rosaldo, and Sylvia Yanagisko. 1992. "Is There a Family? New Anthropological Views." In *Rethinking the Family: Some Feminist Questions, Second Edition* ed. Barrie Thorne and Marilyn Yalom, 31–48. Boston: Northeastern University Press.

Collins, Patricia Hill. 1986. "Learning from the Outsider Within: The Sociological Significance of Black Feminist Thought." *Social Problems* 33 (6): 14–32.

———. 1989. "A Comparison of Two Works on Black Family Life." *Signs* 14 (4): 875–84.

———. 1993a. "Black Feminism in the Twentieth Century." In *Black Women in the United States: An Historical Encyclopedia,* ed. Darlene Clark Hine, Elsa Barkley Brown, and Rosalyn Terborg-Penn, 418–25. New York: Carlson.

———. 1993b. "It's in Our Hands: Breaking the Silence on Gender in African-American Studies." In *Understanding Curriculum as Racial Text,* ed. Willian F. Pinar and Louis Castenall, 127– 41. Albany: SUNY Press.

———. 1994. "Shifting the Center: Race, Class, and Feminist Theorizing about Motherhood." In *Mothering: Ideology, Experience and Agency,* ed. Evelyn Nakano Glenn, Grace Chang, and Linda Forcey, 45–65. New York: Routledge.

———. 1997. "African-American Women and Economic Justice: A Preliminary Analysis of Wealth, Family and Black Social Class." *University of Cincinnati Law Review* 65 (2): 825–52.

———. 1998a. *Fighting Words: Black Women and the Search for Justice.* Minneapolis: University of Minnesota Press.

———. 1998b. "Intersections of Race, Class, Gender, and Nation: Some Implications for Black Family Studies." *Journal of Comparative Family Studies* 29 (1): 27–36.

———. 1998c. "It's All In the Family: Intersections of Gender, Race, and Nation." *Hypatia* 13 (3): 62– 82.

———. 1998d. "The Tie That Binds: Race, Gender and U.S. Violence." *Ethnic and Racial Studies* 21 (5): 918–38.

———. 1999a. "Producing the Mothers of the Nation: Race, Class and

Contemporary U.S. Population Policies." Forthcoming in *Women, Citizenship and Difference*, ed. Nira Yuval-Davis. London: Zed Books.

———. 1999b. "Will the 'Real' Mother Please Stand Up?: The Logic of Eugenics and American National Family Planning." In *Revisioning Women, Health and Healing: Feminist, Cultural, and Technoscience Perspectives*, ed. Adele Clarke and Virginia Olesen, 266-82. New York: Routledge.

Color. 1983. Produced and directed by Warrington Hudlin, written and coproduced by Denise Oliver. New York: Black Filmmaker's Foundation.

The Combahee River Collective. 1982. "A Black Feminist Statement." In *But Some of Us Are Brave*, ed. Gloria T. Hull, Patricia Bell Scott, and Barbara Smith, 13–22. Old Westbury, NY: Feminist Press.

Cone, James H. 1972. *The Spirituals and the Blues: An Interpretation*. New York: Seabury Press.

Coontz, Stephanie. 1992. *The Way We Never Were: American Families and the Nostalgia Trap*. New York: Basic Books.

Cooper, Anna Julia. 1892. *A Voice from the South; By a Black Woman of the South*. Xenia, OH: Aldine.

Cose, Ellis. 1993. *The Rage of the Privileged Class*. New York: HarperCollins.

Cowan, Gloria, and Robin R. Campbell. 1994. "Racism and Sexism in Interracial Pornography. *Psychology of Women Quarterly* 18: 323–38.

———, Jacqueline Anne Rouse, and Barbara Woods, eds. 1990. *Women in the Civil Rights Movement: Trailblazers and Torchbearers, 1941–1965*. Bloomington: Indiana University Press.

Crenshaw, Kimberle Williams. 1991. "Mapping the Margins: Intersectionality, Identity Politics, and Violence Against Women of Color." *Stanford Law Review* 43 (6): 1241–99.

———. 1992. "Whose Story Is It Anyway? Feminist and Antiracist Appropriations of Anita Hill." In *Race-ing Justice, En-Gendering Power*, ed. Toni Morrison, 402–40. New York: Pantheon.

———. 1993. "Beyond Racism and Misogyny: Black Feminism and 2 Live Crew." In *Words That Wound: Critical Race Theory, Assaultive Speech, and the First Amendment*, ed. Mari J. Matsuda, Charles R. Lawrence III, Richard Delgado, and Kimberle Crenshaw, 111–32. Boulder: Westview.

———. 1997. "Color Blindness, History, and the Law." In *The House That Race Built*, ed. Wahneema Lubiano, 280–88. New York: Pantheon.

Cruse, Harold. 1967. *The Crisis of the Negro Intellectual*. New York: William Morrow.

Daniels, Bonnie. 1979. "For Colored Girls . . . A Catharsis." *Black Scholar* 10(8–9): 61–62.

Daniels, Jessie. 1997. *White Lies*. New York: Routledge.

Darcy, R., and Charles D. Hadley. 1988. "Black Women in Politics: The Puzzle of Success." *Social Science Quarterly* 69(3): 629–45.

Daughters of Dust. [1991] 1992. Directed by Julie Dash. American Playhouse and Geeche Gild Productions.

Davenport, Doris. 1996. "Black Lesbians in Academia: Visible Invisibility." In *The New Lesbian Studies: Into the Twenty-First Century,* ed. Bonnie Zimmerman and Toni A.H. McNaron. New York: Feminist Press.

Davis, Angela Y. [1971] 1995. "Reflections on the Black Woman's Role in the Community of Slaves." In *Words of Fire: An Anthology of African American Feminist Thought,* ed. Beverly Guy-Sheftall, 200–18. New York: New Press.

———. 1978. "Rape, Racism and the Capitalist Setting." *Black Scholar* 9(7): 24–30.

———. 1981. *Women, Race and Class.* New York: Random House.

———. 1989. *Women, Culture, and Politics.* New York: Random House.

———. 1997. "Race and Criminalization: Black Americans and the Punishment Industry." In *The House That Race Built,* ed. Wahneema Lubiano, 264–79. New York: Pantheon.

———. 1998. *Blues Legacies and Black Feminism.* New York: Vintage.

Davis, George, and Glegg Watson. 1985. *Black Life in Corporate America.* New York: Anchor.

d' Emilio, John, and Estelle Freedman. 1988. "Race and Sexuality." In *Intimate Matters: A History of Sexuality in America,* 85–108. New York: Harper and Row.

de Lauretis, Teresa. 1986. "Feminist Studies/Critical Studies: Issues, Terms, and Contexts." In *Feminist Studies/Critical Studies,* ed. Teresa de Lauretis, 1–19. Bloomington: Indiana University Press.

Dickerson, Bette J., ed. 1995a. *African American Single Mothers: Understanding Their Lives and Families.* Thousand Oaks, CA: Sage.

———. 1995b. "Introduction." In *African American Single Mothers: Understanding Their Lives and Families,* ed. B.J. Dickerson, ix–xxx. Thousand Oaks, CA: Sage.

Dill, Bonnie Thornton. 1979. "The Dialectics of Black Womanhood." *Signs* 4 (3): 543–55.

———. 1980. " 'The Means to Put My Children Through': Child-Rearing Goals and Strategies among Black Female Domestic Servants." In *The Black Woman,* ed. La Frances Rodgers-Rose, 107–23. Beverly Hills, CA: Sage.

———. 1983. "Race, Class, and Gender: Prospects for an All-Inclusive Sisterhood." *Feminist Studies* 9 (1): 131–50.

———. 1988a. " 'Making Your Job Good Yourself': Domestic Service and the Construction of Personal Dignity." In *Women and the Politics of Empowerment,* ed. Ann Bookman and Sandra Morgen, 33–52. Philadelphia: Temple University Press.

———. 1988b. "Our Mothers' Grief: Racial Ethnic Women and the Maintenance of Families." *Journal of Family History* 13 (4): 415–31.

Dines, Gail. 1998. *Pornography: The Production and Consumption of Inequality.* New York: Routledge.

Diop, Cheikh. 1974. *The African Origin of Civilization: Myth or Reality?* New York: L. Hill.

Dodson, Jualyne E., and Cheryl Townsend Gilkes. 1987. "Something Within: Social Change and Collective Endurance in the Sacred World of Black Christian Women." In *Women and Religion in America, Volume 3: 1900–1968,* ed. Rosemary Reuther and R. Keller, 80–130. New York: Harper and Row.

Dougherty, Molly C. 1978. *Becoming a Woman in Rural Black Culture*. New York: Holt, Rinehart and Winston.

Du Bois, William E. B. 1969. *The Negro American Family*. New York: Negro Universities Press.

duCille, Ann. 1993. "Blue Notes on Black Sexuality: Sex and the Texts of the Twenties and Thirties." In *American Sexual Politics: Sex, Gender, and Race Since the Civil War*, ed. John C. Fout and Maura Shaw Tantillo, 193–219. Chicago: University of Chicago Press.

———. 1996. *Skin Trade*. Cambridge, MA: Harvard University Press.

Dumas, Rhetaugh Graves. 1980. "Dilemmas of Black Females in Leadership." In *The Black Woman*, ed. La Frances Rodgers-Rose, 203–15. Beverly Hills, CA: Sage.

Duster, Alfreda M., ed. 1970. *Crusade for Justice: The Autobiography of Ida B. Wells*. Chicago: University of Chicago Press.

Dyson, Michael Eric. 1996. *Race Rules: Navigating the Color Line*. New York: Vintage.

Eisenstein, Hester. 1983. *Contemporary Feminist Thought*. Boston: G. K. Hall.

Essed, Philomena. 1991. *Understanding Everyday Racism: An Interdisciplinary Theory*. Newbury Park, CA: Sage.

Evans, Sara. 1979. *Personal Politics*. New York: Vintage.

Everyone's Child. 1996. Directed by Tsitsi Dangarembga. Produced by Media for Development Trust, Zimbabwe. San Francisco: Resolution Inc. / California Newsreel.

Fausto-Sterling, Anne. 1992. *Myths of Gender: Biological Theories about Women and Men*, 2d ed. New York: Basic Books.

———. 1995. "Gender, Race and Nation: The Comparative Anatomy of 'Hottentot' Women in Europe, 1815–1817." In *Deviant Bodies: Critical Perspectives on Difference in Science and Popular Culture*, ed. Jennifer Terry and Jacqueline Urla, 19–48. Bloomington: Indiana University Press.

Feagin, Joe R., and Melvin P. Sikes. 1994. *Living with Racism: The Black Middle-Class Experience*. Boston: Beacon.

Featherstone, Elena, ed. 1994. *Skin Deep: Women Writing on Color, Culture and Identity*. Freedom, CA: The Crossing Press.

Feldstein, Ruth. 1994. " 'I Wanted the Whole World to See': Race, Gender, and Constructions of Motherhood in the Death of Emmett Till." In *Not June Cleaver*, ed. Joanne Meyerowitz, 263–303. Philadelphia: Temple University Press.

Femmes Aux Yeux Ouverts (Women with Open Eyes). 1994. Directed by Anne-Laura Folly. Togo. San Francisco: Resolution Inc. / California Newsreel.

Ferber, Abby. 1998. *White Man Falling: Race, Gender, and White Supremacy*. Lantham, MD: Rowman & Littlefield.

Fernandez-Kelly, Maria Patricia. 1983. "Mexican Border Immigration, Female Labor Force Participation, and Migration." In *Women, Men, and the International Division of Labor*, ed. June Nash and Maria Fernandez-Kelly, 205–23. Albany: State University of New York Press.

Fields, Mamie Garvin, and Karen Fields. 1983. *Lemon Swamp and Other Places: A Carolina Memoir*. New York: Free Press.

Fordham, Signithia. 1993. " 'Those Loud Black Girls': (Black) Women, Silence, and Gender 'Passing' in the Academy." *Anthropology and Education Quarterly* 24 (1): 3–32.

Forna, Aminatta. 1992. "Pornography and Racism: Sexualizing Oppression and Inciting Hatred." In *Pornography: Women, Violence, and Civil Liberties,* ed. Catherine Itzin, 102–12. New York: Oxford University Press.

Fortes, Meyer. 1950. "Kinship and Marriage among the Ashanti." In *African Systems of Kinship and Marriage,* ed. A. R. Radcliffe-Brown and Daryll Forde, 252–84. New York: Oxford University Press.

Foucault, Michel. 1979. *Discipline and Punish: The Birth of the Prison.* New York: Schocken.

———. 1980a. *Power/Knowledge: Selected Interviews and Other Writings 1972–1977,* ed. Colin Gordon. New York: Pantheon.

———. 1980b. *The History of Sexuality Vol. I: An Introduction.* Translated by Robert Hurley. New York: Vintage.

Franklin, Aretha. 1967. *I Never Loved a Man the Way I Love You.* Atlantic Recording Corp.

Franklin, V. P. 1992. *Black Self-Determination: A Cultural History of African-American Resistance.* Chicago: Lawrence Hill Books.

Frazier, E. Franklin. 1948. *The Negro Family in the United States.* New York: Dryden.

Funami, Lumka. 1998. "The Nigerian Conference Revisited." In *Sisterhood, Feminisms, and Power: From Africa to the Diaspora,* ed. Obioma Nnaemeka, 411–17. Trenton, NJ: Africa World Press.

Gardner, Tracey A. 1980. "Racism and Pornography in the Women's Movement." In *Take Back the Night: Women on Pornography,* ed. Laura Lederer, 105–14. New York: William Morrow.

Gayle, Addison, ed. 1971. *The Black Aesthetic.* Garden City, NY: Doubleday.

Giddings, Paula. 1984. *When and Where I Enter . . . The Impact of Black Women on Race and Sex in America.* New York: William Morrow.

———. 1988. *In Search of Sisterhood: Delta Sigma Theta and the Challenge of the Black Sorority Movement.* New York: William Morrow.

———. 1992. "The Last Taboo." In *Race-ing Justice, En-gendering Power,* ed. Toni Morrison, 441–65. New York: Pantheon.

Gilkes, Cheryl Townsend. 1980. " 'Holding Back the Ocean with a Broom': Black Women and Community Work." In *The Black Woman,* ed. La Frances Rodgers-Rose, 217–32. Beverly Hills, CA: Sage.

———. 1983a. "From Slavery to Social Welfare: Racism and the Control of Black Women." In *Class, Race, and Sex: The Dynamics of Control,* ed. Amy Swerdlow and Hanna Lessinger, 288–300. Boston: G. K. Hall.

———. 1983b. "Going Up for the Oppressed: The Career Mobility of Black Women Community Workers." *Journal of Social Issues* 39 (3): 115–39.

———. 1985. " 'Together and in Harness': Women's Traditions in the Sanctified Church." *Signs* 10 (4): 678–99.

Gilligan, Carol. 1982. *In a Different Voice.* Cambridge, MA: Harvard University Press.

Gilman, Sander L. 1985. "Black Bodies, White Bodies: Toward an Iconography of Female Sexuality in Late Nineteenth-Century Art, Medicine, and Literature." *Critical Inquiry* 12 (1): 205–43.

Gilroy, Paul. 1993. *The Black Atlantic: Modernity and Double Consciousness.* Cambridge, MA: Harvard University Press.

Giovanni, Nikki. 1971. *Gemini.* New York: Penguin.

———. 1988. *Sacred Cows . . . and Other Edibles.* New York: Quill/William Morrow.

Glenn, Evelyn Nakano. 1985. "Racial Ethnic Women's Labor: The Intersection of Race, Gender and Class Oppression." *Review of Radical Political Economics* 17(3): 86–108.

Golden, Marita. 1983. *Migrations of the Heart.* New York: Ballantine.

———. 1995. *Saving Our Sons: Raising Black Children in a Turbulent World.* New York: Anchor.

Gomez, Jewell, and Barbara Smith. 1994. "Taking the Home Out of Homophobia: Black Lesbian Health." In *The Black Women's Health Book: Speaking for Ourselves,* ed. Evelyn C. White, 198–213. Seattle: Seal Press.

Gramsci, Antonio. 1971. *Selections from the Prison Notebooks.* London: Lawrence and Wishart.

Grant, Jacquelyn. 1982. "Black Women and the Church." In *But Some of Us Are Brave,* ed. Gloria T. Hull, Patricia Bell Scott, and Barbara Smith, 141–52. Old Westbury, NY: Feminist Press.

———. 1989. *White Women's Christ and Black Women's Jesus: Feminist Christology and Womanist Response.* Atlanta: Scholars Press.

Gregory, Steven. 1994. "Race, Identity and Political Activism: The Shifting Contours of the African American Public Sphere." *Public Culture* 7 (1): 147–64.

Gutman, Herbert. 1976. *The Black Family in Slavery and Freedom, 1750–1925.* New York: Random House.

Guy, Rosa. 1983. *A Measure of Time.* New York: Bantam.

Guy–Sheftall, Beverly. 1986. "Remembering Sojourner Truth: On Black Feminism." *Catalyst* (Fall): 54–57.

———. 1993. "A Black Feminist Perspective on Transforming the Academy: The Case of Spelman College." In *Theorizing Black Feminisms: The Visionary Pragmatism of Black Women,* ed. Stanlie M. James and Abena P. A. Busia, 77–89. New York: Routledge.

———. 1995a. "The Evolution of Feminist Consciousness among African American Women." In *Words of Fire: An Anthology of African American Feminist Thought,* ed. Beverly Guy-Sheftall, 1–22. New York: New Press.

———. 1995b, ed. *Words of Fire: An Anthology of African American Feminist Thought.* New York: New Press.

Gwaltney, John Langston. 1980. *Drylongso, A Self–Portrait of Black America.* New York: Vintage.

Hall, Jacqueline Dowd. 1983. "The Mind That Burns in Each Body: Women, Rape, and Racial Violence." In *Powers of Desire: The Politics of Sexuality,* ed. Ann Snitow, Christine Stansell, and Sharon Thompson, 329–49. New York: Monthly Review Press.

Halpin, Zuleyma Tang. 1989. "Scientific Objectivity and the Concept of 'The Other.' " *Women's Studies International Forum* 12 (3): 285–94.

Hammonds, Evelynn M. 1997. "Toward a Genealogy of Black Female Sexuality: The Problematic of Silence." In *Feminist Genealogies, Colonial Legacies, Democratic Futures,* ed. M. Jacqui Alexander and Chandra Talpade Mohanty, 170–81. New York: Routledge.

Hansberry, Lorraine. 1959. *A Raisin in the Sun.* New York: Signet.

————. 1969. *To Be Young, Gifted and Black.* New York: Signet.

Harding, Sandra. 1986. *The Science Question in Feminism.* Ithaca, NY: Cornell University Press.

————. 1987. "Introduction: Is There a Feminist Method?" In *Feminism and Methodology,* ed. Sandra Harding, 1–14. Bloomington: Indiana University Press.

————. 1998. *Is Science Multicultural? Postcolonialisms, Feminisms, and Epistemologies.* Bloomington: Indiana University Press.

Harley, Sharon. 1982. "Beyond the Classroom: The Organizational Lives of Black Female Educators in the District of Columbia, 1890–1930. *Journal of Negro Education* 51(3): 254–65.

————, and Rosalyn Terborg-Penn, eds. 1978. *The Afro-American Woman: Struggles and Images.* Port Washington, NY: Kennikat Press.

Harper, Michael S. 1979. "Gayl Jones: An Interview." In *Chant of Saints: A Gathering of Afro-American Literature, Art, and Scholarship,* ed. Michael S. Harper and Robert B. Stepto, 352–75. Urbana: University of Illinois Press.

Harris, Trudier. 1982. *From Mammies to Militants: Domestics in Black American Literature.* Philadelphia: Temple University Press.

————. 1986. "Introduction." In *Like One of the Family: Conversations from a Domestic's Life,* by Alice Childress, xi–xxxviii. Boston: Beacon.

Harrison, Daphne Duval. 1978. "Black Women in the Blues Tradition." In *The Afro-American Woman: Struggles and Images,* ed. Sharon Harley and Rosalyn Terborg-Penn, 58–73. Port Washington, NY: Kennikat Press.

————. 1988. *Black Pearls: Blues Queens of the 1920s.* New Brunswick, NJ: Rutgers University Press.

Hartouni, Valerie. 1997. "Breached Birth: Anna Johnson and the Reproduction of Raced Bodies." In *Cultural Conceptions: On Reproductive Technologies and the Remaking of Life,* 85–98. Minneapolis: University of Minnesota Press.

Hartsock, Nancy M. 1983a. "The Feminist Standpoint: Developing the Ground for a Specifically Feminist Historical Materialism." In *Discovering Reality,* ed. Sandra Harding and Merrill B. Hintikka, 283–310. Boston: D. Reidel.

————. 1983b. *Money, Sex and Power.* Boston: Northeastern University Press.

Hernton, Calvin. 1985. "The Sexual Mountain and Black Women Writers." *Black Scholar* 16(4): 2–11.

Higginbotham, Elizabeth. 1983. "Laid Bare by the System: Work and Survival for Black and Hispanic Women." In *Class, Race, and Sex: The Dynamics of Control,* ed. Amy Smerdlow and Hanna Lessinger, 200–15. Boston: G. K. Hall.

————. 1994. "Black Professional Women: Job Ceilings and Employment Sectors."

In *Women of Color in U.S. Society*, ed. Maxine Baca Zinn and Bonnie Thornton Dill, 113–31. Philadelphia: Temple University Press.

———, and Lynn Weber. 1992. "Moving Up with Kin and Community: Upward Social Mobility for Black and White Women." *Gender and Society* 6 (3): 416–40.

Higginbotham, Evelyn Brooks. 1989. "Beyond the Sound of Silence: Afro–American Women in History." *Gender and History* 1 (1): 50–67.

———. 1993. *Righteous Discontent: The Women's Movement in the Black Baptist Church, 1880–1920*. Cambridge, MA: Harvard University Press.

Hine, Darlene Clark. 1989. "Rape and the Inner Lives of Black Women in the Middle West: Preliminary Thoughts on the Culture of Dissemblance." *Signs* 14 (4): 912–20.

———. 1995. "For Pleasure, Profit, and Power: The Sexual Exploitation of Black Women." In *African American Women Speak Out on Anita Hill–Clarence Thomas*, ed. Geneva Smitherman, 168–77. Detroit: Wayne State University Press.

———, and Kate Wittenstein. 1981. "Female Slave Resistance: The Economics of Sex." In *The Black Woman Cross-Culturally*, ed. Filomina Chioma Steady, 289–300. Cambridge, MA: Schenkman.

———, Elsa Barkley Brown, and Rosalyn Terborg-Penn, eds. 1993. *Black Women in America: An Historical Encyclopedia*. New York: Carlson.

Hoch, Paul. 1979. *White Hero Black Beast: Racism, Sexism and the Mask of Masculinity*. London: Pluto Press.

Holloway, Karla. 1995. "The Body Politic." In *Codes of Conduct: Race, Ethics, and the Color of Our Character*, 15–71. New Brunswick: Rutgers University Press.

hooks, bell. 1989. *Talking Back: Thinking Feminist, Thinking Black*. Boston: South End Press.

Hudson-Weems, Clenora. 1998. "Africana Womanism." In *Sisterhood, Feminisms, and Power: From Africa to the Diaspora*, ed. Obioma Nnaemeka, 149–62. Trenton, NJ: Africa World Press.

Hull, Gloria T., ed. 1984. *Give Us Each Day: The Diary of Alice Dunbar-Nelson*. New York: W. W. Norton.

———, Patricia Bell Scott, and Barbara Smith, eds. 1982. *But Some of Us Are Brave*. Old Westbury, NY: Feminist Press.

Hunter, Andrea. 1997. "Counting on Grandmothers: Black Mothers' and Fathers' Reliance on Grandmothers for Parenting Support." *Journal of Family Issues* 18 (3): 251–69.

Hurston, Zora Neale. [1937] 1969. *Their Eyes Were Watching God*. Greenwich, CT: Fawcett.

Hurtado, Aida. 1989. "Relating to Privilege: Seduction and Rejection in the Subordination of White Women and Women of Color." *Signs* 14 (4): 833–55.

Imam, Ayesha, Amina Mama, and Fatou Sow, eds. 1997. *Engendering African Social Sciences*. Dakar, Senegal: Council for the Development of Economic and Social Research.

Irele, Abiola. 1983. "Introduction." In *African Philosophy, Myth and Reality*, by Paulin J. Houtondji, 7–32. Bloomington: Indiana University Press.

Iweriebor, Ifeyinwa. 1998. "Carrying the Baton: Personal Perspectives on the Modern

Women's Movement in Nigeria." In *Sisterhood, Feminisms, and Power: From Africa to the Diaspora,* ed. Obioma Nnaemeka, 297–321. Trenton, NJ: Africa World Press.

Jackson, Irene V. 1981. "Black Women and Music: From Africa to the New World." In *The Black Woman Cross-Culturally,* ed. Filomina Chioma Steady, 383–401. Cambridge, MA: Schenkman.

Jackson, Mahalia. 1985. "Singing of Good Tidings and Freedom." In *Afro-American Religious History*, ed. Milton C. Sernett, 446–57. Durham, NC: Duke University Press.

Jackson, Stevi. 1996. "Heterosexuality and Feminist Theory." In *Theorising Heterosexuality,* ed. Diane Richardson, 21–38. Philadelphia: Open University Press.

Jacobs, Harriet. [1860] 1987. "The Perils of a Slave Woman's Life." In *Invented Lives: Narratives of Black Women 1860–1960,* ed. Mary Helen Washington, 16–67. Garden City, NY: Anchor.

Jaggar, Alison M. 1983. *Feminist Politics and Human Nature.* Totawa, NJ: Rowman & Allanheld.

Jahn, Janheinz. 1961. *Muntu: An Outline of Neo-African Culture*. London: Faber and Faber.

James, Adeola. 1990. In *Their Own Voices: African Women Writers Talk*. Portsmouth, NH: Heinemann.

James, Joy. 1996. *Resisting State Violence: Radicalism, Gender, and Race in U.S. Culture*. Minneapolis: University of Minnesota Press.

James, Stanlie. 1993. "Mothering: A Possible Black Feminist Link to Social Transformation?" In *Theorizing Black Feminisms: The Visionary Pragmatism of Black Women,* ed. Stanlie James and Abena Busia, 44–54. New York: Routledge.

————, and Abena Busia, eds. 1993. *Theorizing Black Feminisms: The Visionary Pragmatism of Black Women.* New York: Routledge.

Jarrett, Robin. 1994. "Living Poor: Family Life Among Single Parent, African American Women." *Social Problems* 41 (February): 30–49.

Jewell, K. Sue. 1993. From *Mammy to Miss America and Beyond: Cultural Images and the Shaping of U.S. Social Policy*. New York: Routledge.

Johnson, Charles S. [1934] 1979. *Shadow of the Plantation*. Chicago: University of Chicago Press.

Jones, Gayl. 1975. *Corregidora*. New York: Bantam.

————. 1976. *Eva's Man*. Boston: Beacon.

Jones, Jacqueline. 1985. *Labor of Love, Labor of Sorrow: Black Women, Work, and the Family from Slavery to the Present.* New York: Basic Books.

Jones, Lisa. 1994. *Bulletproof Diva: Tales of Race, Sex, and Hair*. New York: Anchor.

Jordan, June. 1981. *Civil Wars*. Boston: Beacon.

————. 1985. *On Call*. Boston: South End Press.

Joseph, Gloria. 1981. "Black Mothers and Daughters: Their Roles and Functions in American Society." In *Common Differences,* ed. Gloria Joseph and Jill Lewis, 75–126. Garden City, NY: Anchor.

————. 1984. "Black Mothers and Daughters: Traditional and New Perspectives." *Sage: A Scholarly Journal on Black Women* 1 (2): 17–21.

Just Another Girl on the IRT. 1992. Directed by Leslie Harris. Truth 24 FPS and Miramax Films.

Kaplan, Elaine Bell. 1997. *Not Our Kind of Girl: Unraveling the Myths of Black Teenage Motherhood*. Berkeley, CA: University of California Press.

Keller, Evelyn Fox. 1985. *Reflections on Gender and Science*. New Haven, CT: Yale University Press.

Kelley, Robin D. G. 1994. *Race Rebels: Culture, Politics, and the Black Working Class*. New York: Free Press.

————. 1997. *Yo Mama's Disfunktional: Fighting the Culture Wars in Urban America*. Boston: Beacon.

Kennedy, Elizabeth Lapovsky, and Madeline Davis. 1994. *Boots of Leather, Slippers of Gold: The History of a Lesbian Community*. New York: Penguin.

King, Deborah K. 1988. "Multiple Jeopardy, Multiple Consciousness: The Context of a Black Feminist Ideology." *Signs* 14 (1): 42–72.

King, Mae. 1973. "The Politics of Sexual Stereotypes." *Black Scholar* 4 (6–7): 12–23.

Kochman, Thomas. 1981. *Black and White Styles in Conflict*. Chicago: University of Chicago Press.

Kuhn, Thomas. 1962. *The Structure of Scientific Revolutions*. 2d ed. Chicago: University of Chicago Press.

Kuzwayo, Ellen. 1985. *Call Me Woman*. San Francisco: Spinster's Ink Press.

Ladner, Joyce. 1972. *Tomorrow's Tomorrow*. Garden City, NY: Doubleday.

————. 1986. "Black Women Face the 21st Century: Major Issues and Problems." *Black Scholar* 17 (5): 12–19.

————, and Ruby Morton Gourdine. 1984. "Intergenerational Teenage Motherhood: Some Preliminary Findings." *Sage: A Scholarly Journal on Black Women* 1 (2): 22–24.

Lee, Valerie. 1996. *Granny Midwives and Black Women Writers: Double-Dutched Readings*. New York: Routledge.

Lerner, Gerda, ed. 1972. *Black Women in White America: A Documentary History*. New York: Vintage.

Lindsay, Beverly, ed. 1980. *Comparative Perspectives of Third World Women: The Impact of Race, Sex, and Class*. New York: Praeger.

Loewenberg, Bert J., and Ruth Bogin, eds. 1976. *Black Women in Nineteenth-Century American Life*. University Park: Pennsylvania State University Press.

Lorde, Audre. 1982. Zami, *A New Spelling of My Name*. Trumansberg, NY: Crossing Press.

————. 1984. *Sister Outsider*. Trumansberg, NY: Crossing Press.

Lubiano, Wahneema. 1992. "Black Ladies, Welfare Queens, and State Minstrels: Ideological War by Narrative Means." In *Race-ing Justice, En-Gendering Power*, ed. Toni Morrison, 323–63. New York: Pantheon.

————. 1997. "Black Nationalism and Black Common Sense: Policing Ourselves." In *The House That Race Built: Black Americans, U.S. Terrain*, ed. Wahneema Lubiano, 232–52. New York: Pantheon.

MacMillan, Terry. 1992. *Waiting to Exhale*. New York: Viking.

———. 1996. *How Stella Got Her Groove Back*. New York: Viking.

Madhubuti, Haki R, ed. 1990. *Confusion by Any Other Name: Essays Exploring the Negative Impact of the Blackman's Guide to Understanding the Blackwoman*. Chicago: Third World Press.

Mannheim, Karl. 1936. *Ideology and Utopia*. New York: Harcourt, Brace & World.

Marable, Manning. 1983. "Grounding with My Sisters: Patriarchy and the Exploitation of Black Women." In *How Capitalism Underdeveloped Black America*, 69–104. Boston: South End Press.

Marks, Carole. 1989. *Farewell, We're Good and Gone: The Great Black Migration*. Bloomington: Indiana University Press.

Marshall, Annecka. 1994. "Sensuous Sapphires: A Study of the Social Construction of Black Female Sexuality." In *Researching Women's Lives from a Feminist Perspective*, ed. Mary Maynard and June Purvis, 106–24. London: Taylor and Francis.

Marshall, Paule. 1959. *Brown Girl, Brownstones*. New York: Avon.

———. 1969. *The Chosen Place, the Timeless People*. New York: Vintage.

Martin, Elmer, and Joanne Mitchell Martin. 1978. *The Black Extended Family*. Chicago: University of Chicago Press.

Martin, William G. 1984. "Beyond the Peasant to Proletarian Debate: African Household Formation in South Africa." In *Households and the World-Economy*, ed. Joan Smith, Immanuel Wallerstein and Hans-Deiter Evers, 151–67. Beverly Hills, CA: Sage.

Massey, Douglas S., and Nancy A. Denton. 1993. *American Apartheid: Segregation and the Making of the Underclass*. Cambridge, MA: Harvard University Press.

McClaurin-Allen, Irma. 1989. "Incongruities: Dissonance and Contradiction in the Life of a Black Middle-Class Woman." Amherst: University of Massachusetts, Department of Anthropology.

McClintock, Anne. 1995. *Imperial Leather: Race, Gender and Sexuality in the Colonial Conquest*. New York: Routledge.

McIntosh, Peggy. 1988. *White Privilege and Male Privilege: A Personal Account of Coming to See Correspondences through Work in Women's Studies*. Working Paper No. 189. Wellesley, MA: Center for Research on Women, Wellesley College.

McKay, Nellie. 1992. "Remembering Anita Hill and Clarence Thomas: What Really Happened When One Black Woman Spoke Out." In *Race-ing Justice, En-gendering Power*, ed. Toni Morrison, 269–89. New York: Pantheon.

———, Patricia Hill Collins, Mae Henderson, and June Jordan. 1991. "The State of the Art." *Women's Review of Books* 8 (February): 23–26.

McLaughlin, Andree Nicola. 1995. "The Impact of the Black Consciousness and Women's Movements on Black Women's Identity: Intercontinental Empowerment." In *Connecting Across Cultures and Continents: Black Women Speak Out on Identity, Race and Development*, ed. Achola O. Pala, 71–84. New York: United Nations Development Fund for Women.

McNall, Scott G. 1983. "Pornography: The Structure of Domination and the Mode of Reproduction." In *Current Perspectives in Social Theory, Volume 4*, ed. Scott McNall, 181–203. Greenwich, CT: JAI Press.

Mencher, Joan P,. and Anne Okongwu. 1993. "Introduction." In *Where Did All the Men Go?* Female-Headed / Female-Supported Households in Cross-Cultural Perspective, ed. J. P. Mencher and A. Okongwu, 1–11. Boulder: Westview Press.

Miles, Angela. 1998. "North American Feminisms/Global Feminisms: Contradictory or Complementary?" In *Sisterhood, Feminisms, and Power: From Africa to the Diaspora,* ed. Obioma Nnaemeka, 163–82. Trenton, NJ: Africa World Press.

Mills, C. Wright. 1959. *The Sociological Imagination.* New York: Oxford University Press.

Mirza, Heidi Safia, ed. 1997. *Black British Feminism: A Reader.* New York: Routledge.

Mitchell, Henry H., and Nicholas Cooper Lewter. 1986. *Soul Theology: The Heart of American Black Culture.* San Francisco: Harper and Row.

Momsen, Janet H., ed. 1993. *Women and Change in the Caribbean: A Pan Caribbean Perspective.* Bloomington: Indiana University Press.

Moody, Ann. 1968. *Coming of Age in Mississippi.* New York: Dell.

Moore, Lisa C., ed. 1997. *Does Your Mama Know? An Anthology of Black Lesbian Coming Out Stories.* Decatur: Red Bone Press.

Moraga, Cherrie, and Gloria Anzaldua, eds. 1981. *This Bridge Called My Back: Writings by Radical Women of Color.* Watertown, MA: Persephone Press.

Morrison, Toni. 1970. *The Bluest Eye.* New York: Pocket Books.

———. 1974. *Sula.* New York: Random House.

———. 1987. *Beloved.* New York: Random House.

———, ed. 1992. *Race-ing Justice, En-Gendering Power.* New York: Pantheon.

Morton, Patricia. 1991. *Disfigured Images: The Historical Assault on Afro–American Women.* New York: Praeger.

Moses, Yolanda T. 1989. *Black Women in Academe: Issues and Strategies.* Project on the Status and Education of Women. Washington, D.C.: American Association of American Colleges.

Moulton, Janice. 1983. "A Paradigm of Philosophy: The Adversary Method." In *Discovering Reality,* ed. Sandra Harding and Merrill B. Hintikka, 149–64. Boston: D. Reidel.

Moynihan, Daniel Patrick. 1965. *The Negro Family: The Case for National Action.* Washington, D.C.: Government Printing Office.

Mueller, Carol. 1990. "Ella Baker and the Origins of `Participatory Democracy.' " In *Women in the Civil Rights Movement: Trailblazers and Torchbearers, 1941–1965,* ed. Vicki L. Crawford, Jacqueline Anne Rouse, and Barbara Woods, 51–70. Bloomington: Indiana University Press.

Mulkay, Michael. 1979. *Science and the Sociology of Knowledge.* Boston: Unwin Hyman.

Mullings, Leith. 1997. *On Our Own Terms: Race, Class, and Gender in the Lives of African American Women.* New York: Routledge.

Murray, Pauli. 1970. "The Liberation of Black Women." In *Voices of the New Feminism,* ed. Mary Lou Thompson, 87–102. Boston: Beacon.

———. 1987. *Song in a Weary Throat: An American Pilgrimage.* New York: Harper and Row.

Myers, Lena Wright. 1980. *Black Women: Do They Cope Better?* Englewood Cliffs, NJ: Prentice-Hall.

Naples, Nancy A. 1991. " 'Just What Needed to Be Done': The Political Practice of Women Community Workers in Low-Income Neighborhoods." *Gender and Society* 5 (4): 478–94.

————. 1996. "Activist Mothering: Cross-Generational Continuity in the Community Work of Women from Low-Income Urban Neighborhoods." In *Race, Class, and Gender: Common Bonds, Different Voices,* ed. Esther Ngan-Ling Chow, Doris Wilkinson, and Maxine Baca Zinn, 223–45. Thousand Oaks, CA: Sage.

Nash, June, and Maria Patricia Fernandez-Kelly, eds. 1983. *Women, Men and the International Division of Labor.* Albany: State University of New York.

Naylor, Gloria. 1980. *The Women of Brewster Place.* New York: Penguin.

————. 1988. *Mama Day.* New York: Vintage.

Neely, Barbara. 1992. *Blanche on the Lam.* New York: Penguin.

Neverdon-Morton, Cynthia. 1989. *Afro-American Women of the South and the Advancement of the Race,* 1895–1925. Knoxville: University of Tennessee Press.

Nicola-McLaughlin, Andree, and Zula Chandler. 1988. "Urban Politics in the Higher Education of Black Women: A Case Study." In *Women and the Politics of Empowerment,* ed. Ann Bookman and Sandra Morgen, 180–201. Philadelphia: Temple University Press.

Nightingale, Carl Husemoller. 1993. *On the Edge: A History of Poor Black Children and Their American Dreams.* New York: Basic Books.

Nnaemeka, Obioma. 1998a. "Introduction: Reading the Rainbow." In *Sisterhood, Feminisms, and Power: From Africa to the Diaspora,* ed. Obioma Nnaemeka, 1–38. Trenton, NJ: Africa World Press.

————. 1998b. "This Women's Studies Business: Beyond Politics and History." In *Sisterhood, Feminisms, and Power: From Africa to the Diaspora,* ed. Obioma Nnaemeka, 351–86. Trenton, NJ: Africa World Press.

Oliver, Melvin L., and Thomas M. Shapiro. 1995. *Black Wealth/ White Wealth: A New Perspective on Racial Inequality.* New York: Routledge.

Omi, Michael, and Howard Winant. 1994. *Racial Formation in the United States: From the 1960s to the 1990s, Second Edition.* New York: Routledge.

Omolade, Barbara. 1994. *The Rising Song of African American Women.* New York: Routledge.

O'Neale, Sondra. 1986. "Inhibiting Midwives, Usurping Creators: The Struggling Emergence of Black Women in American Fiction." In *Feminist Studies/Critical Studies,* ed. Teresa de Lauretis, 139–56. Bloomington: Indiana University Press.

Oppong, Christine. 1982. "Family Structure and Women's Reproductive and Productive Roles: Some Conceptual and Methodological Issues." In *Women's Roles and Population Trends in the Third World,* ed. Richard Anker, Mayra Buvinic, and Nadia H. Youssef, 133–50. London: Croom Helm.

Page, Clarence, ed. 1986. *A Foot in Each World: Essays and Articles by Leanita McClain.* Evanston, IL: Northwestern University Press.

Painter, Nell. 1993. "Sojourner Truth." In *Black Women in the United States: An*

Historical Encyclopedia, ed. Darlene Clark Hine, Elsa Barkley Brown, and Rosalyn Terborg-Penn, 1172–76. New York: Carlson.

Pala, Achola O. 1995. "Introduction." In *Connecting Across Cultures and Continents: Black Women Speak Out on Identity, Race and Development,* ed. Achola O. Pala, 3–10. New York: United Nations Development Fund for Women.

Paris, Peter J. 1995. *The Spirituality of African Peoples: The Search for a Common Moral Discourse.* Minneapolis: Fortress.

Parker, Bettye J. 1979. "Mississippi Mothers: Roots." In *Sturdy Black Bridges,* ed. Rosann Bell, Bettye Parker, and Beverly Guy-Sheftall, 263–81. Garden City, NY: Anchor.

Perkins, Linda M. 1982. "Heed Life's Demands: The Educational Philosophy of Fanny Jackson Coppin." *Journal of Negro Education* 51 (3): 181–90.

———. 1983. "The Impact of the 'Cult of True Womanhood' on the Education of Black Women." *Journal of Social Issues* 39 (3): 17–28.

Perry, Imani. 1995. "It's My Thang and I'll Swing It the Way That I Feel!" In *Gender, Race and Class in Media,* ed. Gail Dines and Jean Humez, 524–30. Thousand Oaks, CA: Sage.

Petry, Ann. 1946. *The Street.* Boston: Beacon.

Quadagno, Jill. 1994. *The Color of Welfare: How Racism Undermined the War on Poverty.* New York: Oxford University Press.

Radford-Hill, Sheila. 1986. "Considering Feminism as a Model for Social Change." In *Feminist Studies/Critical Studies,* ed. Teresa de Lauretis, 157–72. Bloomington: Indiana University Press.

Ransby, Barbara, and Tracye Matthews. 1993. "Black Popular Culture and the Transcendence of Patriarchial Illusions." *Race and Class* 35 (1): 57–68.

Rapp, Rayna. 1982. "Family and Class in Contemporary America: Notes toward an Understanding of Ideology." In *Rethinking the Family,* ed. Barrie Thorne and Marilyn Yalom, 168–87. New York: Longman.

Reagon, Bernice Johnson. 1983. "Coalition Politics: Turning the Century." In *Home Girls—A Black Feminist Anthology,* ed. Barbara Smith, 356–68. New York: Kitchen Table Press.

———. 1987. "African Diaspora Women: The Making of Cultural Workers." In *Women in Africa and the African Diaspora,* ed. Rosalyn Terborg-Penn, Sharon Harley, and Andrea Benton Rushing, 167–80. Washington, D.C.: Howard University Press.

Richards, Dona. 1980. "European Mythology: The Ideology of 'Progress.' " In *Contemporary Black Thought,* ed. Molefi Kete Asante and Abdulai S. Vandi, 59–79. Beverly Hills, CA: Sage.

———. 1990. "The Implications of African–American Spirituality." In *African Culture: The Rhythms of Unity,* ed. Molefi Kete Asante and Kariamu Welsh Asante, 207–31. Trenton, NJ: Africa World Press.

Richardson, Diane. 1996. "Heterosexuality and Social Theory." In *Theorising Heterosexuality,* ed. Diane Richardson, 1–20. Philadelphia: Open University Press.

Richardson, Marilyn, ed. 1987. *Maria W. Stewart, America's First Black Woman Political Writer.* Bloomington: Indiana University Press.

Richie, Beth E. 1996. *Compelled to Crime: The Gender Entrapment of Battered Black Women*. New York: Routledge.

Rights of Women: A Guide to the Most Important United Nations Treaties on Women's Human Rights. 1998. New York: International Women's Tribune Centre.

Rimer, Sara. 1998. "An Arts Leader for Whom 'Anything Is Possible.' " *New York Times*, December 28, A16.

Roberts, Dorothy. 1997. *Killing the Black Body: Race, Reproduction, and the Meaning of Liberty*. New York: Pantheon.

Rodríguez, Clara E. 1994. "Challenging Racial Hegemony: Puerto Ricans in the United States." In *Race*, ed. Steven Gregory and Roger Sanjek, 131–75. New Brunswick, NJ: Rutgers University Press.

Rollins, Judith. 1985. *Between Women, Domestics and Their Employers*. Philadelphia: Temple University Press.

Rose, Tricia. 1994. *Black Noise: Rap Music and Black Culture in Contemporary America*. Hanover, NH: Wesleyan University Press.

Russell, Diane E. H. 1993. *Against Pornography: The Evidence of Harm*. Berkeley: Russell Publications.

Russell, Karen K. 1987. "Growing Up with Privilege and Prejudice." *New York Times Magazine*, June 14, 22–28.

Russell, Michele. 1982. "Slave Codes and Liner Notes." In *But Some of Us Are Brave*, ed. Gloria T. Hull, Patricia Bell Scott, and Barbara Smith, 129–40. Old Westbury, NY: Feminist Press.

Sacks, Karen Brodkin. 1984. "Computers, Ward Secretaries, and a Walkout in a Southern Hospital." In *My Troubles Are Going to Have Trouble with Me*, ed. Karen Sacks and Dorothy Remy, 173–90. New Brunswick, NJ: Rutgers University Press.

———. 1988. "Gender and Grassroots Leadership." In *Women and the Politics of Empowerment*, ed. Ann Bookman and Sandra Morgen, 77–94. Philadelphia: Temple University Press.

Said, Edward W. 1993. *Culture and Imperialism*. New York: Knopf.

Salt 'n Pepa. 1993. *Very Necessary*. New York: London Records.

Sanders, Cheryl J. 1995. *Empowerment Ethics for a Liberated People: A Path to African American Social Transformation*. Minneapolis: Fortress.

Scales-Trent, Judy. 1989. "Black Women and the Constitution: Finding Our Place, Asserting Our Rights." *Harvard Civil Rights – Civil Liberties Law Review* 24 (Winter): 9–43.

Schroedel, Jean Reith. 1985. *Alone in a Crowd: Women in the Trades Tell Their Stories*. Philadelphia: Temple University Press.

Scott, James C. 1985. *Weapons of the Weak: Everyday Forms of Peasant Resistance*. New Haven, CT: Yale University Press.

Segrest, Mab. 1994. *Memoir of a Race Traitor*. Boston: South End Press.

Shange, Ntozake. 1975. *For Colored Girls Who Have Considered Suicide/When the Rainbow Is Enuf*. New York: Macmillan.

Shaw, Stephanie J. 1996. *What a Woman Ought to Be and to Do: Black Professional Women Workers During the Jim Crow Era*. Chicago: University of Chicago.

She's Gotta Have It. 1986. Directed by Spike Lee. 40 Acres and a Mule Filmworks.

Shockley, Ann Allen. 1974. *Loving Her.* Tallahassee, FL: Naiad Press.

———. 1983. "The Black Lesbian in American Literature: An Overview." In *Home Girls: A Black Feminist Anthology,* ed. Barbara Smith, 83–93. New York: Kitchen Table Press.

Sidran, Ben. 1971. *Black Talk.* New York: Da Capo Press.

Simone, Nina. 1985. *Backlash.* Portugal: Movieplay Portuguesa Recording.

Simonsen, Thordis, ed. 1986. *You May Plow Here: The Narrative of Sara Brooks.* New York: Touchstone.

Smith, Barbara. 1982a. "Racism and Women's Studies." In *But Some of Us Are Brave,* ed. Gloria T. Hull, Patricia Bell Scott, and Barbara Smith, 48–51. Old Westbury, NY: Feminist Press.

———. 1982b. "Toward a Black Feminist Criticism." In *But Some of Us Are Brave,* ed. Gloria T. Hull, Patricia Bell Scott, and Barbara Smith, 157–75. Old Westbury, NY: Feminist Press.

———. 1983. "Introduction." In *Home Girls: A Black Feminist Anthology,* ed. Barbara Smith, xix–lvi. New York: Kitchen Table Press.

———. 1998. *The Truth That Never Hurts: Writings on Race, Gender, and Freedom.* New Brunswick: Rutgers University Press.

———, and Beverly Smith. 1981. "Across the Kitchen Table: A Sister-to-Sister Dialogue." In *This Bridge Called My Back: Writings by Radical Women of Color,* ed. Cherrie Moraga and Gloria Anzaldua, 113–27. Watertown, MA: Persephone Press.

Smith, Beverly. 1983. "The Wedding." In *Home Girls: A Black Feminist Anthology,* ed. Barbara Smith, 171–76. New York: Kitchen Table Press.

Smith, Dorothy. 1987. *The Everyday World as Problematic.* Boston: Northeastern University Press.

Smitherman, Geneva. 1977. *Talkin and Testifyin: The Language of Black America.* Boston: Houghton Mifflin.

———, ed. 1995. *African American Women Speak Out on Anita Hill and Clarence Thomas.* Detroit: Wayne State University Press.

———. 1996. "A Womanist Looks at the Million Man March." *In Million Man March / Day of Absence,* ed. Haki R. Madhubuti and Maulana Karenga, 104–107. Chicago: Third World Press.

Sobel, Mechal. 1979. *Trabelin' On: The Slave Journey to an Afro-Baptist Faith.* Princeton: Princeton University Press.

Soul Food. 1997. Directed by George Tillman. Edmonds Entertainment and Fo 2000 Pictures.

Souljah, Sister. 1994. *No Disrespect.* New York: Random House.

Spelman, Elizabeth V. 1988. *Inessential Woman: Problems of Exclusion in Feminist Thought.* Boston: Beacon.

Squires, Gregory D. 1994. *Capital and Communities in Black and White: The Intersections of Race, Class, and Uneven Development.* Albany: State University of New York Press.

Stack, Carol D. 1974. *All Our Kin: Strategies for Survival in a Black Community*. New York: Harper and Row.

Staples, Robert. 1979. "The Myth of Black Macho: A Response to Angry Black Feminists." *Black Scholar* 10 (6): 24–33.

Steady, Filomina Chioma. 1981. "The Black Woman Cross-Culturally: An Overview." In *The Black Woman Cross-Culturally,* ed. Filomina Chioma Steady, 7–42. Cambridge, MA: Schenkman.

———. 1987. "African Feminism: A Worldwide Perspective." In *Women in Africa and the African Diaspora,* ed. Rosalyn Terborg-Penn, Sharon Harley, and Andrea Benton Rushing, 3–24. Washington, D.C.: Howard University Press.

Sterling, Dorothy, ed. 1984. *We Are Your Sisters: Black Women in the Nineteenth Century*. New York: W. W. Norton.

St. Jean, Yanick, and Joe R. Feagin. 1998. *Double Burden: Black Women and Everyday Racism*. Armonk, NY: M. E. Sharpe.

Sudarkasa, Niara. 1981a. "Female Employment and Family Organization in West Africa." In *The Black Woman Cross-Culturally,* ed. Filomina Chioma Steady, 49–64. Cambridge, MA: Schenkman.

———. 1981b. "Interpreting the African Heritage in Afro-American Family Organization." In *Black Families,* ed. Harriette Pipes McAdoo, 37–53. Beverly Hills, CA: Sage.

Sweet Honey in the Rock. 1985. *Feel Something Drawing Me On*. Chicago: Flying Fish Records.

Takagi, Dana Y. 1996. "Maiden Voyage: Excursion into Sexuality and Identity Politics in Asian America." In *Asian American Sexualities: Dimensions of the Gay and Lesbian Experience,* ed. Russell Leong, 21–35. New York: Routledge.

Takaki, Ronald. 1993. *A Different Mirror: A History of Multicultural America*. Boston: Little, Brown.

Tanner, Nancy. 1974. "Matrifocality in Indonesia and Africa and among Black Americans." In *Woman, Culture, and Society,* ed. Michelle Z. Rosaldo and Louise Lamphere, 129–56. Stanford, CA: Stanford University Press.

Tate, Claudia, ed. 1983. *Black Women Writers at Work*. New York: Continuum Publishing.

Tate, Sonsyrea. 1997. *Little X: Growing Up in the Nation of Islam*. San Francisco: HarperSanFrancisco.

Terborg-Penn, Rosalyn. 1985. "Survival Strategies among African–American Women Workers: Continuing Process." In *Women, Work and Protest: A Century of U.S. Women's Labor History,* ed. Ruth Milkman, 139–55. Boston: Routledge & Kegan Paul.

———. 1986. "Black Women in Resistance: A Cross-Cultural Perspective." In *Resistance: Studies in African, Caribbean and Afro-American History,* ed. Gary Y. Okhiro, 188–209. Amherst: University of Massachusetts Press.

Terrelonge, Pauline. 1984. "Feminist Consciousness and Black Women." In *Women: A Feminist Perspective,* 3d ed., ed. Jo Freeman, 557–67. Palo Alto, CA: Mayfield.

Thiam, Awa. 1978. *Black Sisters, Speak Out. Feminism and Oppression in Black Africa*. London: Pluto Press.

Thompson, Robert Farris. 1983. *Flash of the Spirit: African and Afro-American Art and Philosophy*. New York: Vintage.

Thompson-Cager, Chezia. 1989. "Ntozake Shange's *Sassafras, Cypress and Indigo*: Resistance and Mythical Women of Power." *NWSA Journal* 1 (4): 589–601.

Thorne, Barrie. 1992. "Feminism and the Family: Two Decades of Thought." In *Rethinking the Family: Some Feminist Questions*, ed. Barrie Thorne and Marilyn Yalom, 3–30. Boston: Northeastern University Press.

Torgovnick, Marianna. 1990. *Gone Primitive: Savage Intellects, Modern Lives*. Chicago: University of Chicago Press.

Troester, Rosalie Riegle. 1984. "Turbulence and Tenderness: Mothers, Daughters, and 'Othermothers' in Paule Marshall's *Brown Girl, Brownstones*." *Sage: A Scholarly Journal on Black Women* 1 (2): 13–16.

Tuan, Yi–Fu. 1984. *Dominance and Affection: The Making of Pets*. New Haven, CT: Yale University Press.

2 Live Crew. 1995. "Hoochie Mama." Friday Original Soundtrack: Priority Records.

Van Dijk, Teun A. 1993. *Elite Discourse and Racism*. Newbury Park, CA: Sage.

Vanneman, Reeve, and Lynn Weber Cannon. 1987. *The American Perception of Class*. Philadelphia: Temple University Press.

Wade-Gayles, Gloria. 1984. "The Truths of Our Mother's Lives: Mother-Daughter Relationships in Black Women's Fiction." *Sage: A Scholarly Journal on Black Women* 1 (2): 8–12.

———. 1996. *Rooted Against the Wind*. Boston: Beacon.

Wahlman, Maude Southwell, and John Scully. 1983. "Aesthetic Principles of Afro-American Quilts." In *Afro-American Folk Arts and Crafts*, ed. William Ferris, 79–97. Boston: G. K. Hall.

Walker, Alice. 1970. *The Third Life of Grange Copeland*. New York: Harcourt Brace Jovanovich.

———. 1976. *Meridian*. New York: Pocket Books.

———. 1977. "Zora Neale Hurston: A Cautionary Tale and a Partisan View." Foreword to *Zora Neale Hurston: A Literary Biography*, by Robert Hemenway, xi–xviii. Urbana: University of Illinois Press.

———, ed. 1979a. *I Love Myself When I Am Laughing, And Then Again When I Am Looking Mean and Impressive: A Zora Neale Hurston Reader*. Old Westbury, NY: Feminist Press.

———. 1979b. "One Child of One's Own: A Meaningful Digression Within the Work(s)." *Ms* 8 (August): 47–50, 72–75.

———. 1981. "Coming Apart." In *You Can't Keep a Good Woman Down*, 41–53. New York: Harcourt Brace Jovanovich.

———. 1982. *The Color Purple*. New York: Washington Square Press.

———. 1983. *In Search of Our Mother's Gardens*. New York: Harcourt Brace Jovanovich.

———. 1988. *Living by the Word*. New York: Harcourt Brace Jovanovich.

Walker, Margaret. 1966. *Jubilee*. New York: Bantam.

Wallace, Michele. 1978. *Black Macho and the Myth of the Superwoman*. New York: Dial Press.

———. 1990. *Invisibility Blues: From Pop to Theory*. New York: Verso.

Walton, Ortiz M. 1971. "Comparative Analysis of the African and Western Aesthetics." In *The Black Aesthetic*, ed. Addison Gayle, 154–64. Garden City, NY: Doubleday.

Washington, Mary Helen, ed. 1975. *Black-Eyed Susans: Classic Stories by and about Black Women*. Garden City, NY: Anchor.

———, ed. 1980. *Midnight Birds*. Garden City, NY: Anchor.

———. 1982. "Teaching *Black-Eyed Susans:* An Approach to the Study of Black Women Writers." In *But Some of Us Are Brave*, ed. Gloria T. Hull, Patricia Bell Scott, and Barbara Smith, 208–17. Old Westbury, NY: Feminist Press.

———. 1984. "I Sign My Mother's Name: Alice Walker, Dorothy West and Paule Marshall." In *Mothering the Mind: Twelve Studies of Writers and Their Silent Partners*, ed. Ruth Perry and Martine Watson Broronley, 143–63. New York: Holmes & Meier.

———, ed. 1987. *Invented Lives: Narratives of Black Women 1860–1960*. Garden City, NY: Anchor.

Wattleton, Faye. 1996. *Life On the Line*. New York: Ballantine.

Webber, Thomas L. 1978. *Deep Like the Rivers*. New York: W. W. Norton.

Weems, Renita. 1984. " 'Hush. Mama's Gotta Go Bye Bye': A Personal Narrative." *Sage: A Scholarly Journal on Black Women* 1 (2): 25–28.

Wekker, Gloria. 1997. "One Finger Does Not Drink Okra Soup: Afro-Surinamese Women and Critical Agency." In *Feminist Genealogies, Colonial Legacies, Democratic Futures*, ed. M. Jacqui Alexander and Chandra Talpade Mohanty, 330–52. New York: Routledge.

Wells, Julia. 1998. "Maternal Politics in Organizing Black South African Women: The Historical Lessons." In *Sisterhood, Feminisms, and Power: From Africa to the Diaspora*, ed. Obioma Nnaemeka, 251–62. Trenton, NJ: Africa World Press.

West, Cheryl. 1987. "Lesbian Daughter." *Sage: A Scholarly Journal on Black Women* 4(2): 42–44.

West, Cornel. 1977–78. "Philosophy and the Afro-American Experience." *Philosophical Forum* 9 (2–3): 117–48.

———. 1993. *Race Matters*. Boston: Beacon.

West, Dorothy. 1948. *The Living Is Easy*. New York: Arno Press/New York Times.

White, Deborah Gray. 1985. *Ar'n't I a Woman? Female Slaves in the Plantation South*. New York: W. W. Norton.

White, E. Frances. 1984. "Listening to the Voices of Black Feminism." *Radical America* 18 (2–3): 7–25.

———. 1990. "Africa on My Mind: Gender, Counter Discourse and African-American Nationalism." *Journal of Women's History* 2 (Spring): 73–97.

White, Evelyn. 1985. *Chain Chain Change. For Black Women Dealing with Physical and Emotional Abuse*. Seattle: Seal Press.

―――, ed. 1994. *The Black Women's Health Book: Speaking for Ourselves*. Seattle: Seal Press.

Williams, Fannie Barrier. 1987. "The Colored Girl." In *Invented Lives: Narratives of Black Women 1860–1960*, ed. Mary Helen Washington, 150–59. Garden City, NY: Anchor.

Williams, Patricia J. 1991. *The Alchemy of Race and Rights: Diary of a Law Professor*. Cambridge, MA: Harvard University Press.

―――. 1995. *The Rooster's Egg: On the Persistence of Prejudice*. Cambridge, MA: Harvard University Press.

Williams, Rhonda. 1997. "Living at the Crossroads: Explorations in Race, Nationality, Sexuality, and Gender." In *The House That Race Built: Black Americans, U.S. Terrain*, ed. Wahneema Lubiano, 136–56. New York: Pantheon.

Williams, Sherley A. 1979. "The Blues Roots of Afro-American Poetry." In *Chant of Saints: A Gathering of Afro-American Literature, Art and Scholarship*, ed. Michael S. Harper and Robert B. Steptoe, 123–35. Urbana: University of Illinois Press.

―――. 1986. *Dessa Rose*. New York: William Morrow.

Williams, Shirley. 1990. "Some Implications of Womanist Theory." In *Reading Black, Reading Feminist: A Critical Anthology*, ed. Henry Louis Gates, 68–75. New York: Meridian.

―――. 1992. "Two Words on Music: Black Community." In *Black Popular Culture*, ed. Michele Wallace and Gina Dent, 164–72. Seattle: Bay Press.

Wilson, William Julius. 1987. *The Truly Disadvantaged: The Inner City, the Underclass, and Public Policy*. Chicago: University of Chicago Press.

―――. 1996. *When Work Disappears: The World of the New Urban Poor*. New York: Vintage.

Yuval-Davis, Nira. 1997. *Gender and Nation*. Thousand Oaks, CA: Sage.

Zinn, Maxine Baca. 1989. "Family, Race, and Poverty in the Eighties." *Signs* 14(4): 856–74.

―――, Lynn Weber Cannon, Elizabeth Higginbotham, and Bonnie Thornton Dill. 1986. "The Costs of Exclusionary Practices in Women's Studies." *Signs* 11 (2): 290–303.

Index